# GLOBAL DIMENSIONS OF INDO-NEPAL POLITICAL RELATIONS
## Post Independence

# GLOBAL DIMENSIONS OF INDO-NEPAL POLITICAL RELATIONS
## Post Independence

**Rajkumar Singh**

GYAN

Global Dimension of Indo-Nepal Political Relations : Post Independence

Rs. 850



ISBN: 978-81-212-1025-6



Published in 2009 in India by
Gyan Publishing House,
23 Main, Ansari Road, Darya Ganj,
New Delhi-110002
Phones : 23282060, 23261060
Fax : 011-23285914
E-mail: books@gyanbooks.com
Website: www.gyanbooks.com

*Lasser Type Setting by*: Quick Media, Delhi
*Printed at:* Singhal Print Media, Delhi

**Dedicated to**

*Late Ram Bilas Singh*

*Father*

# CONTENTS

# LIST OF ABBREVIATIONS

| | |
|---|---|
| AD | Annie Domini |
| AICC | All India Congress Committee |
| ASEAN | Association of South East Asian Nations |
| CBM | Confidence Building Measures |
| CCS | Cabinet Committee on Security |
| CPC | Communist Party of China |
| CPN | Communist Party of Nepal |
| CSC | China Study Center |
| CTBT | Comprehensive Test Ban Treaty |
| DPR | Detailed Project Report |
| HMG | His Majestic Government |
| IDSA | Institute for Defence Studies and Analysis |
| ICCPR | International Covenant on Civil and Political Rights |
| ILO | International Labour Organisation |
| IMF | International Monetary Fund |
| IMLG | Indian Military Liaison Group |
| IMM | Indian Military Mission |
| IMTAG | Indian Military Training and Advisory Group |
| INC | Indian National Congress |
| IPKF | Indian Peace-keeping Force |
| ISI | Inter Services Intelligence |
| JTMM | Janatantrik Tarai Mukti Morcha |
| JWG | Joint Working Group |
| MFN | Most Favoured Nation |
| MJF | Madhesi Janadhikar Forum |
| ML | Marxist Leninist |
| NC | Nepali Congress |

| | |
|---|---|
| NMKP | Nepal Majdoor Kisan Party |
| NPC | National People's Congress |
| NPT | Non-Proliferation Treaty |
| PRC | People's Republic of China |
| RAW | Research and Analysis Wing |
| RNA | Royal Nepal Army |
| SAARC | South Asian Association for Regional Cooperation |
| SPA | Seven Party Alliance |
| SP | Sadbhavna Party |
| TCM | Technical Assistance Cooperation Mission |
| TMLP | Tarai Madhes Loktantrik Party |
| ULFA | United Liberation Front of Assam |
| UML | United Marxist Leninist |
| UNO | United Nations Organisation |
| UPFN | United Peoples Front of Nepal |
| USAID | United States Assistance for International Development |
| USIS | United States Information Service |
| WHO | World Health Organisation |

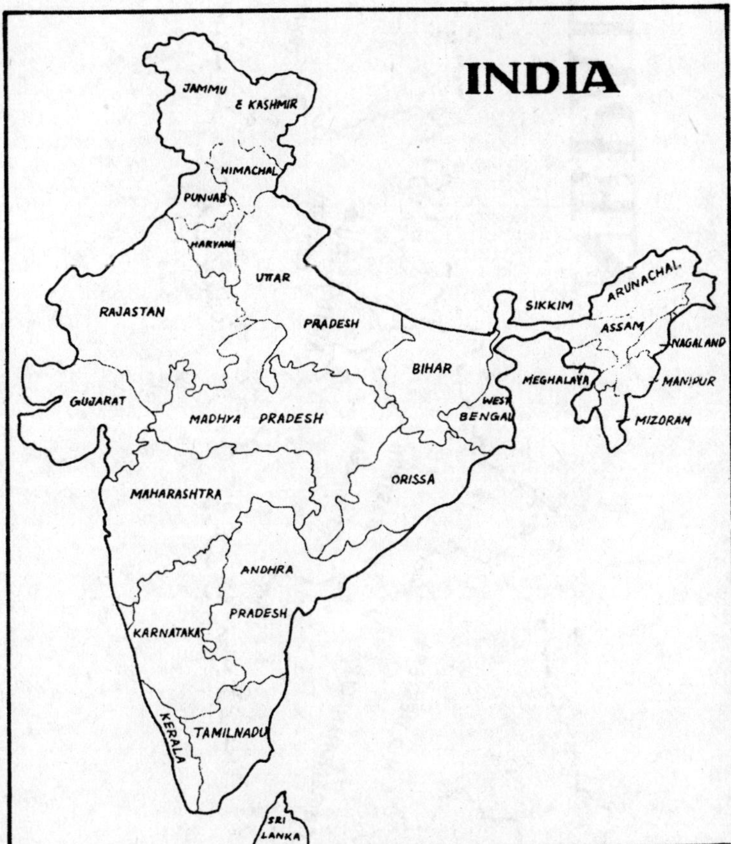
INDIA
JAMMU
& KASHMIR
HIMACHAL
PUNJAB
HARYANA
UTTAR
PRADESH
RAJASTAN
GUJARAT
MADHYA PRADESH
BIHAR
SIKKIM
ARUNACHAL
ASSAM
NAGALAND
MEGHALAYA
MANIPUR
MIZORAM
WEST
BENGAL
ORISSA
MAHARASHTRA
ANDHRA
PRADESH
KARNATAKA
KERALA
TAMILNADU
SRI
LANKA

# NEPAL

DIPAYAL
FAR WESTERN
MID WESTERN
BIRENDRANAGAR
WESTERN
POKHARA
KATHMANDU
CENTRAL
EASTERN
DHANKUTA

# PREFACE

The book Global Dimension of 'Indo-Nepal Political Relations: Post Independence' is a sincere attempt of the author to look into the complexities of India's foreign relations with the Himalayan Kingdom. Even in the situation when Nepal has been changed radically India needs to be more conscious and alert due to its ideological proximity with the People's Republic of China. In yesterdays' Nepal almost all the democratic parties of the country and Nepali Congress, due to its identity of views with the Indian leaders, have been faithful to the throne of New Delhi irrespective of party position there. As from the beginning India adopted the policy of promoting and protecting the democratic aspirations and activities of the Nepalese people the Kings of Nepal remained critical to New Delhi's role in Nepalese politics and for their safety, in case of emergency or assertiveness on India's part, sided with China to have a political leverage against India. For decades Kathmandu was benefited from its 'China Card' policy, it however, lost relevance when India's relations with China began to improve in other spheres and several round of talks conducted successfully on border issue. Since then China has hesitated to get itself involved in India-Nepal affairs and always suggested the kingdom to maintain friendly terms with New-Delhi.

Emergence of the Maoists as number one ideological force which was succeeded by the end of 240-year old system of monarchy in the country cast a long and deep shadow on India's erstwhile relations with Nepal. Except for some brief interlude, the Maoists are, in general, not happy with the mode of New Delhi's relations with Kathmandu and have been pleading for a basic change in India's attitude towards Nepal. Although they know it well that still India matters most in kingdom's economic development and internal politics, the Maoist in the changed circumstances, are prepared to put their demands in assertive and aggressive way in tune of their ideological faith and working style. At present a Maoist-led coalition has formed a government in Nepal that would, perhaps dominate the proceedings of writing a Constitution for the new republic of Nepal. To have a fruitful relations with Nepal, India needs to get rid of its traditional mind-set and requires to cooperate with Kathmandu who is not a small neighbour but a strategic partner too.

Encouragement, co-operation and goodwishes of the institutions and individuals that I received are acknowledged with gratitude. Several central libraries as well as the book-stocks of different Departments have been consulted in the completion of the book. Librarians and staff of the institutions deserve cordial thanks.

Among teachers Dr. D.N. Mallik, Dr. Kirtyanand Singh, Dr. R.N. Kumar and Dr. M.R. Kazami, retired Professors of the University Department of Political Science, BRA Bihar University, Muzaffarpur, Prof. (Dr.) R.P. Singh Rahi, Chief Consultant, School of Social Sciences, Nalanda Open University, Patna, have been a constant source of guide and encouragement at every stage. Colleagues Dr. Chandra Prakash Singh, University Department of History, BN Mandal University, West Campus, Saharsa, Dr. Ram Naresh Kumar, Professor and Head, University Department of Chemistry, BN Mandal University, Madhepura, Dr. Dhirendra Narayan Singh, Department of Political Science, MLT College, Saharsa, are thankful for their cooperation and goodwishes. Eldest brother the late Suryanath Singh, elder brother Shri Bhuvneshwar Prasad Singh, father-in-law Shri Ramanand Singh, retired Professor and Head, University Department of Physics, BRA Bihar University, Muzaffarpur, deserve deep sense of gratitude for their sincere goodwishes. The author is also grateful to colleagues and staff of the BN Mandal University, West Campus, P.G. Centre. Saharsa.

I must extend my honest goodwishes and gratitude to the family members including my wife Dr. Hemlata Singh, son

Aditya Priyadarshi and Apurv Adarsh in the completion of the book.

All responsibility for the defects and misjudgements, however, rests with me alone.

Date: 26.09.2008 **Rajkumar Singh**

# 1

# ABOUT NEW NEPAL

## Introduction

The centuries-old monarchy of Nepal came to an end in May 2008 in a transparent, democratic and dignified manner when the newly elected 575—member Constituent Assembly unanimously passed the resolution. It is now a Federal Democratic Republic and unlike the previous elections, this time the people of Nepal had voted for much more than an end to the monarchy and at the point the real challenge for the ruling allies lies. The popular mandate is in favour of a coaliton government that would oversee the writing of a constitution that enshrines the desires and aspirations of the country's peoples for an inclusive republic in which the economic, political and social rights of all are guaranteed. In today's circumstances political parties of the country are entitled to bargain hard over the conditions but the truth is that they would have to agree to join the new Maoist-led government. Hence, the incumbents to come would have to face an extremely difficult task of balancing the forces internal as well as external.

## The Antecedents

The Shah Dynasty of Nepal has a recorded history of over 450 years beginning in 1559 after Drabya Shah, the progenitor of Shah Dynasty, wrested Gorkha from local tribal chiefs and established Gorkha kingdom. The Shahs remained confined for the next 183 years but it changed once and for all when an audacious Prince Prithvi Narayan Shah ascended to the throne in 1742 at the age of 20 and initiated the unification drive, the same year. At the time the kingdom was fragmented into more than 60 tiny principalities and the dynasty was marred by internal fends, betrayals and killings. The new king was a shrewd, strategic in his thinking, meticulous in his planning and ruthless in obtaining his military objectives. He inified these principalities through conquest and conquered the present Kathmandu Valley in 1768 that led to the establishment of the modern state of Nepal. He defeated the small hill principalities either voluntarily or after unsuccessful resistance to the Gurkha armies. It was the Gurkha conquest under his leadership that gave the country a single name and a strong central government in modern times. His emergence as a strong monarch out of the prevailing chaos and uncertainty, made the kingdom state-centric and not society-centric.[1]

The state centric-approach is described as the perception that operators of the state system play the most decisive roles in the determination of public policies. In the system even state is defined as all those individuals who occupy political offices that authorise them and them alone to make and apply decisions.[2] The system so established, checked the development of political consciousness and a clear sense of identity with the symbol of nationalism. For hundreds of years, the central government in Nepal was run by a number of interrelated families, with the most influential and powerful of them keeping the Prime Ministership or to chief executive postion to themselves.[3] The founder-king Prithvi Narayan Shah died in 1775 at a relatively young age of 53 without completing his unification project, but more importantly, without providing a people of vast cultural diversity within the newly acquired frontiers, a sense of belonging to the new kingdom.[4] After the death of Prithvi Narayan Shah Nepal lost direction, the principal actors lost their character, and the newly unified but still unconsolidated state fell into an era of uncertainty and chaos.

Soon after the demise of Prithvi Narayan Shah his successors established an absolute political system in which the monarch was the centre of power. The words and commands of the king constituted the rules and regulations of the country and these took the shape of laws. In the highly segmented pyramidal structure of the political system that evolved, the king was advised by a number of prominent Brahmin families which came to occupy dominant position in quick succession. The coming periods witnessed the direct rule of king with authority and under the circumstances a political system was evolved which relied for its effectiveness on plots and rumour, mongering bluster and bullying, and primarily on manoeuvres and counter manoeuvres. It was the primary obligation of the common people or the masses to support the elite in the government and in the landed aristocracy. The government existed for the elite rather than for the people. The organs of the government were used largely for the personal gain and the masses were explotied rather than benefited.[5] The modern Kingdom of Nepal began to be ruled by kings and regents who were either insane, inept profligate or promiscuous—or all four.

However, the furthering of the expansion of the Gurkha Kingdom was checked first by the Chinese empire in the 1790s and then by the British East India Company in the 1814-16. In its war with the British Gurkhas were defeated that determined the further course of action in the history of Nepal. It was during this period that Nepalese interests clashed to that of the Britishers who also wanted to expand towards north. As a result of the Nepalese defeat the famous Treaty of Sugauli was made in 1816 with the British East India Company and Nepal became a Himalayan Empire, streteching from Kashmir in the west to Tista, now in India, in the east. It relinquished much of its newly acquired territory and agreed to allow a British residency to be established at Kathmandu. The war followed a cordial relation between them and the British in India guaranteed the survival of Nepal as a state.[6] After the treaty Nepal was squeezed into the boundaries that it has today. Several British historians including John Pemble had considered the treaty in Nepal's favour. He writes, "In the space of half a century, the Gurkhas had unified, for the first time in history, a belt of territory which was the most beautiful, the most inaccessible and traditionally the most fragmented in Asia. There seems no reason to suppose that had the war with the British not intervened, this empire would not have proved viable"[7] The Gurkhas also provided the British with soldiers who fought in the defence of British imperial interest.

But the internal struggle for power within the ruling family weakened the position of monarch. King Rajendra, the last in the line of ruling Shahs, engaged himself too much in intriguing politics-playing one political faction against the other. As a result, the country came to the verge of a civil war and total disintegration. In those years, Bhimsen Thapa (1806-37) was the Prime Minister of Nepal who greatly increased the power of his office at the expense of monarch and paved the way for the establishment of the Rana line of hereditary Prime Ministers. The deteriorating situation was exploited by a remarkable man in the history of Nepal, Jang Bahadur Kunwar, better known as Jang Bahadur Rana. Following the Kot massacre in which a fighting broke out at a gathering of the members of the military and administrative establishment of Kathmandu in the court yard of the palace armoury (Kot), Jang Bahadur became the Prime Minister assuming all powers on 17 September 1846. He soon eliminated all major rivals, imprisoned the king and elevated Rajendra's son to the throne as Surendra Bikram Shah.

Jang Bahadur, the first ruler of Rana family, adopted a friendly and cooperative attitudes towards British India and during India's first struggle for freedom (1857-58) he stood firm as a friend of the British. Although he died in 1877, his policy towards the British survived. The Ranas used to say that they are Rajputs and trace their ancestry back to the Suryavanshi royal family of Mewar (Udaipur). Though they are Nepalese after generations of living in that country, many members of the Rana family take care to point out that they don't look entirely Nepalese pointing to the circular shape of their eyes—a distinction that is usually lost on non-Ranas. Jang Bahadur started a dynasty that modernise Nepal while allowing the kings to continue as figureheads.[8] However, the contradictions between the king and the Rana Prime Ministers and within the Rana family, were internal to their system of family oligarchy. Externally, the Rana regime was hostile to and incompatible with the modern concepts of power, authority and legitimacy which, in nutshell, required the broadening of the regime's base by making it people-oriented.[9]

Several factors were responsible for the fall of Ranacracy in Nepal. The British withdrawal from India weakened the Rana regime which drew support from the British in times of crisis. The rise of communist to power in China also made the ruling class panickly. Earlier winds of change began blowing in thirties-anti-Rana organizations were formed when the Prachanda Gurkha in 1931 and the Praja Parishad in 1935. Young Nepalis, who studied and lived in India and participated in Indian independence struggle became fired up for the liberation of their own country from the clutches of the Ranas. B.P. Koirala, Subarna Sumsher and other energetic youths started an armed insurgency. In the changed circumstances they began to think of founding an organization to carry on the struggle for democracy in Nepal. They founded the 'All India Nepali National Congress' at Varanasi on 31 October 1946 with the guidance and support of Indian socialists. Further for a number of years Kathmandu witnessed political instability which resulted in Delhi Settlement with the help and interference of the then Indian government. Thus Rana oligarchy was put to an end through a tripartite agreement reached in 1951.

**Region, Caste and Ethnicity**

Broadly speaking Nepal, which is the third biggest country in South Asia is divided into three markedly different topographical and ecological regions: the Mountain region, the Hill region, and the Terai region. The mountain region or Parbat is situated at 4.000 meters or more above sea level to the north of the Hill region. Throughout the year this region is covered with snow. The Inner Himalaya or the mountain region in the middle is formed by the Mahabharat range that soar to about 16,000 feet at several places. It lies between the great Himalayas and the Churia Hills (Siwalik) bordering the Terai.[10] The region is sparsely populated and whatever farming activity exists is mostly confined to the low-lying valleys and the river basins, such as the upper Kali Gandaki Valley.

South of the Mountain is the Hill or Pahar region. With fluctuating altitudes this region includes the Kathmandu Valley, the country's most fertile and urbanized area. Two major ranges of hills, commonly known as the Mahabharat Lekh and Siwalik Range occupy the region. Although the region is geographically isolated and has little agricultural potential, the region has been historically the political and cultural centre of Nepal. It is a sub-tropical belt beginning from the Mahabharat range upto the great Himalayas in the north. The extreme northern part of the

Hill region consists of snow clad mountains with big glaciers sliding downwards and, thus providing marginal areas for human settlement. For centuries, bulk of the ruling elite has come from the Hills. The Kathmandu Valley though forms a part of the Hill region, also has a separate identity because it has been the seat of power and in modern times its distinctiveness has further increased due to its urbanization and development activities.[11] In short, this region is different from the Terai region also in terms of their economies and the way of life.

South of the Hill region, stretching along the Nepal- India border is the Terai region. It is a lowland tropical and subtropical belt of flat, alluvial land. Commencing at about 300 meters above sea level and rising to about 1,000 meters at the foot of the Siwalik Range, the region is the life line of the country. Rivers rising in the Himalayas emerge in the Terai and continue southward, some of them becoming tributaries of the Ganges in northern India. The fertile soils of the Terai make it the richest economic region, both in terms of farm and forest land. Nearly half of the country's population lives in this region highest being in the Eastern Terai and lowest in Western Terai.[12]

The two regions-the Terai and the Hills of Nepal represent two important dimensions of regionalism in the country. The Terai region is agriculturally and industrially, the most developed region of the Kingdom. But the benefits of development have not gone to the people of the Terai owing to dominance of the people of the Hills over the economy of the Terai. This dominance of the Hill people has also led to their political dominance. The place of the people of the Terai in politics, administration, defence services is not commensurate to their population and economic strength. The attitude of the Hill people towards the Terai, in general, has been guided with a psychological feelings that the people of the Terai do not represent the Nepalese culture. Organised movements have not succeeded in the Terai because it does not provide as a composite group, socially and culturally.[13] As a result it has lacked that political consciousness which is essential for interest articulation and interest aggregation.

In the present time, with the changes in economic activities of the people, the social change is gradually taking place in the

Nepalese society. In the Terai region because of the concentration of modern economic activities, social mobilization is growing on faster scale and it is passing through a transitional phase. A large number of the Hill people are migrating to the Terai and they are also bringing with them their own way of life. This process has been termed more recently as 'Nepalisation' of the Terai because for a long time there has been a psychological feeling that the Hills represent Nepalese way of life, while the Terai is mainly Indian.

The migration from the Hills to the Terai is not a new phenomenon. During the early days when the Terai region was not suitable for human settlement, people of the Hill region of Nepal had been migrating to the northern plains of Inida, Sikkim and Bhutan. After 1860 Nepalese government thought of developing the neglected Terai region. It began providing incentives for the economic development of this region. At that time the Hill people were not attracted to such incentives because of the fear of malaria, dense forests, wild beasts and the swamps. Therefore, the Nepalese government encouraged the people of the Indian plains to settle in the Terai. Consequently a large number of Indians had migrated to the region. They cleared the dense forests and swamps and began cultivation. The neighbouring Indian industrialists and business men also extended their activities to the Terai.[14] It was also the time when the neighbouring Indian regions were undergoing rapid development in transportation and communication which further encouraged the Indians to settle in the Terai. In the region the industrial development has largely been encouraged by the industrial development of the neighbouring states of Uttar Pradesh and Bihar in India, and the infra-structure facilities provided by them.[15] Most of the industries in the Terai are located towards the Indian borders. They have not only been facilitated by the capital and technology from India, but also the market facilities in the neighbouring Indian cities.[16] Thus, India provided input and output facilities to the industries of the Nepalese Terai. The transportation facilities and open border between the two countries have further encouraged this process.

However the migration of the Hill people to the Terai region has given rise to certain problems in the area. The migrated people have lived in different social environment and they find it difficult to adjust themselves in the new environment and it gave birth to social tension in the region. With this the problem of identity arose and people began to say who is a local Nepali and who is outsider.[17] In this connection the Hill people considered themselves the true Nepali and the Indian settlers an outsiders. Further it made the population of Terai more densed than earlier that resulted in the increased pressure on the means of production followed by the problem of unemployment and an increase in regional economic disparities. Along with these caste composition of the Terai had also undergone a change. The Hill migrants mostly belong to the high caste, like Brahmin, Chettri and Newar. The migrants from the Indian plains are mostly from low castes.[18] The migrants of the Hills are generally educated and economically rich and they have access to the centres of political power. In fact the Nepalese government has encouraged the migration of the Hill people to the Terai and facilitated their settlement in that region. The Hill migrants have been favoured in distributing the surplus land instead of local people of the Terai. Excess favour of the Hill migrants has further accelerated control of the Hill people over the economy of the Terai.

The Nepali society has, through the years, have been successful in synthesising the various religious and cultural strands into a uniquely Nepali compound. The basis of the Nepalese comprehension is that they link with both south and east Asia rather than connect exclusively to either.[19] The main social groups in the Hills are the Hill Brahmin, Chettri, Newar, Rai, Limbu, Gurung, Tamang Magar, Sherpa Thakali, Dolpa, Gola, etc. while the main communities of the Terai are the plain's Brahmin, Rajput, Rajbansi, Sutar, Muslim, Tharu, Dhimal, Bodo, etc. Most of them belong to the Indo-Aryan racial stock. Their social life and belief systems are influenced by the neighbouring Indian culture.[20] The linguistic diversity seems greater in the Terai, where several languages and dialects spoken in neighbouring Indian region are prevalent, such as, the Maithili, Bengali, Bhojpuri, Hindi, Urdu, Tharu, Awadhi, and Marwari.

Nepal is a nation said to be materially poor but culturally rich. Because of its geographical location, Nepal has been a meeting point of races. From the point of view of their ethnic character they can be classified into three broad categories. The first group consists of the Indo-Aryans who, migrating from northern India, mostly inhabited the Terai region of the country. The second group is of Mongoloid origin and the people of this stock chiefly inhabit the high mountains of the north where, migrating from Tibet, they had settled. The third major group has been formed by the admixture of the Indo-Aryan and Mongolian strains.[21] The first group consists of high-caste Hindu families mostly Kshatriyas and Brahmans, which migrated to Nepal in the wake of the Muslim invasions of north India, however, spread all over Nepal with the exception of the areas in its extreme northern part. They constitute a significant proportion of the local elites wherever they reside. Frequently they are also the largest land-owners. Numerically, socially, and politically this is the most important racial group in Nepal. Of late Nepal had continued to be ruled by families having Indo-Aryan and Hindu background, the Indo-Aryan ancestry has been a source of prestige in Nepal.

Among the second Gurungs, the Magars, the Limbus, the Rais, the Sunwars and the Bhotias are the prominent ethnic groups. The Bhotias include a number of ethnic groups made up of recent Tibetan migrants, the Sherpas being its most known subdivision. Being of the Mongoloid origin, people of this group resemble their Tibetan neighbours in physical features and have similar language, dresses, customs and culture. Inhabiting the largely inaccessible regions of the country, they are politically, socially and economically very backward. The third group bears the traits of Mongoloid as well as Aryan physical features and of Tibetan and Indian culture. They mostly inhabit the central mid-mountain region of the country where, moving from the opposite directions, these two races met. The Newar and Chettri communities fall under this category.

There have been major groups—the Gorkhas as the ruler, the Brahmins as the administrators and men of educated professions and the Newars controlling the economy and the arts and crafts.[22] The Shah Kings quite clearly realized that they could rule Nepal only with a working coalition of these three major groups with the Gorkhas holding the balance between the Newars and the Brahmins. With this aim in view King Prithvi Narayan Shah took a few significant decisions to which his successors remained faithful. He decided that the army should almost exclusively be offered by the Gorkhas. Secondly, he decided to reduce the preponderance of the Brahmins in the administration, if possible, by bringing in more Gorkhas and other Chettries and, if necessary by brining in more Newars.[23] It is worth mentioning here that the Newars as a group entertain and vigorously support anti-Indian sentiment in Nepal.[24] This anti-Indian attitude is mainly responsible for their pro-China leanings.[25] Caste status and economic position do not always correlate, but high caste status is generally a prerequisite for belonging to the economic and particularly the political-administrative elite.[26] In other words, Nepal is a society highly stratified by caste and economic concentration. It is also a society highly stratified in political terms.

Before 1990, the regime form in Nepal was the so-called Panchayat system under which the king held a very strong position and was advised by a Council of Ministers and by his own palace secretariat. The partyless Panchayat system was dominated by traditional elites mainly drawn from the three major upper castes. These elites benefited from the ban on political parties and autonomous trade unions and other interest organizations, because these bans effectively constrained the organising abilities of most non-elite groups in the country while the traditional elites could exploit social networks and formal political and administrative positions.[27] In addition the two special variant of social exclusion and inclusion called *afno manchhe* and the tradition of *chakari* have reinforced political inequalities. Afno manchhe literally means 'one's own people.' It refers to the predominant form of social interaction and organisational in Nepal whereby people act on the basis of strong attachment to each other within a particular group while at the same time treating other citizens as outsiders.[28] The practice of Chakari (sycophancy) implies that people less well off and less powerful tend to spend a lot of time and energy just to show their obedience and dependence on high-status persons in powerful positions.

The Panchayat system of Nepal exhibited the extreme concentration of political power under it that provoked protests on several occasions from 1979 onwards. Both elite groups and representatives of resource-poor segments of society gradually emerged as strong oppositions to the partyless panchayat system. Despite dissatisfaction and resentment at large it took more than ten years for the opposition parties to unite in the Movement for the Restoration of Democracy, consisting of the Nepali Congress Party and the United Left Front, a coalition of communist factions. The movement's objective included the ending of the partyless system and the dismissal of corrupt officials but it did not advocated the abolition of the monarchy. In November 1990 a new constitution was promulgated which guaranteed the multi-party system and changed the king's position to that of a constitutional monarch - although he retained his position as the effective commander of the armed forces. Party-based elections were held after more than thirty years on 12 May 1991 which resulted in the victory of Nepali Congress Party. In the election the Nepali Communist Party won 69 seats and emerged as the largest opposition party of the country. Gradually position and influence of the Maoist forces strengthened in Nepal and from mid-Nineties it started campaigning for the abolition of monarchy and establishment of Nepal as a federal republic. Over decades of insurgency paved the way for Nepalese republic in May 2008. The new Nepal faced two major problems—the Madhesism and Maoism and they would continue to haunt Nepalese politics and society in days to come.

**The Madhesi**

Madhesi is an amorphous term referring to caste categories of the eastern Terai in particular. The Terai belt is Nepal's most densely populated region and accounts for half the country's 29 million people. Not all of its residents are Madhesis, however, Janajati groups like the Tharus—the original inhabitants before the swamps were cleared and Avadhi, Bhojpuri and Maithili-speaking migrants moved up from India have a strong presence in the western planes districts. In addition to them there are Limbus and throughout the region, the Nepali-speaking Pahadis are present in significant numbers. The Madhesis in particular, form 31.2 per cent of Nepal's population and they are as stratified in terms of language and caste as the Pahadis, a shared sense of grievance inheres in all of them, 'We have never been accepted as Nepalis. Despite being Nepali citizens, we have always been called Indians.[30]

In past the people of the Terai region have sometimes opposed the policies of the government, but their resentment against it never developed to an extent which could be termed as a separatist movement. On many occasions after 1950 people of the Terai region raised their voices against the economic policies of the government. One of the major issue of their resentment has been the land reform policies of the government. In fact, the people of the Terai, most of whom have migrated from the Indian plains continued to maintain their socio-cultural links with their Indian counterparts. They also do not possess similar linguistic, ethnic and economic background. Because of different socio-economic background the interests of the people of the Terai do not coincide with each other. It had in turn, discouraged them from organising themselves into a cohesive group.[31] However, an organisation named Terai Liberation Front' was formed in 1964 to fight the causes of the Terai. But as the movement was politically motivated it never gained mass support and faded out.

The turn of events moved fastly in Nepal at the close of the century and thereafter as well. Multi-party democracy with constitutional monarchy was adopted in 1990 and the Maoist's movement initiated in 1996 had changed the social feeling and political fate of the nation. Gyanendra, the last king of Shah dynasty who took over the throne following the palace massacre in which King Birendra was gunned down in June 2001, miscalculated three things : First, he thought the Maoists and mainstream parties would never join hands and form a collective front against him. Secondly he hoped that given a choice between the Maoists and the monarchy, the international community, particularly India and the United States, would eventually choose monarchy. And lastly, he underestimated the consciousness of the Nepali people, which had grown by leaps and bounds in the post-1990 open society and during the decade-long Maoist insurgency.[32]

After a long gap the Madhes awakened in April, 2006 when the mass upsurge of the people's movement sought peace and pluralism, and mandated the writing of a new constitution to redraw state-society relations. The agitation of Madhes was a spontaneous uprising by the people of Terai plains origin who have long felt excluded amidst the high lander identification of the nation state. The exclusion that Madhesi activists speak about is not just nomenclatural. There is bitterness over the extent to which Madhesis have been kept out of the state administration, and over the fact that Hindi—the link language between Maithili, Bhojpuri and Avadhis finds no official recognition in Nepal. They in common with the rest of the erstwhile kingdom's citizens, wanted the Constituent Assembly to provide them the rights they have been denied all these years. Their demands included proportional representation in state organs including the army, changes in electoral laws to enhance Madhesi participation and so on. Sensing the government's mood they have also enlarged their aspirations to the level of utopia and included self-determination and the declaration of the 500-by-20 mile Terai plains as a single province "Ek Madhes, Ek Pradesh."[33]

Initially, the Maoists of Nepal kept a sympathetic view towards the problems of Terai region and in the areas where janajatis were dominant and demanded for a Constituent Assembly to be elected on the basis of proportional representation. It gave a wide mass support to the Maoists who were in keen contest with the Nepali Congress. But after the Jan Andolan–II of March-April 2006 when Parliament was restored and the Maoists joined the government, the Nepali Congress and the Communist Party of Nepal (UML) forced the former rebel to drop their demand for proportional representation. A compromise was struck among them for only half the seats to the Constituent Assembly to be allotted on proportional representation basis. By this understanding the Maoists were not in greater loss because they promised ethnic rights, its impact on Madhesis became sparking and they immediately started their movement which paved the way for further developments in Nepalese politics.

There are three forces in Nepalese national life who are attached to the issue of Madhesis—the Maoists, the Nepali Congress along with Communist party of Nepal (UML) and the palace politics. They all tried to compete and gain the favour of Madhesis for no other purposes but political. As the movement of Madhesis was erupted due to Maoists consensus with the other forces, they remained soft throughout the movement. On their part they have put forward a map which comprises more than a dozen provinces, including a part of the Terai called 'Madhes' which divided the region into three sub-provinces of Abadh, Bhojpura and Mithila. The Tharus and Limbus got their own provinces in the western and eastern Terai. The Nepali Congress and its allies, found the agitation of Madhes as useful since its immediate target was the Maoist but in due course they felt that it was unable to countenance the identity-led nature of the agitation in the Terai. Therefore, Girija Prasad Koirala, the Prime Minister became slow in addressing the Madhesi demands. The Nepali public across the country also doubted the sincerity of Nepali Congress to the republican cause. Earlier Koirala floated the idea of 'baby king' and his daughter Sujata who was contesting the election from Sunsari district in the Terai was also in favour of constitutional monarchy.

With the violent movement of the Madhesis, over night new political groups emerged which took up the demands for, *inter alia,* a fully proportional electoral system. Eventually, two armed groups also emerged—the Janatantrik Tarai Mukti Morcha (JTMM) and Jai Krishna Goit. While the Maoists wanted to tackle the problem of Madhesis domestically these extremist outfits have operated with impunity from Indian towns of Sitamarhi, Raxaul, Darbhanga and Gorakhpur. But having facilitated the discussions in New Delhi in the autumn of 2005 that brought the Maoists to an understanding with the parliamentary parties, New Delhi had been asked, specifically, to rein in militants who have been engaged in bombing and targeted killings in Nepal's Terai plains and taking refuge across the open border.[34] As time went on, it became clear that quite a few among the Madhesi leadership were seeking consortium with the royalists of Kathmandu, as well as the Hindutva forces across the border.

By these developments the Narayanhiti royal palace or Gyanendra seemed energised and viewed the events as a last silver line to save the fortunes of monarchy in Nepal. He sent emissaries to meet with Hindutva and BJP stalwarts in India in a bid to revive the near-end system of the country. But at this stage the Foreign Ministry in South Block played its card in favour of a pluralistic, representative evolution in Nepal. By extending the tenure of Indian Ambassador to Nepal until after the election the government had sent a message committing its own agenda and standing to the holding on elections on schedule in Nepal.

However, the demand of 'Ek Madhes, Ek Pradesh' is problematic because it will foreclose the real devolution and inclusion that Nepal's diverse ethno-linguistic groups aspire to. The three Madhesi parties - Madhesi Janadhikar Forum (MJF), Tarai Madhes Loktantrik Party (TMLP) and the Sadbhavna Party will also do their job differently making the situation bad to worse. An added cause for wariness is the interest some United Nations officials as well as U.S. government agencies and non-governmental organisations have begun to show in the Madhesis. Sensing the prospect of the larger payoff that internationalisation might bring, the Madhesi leadership and a section of the people are prepared that if Nepal fails to grant autonomy, they would look to India. 'We are offering Kathmandu control over only defence, foreign affairs and communications and he also added further that if Kathmandu does not want this we can always offer Delhi the same.'[35]

In the circumstances all hopes pinned on the formation and efficiency of a 601-member House that has the dual responsibility of drafting a new constitution and serving as parliament during the interim. The Constituent Assembly is a necessary condition for the country to achieve political stability, peace and a return to pluralism. The general expectation is that the Constituent Assembly will define a democratic constitution that will simultaneously address the many conflicting and complementary demand of marginalized minorities and, at long last, provide politics as a platform for economic progress. Whatever the origins of the recent Madhesi movement, the Terai region is in ferment and will not settle for second-class status. If the Constituent Assembly fail to design federal structures which guarantee autonomy and dignity to all regions of Nepal and economic justice for the poor and the landless, new faultlines and conflicts will emerge. With the right approach, Madhesi aspirations can easily be accommodated within the federal Nepal that all parties there are officially committed to. Earlier India played a good role in helping to broker the last agreement between the Nepal government and the Madhesi parties and now it should ensure that its territory is not used by extremist forces bent on sabotaging the possibility of a democratic solution in a peaceful way.

**The Maoists**

The success of the Chinese revolution had a profound impact on the world, creating a wave of joy amongst the oppressed countries in South Asia on the one hand and sending shivers down the spine of the developed capitalist countries of Europe and especially America on the other. Personalities like Mao Zedong and Zhou En Lai started to be worshiped as cult figures, not only in China, but in many other countries as well.[36] Chinese revolution served as the required fuel to ignite the hidden passions of freedom for many a third world countries and the kingdom of Nepal is one of them. But the success of the Maoists in Nepal should not be overemphasised as a stupendous achievement of Maoism. In fact it is a product of more than 50, if not 200, years of political distortions. Monarchy in Nepal has reigned supreme for 40 years, governing through a corrupt, inefficient and repressive Panchayat order. During the last 14 years, while managing to arouse popular aspirations for economic well being and social justice, the parliamentary political system utterly failed to keep its promises.[37] In addition the military potential of Nepal should be kept in the backdrop before arriving at any abrupt conclusion. Moreover, the uniformity in the ethnic composition and the overall uniformity in their economic profile and hence lack of many classes in society makes it easier for Maoism to thrive in Nepal. But for many Maoists, even accepting to take part in elections of the Constituent Assembly in a bourgeoisie set up is a revisionist attitude, although it was the Nepali Maoists who forced the so-called bourgeoisie democracy to accept their terms and conditions. Monarchy has been abolished in Nepal and the Maoists have won the elections.

Politically, diplomatic relations between the peoples Republic of China and Nepal was established in 1955, the year King Mahendra became the King of Nepal after the death of his father King Tribhuvan. It was the period when Nepal had a passionate quest for independence and status in international society and its big strategic understanding with China gave Kathmandu an opportunity to balance its relations with India. The new King Mahendra also appointed T.P. Acharya as the new Prime Minister of Nepal who was known for his Pro-China and anti-India inclinations. Presumably India considered the immediate danger not from common border with China but from its extension in Nepal as the latter was a relatively weak country.[38] The new dispensation of Nepal introduced Panchayat system and put several restrictions on the activities of political parties. The system of panchayat continued in Nepal for next thirty years and after an intense movement for the restoration of democracy the existing system was replaced by the system of a constitutional monarchy based on multiparty formula. Political relations between China and Nepal touched a new height during the period, Maoists activities remained limited to influencing public opinion in ways more than one. The left wing communist organizations kept themselves active and often raised voices in support of the popular grievances and also against the land reform policies of the government. Initially they had lacked mass support because of their violent means and ideological preoccupations.

In 1990 the Partyless Panchayat system was replaced by Parliamentary democracy and a fresh constitution was enacted which paved the way for competing party politics. Since the process of democratization started in early Nineties, Nepal witnessed a plethora of contentious activities, both violent and non-violent. Contentious activities include identity and gender movements numerous public protests and strikes and the Maoist rebellion. But to a large extent these contentious activities were an urban phenomenon in Nepal. They occurred around Kathmandu and other urban centres. Many of the people engaged in these activities belonged to middle class or elite section of the society.

The Maoists stood first in the mobilization of the rural poor and their issues. No political party or movement had mobilized the rural people more than the Maoists. This is significant because the mainstream movements and political parties, despite their claim of representing the rural people, were mostly led by urban and rural elite. If the mobilization of hitherto largely neglected people is a contribution towards democratization, the Maoists have played a significant role.[39] The Maoists controlled a large part of Nepal's geographical space and enjoyed public sympathy for their proposed socio-economic programme. However, the violent methods adopted by them undoubtedly undermined electoral democracy and put a question mark on the future of democracy.

Even in the first general elections held in May 1991 the Nepali Congress and the United Marxist Leninist Communist Party of Nepal (UML) shared most of the votes and Girija Prasad Koirala, leader of the Nepali Congress became the Prime Minister. But unfortunately factionalism soon engulfed the Nepali Congress and it became difficult for Koirala to implement policies and programmes of the government. He lastly resigned and called for mid-term election in 1994. The United Marxist Leninist Communist Party of Nepal won 89 seats in the general elections held in November 1994 and Man Mohan Adhikari of the UML formed a minority government with the help of small parties like the Nepal Majdoor Kisan Party and Communist Party of Nepal (Masal), Nepal, thus, became the first communist monarchy.

The minority government of Man Mohan Adhikari assumed power after an election campaign dominated by issues mostly India centred and based on anti-India planks: abrogation of the 1950 treaty, ending the special relationship with India, renegotiating agreements on cooperation in water resources, and ending the recruitment of Nepalese Gurkhas in the Indian Army—exactly the issues raised by the Maoist in 2008 when they formed the government under the Premiership of Pushpa Kamal Dahal 'Prachanda'. In his election campaign, before the polls, Adhikari was to seek the review of Nepal's 1950 treaty with India because it proved convenient to him in an atmosphere which was anti-India.[40] He found in the treaty a tilt in India's favour and declared it to be reviewed.[41] The new Prime Minister also refused to accept Indian security umbrella and expressed the wish to have free trade with both Pakistan and Bangladesh.[42] Going a step further the then Adhikari government of Nepal made an institutional arrangement at the Foreign Secretary level set up in March 1995; but after a few rounds of discussions, it became clear that India was not interested in amendment: the treaty had either to be abrogated or maintained in its present form, as the text of the treaty did not provide for modifications.[43] India made its stand clear 'either we keep it or you abrogate it'. However Nepalese leaders did not go beyond making proforma noises about review of the treaty being under active discussion. At the moment the best New Delhi could do was to watch the new Nepal which had turned red recently[44] but at the same time India, on its part, took great care in not giving any impression of big brotherliness.

The Maoists of today were once a part of the mainstream politics under the banner of United Peoples Front of Nepal (UPFN) led by Baburam Bhattarai. In a split in the party, the Baburam faction failed to get the recognition of the Election Commission to participate in the mid-term elections in 1994. This group joined hands with the Communist Party of Nepal (Maoists). The declared aim of the Maoists is to establish a people's government through peoples war that is inspired by Marxism-Leninism-Maoism. In 1996 the Maoists launched the 'Peoples Movement' or Jana Andolan by carrying out attacks in different parts of Nepal. Indeed they launched insurgency after the state repeatedly ignored their demands and received support from the population ignored by the state. Like other leftists, the Maoists of Nepal considered the states as a semi-feudal organisation and held it responsible for the prevailing socio-economic ills within the country. The Maoists of Nepal have also projected India and the US as the imperialist powers trying to subvert the interests of the people of Nepal by aligning with the rightist forces within Nepal.

By the time the peoples movement was started by the Maoists the systems of the country as whole provided them a convenient phenomenon. With the democratic politics in Nepal being extremely factionalised successive governments in Nepal found it difficult to implement governmental policies and programmes. One result of this was the rate of economic growth was modest, but it did not match the rate at which population grew. Particularly in the Ninth Plan (1998-2002) which was planned to make Nepal a competitive, competent and technologically oriented society failed to achieve the target due to the violence unleashed by the Maoist insurgency. The Peoples Movement cast a dark shadow on the development in all sectors. It resulted in massive unemployment and illiteracy in a society that had an ethnically and religiously fragmented population. It all favoured the Maoists because those who mobilize often seek resources or comfortable policies from the state. This situation helped them in intensifying conflict among groups who control the state and its resources and those who want a voice in the state and a share of its resources. The Maoists used terror tactics to spread their influence in the rural areas and taken effective control of administration in several districts. By the end of 2000, the Maoists were active in over two thirds of the 75 districts of Nepal. They had set up people's government in five districts of western Nepal. In the areas under their control, the Maoists do local policing, settle local disputes, collect levies from the people and even set up banks.

In the early years of the Maoist movement, Nepalese politicians belonging to the leftist camp displayed a fraternal resistance to taking any harsh measures toward the Maoists. The Communist Party of Nepal Marxist-Leninist, the third largest political party in Nepal, openly endorsed the aims of the Maoists even while disapproving of its working style. The majority ruling party, the Nepali Congress, beset with internal problems, could not take concrete action to deal with the Maoist problem. The Maoist insurgency added confusion in the democratic politics of Nepal that was already reeling under factionalism which ultimately led to a constitutional crisis. The key problem for Nepal at the time was the absence of linkage between the people at large and their government. Consequently the formation of a healthy civil society in Nepal has been held in check. The conflicts in Nepal have been the outcome of incongruence between societal aspirations and state institutions.[45]

The Maoists of Nepal took maximum benefit of the prevailing political instability of the Kingdom and from 2001 onwards began to dominate the politics and political events of the country. It assumed grave proportions became number one problem of Nepal and government's measures such as, force, persuasion and negotiation to tackle the Maoist problem proved both useless and counterproductive as well. Since March 2001, several rounds of peace negotiations have been held between the government and the Maoists. But due to irreconcilable differences and mutual suspicion, these efforts have not borne result. Terror and violence by the insurgents continued and the security forces have stepped up counter insurgency operations. However, the Maoists activities had restricted the democratic rights of the common people even when they were conducted in the name of protecting democratic rights. The most well-known public protests were the *bandhs* which called for closure of markets, towns, cities or the whole country. Those who dared to continue with regular activities were often violently stopped. The common people were thus denied their fundamental political rights and civil liberties.

For long the Maoists of Nepal had held the normal political processes under seize as prescribed in the constitution of 1990. In May 2002, the Deuba government recommended the dissolution of the parliament but found it difficult to hold elections because of the Maoist insurgency. Taking advantage of the situation King Gyanendra invoked Article 127 of the constitution to dismiss the Prime Minister and his cabinet for 'incompetence' in October 2002. He nominated Lokendra Bahadur Chand to head a nine-member interim government but in March 2003 the mainstream forces of the country launched a movement against the monarchic takeover. Since then, a tripartite power struggle has dominated Nepali politics, between the king, the mainstream political parties and the Maoists. Even during this period the Maoists remained adamant in their demand for the creation of a Constituent Assembly to draft a drastically revised constitution. As the Maoist insurgency raged, the King declared a state of emergency on 1 February 2005 arresting mainstream political leaders and assumed absolute power.

When King Gyanendra decided to dismiss the Government of Sher Bahadur Deuba and declare emergency in the Himalayan Kingdom in 2005, it was clear that his days were numbered. Although the country was passing from the worst form of political instability and dilemma, dismissing the government was not the best option. The Maoists have been able to grow, in part because of the factious nature of the mainstream parties but a major share of the blame surely rests on the king who had not given any administration in Kathmandu room for negotiation[46] The king had also betrayed the expectations that the country had from him following his incarnation in 2001. To falcify the king's calculations the Maoists and the democratic forces joined hands together and after a nineteen days mass demonstration in April 2006 the king had to left his executive powers and agree to work with an interim government. In a grand alliance of seven parties and the Maoists, the latter had consented to join the interim government. This grand alliance was entrusted to conduct elections to a Constituent Assembly. The interim government would have also to administer the country till the formation of a new government elected on the basis of the Constitution which will emerge from the Assembly's deliberations.[47] The 8-point agreement between Seven Party Alliance (SPA) and the Maoists explicitly provided for the United Nations to help in the management of arms and armed personnel of both the sides and to monitor it in order to conduct elections for the Constituent Assembly in a free and fair manner.[48] It was the best chance ever provided for the peaceful democratic change in the Himalayan Kingdom.

The election to the members of Constituent Assembly was held on April 10, 2008 that saw more than 60 per cent participation of the 17.5 million-strong electorate in 21,000 polling centres. In results the Nepali citizenry surprised itself and the world on occasion with a show of people's will that was unprecedented and path-breaking. It had brought a rebel force barely out of the jungle into the driver's seat of national politics. The Maoists has achieved a massive win over its rivals, the Nepali Congress and the mainstream left Communist Party of Nepal (UML). By voting in the Maoists as the single largest party, the electorate has sent a clear message that it favoured the new. But voters tempered this message by denying the former rebels an absolute majority of their own. Under the rules of Nepal's interim constitution a two-thirds majority was needed for any major decision, including the election of Prime Minister and President. By giving the Maoists a little more than one-third of the seats, the electorate said that it wanted the Maoists to keep alive the principle of consensus that had served Nepal's parties so well in the struggle against the monarchy.

Several factors seem to explain the crushing success of the Maoists in Nepal. To begin with, the Maoist win is the result of a well-oiled campaign machinery worthy of a politico-military organisation. There was country-wide deployment of threat and intimidation during the run-up to the elections, which demoralized competing party activists and civil servants alike. A major reason for the win seems to be voter's desire to keep the Maoists from returning to the people's war and suffering attendant miseries. The imperfect peace process, made so by the absence of the rule of law and state administration over the last two years, left the population beleaguered and worried of a return to that horrific period. It is said that urban people were convinced of the Maoists' popular promise in a country whose workforce continues to migrate in massive numbers to India and overseas because of high levels of poverty. The Maoists projected themselves as true agents of change.[49] Lastly they also filled their candidates from the members of the deprived communities, including the Dalits, the Janajati ethnic category and women. They laid claim with justification, to having introduced all the salient issues that had been placed before the electorate, including the demands for inclusion, federalism, secularism and an overturning of economic relations to serve the underclass.

Emergence of the Maoists as the single largest party had paved the way for formation of a Maoist-led coalition government in Nepal. Having confirmed that he would lead the Maoists in the government Pushpa Kamal Dahal 'Prachanda' began to speak on its relations with neighbouring countries and at the same expressed his party's vision of a new Nepal. Apart from underlining his desire to follow the policy of 'equidistance' in relationship with giant neighbours India and China[50] he also wanted to change the image of the Maoists among the middle classes in Nepal and among the international community. There was some suspicion about the Maoists' intentions, given their background as insurgents against the monarchy and it was thought that they would be autocratic when they assumed power. Initially there were doubts whether they would participate in the democratic process of elections as it was assumed their strength lay only in the power of arms. After emerging as the largest party there was still some concern that would turn autocratic, Prachanda emphasised that they would again proved the critics wrong by demonstrating their commitment to multi-party democracy and democratic rights and freedoms.[51] However, with some delay in forging the alliance the Maoists had reached an agreement with the Communist Party of Nepal (UML) and Madhesi Janadhikar Forum (MJF), the two major parties, to support Prachanda's candidacy first and later the government. In afterwards his candidacy was also backed by other small parties. He took the oath of office of the Prime Minister with eight ministers in the third week of August 2008.[52] Now the time has come to rectify the past misdeeds and address the question of disjunction with utmost care and importance.

## Challenges Ahead

Nepal was brought together territorially by the Gorkha conquest. It had not been unified psychologically and economically even after more than two centuries. This is partly because the Nepali state was captured and exploited by a small elite caste group ever since its formation. The ruling group defined the rights and duties of citizens towards the state to promote its own interests. This disjunction between the state and society has been the underlying cause for the eruption of many contentious activities in present day Nepal, which have directly or indirectly affected the recent trend towards democratization.[53] The Maoists who are assigned to seat on driver's position by the power of the ballot have every right to feel betrayed and cheated, they must make one last attempt to foster a consensus. For the better or worse, the former rebels are the only party with the ability to manage the contradictions and faultlines which lie at the base of Nepali society. A just beginning initiated with cooperation from all corners need to be upheld.

Earlier the Maoists attempt to lead a coalition government was frustrated by the arch rivals the Nepali Congress, the Communist Party of Nepal (UML), and the Madhesi Janadhikar Forum (MJF) who banded together to defeat the candidature of Ram Raja Prasad Singh, the Maoist nominee for President in July 2008. In this month Ram Baran Yadav, a Madhesi and Nepali Congress candidate for President and Parmanand Jha of the MJF were elected first President and Vice-President of the new republic of Nepal. However, internal politics in the Kingdom took a turn and in less than a month Pushpa Kamal Dahal 'Prachanda was elected the Prime Minster of the Federal Democratic Republic of Nepal by a four-fifth majority of the Constituent Assembly. It represents the ultimate victory of sobriety, accountability, and morality over the politics of cynicism and distrust.[54] Although governing Nepal at a time of global economic uncertainty will be challenging, the most important task before Prachanda is to lead the writing of a new constitution. The key challenges will be here to articulate robust mechanisms for the exercise of citizens' political social, cultural, and economic rights; working out a federal structure that can address the needs and aspirations of different ethnic groups, including the Madhesis; and ensuring that the army remains subordinate to civil authority.[55] The new government and Constitution are likely to place Nepal's relations with the outside world and with India on a sounder footing.

Despite instability of the successive governments the Nepali Congress and the Communist party of Nepal (UML) had in fact since 1990 developed values of responsible politics and Parliamentary practice and the expectation was that particularly with the new entrants—the Maoists and the new the Terai/

Madhes, the people now wait to see how the leadership takes the lead vis-à-vis the grave responsibilities of writing a new democratic constitution and running the state administration. It poses a challenge before the new dispensation to continue required majority in the Constituent Assembly to incorporate their radical reforms into the new constitution. Without sufficient number in the constituent the opposition would not be willing to be a party to the programme of the Maoists and would try to subvert any radical changes aimed at curtailing their own class interests. Hence no radical restructuring of the system is possible without the militant mobilisation of the vast masses into bitter class struggle. It is impossible to make changes through measures initiated from above; that is through state decrees and laws.[56]

Army integration is another issue that needs to be dealt with. The Maoists must also assure all on a sober and responsible approach to the national security forces—the Nepal Army, the Armed Police and the Nepal Police. Related to it is the integration of the People's Liberation Army with the Nepal Army. Integration is a formal part of the peace process and the seven party alliance is formally committed to seeing it through. Until now, the Nepal Army brass has publicly opposed integration. The Maoist leader Prachanda himself had said in the past that Nepal did not need such a large army but any drawing down of numbers will have to be accompanied by a plan to reabsorb those being demoralized in some kind of productive employment. What form integration will take and what the overall size of the Nepal Army should be are issues that need sorting out. The Maoist leadership needs to handle this question with a great deal of sensitivity and tact. Already, the decision to deploy the People's Liberation Army for the Prime Minister's security has irked the Communist party of Nepal (UML) MJF and Nepali Congress. Arjun Narsingh, the spokesperson of the main opposition party Nepali Congress, has also said that if the integration did not meet international standards, it could demoralise the Army.[57] He added further, How can they control both state and non-state armies? It has continued to be a deadlock point among the coalition-partners and needs to be handled carefully.

The Maoists faced an extremely difficult task ahead in balancing all the external forces and carrying on with their people's agenda. Basically the Maoists were apprehensive of the US and Indian motives and designs with whom it has to deal tactfully. As disclosed by Prachanda in May 2008 in course of an interview to *The Hindu* 'We will be living in a fool's paradise if we believe that the US and India will be comfortable with the Maoists in Nepal or that they will adjust to the new reality. Although they will continue diplomatic relations, they will create an adverse situation if the new government does not obey their dictates. The US tried its best to keep the monarchy alive as the king was a pawn to rule by proxy. As for India it received a slap in its face when G.P. Koirala and his NC faced a defeat'[58] However, he did not miss the opportunity to add the fact that both India and the US can hit at Nepal's belly—its economy by paralising industrial production, blocking trade and supply lines thereby creating food shortages and shortage of consumer goods. Towards the US perhaps it is because of its continuing designation of the Maoists as a terrorist organization. Former President Jimmy Carter has publicly called for this designation to be withdrawn but no organization that has been so named has ever been taken off the terrorist list. From strategic points of view the Indian government should approach the US to get Nepal removed from the list of terrorist organisation. This designation is a major hurdle in developing Nepal's relations with many developed western countries.

Not only on several internal and foreign policy counts but the present dispensation will also face difficulty in solving its own party's problems. The major challenge for the Maoist—led government would be to reinstate hundreds of families displaced by their war. Of the estimated 2100 displaced families, only 700 have got their homes back. The Maoists also have to return the public and private land and properties seized during their war. Here, it is necessary to separate this issue into two. Certain properties such as private dwellings are easier to return but land seized from landlords is not. In the case of land that is being tilled by persons other than legal owners, a solution of a longer-term nature can be found through the constitutional process itself rather than through bargaining outside the Constituent

Assembly. Article 19 of the Interim Constitution speaks of compensation to be paid by the state for any property requisitioned as part of scientific land reform'. The question of land is central to the livelihood of millions of ordinary Nepalis and land reform will be a major pre-occupation of the Constituent Assembly. Earlier, on the day of Prime Ministerial election, senior leader Babu Ram Bhattarai reiterated the party's commitment to return those confiscated land and properties.

**India-Nepal Relations**

India and Nepal have a deep and abiding special relationship without parallel in the world. But with the end of 240-year old monarchy rule the new republic of Nepal has made a fresh beginning in its wholesome relations with India. To make any engagement with new Nepal constructive and mutually advantageous, India has to grasp the degree and depth of the radical transformation that Nepal has gone through in the last couple of years. The former Kingdom has witnessed the spread of political consciousness at the grass roots, up surge of socio-economic aspirations and the unprecedented rise of peoples power. Now India can no longer pursue its vital strategic and economic interests in this radically transformed Nepal on the basis of its old colonial policy mindset and bureaucratized traditional tools of diplomacy. It can no longer play the king against the Ranas; political parties against the king; one set of Koiralas against the other; and one political party against the other. The old chess-board politics of cultivating coteries and promoting cronies or pitting feudal, corporate and sectarian vested interests against one another would be grotesque and counter-productive.[59] Although the new Nepal is not free from political cleavages and faultlines like the 'Madhesh' versus the 'Paharis;' the Janjatis versus the dominant castes and the prosperous versus the paupers. There are also disgruntled feudal and discarded political interest groups that would like to sabotage the new and emerging Nepal. The traditional strategic mindset in South Block and operations experts in the security agencies may want these new faultlines to be exploited to promote India's short term interests. But following such will harm India more than help it.

Despite the fact that landlocked Nepal was surrounded by both India and China, the Kingdom's geographic, economic, and cultural orientation was more closely linked to India. Under geo-strategic compulsions, Nepal's importance in India's security concerns is enhanced due to its relations with China. Though the Chinese have settled their boundary issue with Nepal through the Sino-Nepal boundary agreement and efforts are being made to normalize Sino-India relations through diplomatic talks in the wake of an armed conflict with India, the Chinese may not hesitate to pass through Nepal and carry out operations against India.[60] Keeping it in view India's policy makers tended to stress the similarities that bound the two countries together as Jawaharlal Nehru, the Prime Minister of India, stated in Indian Parliament in 1950 that we respect the independence of Nepal but we can not allow anything wrong to be happened in Nepal because that would be a risk to our own security. Nehru and his successors subsequently stated that any Chinese attack on Nepal would be regarded as aggression against India. According to New Delhi's perception, South Asia constituted an integral security unit in which India played the lead role.

On the other many Nepalese stressed the differences that defined Nepal's national existence and resented Indian interpretation and accused the latter of being insensitive to Nepal's status as an independent nation. Despite New-Delhi's insistence that stable, independent neighbours were vital to India's security, many Nepalese regarded India as a regional bully. Because of these differing attitudes, Nepal's relations with India oscillated considerably over the years, particularly in matters of security. Geography, British colonial history commonalities of civilization and an inner quest for a unique national identity, given Nepal's history as an independent country since its founding in 1769, are the structural and psychological factors behind the mistrust and unstable bilateral security relations between India and Nepal after India's independence in 1947. Nepalese national politics are best understood against the background of these forces coupled with the normal big power-small power asymmetry in the relationship that is common to all nations.

India after 1947 started its relations with Nepal on a very happy note and during the regime of King Tribhuvan it enjoyed a privileged position in comparison to other powers of the world. In view of the danger posed by Chinese annexation of Tibet by force in 1950 India and Nepal both felt the need of a comprehensive treaty. Fearing that China might eventually subvert or invade Nepal, India signed a Treaty of Peace and Friendship with the Rana regime in 1950. Although not a formal military alliance, the treaty required both parties to consult and 'devise effective countermeasures' in the event of a security threat to either country. In the exchange of secret letters that was made later public it was provided that neither government shall tolerate any threat to the security of the other by a foreign aggressor. To assuage Nepalese fears of Indian domination, the treaty also stipulated that Indian forces could be introduced into the country only at the invitation of the Nepalese government. At the same time they also signed a trade and transit agreement that extended reciprocal rights with regard to bilateral trade and residential arrangements as well as trans-shipment of Nepalese goods through India.

As a section of the Nepalese people was not happy with the special relationship, following the demise of King Tribhuvan in mid-1950s who was a prime mover in the evolving India-Nepal relation, tensions were bound to be high. In this period Indian businesses started to pour into Nepal in the 1950s bringing in their own managers and labourers: and when migrant Bihari labourers, chose to settle in the bordering Terai region as tenants. Fear, suspicion of foreigners, and a complex of inferiority among the general population were inevitable psychological reactions to these new developments when Nepal had just opened its gates to the outside world after 104 years' of a closed-door foreign policy pursued by the Rana regime. The open border policy created insurmountable difficulties for Nepal in implementing a development policy based on market liberalism because it was not ideologically palatable to India throughout the period. Later the open border system also created serious troubles for India from mid-1980s when ISI activities increased in India through Nepal and the most wanted criminals made Nepalese territory their safe centre where Indian police can not reach easily.

In spite of close military ties on the basis of 1950 treaty between the two countries Nepal has never allowed garrisoning of Indian troops or joint military exercises in the country. A bilateral strategic divide arose, for the first time, when King Mahendra assumed direct rule in 1961 and in 1962, during the Sino-Indian border war. In post-1962 period Nepal tilted towards the Peoples' Republic of China as the latter had defeated India in the war. King Mahendra, strengthening country's strategic relations with China, took the bold and far-reaching decision to allow China to build the north-south or Arniko highway to link Lhasa to Kathmandu, which was started in 1963 and completed in 1965. Further this divide between them arose prominently, once again, when India adamantly refused to recognize King Birendra's 'Zone of Peace' concept. The stridency of its Nepal policy against the peace zone concept of 1975 was to be witnessed by the fact that although it had been endorsed by 116 countries of the United Nations, and King Birendra, the then king, considered that the 1950 treaty of peace and friendship was not incompatible with it. The genesis of this policy lay, most probably, in the annexation of Sikkim by India in 1975 as a part of the Indian Union.

The India-China war of 1962 and the later developments had reinforced Nepalese perceptions of their country's perilous role as a Sino-Indian security buffer. Because of India's growing influence and Nepal's corresponding dependence on India, international diplomacy has always been a vital element of Nepal's survival strategy. Nepal was an active participant and a voice of moderation in the United Nations and the Non-aligned Movement. At the UN the late King Birendra proposed to declare Nepal a Zone of peace, where military competition would be off-limits. In his view, the proposal symbolized Nepal's desire to maintain cordial relations with both its neighbours by placing internationally sanctioned restrictions on the use of military force. Later Nepal became less emphatic on the issue and firmly supported the South Asian Association for Regional Cooperation (SAARC) headquartered in Kathmandu. However, the SAARC eschewed any role in regional security because the threats perceived by Nepal and the other small states of the region were often at variance with those perceived by India.

Relations between India and Nepal received a major jolt over a protracted period starting in 1988 when in the month of June King Birendra concluded a secret arms purchase with China to supply obsolescent air defence artillery at bargain prices. In India's view King Birendra had violated the spirit, if not the letter, of the 1950 treaty and hence protested vigorously the agreement. New Delhi interpreted the sale as a dangerous precedent that could not go unchallenged. King Birendra, capitalizing on nationalistic fervor, was intransigent and insisted that Nepal had the sovereign right to determine its own defence requirements. When India raised other issues of vital interests Nepal also pointed out that its use of air defense assets against India would never arise as long as Indian fighters respected Nepalese air space.

Within a year of the dispute India's hardening attitude towards Nepal became known to all when in March 1989 India refused to renew the India-Nepal trade and transit agreement unless Nepal agreed to meet India's commercial and defence concerns. After both sides refused to back down India allowed the agreement to lapse and closed thirteen of the fifteen border check-posts that regulated most of Nepal's trade with the outside world. The blockade was a severe blow to Nepal because there were no other reliable transit routes. Apart from difficulties with China, Pakistan and Bangladesh were hardly in a position to supply major assistance because of their only land routes to Nepal traversed India. Other world powers including the US and USSR had declined to take sides and urged India and Nepal to return to the bargaining table. Many Nepalese saw New-Delhi's action as 'punishment' for Birendra's show of independence and as a manifestation of India's supposed policy of isolating and subjugating its smaller neighbours. Ultimately after fifteen months of economic dislocations and diplomatic recriminations, both sides reaffirmed the 1950 treaty and Kathmandu agreed not to purchase defence items abroad without consulting New Delhi. King Birendra also requested the China to stop the delivery of a final shipment of air defence equipment. However, relations between the two returned to normalcy and improved significantly in May 1991 when a democratically elected government assumed office in the

Kingdom. The entire episode convinced many Nepalese that India had the capacity and will to pressure small neighbours in pursuit of its foreign policy objectives-a message that New Delhi clearly intended to convey to Beijing.

In 1990 Nepal adopted a new Constitution and in the multi-party elections held in May 1991 a democratic government was intalled in the country. The new Constitution was based on the principles of constitutional monarchy in which real power of the administration was vested in the elected government. Especially from mid-nineties the Maoist insurgency began to spread in Nepal and apart from forming a coalition government earlier after fifteen years they reached in commanding position. In these long years many of the senior Nepali Congress and the Communist Party of Nepal (UML) were in close companies and fondly swear by the old politics and cozy alliance with the feudal vested interests. These leaders had the chance to initiate and lead the agenda of a new Nepal after the first Jan Andolan, if they had any sincere commitment to it. When the Maoists gained strength and seemed to halt democratic process of the country and it became almost impossible to hold general election. In that kind of situation, the then King Gyanendra began asserting his authority from 2002 as the successive governments failed to defeat the Maoists insurgency. After six years of armed struggle, the People's Liberation Army and the Royal Nepal Army had fought each other to a standstill. Each side was capable of staging punishing strikes on the other but in strategic terms, an impass had set in which could have dragged on for years.[61] While Gyanendra chose to press for an outright military victory, the Maoists sought to break out of this stalemate by opening a political front of struggle.

Until February 2005, the dominant section of the Nepali Congress and the Communist party of Nepal (UML) leadership continued to work closely with the palace. But the Indian approach to the whole issue remained myopic and confusing-chanting the ideal of constitutional monarchy while lending almost total support to the King's authoritarian moves. Behind this policy was India's somewhat imprudent and unrealistic dislike for corrupt and power hungry political leaders as well as its near hatred for the Maoists who are seen as supporters and abettors of the Naxalite and insurgent groups in India.[62] For a while India's assertive stance during the Kathmandu blockade was understandable but that can not be the long-term response. It would be an adventure on the part of India and foolhardy, if not suicidal move to support the military methods of King Gyanendra. What India could do at the juncture was to work as a quiet and honest facilitator and it should try and set a sincere peace process, involving all the three important players moving in Nepal. Towards that end, it should lean heavily on the king to make him accept the role of a genuine constitutional monarch.[63] New-Delhi also needs to engage constructively with the political parties as well as the Maoists without any prejudices on its part.

In a desperate move King Gyanendra declared emergency in the country and took over all executive powers of the government on February 1, 2005. Earlier the NC and the UML leadership had cooperated with the king in the hope that the latter would win over the Maoist but their expectations too belied as the king had imposed several restrictions on political activists of all shades. The Maoists forces are also ready to open a political front leaving their earlier path of violence and intimidation. The situation left the NC and UML in a dilemma. To the extent to which they rejected the Maoists demands and use of violence, a section of their leadership found the king's call for a fight to the finish appealing. But another section also knew that the violence of the Maoists was not merely nihilistic and that the rebels' demands enjoyed support amongst the poor and marginalised. In addition they were suspicious that if some way could be found to get the Maoists to enter the political arena, they believed, not only would this help to bring peace to Nepal but a new power equation might get established which would further the struggle against autocratic monarchy.

But the foolishness of the king had left no alternative before them than to fight jointly against the misrule of the ruling monarchy. In the situation collaboration with the monarchy was not longer tenable. Slowly but surely, the centre of gravity within these two establishment parties began to move in the direction of peace negotiations with the Maoists. With the assistance of Nepali civil society leaders an atmosphere of trust and confidence between the parties was built up, grounded in the twin objectives of peace and constitutional reform. Ultimately the leaders like Girija Prasad Koirala and Madhav Kumar had showed the courage to place the future of the country above their partisan concerns and with the backing of India, they entered into a major understanding with the Maoists in November 2005. It led to the launching of second Jan Andolan in April 2006 which succeeded and the king agreed to hand over the executive powers to a coalition which would form a government.. The Parliament suspended in 2002 was also restored and a schedule of the election of Constituent Assembly announced which held finally in April 2008. The elected members of the Constituent Assembly would also act as a legislature till the constitution is written.

The results of the election went in favour of the Maoists who emerged as the single largest party. The Maoists formed a coalition government with the support of the Communist Party of Nepal (UML) and Madhesi Janadhikar Forum (MJF) who also participated in the government. In August 2008 Pushpa Kamal Dahal 'Prachanda' was elected the first Prime Minister of the new federal republic of Nepal. All told, the election results are good news for both India and Nepal. Rather than looking at the rise of the Maoists with fear and trepidation, the Indian establishment needs to do what it can to help Nepal's new coalition government fulfil its democratic mandate.

The entire gamut of India-Nepal relations underwent a radical change with turnings in Nepal's national politics which led to the end of monarchy and establishment of a Maoist - led coalition government formed in August 2008. One of the major demands of the new dispensation in Nepal is the revision of Indo-Nepal Treaty of Peace and Friendship signed in 1950. Earlier even the first Communist government of Nepal which was formed in 1994 demanded the revision of the treaty and later on times without number the issue of revision of the treaty has been raised by individual persons and organisations as well. The present Maoists government, particularly after emerging as the single largest party had assertively reiterated the demand in view of changed perspectives. In past the treaty had found unequal treatment by the ruling elites of Nepal. Its criticism at any given time has depended on the degree of hostility or political insecurity felt by a particular power centre in Kathmandu vis-à-vis India. Except in the brief period of King Tribhuvan, the monarchy in Nepal was actively engaged for several decades in undermining the treaty in letter or spirit or both. But even when Nepal had a democratic dispensation, there was a certain unity across the political spectrum that, while the economic benefits accorded by the treaty were essential for Nepal, the treaty in its existing shape was not compatible with national self- respect.[64]

In letter and spirit the treaty of 1950 between India and Nepal represented a straightforward imitation of understandings dated back to British India days, and basically offered economic opportunities in India for Nepalese nationals against Nepalese assurances that India's security concerns would be respected, became an irritant in relations between the two countries as soon as it was signed. In Nepalese view, India's growing sense of insecurity, generated by an apparently aggressive and expansionist China, had compelled it to yield to expediency, abandon its support for the incipient democratic movement against the autocratic Rana regime and seek to constrain Nepal's sovereignty so that it was compatible with India's security perceptions. The new incumbent which took over in August 2008 had also reiterated the demand and Prime Minister Pushpa Kamal Dahal 'Prachanda' even before taking the oath of office in June 2008, emphasized stronger relations with India on the basis of new realities.

In tune with the Nepalese sentiments and changed context the Government of India had agreed to review the treaty of 1950. Pushpa Kamal Dahal 'Prachanda', the first Prime Minister of the new federal republic of Nepal came to India on a four day official visit 14-17 September 2008 along with Nepalese Foreign Minister Upendra Yadav. They met leaders of the different political parties and held discussion on wide range of subjects covering bilateral and multilateral issues. India's Foreign Secretary Shiv Shankar Menon said that Nepal is keen to look at the 1950 treaty and we have said that we are ready to revise and update it. At a separate news conference the Foreign Minister of Nepal had said, 'Times have changed. We have to upgrade and revise it to make our friendship stronger.[65] Above all the successful visit of Nepalese Prime Minister has set the—stage for a new chapter in the relationship between New-Delhi and Kathmandu. While the joint press statement suggests that substantive decisions have been taken, the real significance of the visit lies in the fact that it has allowed the Indian establishment to see first-hand the statesman like approach of the Maoist leader towards issues that animate the bilateral relationship.[66] Given the big political changes that have occurred in Nepal and India over the past six decades, a new treaty is needed to better reflect the challenges and opportunities. Both sides need to ensure that the work of developing a new treaty is handled in friendly and cooperative spirit. In the long run, India will find that a democratic, self-confident Nepal will be a far better friend and partner than the monarchy which it supported for years ever was. What is needed on both sides is a creative political approach towards each other, free from ideological obsessions and past prejudices.

## Notes and References


1. Dr. Rajkumar Singh, "Democratic Experiments in Nepal," Babuddin Khan, ed., *Third Concept*, Vol. 21, No. 251, January 2008, New Delhi, 2008, p. 13.
2. J.W. Bjorkman, "Changing State-Society Relations: Broad-Brush Approaches and Analytical Models," Ramesh K. Arora, ed., *Administrative Change*, Vol. X X VIII, No. 2 and Vol. XXIX, No. 1, January-December 2001, Jaipur, 2001, pp.12-13.
3. Rishikesh Shaha, *Nepali Politics: Retrospect and Prospect*, Delhi, 1978, p. 2b.
4. Ameet Dhakal, "A Republic at Last," *The Hindu*, 22 June, 2008.
5. Rajkumar Singh, *Less Tasty Indo-Nepal Political Relations 1947-1997*, Patna 1998, p. 18.
6. Takashi Inoguchi, "Political Security: Toward a Broader Conceptualization" Bansidhar Pradhan, ed., *International Studies*, Vol. 40, No. 2, April-June 2003, New Delhi, 2003, p. 114.
7. As quoted in Ameet Dhakal's article, *op. cit.*
8. *The Hindustan Times,* 4 June, 2001.

9. S.D. Muni, ed., *Nepal: An Assertive Monarchy,* New Delhi, 1977, p. 4.
10. Dr. Kirtyanand Singh, *Small Neighbours of Big Powers, India's Attitude Towards Nepal September 1946-March 1963*, Delhi, 1988, p. 74.
11. Mohan N. Shrestha, "Internal Migration of People in Nepal," *Eastern Antropologist*, Vol. 32, No. 3, July September, 1979, p. 163.
12. *Ibid.,* p. 164.
13. Dr. Ramakant and B.C. Upreti, "Regionalism in Nepal: A Study of the Terai Region," Ramakant, ed; *Regionalism in South Asia*, South Asian Studies Series, No. 5, Jaipur, 1983, p. 139.
14. *Ibid.,* 149.
15. See: *The Election Manifesto of Nepal Terai Congress*, Raxaul, 1959.
16. Nagendra Goyal, *The King and His Constitution*, New Delhi, Nepal Trading Corporation, 1959, p. 97.
17. Rishikesh Shaha, *op. cit.,* p. 23.
18. Fredrick H. Gaize, *Regionalism and National Unity in Nepal*, Berklley, 1975, p. 73.
19. K.K. Bikram Shah, "Nepal in the South Asian State System: Foreign Policy Dimension," Shelton U. Kodikara, ed., *External Compulsions of South Asian Politics*, New Delhi, 1993, p. 171.
20. Dor Bahadur Bisht, *op. cit.,* p. 109.
21. Dr. Kirtyanand Singh, *op. cit.,* pp. 76-77.
22. Pran Chopra, "The Living Goddess," *The Times of India,* 12 March, 1978.
23. Ramakant, *Nepal-China and India*, New Delhi, 1976, p. 41.
24. *Ibid.*
25. Shriman Narayan, *India and Nepal: An Exercise in Open Diplomacy*, Bombay, 1970, p. 117.
26. John Martinussen, *Democracy, Competition and Choice-Emerging Local Self-government in Nepal*, New Delhi, 1995, p. 36.
27. *Ibid.,* pp. 37-38

28. For detail see Dor Bahadur Bista, *Fatalism and Development: Nepal's Struggle for Modernization*, Hyderabad, 1991.
29. John Martinussen, *op. cit.,* pp. 38-39.
30. Siddharth Varadarajan, "The Rumblings in Nepal's Tarai," *The Hindu*, 9 April, 2008.
31. Dr. Ramakant and B.C. Upreti, *op. cit.,* pp. 158-60.
32. Ameet Dhakal in *The Hindu*, 22 June, 2008
33. Kanak Mani Dixit, "India and Nepal's Constituent Assembly," *Ibid.,* 7 March, 2008.
34. *Ibid.*
35. Siddharth Varadarajan, *op. cit., The Hindu*, 9 April, 2008.
36. Uddipan Mukherjee, "Maoism and Its Future in India," Subhash C. Kashyap, ed., *South Asia Politics*, Vol. 7, No. 3, July 2008, New Delhi, 2008, pp. 26-27.
37. S.D. Muni, "On a Hot Tin Roof," *The Hindustan Times*, 30 August, 2003.
38. *The Times of India* (editorial), 5 July, 1960.
39. Raj Kumar Kothari, "Democratic Transition in Nepal Banes and Boons for India, Subhash C. Kashyap, ed., *South Asia Politics*, Vol. 7, No. 2, June 2008, New Delhi, 2008, pp. 24-25.
40. Kuldip Nayar, "Estranged Neighbour: The Arrogant India," *The Indian Express*, 12 December, 1994.
41. *The Times of India*, 21 November, 1994.
42. *The Indian Express*, 22 November, 1994.
43. K.V. Rajan, "Should the 1950 Treaty Be Scrapped?" *The Hindu*, 3 May, 2008.
44. *Ibid.,* 22 November, 1994.
45. Raj Kumar Kothari, *op. cit.,* p. 26.
46. *The Hindustan Times*, (editorial), 2 February 2005.
47. Siddharth Varadarajan, "In Nepal Times to Check the Dangerous Drift," *The Hindu*, 20 September 2006.
48. *Ibid.*
49. Kanak Mani Dixit, "Enter Nepal's Maoist Establishment," *The Hindu*, 14 April, 2008.
50. *Ibid.,* 14 June, 2008.
51. *Ibid.,* 30 June, 2008.

52. *The Times of India*, (Nagpur), 23 August, 2008
53. Raj Kumar Kothari, *op. cit.,* p. 26.
54. *The Hindu*, (editorial), 16 August, 2008.
55. *Ibid.*
56. K. Srinivas Reddy, "Uphill Task for Nepal Maoists," *Ibid.,* 16 May, 2008.
57. *Ibid.,* 31 August, 2008
58. K Srinivas Reddy, *op. cit.*
59. S.D. Muni, "Dealing With a New Nepal," *Ibid.,* 15 September, 2008.
60. Sangeeta Thapliyal, "Nepal in India's Security Parameters," *Strategic Analysis*, Vol. XVIII, No. 9, December 1995, Islamabad, 1995, pp. 1194-95.
61. Siddarth Varadarajan, "A Lesson in Statecraft, From Nepal to India," *The Hindu*, 25 April, 2008.
62. S.D. Muni, *op. cit.,* 30 August, 2003.
63. *Ibid.*
64. K.V. Rajan, *op. cit.,* 3 May, 2008.
65. *Ibid.,* 17 September, 2008
66. *Ibid.,* (editorial), 19 September, 2008.

# 2

# THE FOUNDATIONS INDIA-NEPAL

## INDIA

### Geographical Position

India is a great subcontinent of Asia with a distinct geographical entity. Bounded by the great Himalayas in the north it stretches South-wards and at the Tropic of Cancer, tapers off into the Indian Ocean between the Bay of Bengal on the east and the Arabian sea on the west. It covers an area of 32,87,263 sq. km, and a population. Lying entirely in the northern hemisphere, the mainland extends, between latitudes 8° 4′ and 37° 6′ north and longitudes 68° 7′ and 97° 25′ east and measures about 3,214 km from north to south between the extreme longitudes. It has a land frontier of about 15,200 km. The total length of the coast line of mainland, Lakshadweep Group of Islands and Andaman and Nicobar Group of Islands is 7,516,5 km.[1]

### People

Situated between an Islamic cultural area to the west and a Buddhist cultural area to the east, India is Aryavarta—the homeland of the Indo-Aryan people and their highly structured, complex social and religious system. The Indians can scarcely be said to have a word of their own by which to express their common country. In Sanskrit it is called Bharatvarsha, from Bharata, a legendary monarch of the lunar line. The name, Hindustan, which was at the time adopted by European geographers, applies properly only to that portion of the penninsula lying north of the Vindhya mountains or yet more strictly to the upper basin of the Ganges, where Hindi is the spoken language. India, a word derived from the Sanskrit

Sindhu, "river" predominantly the Indus became familiar only after the British connection.[2]

Modern India, in its political aspects, is a product of a variety of influences spread over a long period of time. Three historical strands, stand out distinctly as substantial influences. The first is Hinduism, the solid bedrock and unifying framework of Indian society. The second is the British impact of rational level authority wielded by a central power that managed to consolidate the whole of the pre-independence era, generated in response to the impact of new world order as transmitted through the colonial power and developed as a means to political independence and social reform in the context of a slowly expanding framework of democratic institutions.

The Muslims (Arabs, Afghans, Mongols) came as raiders and conquerors starting sporadically as early as the eighth century in Sind and then more massively in the tenth and eleventh centuries, followed by the founding of the Delhi Sultanate in 1206 and the long rule of the Moghal dynasty from 1526 to 1707. The political organisation of Muslim rule, though it made great strides in civil administration, retained a hard core of military character. The period taken to install Muslim rule in India was very long and even then the whole of India was not brought under one political authority. The long period of fighting that resulted led to much dislocation of life and economic misery.[3] India's population, apart from Hindus and Muslims includes several large minority communities of various types, such as, Christians, Sikhs, Tribals etc.

**Strategic Position**

The strategic location of India has helped her to acquire a central position in Asia and in world politics. All the major sea and air routes of the world pass through India. It has some importance because it has placed her within easy reach of many sensitive areas in the world including China, the South-east Asian nations, West Asia and East Africa. On the extreme, west of the northern frontier is the Pakistan Occupied Kashmir, which is contiguous to the Sinkiang province of China and almost contiguous to the Tadzhik Republic of the Soviet Union. There are at least eight important passes in the Karakoram mountain range linking this area with Sinkiang, and an all weather motorable road, roughly following an ancient trade and pilgrim route, now connects Gilgit with Sinkiang. It is felt that the security problem in this sector is more political than military, arising mainly after the formation of Sino-Pak-Axis. The Soviet Union is, however, capable of seriously challenging the Chinese troops in Sinkiang from the western flank and thus frustrating any Chinese designs on the Indo-Pakistan sub-continent in this sector.[5]

India's geopolitical situation in the northern border area was undermined, to some extent, by two factors in the immediate Post-Independence period. The first of these was the partition of Bengal and the merger of the Muslim majority area of East Bengal into Pakistan. This virtually isolated India from Assam and the eastern and north-eastern borders with Burma and China (i.e., Tibet) except for a narrow corridor between East Bengal and the Sub-Himalayan hill area with disastrous consequences in the brief 1962 war on the north-eastern border with China. The second was the decision by New Delhi to allow the Himalayan border states of Nepal, Sikkim and Bhutan to maintain a separate political identity rather than to insist upon their accession into the newly formed Indian Union. While India has continued to exert a dominant influence in the border states, its position has been seriously weakened by the presence of China across the Himalayan border in Tibet. Chinese determination to wield at least a minimal influence in this "buffer" area has led to a limited confrontation that has had an adverse effect upon Indian interests in the border states.[6]

However, India need not rely solely upon a strategic position for political importance. The adequate size and compact form of the country is favourable and optimum for purposes of defence as well as effective policy. The larger a state is, the greater is the possibility of its containing a large population and a rich array of natural resources, and therefore the greater is its likelihood of being politically strong and economically wealthy.

**Political Culture**

A Political culture is defined as "the pattern of individual attitudes and orientations towards politics among the members of a political system".[7] The people of a society share a common human nature like emotional derives, intellectual capacities and moral perspectives. The common human nature expresses itself in the form of certain values, beliefs and emotional attitudes which are transmitted from one generation to another though with greater or lesser modifications, and thus constitute the general culture of that society. "Certain aspects of the general culture of a society are especially concerned with how government ought to be conducted and what it shall try to do. This sector of culture we call political culture."[8] It "is the set of attitudes, beliefs and sentiments that give order and meaning to a political process and that provides the underlying assumptions and rules that govern behaviour in the political system."[9]

In the Post-Independence India there have emerged two political cultures operating at different levels of Indian society. The first political culture can be characterized as an emerging mass political culture; the second as an elite political culture. The first is in the districts. It permeates local politics, both urban and rural, local party organization, and local administration. It is an expanding political culture which reaches out into the state legislatures, state governments and state administrations. Although it is permeated with traditional elements, it is not wholly traditional, for it has many modern components.

The nationalist leaders who took power from the British in 1947 set out to remake India in their own image. Their policies and actions are well known to those who have followed political events in Asia—five year plans for economic development, the community development programme, a spate of land reforms legislation, new institutions of local government, a national constitution, free state and national elections, the abolition of the princely states, the reorganization of states along linguistic lines. What is less known is the impact which these various policies have had upon the attitudes and behaviour of Indians towards the state and towards politics generally. Political attitudes in a country as large and complex as India are bound to be diversified. Along side the gentle, Gandhian style of politics in the state of Gujarat in the northwest one finds both the more emotional, violent and calculating politics of the delta of Andhra in the South and the uncompromising ideologically oriented politics of West Bengal in the northwest. However, the most significant change is the increase in the amount of contact between individual Indians and their government, with a consequent change in the character of their relationship. Three aspects of governmental activity have been vital in this changing relationship: the expanding activities of all levels of government, the dispersion of power and the democratisation of power.

The second political culture is personified by India's planners, many of the national political leaders, and the senior administrative cadre. It is also widespread in the army and it is shared by most of the English-speaking intelligentsia. It becomes less evident as one moves into state capitals, though it can be found there too, and almost disappears as one moves into rural areas or municipal government. It is a defensive political culture. It is critical of the emerging more popular, mass political culture which in large measure is its own creation. But though this culture is expressed in modern language and is permeated with elements which we ordinarily think of as modern, it is not wholly modern, for it has many traditional components.[10]

The elite political culture of India is clearly heavily influenced by the British view of politics. It is a politics of ideas and of men who personify ideas. There is room for personal foibles but not for irrational and irrelevant ethnic loyalties. From the view point of the Indian elite the most serious defect of the mass culture is that political action seems to be so heavily based upon loyalty to caste, religion, tribe and region at the expense of national loyalties. Caste and religious groups oppose one another. The elite considers that such ambitions and loyalties have no place in a modern democracy and that if they continue they could destroy the democratic system and the national state. The national movement certainly strengthened the ideal of India as one nation, and men because willing to sacrifice for a common cause without concern for the parochial loyalties to caste, religion, tribe, or language. In other words, the elite shares a belief or at least a predisposition, to judge men by their motives rather than by the equality of their work."[11]

The Post-Independence India's cultural tradition has involved an interplay and mixture of elite and mass culture, though in the realm of politics—a sharp division was maintained. The dispersion and democratization of power which has occured in recent years in India makes it impossible to maintain such a division. Today the elite culture—even while it maintains itself through its own socialization processes—has been losing political ground to the mass culture. The expansion of the mass and the entrance of rural leaders into state and national life suggests that if the gap is to be bridged, it is more likely to be done by creative leadership from the country side. If such men whose political carrers have largely been in the local party organisation, take control over the national government, they will have the formidable task of making the emerging mass political culture acceptable to the national elite which at the same time modifying that culture so that it is truly conducive both to modernisation and to stable democratic government.

**Essence of Foreign Policy**

An independent thinking on foreign policy—independent of the British Indian Government started with the beginning of the 1920s. In 1921 the All India Congress Committee at its Delhi session held on 4-5 November passed Resolution VI which could be regarded as a "landmark in the history of India's foreign relations".[12] It was for the first time that the Congress had passed a general resolution on foreign policy which made it clear that the British Indian Government in no way represented Indian opinion.[13] The resolution laid down the basis of an independent foreign policy.

India's outlook in regard to the foreign policy came to have a crucial turning point in 1926-27 when it began to acquire international perspectives under the able guidance of Jawaharlal Nehru who played the most notable role in the formation, growth and development of this outlook as also in the conduct of the foreign policy of independent India in the early years. Nehru attended the Brussels Congress of Oppressed Nationalities as a delegate of the Indian National Congress. At Brussels Congress, as Nehru wrote in his autobiography, "it was felt more and more that the struggle for freedom was a common one against the thing that was imperialism, and joint deliberation and where possible, joint action were desirable."[14]

However, the basic tenets of India's foreign policy found expression for the first time in the statement of Jawaharlal Nehru which he made on 7 September 1946 on All India Radio as the Vice-President and Member-in-charge of External Affairs in the Interim Government which had taken over on 2nd September, 1946. He said :

We propose, as far as possible to keep away from the power politics of groups, aligned against one another, which have led in the past two world wars and which may again lead to disasters on an even vaster scale. We believe that peace and freedom are indivisible and the denial of freedom anywhere must endanger freedom elsewhere and led to conflict and war. We are particularly interested in the emancipation of colonial and dependent countries and peoples, and in the recognition in theory and practice of equal opportunities for all races. We repudiate utterly the Nazi doctrine of racialism wheresoever and in whatever form it may be practised. We seek no domination over others—and we claim no privileged position over other peoples. But we do claim equal and honourable treatment for our people wherever they may go, and we can not accept any discrimination against them.[15]

Nehru's statement spelt out the basic format and directions of free India's foreign policy. He laid down the basic tenets that would guide India's foreign policy. These could be identified as (*i*) keepig away from power politics of groups aligned against one another, (*ii*) support for the emancipation of colonial and dependent countries, and (*iii*) repudiation of racialism and recognition of the theory and practice of equality of all races. These principles could further be summarised as those of non-alignment, anti-colonialism and anti-racialism.

Initially, for want of better, popular name, it was called an "independent policy or a policy aiming at freedom of action and judging every international question or problem on its own merit—with no advance ideological or military commitments. Even so, Nehru was at pains to assert that it was not a policy of 'neutrality' for, according to him, "neutrality as a policy has little meaning except in times of war". The concept of non-alignment as he made it clear had negative as well as positive elements. The negative element envisaged a course of refusal to take side in any military line-up of world powers. Non-alignment was meant to keep away from bipolarity, the cold war, ideological crusades, the arms race, and military blocs which were the chief characteristics of international politics of the era following the second world war.[16]

The preservation and promotion of national interest was the most important positive element of the concept of non-alignment. It should be noted here that the furtherance of national interest had traditionally been considered to be an object of all international relations. The national interest of nations constituted the foundation of the concept of non-alignment. In determining national interest, the leaders of the nations attempted a synthesis of nationalism and internationalism, a combination which gave much of the positive content to the concept of non-alignment. This enlightened national self-interest became the most important aspect of non-alignment.

Fight against colonialism and imperialism became one of the primary and overriding goals of free India's foreign policy.[17] This goal could be achieved only through the promotion of solidarity among the entire non-western world, hence the emphasis was on unity and co-operation among Afro-Asian countries. India required peace for its development. The other countries of Asia and Africa as they became free would also require peace for their development. But there could be no peace, as Nehru said so long as there was continued domination of one country by another. In his view the end of colonial domination was essential for the establishment of peace in the world.[18] The Indian National Congress in its various resolutions, condemned colonialism, in any form, and extended its support to the ongoing freedom struggles in many countries before and after independence.

It should be noted here that India's interest was not confined to the political emancipation of Afro-Asian countries alone. It did not overlook a related aspect of the problem, the problem of their economic emancipation. Nehru understood the link between political freedom and, economic emancipation. He knew that if they lagged behind in economic development, they would not be able to retain their independence, or else, one kind of domination would be replaced by another, that is, political domination would be replaced by economic domination. As such, he put emphasis on the economic development of these countries.

To Asia and Africa colonialism meant the domination of white powers over the coloured countries of the world.[19] India's opposition to colonialism was well known. Its opposition to racialism was a logical extension of that same policy. Nehru said in the Constituent Assembly on 16 May, 1949 that fight against racial discrimination was one of the pillars of India's foreign policy. Describing the situations in South Asia as grave he extended India's full co-operation and support to the people who were putting up a heroic struggle against the tyranny of a racial minority.[20] He opposed vehemently both tolerance as well as continuance of racialism as it was directly related to world peace and urged the nations to understand the problem properly and said, "Racialism has been, and is even today, the policy of some other countries. We in Asia who have suffered so much from it are not going to encourage it, but will cambat it, believing as we do that it is not only a negation of democracy, but also the seeds of conflict."[21]

The pursuit of the policy of racial discrimination by the Government of India could be seen in major decisions and transactions in the realm of Indian diplomacy and international relations that unmistakably demonstrated its impact. As a mark of protest against the policy India recalled its High Commissioner from the country and took the pioneering step of raising the issue of racial discrimination in the United Nations General Assembly under Article 10 to 14 of the UN Charter. India was also the first country which discontinued trade and diplomatic relations with South Africa.

## Political History

The Indus Valley civilization, is the earliest picture that we have of India's past. Impressive remains discovered at Mohenjo-daro in Sind and at Harappa in the Western Punjab have revolutionised the conception of ancient history. The Indus Valley civilization, as we find it, was highly developed and must have taken thousands of years to reach that stage. It was surprisingly enough, a predominantly secular civilization, and the religious element, though present, did not dominate the scene. It was clearly also the precursor of later cultural periods in India. This civilization connected and traded with its sister civilization of Persia, Mesopotamia, and Egypt, and superior to them in some ways. It was an urban civilization, where the merchant class was wealthy, and evidently played an important role. The system of an organized government over a large area, also developed almost simultaneously around the river valleys of Nile, Euphrates and Indus.[22] Gordon Childe adds that well planned streets and a meaningful system of drains, regularly cleared out, reflect the vigilance of some regular municipal government. Its authority was strong enough to secure the observance of town-planning by laws and the maintenance of approved lines for streets and lanes over several reconstructions rendered necessary by floods."[23]

While there is a definite sense of continuity between the Indus Valley civilization and later periods, there is also a kind of break or a gap, not only in point of time but also in the kind of civilization that came next. The Aryan migrations are supposed to have taken place about a thousand years after the Indus Valley period from the north west. The first great cultural synthesis and fusion took place between the incoming Aryans and the Dravidians, who were probably the representatives of the Indus Valley civilization. The coming of the Aryans into India raised new problems—racial and political. The conquered race, the Dravidians, had a long background of civilization behind them, but there is little doubt that the Aryans considered themselves vastly superior and a wide gulf separated the two races.

Caste began with a hard and fast division between Aryans and non-Aryans. The Aryans, to begin with, formed one class and there was hardly any specialisation. Aryans as a whole were agriculturist and agriculture was considered a noble occupation. The caste divisions, originally intended to separate the Aryans from non- Aryans, reacted on the Aryans themselves, and as division of functions and specialization increased, the new classes took the form of castes.[24] The four varnas in which the Aryans divided the caste system, Brahmin, Kshatriya, Vaisya, and Sudra, meant to correspond to the four functions of knowledge, defence, wealth, and labour respectively. The Indo-Aryans developed a special organization that answered to the several needs of the people. It became structured along a hierarchy of four varnas which were superimposed on a loose and primitive system of "castes" that existed before the Aryans came. Such a hierarchy, while based upon primary ties of marriage and family, assumed importance in the division of secondary functions, including "Political" functions such as the resolution and adjudication of disputes.

All the battles, the different tribes of the Aryans waged, whether among themselves or against the non-Aryans, were under their chief termed 'rajan'. The word is almost automatically translated as 'King' but we must remember that at this period the word signified a tribal chief rather than a king for there were no kingdoms as such. Nor did the 'rajan' exercise unfettered power which we normally associate with a king. The Rig Veda makes frequent references to the 'Sabha' and the Samiti whose voice the 'rajan' had to listen to. In all probabilities, the 'Sabha' was an assembly of the elders and the more powerful where as the 'Samiti' was a general assembly of the entire tribe.

The tribe consisted of families, the Kula, which was the basic unit of the society. The Kula was led by the Kulapati or Kulapa, and a member of Kulas formed a grama led by the gramani. A cluster of gramas with the gramani as the chief formed the Visah. There is mention of another unit, the Jana put the precise nature of the visah or the Jana is now difficult to determine. These constituted the rashtra with the 'rajan' as the chief. Although the institution of the rajan had become hereditary during this period, there are references to the rajan being selected by the visah.[25]

From the early until about the tenth century A.D., the Aryans formed several Kingdoms and ruled over the area, giving rise at times to empires such as the Mauryas, the Gupta, and the Harsha dynasty in the north, and the Cholas and Pallavas in the South. Hindu dynasties persisted in some areas long after the tenth century when the Muslim invasions began to undermine the political supremacy of the Hindus. Taking the subcontinent as a whole, however, a decline had set in after the tenth and eleventh centuries. The memory of a great past and its reinterpretation strengthened the awakening of modern India, and in that lies the political significance of the long Hindu period. Its real achievements, however, are in directions other than strictly political—in the perfecting of a remarkable social order and in the development of traditions and values that have had lasting effect on all subsequent periods.

Babar, a Turco-Mongols and a prince of the Timurid line in Central Asia won the throne of Delhi in 1526. With him begins the Mughal Empire of India. The impact of this invader, who came from the north-west and of Islam on India had been considerable. It had pointed out and shown up the abuses that had crept into Hindu society—the petrifection of caste, untouchability exclusiveness carried to fantastic lengths. On the otherhand, Babar's success was probably due not only to the weakness of the Delhi Sultanate but to his possessing a new and improved type of artillery which was not in use in India then. However, the Moslems, brought from outside, know new technique and political structure. Inspite of a religious belief in the brotherhood of Islam, they were class bound and feudal in outlook. In technique and in methods of production and industrial organization, they were inferior to what prevailed then in India. Thus, their influence on the economic life of India and the social structure was very little. The Afghan and Mughal rulers took special care not to interfere with old customs and conventions and no fundamental changes were introduced, and the economic and social structure of Indian life continued as before.

The Muslim rule in India considerably disturbed the pre-existing balance of the Hindu system. From the first raids of Afghans, internal peace was upset by periodic fighting, ravaging, plundering, the destruction of holy-places, general disorder, and lawlessness. Military affairs were ferociously conducted by both Muslims and their Hindu adversaries— and often involved much local suffering and hardship. In many ways the whole period was characterized by lack of peace and a disturbance of the morale of the people. It greatly upset the self-confidence of leaders of society and religion and threw Hindu society into a state of confusion and defeatism. Hindu responded by withdrawing into the web of exclusiveness provided by caste and kinship and thus managed to survive.

Even before the Mughals, attempts were made by outstanding monarchs like Ashoka, Samudra Gupta, to bring the whole of India under a single state regime and administrative system. Again, Akbar, who was the third of the Mughal dynasty in India, as a warrior, conquered large parts of India, but his eyes were set on another and more enduring conquest, the conquest of the minds and hearts of the people. In him the old dream of a united India took shape, not only politically in one state but organically fused into one people.

They all, however, succeeded in bringing greater portion of India under their rule, the political and administrative unity achieved was of a normal character only, since legion of self-governing villages wherein the preponderant portion of the Indian population resided were not thereby affected. In fact, these villages, from times immemorial, had been so many self-governing republics. The village committee reinforced with the caste committees constituted the defacto government of the village population.

The main reasons why effective political and administrative unification of India in the pre-British period did not take place, were the absence of a unified national economy and efficient, well ramified, and extensive means of communications. The history of the rise of centralized states in European countries shows how the growth of such state structures is closely bound up with the growth of unified national economies and the development of rapid and efficient means of communications.[26]

The establishment of British rule in India was an entirely novel phenomenon for her, not comparable with any other invasion or political or economic change.[27] Every previous ruling class, whether it had originally come from outside or was indigenous, had accepted the structural unity of India's social and economic life and tried to fit into it. It had become India-nised and had struck roots in the soil of the country. The new rulers were entirely different, with their base elsewhere but between them and the average Indian there was a vast and unbridgeable gulf—a difference in tradition, in outlook, in income and ways of living. The feudal landlords and their kind who came from England to rule over India had the landlords view of the world. To them India was a vast estate beloging to the East India Company, and the landlord was the best and the natural representative of his estate and his tenants. That view continued even after the East India Company handed over its estate of India to the British Crown.

In 1858, after the shock of the Indian mutiny and revolt; the East India Company transferred its domain of India to the British Crown. That transfer did not involve a separate transfer of the Indian states apart from the rest of India. The whole of India was treated as a unit and the British parliament functioned in India through the Government of India which exercised a suzerainty over the states. The states had no separate relations with the British Crown or Parliament. They were part and parcel of the system of government, direct and indirect, represented by the Government of India. This government, in later years, ignored those old treaties whenever it suited its changing policy to do so, and exercised a very effective suzerainty over the states.[28]

The establishment of British rule in India brought about an extensive and basic political, administrative, and legal unification of the country for the first time in Indian history. It established uniform reign of law in the country. They enacted laws and codified them. These laws were applicable to every citizen of the state and were enforced by a hierarchically graded system of tribunals which constituted the judicial section of the state. Judicial officials appointed by the state interpreted and enforced the laws of the state incorporated into various codes in every village, town, and city. In establishing the new system of law and tribunals, the British had to supersede the customary law which prevailed in pre-British India and expropriate village and caste committee of their power to enforce the customary law which further varied from place to place in the absence of a uniform system of law. The new legal system was based on the democratic conception of equality of all citizens before the laws of the state.

In determining the first step in the development towards parliamentary government in India was the mild measure of reform introduced by the British and known as the Indian Council Act of 1909, by which for the first time some elected members were taken in the Viceroy's and Governor's council. It led to a demand for more representation and greater power to the elected elements who as yet, were greatly outnumbered by the official and nominated members of the council. The demand for "Home Rule" became more intense.

The Indian Council Act of 1919 established a moderate form of parliamentary government under foreign tutelage. A central legislature was constituted with two chambers, both of which included nominated members as before. It had also a substantial number of representatives elected on the basis of general and "special" electorates. At the Provincial level, there were further concessions in the direction of self-government. There came into being a symbol of "Dyarchy" according to which certain regulative and extractive functions of government were reserved for the Governor and others were transferred to ministers who were to be responsible to the Provincial Legislative Council, a majority of whose members were elected. The Act, as with all subsequent British attempts at conciliation, received a cold response in the country. The Indian National Congress in considering the Act of 1919 passed a resolution saying that the Act was "disappointing and called upon the parliament in Great Britain to establish "full responsible government" in India "in accordance with the principles of self-determination". The Congress in effect, declined to co-operate on the basis of the Act.

The British Parliament after some years of commissions, committees, and debates, passed a Government of India Act in 1935. They provided for some kind of provincial autonomy and a federal structure, but there were so many reservations and checks that both political and economic power continued to be concentrated in the hands of the British Government. Indeed in some ways it confirmed and enlarged the powers of an executive responsible solely to that government. The federal structure was so envisaged as to make any real advance impossible and no loophole was left for the representatives of the Indian people to interfere with or modify the system of

British administration. Any change or relaxation of this could only come through the British Parliament.

The Act strengthened the alliance between the British Government and the princes, landlords and other reactionary elements in India; it added to the separate electorates, thus increasing the separatist tendencies; it consolidated the predominant position of British trade, industry, banking and shipping and laid down prohibitions against any interference with this position. It retained in British hands complete control over Indian finance, military, and foreign affairs; it made the Viceroy even more powerful than he had been.

The Act of 1935 was bitterly opposed by all sections of Indian opinion. While the part dealing with provincial autonomy was severally criticized for its many reservations and the powers given to the Governors and the Viceroy, the federal part was even more resented. Federation as such was not opposed and it was generally recognized that a federal structure was desirable for India, but the proposed federation petrified British rule and vested interest in India.

As the Indian people became politically conscious, organized movements to secure demands for the transfer of power intensified and the end came quickly. The India Independence Bill, introduced in the House of Commons on 4 July, 1947, was hurried through both Houses in twelve days. On August 14, the India (Provisional Constitution) Order, 1947, was passed and the next day Pakistan and India were declared the two new dominions to which power was transferred. Now India is a Sovereign Socialist, Secular Democratic Republic with a Parliamentary system of government. The Republic is governed in terms of the constitution, which was adopted by the Constituent Assembly on 26 November 1949 and came into force on 26 January 1950.

## NEPAL

### Geographical Position

Nepal is an independent country, situated on the north eastern frontier of India. It is lying between 80° 15′ east longitude and between 26° 20' and 30° 10' north latitude. It has an area of 54,717 square miles.[29] It is 500 miles long from the east to west and 90 to 150 miles wide from the south to the north.[30] It is bounded in the north by Tibet; on the east by Sikkim; on the south by Bengal and west by Bihar and Uttar Pradesh. It is separated from the Tibetan region of China by the main Himalayan Range and is surrounded by Indian territory on other three sides. Nepal has 500 miles long free and open border with India. With its location in the centre of the Himalayas, between the Tibetan regions of China and India, it is a land-locked country, cut off from the rest of the world by high mountains. Among these distinct states, Nepal happens to be the largest on the Southern slopes of the great mountain divide which has always been regarded vital from the viewpoint of Indian security.

## People

The People of Nepal on the basis of three distinct geographical regions, have been categorized as the middle hill and valley people, the Terai and the northern border people. Socially and politically the Brahmans and Kshatries have been for a long time the dominant groups in Nepal. They form the local elite, and have also for many years dominated politics at the central level. In the high mountains region of the north the people are mainly of pure Mongoloid stock. Prominent among them are the Magars, the Gurungs, the Limbus, the Rais, the Tamangs, the Sherpas and the Thakalis. Their language, dress and customs are similar to those in Tibet. In southern Nepal the people are of Aryan stock.

In the central region there is mixture of Mongoloids and Aryan traits. The Newars belong to this category. They are concentrated in Kathmandu Valley. They are charactically an urban group. There are both Hindu and Buddhists sub-groups among the Newars. Living among these people, but apart from them, are clusters of high caste Hindu mostly of the Brahmin or Kshatriya castes. The Hindus of Nepal have regarded themselves as a different people because they had always remained independent while the Hindus of India had become subjects of the Moghuls and the British at different periods of our history. Long neglected by the Hindu community of India the Nepalese Hindus developed an independent approach and outlook in their political affairs.

**Strategic Position**

The geo-political situation of Nepal has considerably influenced Indian attitude because it forms a rectangle along the Himalayas. Like its nighbouring kingdom, Nepal is sharing borders with both India and Tibet. To the north the great Himalayas present a physical barrier which may be penetrated in only a few places. To the south the inhospitable swamps of the terai and the rocky inclines of the Siwalik ranges impede passage into the interior with the Tibetan plateau. Occupied by the troops of the Communist China and the construction of Lhasa - Kathmandu road, the less penetrable northern borders become geo-politically the more important of the two, not only to Nepal but to India as well.[31]

Nepal, by virtue of its strategic position has always felt that it could influence the course of events in central Asia. This feeling in the Nepalese mind is part of its ancient heritage. It was rooted in the awareness that one of the main land routes between India and China lay in Nepalese territory. In ancient times the main land route between India and China lay across Kashmir. But in 700 A.D. and with the discovery of Keyrong pass in west Nepal Himalayas, the main route shifted to Nepal. Britain's main interest in Nepal in the 18th and 19th century arose from the fact that the Kingdom controlled the access to the route for the entry of British merchandise into the Tibet market. When, early in the 19th century the Nepalese resisted British pressure to make inroads into Kathmandu, Britain switched over to the Chumbi valley route to Lhasa that lay in the Sikkim Himalayas. Again in 1902-4 Kathmandu demonstrated its ability to influence Lhasa in the dispute between Britain and Tibet. Though the opportunities to exploit the geographical influence was rare Nepal, however, was aware of its immense potential. For China, Nepal had all along been a distant neighbour with it could come into contact only through Tibet. In the early 'fifties' Pekings security interests in Nepal could no longer be regarded peripheral as the USA was setting up bases, wherever possible, encircling China. The Americans had found a foothold in 1949 at Kathmandu by Technical Assistance Co-operation on Mission. To New Delhi, Nepal had become part and parcel of the security system on India's northern fringe.

**Political Culture**

The people of Nepal have fairly low level of political consciousness. They neither have a clear sense of identity with the symbol of nationalism nor strong attitudes regarding the proper limits of political activity. For hundreds of years, the central government in Nepal was run by a number of inter-related families, with the most influential and powerful of them keeping the Prime Ministership or to chief executive position to themselves. Centrally appointed governors provided the link between Kathmandu and the rest of the country. The principal functions of the government were to maintain law and order and a semblance of justice within the territory to protect it against encroachment from outside, and to raise revenue from the inhabitants of the territory for the services of order and protection.[32]

The system was feudal in nature and to promote one's status, it was necessary to become part of the ruling hierarchy or to undertake some activity with its favour and sanction. For those who could not belong to the ruling hierarchy, the landed aristocracy was the second best choice as long as opportunities for reclaiming new land in the Terai and the hills existed. Under the circumstances, a political system was evolved which relied for its effectiveness on plots and rumour-mongering, bluster and bullying, and primarily on manoeuvres and counter manoeuvres. It was the primary obligation of the common people or the masses to support the elite in the government and in the landed aristocracy. The government existed for the elite rather than for the people. The organs of the government were used largely for the personal gain and the masses were exploited rather than benefited.

Thus, the political culture of Nepal has always been characterized by authoritarian tendencies. Both religion and general societal norms have reinforced the authoritarian tradition by encouraging blind obedience to autocratic authority of some kind or the other. Just as the will of the head of the family had to be obeyed under all circumstances, the ruler's wish was a law and command to the people. Nepal was ruled for centuries by the personal fiat of one strong man or the other. Considerations of the common people seldom figured in the calculations of the rulers. Peasants were associated merely with the ceremonial functions of the central government. Successful politics implied well-thought out and determined use of force aimed at the immediate gain of office for those involved in the adventure. However, under the impact of modern ideas and the limited application of science and technology to societal problems, the family's over all influence on the individual and on society is gradually declining.

## Essence of Foreign Policy

King Prithvi Narayan Shah, the founder of modern Nepal, not only unified the Kingdom, but also laid down the basic tenets of its foreign policy. He described the kingdom of the Kathmandu valley as "a fort built by God himself" and "a root between two stones". Giving a guide line to his successors about the foreign policy, the King said, "The Kingdom is like a yam between two stones. Maintain friendly relations with Emperor of China. Great friendship should also be maintained with the Emperor beyond the southern seas, but he is very clever. He has kept India suppressed. He is entrenching himself in the plains. One day that army will come. Do not engage in offensive attack. Fighting should be conducted on a defensive basis...... If it is found difficult to resist in the fight, then even means of persuasion, tact and deceit should be employed".[33]

The King himself followed this policy in his dealings with the British in India. From the emergence of Nepal as a modern nation state its most formidable problem in the formulation and implementation of foreign policy had been the preservation of its independence in the face of the two concurrent but separate threats posed by the newly emerging dominant power in northern India, the British East India Company, and the slowly but steadily expanding Chinese presence in Tibet. This was precisely the policy adopted by Nepal in the first half of the 19th century. Whenever, relations with the British reached a critical stage, the Nepalese did their utmost to dramatise their relationship with China. Although Nepal's policy of balancing China against British India could not succeed to the extent desired by Kathmandu. Nevertheless, Nepal persisted in its game of balancing the one against the other with a view to preserve at least its internal independence. Even during the period of Bhimsen Thapa (1806-37) the policy of friendly neutrality with British government was followed. Thus the utilisation of the balance of power and isolationism were the twin pillars of Nepal's foreign policy in the region.

The second pattern of Nepal's foreign policy, namely, the acceptance of a limited degree of domination by its more powerful neighbour, is evident after 1846. China's power and prestige declined to a great extent following the opium war (1840-42) and by 1846 Kathmandu realised that China was both unable and unwilling to provide the type of assistance required to preserve Nepal against British expansion. Under the circumstances Nepal adopted a new foreign policy of friendship and co-operation with the British India and moved into the British sphere of influence. Jung Bahadur Rana was the first Rana Prime Minister who assumed power on 17 September 1846. This marked a great dividing line in the history of Nepal's relations with British India. Jung Bahadur died in 1877 but his policy survived. Almost all Rana Prime Ministers followed his suit. In the subsequent years co-operation between the two increased further. While the Rana rulers helped the British government in dealing with the anti-British forces in India, the British in India helped the Rana rulers in curbing the anti-Rana activities of some young educated Nepalese in India.[34]

In the post-Rana regimes, particularly after the death of King Tribhuvan (1955) Nepal has been motivated in the formulation and execution of its foreign policy, by three strong urges. They are, as described by Liska—are the urges for "security, stability and status".[35] The urge for "security" has found expression in the objectives of (*a*) Preservation of autonomy and independence in taking and implementing foreign policy decisions; and (*b*) Preservation of territorial integrity. The first objective has a politico-diplomatic connotation and its task may be described as one of counteracting undesirable external pressures and influences. The second objective has a politico-military-strategic connotation and its task is defence against external aggression for the preservation of territorial integrity. The urge for "stability has also two dimensions, namely, (a) stability of the domestic power structure in which every ruling group has the highest stakes, and (b) stability through economic development. These dimensions have been accordingly expressed as objectives of foreign policy. The urge for "status" is psychological in nature and it has been one of the forceful drives behind Nepal's foreign policy behaviour.[36]

## Political History

Nepal is one of the oldest nations in Asia. In the beginning of the Kaliyuga, the Gupta dynasty is said to have been founded by Ne-Muni, from whom the country takes its name of Nepal. The modern history of Nepal has been shaped by three important periods : first, the conquest of the Kathmandu Valley by Prithvi Narayan Shah in the 1760s that led to the unification of Nepal under one rule. Secondly, the usurpation of power by Jung Bahadur in 1846, which resulted in the hegemony of the Rana family for 104 years without a break and finally, the sequence of events from 1950 onwards.

The Gurkhas were driven from their own country by the victorious Muslims and took refuge in the hilly districts of Kumaon, from where they gradually pushed their way eastward to Lamjung, Gurkha, Nayakot and ultimately the Valley of Nepal. In the latter half of the eighteenth century, the tiny principality of Gurkhas under the leadership of a King belonging to one branch of shah family began to expand its domains. All of the sub-Himalayan hill areas between Bhutan in the east and the Sutlej River in the west had been brought under control. More than seventy-five small hill principalities submitted, either voluntarily or after unsuccessful resistence to the formidable Gurkha armies. Prithvi Narayan Shah integrated the Kathmandu Valley in 1769 and thereafter undertook to unify the country and created the present state of Nepal. Thus it was the Gurkha conquest that gave the country a single name and a strong central government in modern times. The emergence of Prithvi Narayan Shah as a strong monarch out of the prevailing chaos and uncertainty, attendant upon the breakdown of the tribal era, was a major factor in the growth of Nepali nationalism and made a distinct advance from the state of a tribe to that of a kingdom.[38]

Prithvi Narayan Shah died in 1774. But from 1769 to 1846, the King both ruled and reigned. Though the post of Prime Minister was not unknown during this period, the Kings of Nepal undertook to rule directly and with authority.

After the conclusion of the Anglo-Napali war in 1815, the strong Prime Minister of Nepal Bhimsen, greatly increased the power of his office at the expense of the Monarch. His strengthening of Prime Minister's office paved the way for the establishment of the Rana line of hereditary Prime Ministers. The famous Treaty of Sugauli (1815) was ratified in March 1816, by which the Nepalese relinquished much of their newly acquired territory and agreed to allow a British residency to be established at Kathmandu. In 1839 Bhimsen's enemies succeeded in driving him from power, and he committed suicide, or was murdered, in prison. Ultimately, Jung Bahadur, a member of Bhimsen's family, obtained a prominent position in the government and soon after destroyed his enemies by what is known as the Kot massacre and assumed power on 17 September 1846. From that time till the day of his death Jung Bahadur was in reality the ruler of Nepal. In 1850 Jung Bahadur paid a visit to England and there proved himself to be a staunch friend of British. On his return in 1851 he devoted himself to reforming the administration of the country, and it must be allowed that he eventually proved himself the greatest benefactor his country ever possessed. In 1854 the Nepalese commenced a war against Tibet, which ended with a peace favourable to Nepal in March 1856.

Jung Bahadur's friendly and co-operative attitude towards British India was fully vindicated during India's first struggle for freedom in 1857-58. Inspite of great opposition he stood firm as a friend of the British. On 26 June, 1857, 4,000 troops were dispatched and rendered excellent service. Later on, he himself led the troops and broke up much of the rebel army. He played a great role in the final battle of Lucknow and Delhi.[39] Jung Bahadur was knighted and decorated for his services and his troops received pay and handsome donations if wounded. Jung Bahadur died suddenly in 1877 but his policy earned him much British appreciation. The large part of Terai low land, wrested from Nepal in 1816, was restored to Kathmandu.[40] His help to the British in the internal uprising in India also paved the way for recruitment of the Gurkha soldiers into the Indian army. Thus Jung Bahadur initiated the Nepalese policy of active co-operation with a view to earning prestige, money and territory. The Nepalese government had now finally abandoned the earlier policy of taking advantage of British difficulties. Nepal was now not only a safe neighbour but also a dependable ally.[41]

Even after the death of Jung Bahadur his policy survived. Almost all Rana Prime Ministers followed his suit. The most notable among whom was Chandra Shamsher, who ruled Nepal with much ability. He gave effective aid to the British during the Tibet war of 1904 and the relations with the Government of India became cordial after his accession. He also visited England in 1908 as a guest of the British Government.

During world war I, Sir Chandra Shamsher Jung placed the entire resources of his country at the disposal of the Allies. From 1915 to 1918 about 10,000 men of the Nepalese army served in India and on the Indian frontier. The 20 Gurkha battalions of the Indian army were increased to 40. In the brief Afghan war (1919) 2,000 Nepalese troops assisted the Indian government. Chandra Shamsher Jung was also responsible for the abolition of slavery in Nepal.

In addition to the old treaty of Sugauli a new treaty of friendship was signed on 21 December 1923, an important provision of which was the recognition by the British government of the complete independence of Nepal. In world war II as in world war I the Government of Nepal supported the Allied war effort with men and money. After war with a new situation having arisen in consequence of the partition of British India, the Republic of India and Nepal signed two treaties (1 August, 1950) regulating their political and commercial relations.

## Notes and References

1. India 1983, compiled by *Research and Reference Divison* (Publication Division, Ministry of Information and Broadcasting, Government of India, New Delhi, 1983), p. 1.
2. *Encyclopaedia Britannica*, Vol. 12 (Encyclopaedia Britannica, London, 1768), p. 150.
3. Rajni Kothari, *Politics in India* (Orient Longman, New Delhi, 1970), p. 31.
4. S.S., Bindra, "Foundations of Sino-Pak Axis", *Kurukshetra University Research Journal*, Vol. IX. 1975.
5. J., Bandyopadhyaya, *The Making of India's Foreign Policy*, (Bombay, 1980), pp. 34-35.
6. Wayne Wilcox, Leo E., Rose, Gavin Boyd (eds.), *Asia and the International System* (Winthrop Publishers, Cambridge, Massachusetts, 1972), p. 64.
7. G.A., Almond and Powell : *Comparative Politics : A Developmental Approach* (Boston : Little Brown, 1966), p. 50.
8. Beer and Ulam, *Patterns of Government* (Newyork, Random House, 1962), p. 32.
9. Lucian W., Pye, *Aspects of Political Development* (Boston, Little Brown, 1966), p. 104.
10. Myron Weiner, "India : Two Political Cultures", Lucian W. Pye and Sidney Verba (eds.), *Political Culture and Political Development*, (Princeton University Press, Princeton, New-Jersey, 1965), p. 199.
11. *Ibid.*, pp. 231-32.
12. Norman, D., Palmer, *"Foreign Policy of the Indian National Congress Before Independence"*, K.P., Misra, ed., *Studies in Indian Foreign Policy* (Vikas Publishers, Delhi, 1969), p. 22.
13. *Ibid.*
14. Jawaharlal Nehru, *An Autobiography* (Oxford University Press, London, 1936), p. 161.
15. Jawaharlal Nehru, *India's Foreign Policy, Selected Speeches, September 1946-April 1961* (The Publication Division, New Delhi, 1961). p. 2.

16. K. P., Misra, "*The Concept of Non-alignment Its Implications and Recent Trends*", *op. cit.*, pp. 91-92.
17. Jawaharlal Nehru *op. cit.*, p. 2.
18. *Ibid.*, p. 48.
19. Adda B., Bozeman, "India's Foreign Policy Today : Reflections upon its Sources", K.P., Misra, ed., *op. cit.*, p. 34.
20. Jawaharlal Nehru, *op. cit.*, p. 3.
21. *Ibid.*, p. 410.
22. A. L., Basham, *The Wonder that was India* (Newyork, 1959), p. 15.
23. Jawaharlal Nehru, *The Discovery of India* (Jawaharlal Nehru Memorial Fund, (Oxford University Press, New-Delhi, 1982), pp. 71-72.
24. *Ibid.*, p. 85.
25. O. P., Kejariwal, "The Vedic Age", 1-7 March 1997, *Employment News* (Publication Division, Ministry of Information and Broadcasting, New Delhi, 1997), p. 1.
26. A. R., Desai, *Social Bạckground of Indian Nationalism* (Popular Prakashan, Bombay, 1989), pp. 166-67.
27. Jawaharlal Nehru, *op. cit.*, p. 302.
28. *Ibid.*, p. 309.
29. Rishikesh Shaha, *An Introduction to Nepal* (Ratna Pustak Bhandar, Kathmandu, 1976), p. 1.
30. P. P., Karan and W. M., Jenkins, *The Himalayan Kingdom: Bhutan, Sikkim and Nepal* (Princeton : Van Nostrand, 1963), p. 79.
31. Dr. S. S., Bindra, *India and Her Neighbours : A Study of Political, Economic and Cultural Relations and Interactions* (Deep and Deep Publications, New Delhi, 1989), p. 203.
32. Rishikesh Shaha, *Nepali Politics : Retrospect and Prospect* (Oxford University Press, Delhi, 1978), p. 26.
33. Yogi Narahari Nath and Babu Ram Acharya (eds.), *Rastrapita Shri S., Bada Maharaja Prithvi Narayan Shah Ko Divyanpdesh* (Prithvi Jayanti Samaroha Samiti, Kathmandu, 1951), pp. 15-16.
34. Shashi Bhushan Prasad, *The China Factor in Indo-Nepalese Relations : 1955-72* (Janaki Prakashan, Patna, 1988), pp. 49-56.

35. George Liska, *Alliance and the Third World* (USA, 1968), p. 27.
36. S. D., Muni, (ed.), *Nepal : An Assertive Monarchy* (Chetana Publications, New Delhi, 1977), p. 127.
37. Dr. P., Sharan, *Government and Politics of Nepal* (Metropolitan Book, New Delhi, 1982), pp. 10-11.
38. Rishikesh Shaha, *Nepal and the World* (Neya Nepal Prakash, Kathmandu, 1962), p. 7.
39. B. D., Sanwal, *Nepal and the East India Company* (Asia Publishing House, Bombay, 1965), p. 285.
40. D. R., Regmi, *A Century of Family Autocracy in Nepal* (The Nepali National Congress, Varanasi, 1950), p. 88.
41. Shashi Bhushan Prasad, *op. cit.*, p. 50.

# 3

# TRANSITION AND CONSOLIDATION (1947-1951)

## Diplomacy

The establishment of Rana rule in 1846 witnessed a radical change in Nepalese Policy towards the British India. By the time all potential allies of Nepal in.India had come under British dominance. After its defeat in the Opium War, China was both unable and unwilling to come to the rescue of Nepal against British expansion. Under the circumstances a change in policy towards the British became imperative. Jung Bahadur Rana, the first Rana Prime Minister, initiated a policy of friendship and co-operation with the British appeared to him to be the only way to save Nepal's independence from British imperialism.[1] The two most significant political considerations which conditioned Nepal's relations with the British were the preservation of its territorial integrity and the maintenance of internal political status quo.[2] But the contradictions between the King and the Rana Prime Minister, and within the Rana family, were internal to their system of family oligarchy. Externally, the Rana regime was hostile to and incompatible with the modern concepts of power, authority and legitimacy which, in a nutshell, required the broadening of the regime's base by making it people-oriented.[3]

Initially, protests against the Ranas were made in the form of condemnation of regime's activities. In 1930s two clandestine anti-Rana organisations were formed in Nepal the Prachanda Gurkha in 1931, and the Praja Parishad in 1935. In addition, many of the young Nepalese students studying in India including B.P. Koirala and D.R. Regmi who later became Nepal's Prime Minister and Foreign Minister respectively, joined the Indian Nationalist movement were even imprisoned by the

British for their active participation in the Indian freedom struggle during the Second World War. The active support and suffering of the Nepalese leaders for the cause of India's freedom and their contacts with the Indian leaders helped create a strong public opinion in India in their favour. Almost all important political sections in India barring the Hindu Mahasabha which was sympathetic to the Rana regime[4] and some others having vested interests in Nepal who feared the socialistic stance of the movement and hence favoured the status quo were supporting the Nepalese movement.

It was the time when the Nepalese leaders began to think of founding an organisation to carry on the struggle for democracy in the country. The result was the founding of the "All India Nepali National Congress" at Varanasi on 31 October 1946, with the guidance and support of the Indian Socialist leaders, notably Jaya Prakash Narayan and Ram Manohar Lohia.[5] Later on, at a conference held at Bhawanipur near Calcutta on 25 January 1947 the word "All India" was dropped but the aim of the Party was proclaimed to be the achievement of independence for India and a constitutional monarchy in Nepal.[6] However, during the long Rana rule in Nepal, the British extended their support lo the Rana government, and tried to keep Nepal within their sphere of influence. The Rana rulers, on the other hand, showed their loyalty to the British and cooperated with them until the British left India.

By the time the Interim Government came to be formed in India headed by Jawaharla! Nehru was also quite sympathetic-being morally bound to champion the cause of those who fought shoulder to shoulder with Indians in the freedom movement. Besides, the objectives of the Nepali Congress were in conformity with the policy of the Indian National Congress to help the democratic and progressive forces in Afro-Asian countries.[7] India had been wanting to lead the new states of Asia and Africa along the path of democratic liberalism and socialism which had been central to its national movement.[8] However, the Government of India's sympathy was bound to be restrained lest it should be charged with interference in the internal affairs of Nepal. But the Socialist Party of India being out of government suffered from no such restraint and, therefore, actively associated itself with the Nepalese struggle.

The British withdrawal from the Indian subcontinent in 1947 constituted a big setback to the Rana system. It deprived the Ranas of powerful external backing and placed in Power, in New Delhi, a government whose attitude towards the Ranas could not be sympathetic. Following its independence India was engaged in planting the institutions of democracy in its own land and desired that these be planted and may take firm roots and flourish in all the newly emerging states of Asia and Africa and more so, in India's backyard. It looked for democratisation of Nepal for the political health of that country as much as for the prospects of its own security.

Even though the Government of India favoured liberalisation and democratisation of the authoritarian Rana regime, in the early stage it did not extend any direct help to the democratic forces struggling for establishment of a democratic regime in Nepal.[9] Nehru himself as a result of his liberalism treated Nepal, which had a status of doubtful independence in the British days, as a fully independent country and clearly envisaged close co-operation between India and Nepal. As early as on 27 September 1946, as the vice-President of the Interim Government he remarked at a Press Conference on Indian foreign policy. "Nepal is an independent country so far as we are concerned. If, in future, Nepal choses to have some kind of close union with India, we shall welcome it".[10] A few months before independence when Indian leaders organised an Asian Relations Conference in Delhi in March-April 1947, Nepal was also invited to participate for the first time in an international Conference. India's views on the status of Nepal became crystal clear when in 1949, the Government of India promised full support to the latter in seeking admission into the United Nations.[11]

The Government of India avoided for about two years doing anything that might invite the charge of interference in the internal affairs of small neighbour. It did not extend any substantial support to the democratic forces struggling in Nepal and confined its role to offering "friendly advice" to the Ranas to keep pace with the democratic forces. Instead it choose to exercise in vain its persuasive influence with the Ranas to make at least "some advance in the ways of democracy". Even as late as February 1950 when Mohan Shamsher was in New Delhi on India's request, Nehru "exercised his persuasive talents on the Nepali Prime Minister but was not able to convince him of the necessity of reforms."[12] The second line of India's approach which, at times, went side by side with the first, was to exert pressures on Nepal for the liberalisation of its regime. And finally, when the first two lines of approach failed to produce satisfactory results, India sided with the democrats of Nepal.

Despite India's well meaning advice the Ranas refused to change with the times and associate the people with governmental administration in any vital way. Free India was committed to a policy of helping the cause of nationalism and democracy in Nepal. In a very real sense, the movement for democracy in Nepal had its origin on Indian soil and, to a large extent, the Indian nationalist movement served as a model and an inspiration to the Nepalis. The small but vocal group of anti-Rana Nepalis in India got for the first time an opportunity to organise politically and to use India as a base from which to subvert the Nepali government. Internal discontent also began to assume dangerous proportions, both in Kathmandu as well as in the districts adjacent to India where Rana authority could be effectively challenged.[13] When all hopes of reforms were belied, the Nepali Congress, which had come into existence through the merger of the Nepali National Congress and the Nepali Democratic Congress in April 1950, had decided to launch an armed struggle in Nepal and had quickly started preparations for it with the support of the Indian socialists.[14]

However, New Delhi was not indifferent towards Nepal and it was doing whatever it could without exposing itself to the charge of interference. Persistently, but unsuccessfully, New Delhi used its influence with the Government of Nepal to persuade it to democratise the regime.[15] Nehru, on the request of Padma Shamsher, the then Prime Minister of Nepal sent a team of constitutional experts, headed by Sri Prakash, and the other two members being Raghunath Singh and R.U. Singh, on behalf of the Government of India in 1947 to advise the Darbar on constitutional reforms. The new constitution was promulgated on 26th January 1948.[16] But a powerful section of the Rana family led by Commander-in-Chief, Mohan

Shamsher, was not prepared to accept this limited reforms and before it could be implemented, took over from Padma Shamsher, quietly postponed the execution of the constitutional provisions.

New Delhi continued to look for liberalisation and democratisation of the administration in Nepal whereas Mohan Shamsher continued to evade. This made New Delhi increasingly critical of the Rana Government. In Nepal too, opposition to the Rana rule was rapidly growing and crystallising into hostility. The Nepalis Congress was engaged in the collection of arms and was making preparations for armed struggle. It was in contact with the King Tribhuvan who sympathised and co-operated with the anti-Rana elements. On the other hand Nepal's policy towards India, in the circumstances exclusively aimed at winning over the Indian Government's sympathy for the Rana rule. The Ranas repeatedly pleaded with New Delhi that they would always remain friendly and loyal to the new government in India as they had been to the British.[17] To demonstrate their credibility in this respect they accepted the Indian advice on some modest political reforms in Nepal, promptly dispatched a contingent of Nepali troops to help the Indian government in dealing with thc Hyderabad Question in 1948 and readily agreed to the Indian proposal for a new treaty instead of old one of 1923. Obviously the Ranas were doing all this to appease India, though in fact, they hardly had any alternative choice.

In fact, New Delhi was not for any "major unpheaval"; it was not for the "total uprooting of the ancient order" and wanted simply to ensure "the introduction of some advance in the ways of democracy in Nepal".[18] Initially Kathmandu reacted sharply and offered resistance to Indian pressures. But soon it realised that it could not ignore New Delhi and in the last week of November 1950, sent a team consisting of Bijay Shamsher, Director-General of Foreign Affairs, and Kaiser Shamsher, the Defence Minister to Delhi for discussions with the Government of India.[19] At the end of the discussion the Government of India, at the request of the Nepalese delegation, submitted a memorandum embodying the suggestions for political reforms in Nepal.

As no concrete result had come to the satisfaction of all concerned, another round of negotiations between King

Tribhuvan, the Ranas and the Nepali Congress began in New Delhi in February 1951 under the auspices of the Government of India. It was conducted largely in the presence of Nehru. A week of negotiations for constituting an Interim Ministry in Nepal ended on 12 February 1951 with an agreement that the Ministry would consist of ten members in all, with the Ranas and the Nepal's Congress having equal representation. The Prime Ministership would, however go to King Tribhuvan and accordingly a new ministry was sworn in on 18 February 1951. The understanding amongst the King, the Rana rulers and the Nepali Congress leaders, evolved through the efforts and influence of the Government of India came to be known as the "Delhi Settlement". Thus a semi-democratic regime was born in Nepal in which India played a major role.

**Strategy for Security**

Immediately after independence, India had apparently no security problem on her northern border. The British had left India with a peaceful Himalayan frontier, an independent but friendly and co-operative Nepal. Sikkim and Bhutan as Indian protectorates, and Tibet as an autonomous buffer state guaranteeing India's commercial and strategic interests in that country. Therefore, the Government of India allowed the old British pattern of Indo-Nepalese relationship to continue for the time being. Even China, which had vital strategic interest in that area, was not active there on account of domestic political instability. However, certain developments in the subsequent years made India alive to the dangers on her northern frontier and shattered Nehru's notion of the impregnability of the Himalayas. The developments, which brought about a complete reorientation of India's Nepal policy, can be mentioned as follows :

(i) rising tempo of the Nepalese movement for political reforms and Prime Minister Mohan Shamsher's uncompromising alttitude to it;

(ii) growing influence of the Big Powers, especially the United States and the United Kingdom in Nepal, and

(iii) rise of Communists to power in China and the seizure of Tibet.[20]

Apart from the above two factors, the success of Communists in China early in October 1949 leading to the establishment of the People's Republic, abruptly changed the picture and posed a new challenge to India's security. The activities of the Chinese army in Tibet brought to the fore the problem of security of India's Himalayan frontier. The two pillars of India's northern security during the British days were an autonomous Tibet and an independent Nepal as effective buffers. The fall of the first was a serious indication of the likely fate of the second, contemporaneously weakened by political disorder and discontent, if suitable preventive measures were not taken promptly.

Indian press and political leaders perceived the danger and raised an alarm which became louder after People's Republic of China occupied Tibet by force in October 1950. Dr. Ram Manohar Lohia, perceived the danger quite early and on 14th January, 1949 sounded a warning to the Government of India and "drew attention to the increasing communist threat from across our northern borders". He lamented that the Indian people were not being made aware of "the developments in Nepal Sikkim and Tibet", where the activities of the Chinese Communist had increased.[21] Following Chinese action in Tibet, Sardar Patel, the Deputy Prime Minister of India, in a letter drew Pandit Nehru's attention to the problems of India's security in the north and suggested measures to strengthen them. He expressed the apprehension that the Chinese and the Russians would not miss any opportunity to exploit weak spots in the north. In his opinion, therefore, India could not "afford to be complacent or to be vacillating" and hence he advocated "enlightened firmness, strengthen and a clear line of policy" in respect of Nepal.[22] The Delhi correspondent of *'The Hindu'* on the eve of the Nepalese Prime Minister's visit, highlighted the problem of security of this "small but strategically vital mountain state (Nepal) guarding the northern entry into India.[23]

India responded in two ways to meet the emergent threats to its security from the north which had their bearings on Nepal. In the first place, it took steps to bring Nepal, along with the two other Himalayan states of Sikkim and Bhutan,[24] closer to itself through treaties. Secondly, it started taking keen interest in the "internal conditions" of Nepal. Earlier when New Delhi sounded Nepal, Bhutan and Sikkim for the conclusion of formal treaties to replace those they had with the British Government, Mohan Shamsher grew circumspect over the Indian motives and it took him sometime to respond to Nehru's invitation. But reports of Communist military success in Tibet and the birth of the Communist Party of Nepal forced Nepalese Prime Minister to hasten the conclusion of a new Friendship and Peace Treaty with India.[25]

It was only after prolonged deliberations that the Government of India signed with the Government of Nepal two treaties—The Treaty of Peace and Friendship and the Treaty of Trade and Commerce on 31st July 1950.[26] The Treaty of Peace and Friendship which, though not a formal military alliance, was almost a defence pact between the two countries. By Article 2 of the treaty, the two Governments undertook "to inform each other of any serious friction or misunderstanding with any neighbouring state likely to cause any breach in the friendly relations subsisting between the two Governments".[27] An exchange of letters on the same day made the binding more specific by further laying down that "neither Government shall tolerate any threat to the security of the others by a foreign aggressor. To deal with any such threat the two governments shall consult with each other and advise effective counter-measures".[28]

Thus the Treaty of Peace and Friendship provided for joint action for mutual security and defence between the two countries. It cancelled all the previous treaties, agreements and arrangements which had been regulating Indo-Nepal relations till then and laid the foundations of a fresh relationship. It also included new clauses promising the furtherance of friendly relations between the two countries on popular level. Articles 6 and 7 of the treaty bound the Government of India and Nepal to grant to the nationals of one country in the territories of the other "the same privileges in the matter of residence, ownership of property, participation in trade and commerce, movement and other privileges of a similar nature".[29]

Nehru faced a dilemma for the situation in Nepal at the time in as much as he had all his life championed the cause of freedom and independence of all nations, big and small, while at the same time, as Prime Minister of India, he had acquired a deep concern for the security of India's frontiers. In his relations with Nepal as with other countries on India's periphery, he found it difficult to resolve the dilemma in a practical and expeditious manner.[30] As Nehru said in Parliament on 6th December 1950: "And now our interest in the internal conditions of Nepal became still more acute and personal. If I may say so, because of the developments in China and Tibet, to be frank".[31] India now started taking active interest in strife-torn Nepal with a view to promoting democracy[32] and, thus, ensuring political stability in the country.

**Politics**

By the end of the Second World War it became quite clear that the century-old British dominance in Nepal, as in Asia was coming to an end, and that a new basis would soon have to be found for relation between the two countries in the light of the new realities of international political situation in general, and those of Asia in particular. Prior to 1947, the British Government in India hardly allowed Nepal any liberty to handle its foreign policy. The British withdrawal from India, and the emergence of Communist China two years later, confronted Nepalese isolationism with new realities, the socio-political changes in India, the postwar technological revolution, and the presence in the immediate neighbourhood of a state founded on the concept of class war.[33] With Britain's exit from the Indian sub-continent, the old world, based on the shadowy concept of Nepalese independence, stood almost shattered as new political undercurrents found entry into the once-closed Kingdom. The new phenomenon portended convulsive changes, giving rise to a desire to break with the past. Kathmandu felt compelled to respond to the changed perspective-both national and international.

The test of independence of a country being its relationship with other countries, the Ranas were aware of this weakness of Nepal. Nepal's closed-door policy with regard to the outside world underwent a noticeable change after India became free. As the British were transferring power to Indian hands, the Rana rulers of Nepal were attempting to establish new international contacts in an effort to protect and perpetuate their rule. They were quite naturally fearful and suspicious of the new Indian rulers, who were natural allies of the nascent democratic forces in Nepal. It was apprehended that their country might meet the fate of the Indian native states which were forced to accede to the Indian Union between I947 and 1948.[34] So, to counteract, the Rana Government of Nepal deemed it necessary to expand international contacts and seek recognition abroad as an independent member of the comity of nations.[35]

However, Britain moved quickly even before its withdrawal, to safeguard its residual interests in Nepal. In sharp contrast to the policy traditionally followed by the British Government of India, the British tended to emphasise Nepalese independence, especially from India[36], to have it reinforced with recognition by other countries the US, France and generally to facilitate Nepal's contacts abroad towards this end.[37] The Ranas who shared with the British their (India's) distrust of the Congress politicians, did not require any encouragement, as they were already keen to diversify Nepal's foreign relations.

The implementation of this policy was skillfully timed. In July 1947, the British government reaffirmed Nepalese independence when their respective legations in Kathmandu and London were raised to the embassy level.[38] In early August 1947 the Tripartite Agreement was arrived at between India, the United Kingdom and Nepal on Gorkha troops[39] and on 9 November 1947, it was finally signed[40] as a result of which the British retained their foothold in Nepal.

The internal threat to the Rana regime, at a time when the cold war between the blocs was at its height, lent a new sense of urgency to increase the US interest and involvement in Nepal.[41] In 1946, a delegation of senior Ranas, a few of them figuring in the roll of succession, paid a visit to Washington. This resulted in the US recognition of Nepal in April 1947. Nepal's resident ambassador at London was concurrently accredited to

Washington, and the US Ambassador at New Delhi was accredited to Kathmandu. At the same time, Joseph Satterthwaite, as a personal representative of President Truman with ministerial status, handed to the Nepalese Prime Minister a personal letter from the American President wherein the complete independence of Nepal was recognised by the United States.[42] In 1949 the Nepalese Prime Minister, Maharaja Mohan Shamsher concluded with US Government the Technical Co-operation Mission agreement, the first aid pact signed by the Himalayan Kingdom. During 1949-51, Washington extended its friendly interests in Nepal. As the leader of the Post-War Western Camp, the US was directly involved in a cold war. It could well see that Peking was going to grow into a new centre in the opposite camp. American foreign policy under John Foster Dulles had the containment of communism as one of its major goals. Nepal lay on the periphery of China and could serve as a listening-post on Tibet. The fact that King Tribhuvan favoured a democratic system of government could have been overlooked. Incidentally with the American entry into Nepal, New Delhi's influence began to wane.

After Mohan Shamsher assumed the office of Prime Minister in February 1948 Nepal pursued the policy of diversifying its diplomatic contacts at an address in April 1948 regretted the isolation of Nepal in world politics and expressed his desire of establishing his country's diplomatic contacts with China, Tibet, France; the Netherlands, Brazil and Belgium.[43] In 1949 diplomatic relations were established with Brazil and France and the Brazilian Minister to India was decorated with a Nepali medal. The same year Nepal sent observers to the Asian Conference on Indonesia in New Delhi, opened a consulate in Burma and applied for the membership of the UN. By this time it had already become a member of some of the agencies of the UN, such as, the ILO and the WHO. Relations with China could not develop, though a Chinese goodwill mission had visited Kathmandu in December 1946 which Kathmandu had returned in 1947. All these measures of the Rana Government were aimed a strengthening and asserting Nepal's sovereign independent status. However, contrary to the apprehensions of the Ranas and despite the fact that Nepal had a doubtful sovereign status, the Government of free India treated it as a sovereign nation and never came in the way of Nepal developing relations with other countries. Instead, it patronized Nepal with the encouragement to develop such relations.[44]

**Analysis of the Attitude**

India's attitude towards Nepal was conditioned largely by political motives. Acute concern for the security of India's northern border was the uppermost consideration in New- Delhi. It led India to take keen interest in the internal political crisis in Nepal. The Government of India wanted both stability and change in the Nepalese political system. This is not to deny that India felt sympathetic to democratic movements everywhere, including Nepal. Free India was committed to a policy of helping the cause of nationalism and democracy in Nepal. In a very real sense, the movement for democracy in Nepal had its origin on Indian soil and, to a large extent, the Indian nationalist movement served as a model and an inspiration to the Nepalis. India's behaviour towards Nepal during the period varied from patting on the latter's back to resorting to pressures. If New-Delhi thought that Kathmandu was moving along the lines which it viewed desirable it stood to encourage. Offering good-intentioned advice to Kathmandu was, however, more frequent. But when such advice did not work New Delhi used its persuasive power, when even persuasion failed, New Delhi did not hesitate to use pressures.

On the other hand, people were impatient for a change in Nepal. Repression of the worst type had failed to curb their desire for a change. To a people frustrated by ruthless repression, the only alternative seemed to be recourse to extremist means which may eventually wipe out the values preserved by the traditional Nepalese society. Internal stability was not only vital for Nepal's independence and territorial integrity but also the best guarantee against the threat of external aggression. It was difficult to ignore the threat posed to internal stability by elements drawing their inspiration from international movements. At the time the Rana rule was faced with the greatest crisis in its history, caused by the withdrawal of the British from India. The hereditary Rana Prime Minister of Nepal proved incapable of the courage, foresight and statesmanship demanded by the circumstances. The fate of Rana rule was closely bound up from the very beginning with the fate of British imperialism in India. Prior to the conclusion of the treaty of 1950 between Nepal and India, as well as for sometime following conclusion of the treaty. However, the Nepalese Prime Minister declared in May 1948 that as it was not possible in the present times to remain completely detached from the world-wide developments, they would adopt "the policy of searching friends and establishing diplomatic contacts with various countries; and practically, the Government of Nepal had already been pursuing this policy.

For various reasons, Nepal continued to be helplessly dependent upon India in economic matters. But it cannot be said that New Delhi was guided in its behaviour towards Nepal by the motive either of economically exploiting the latter or of keeping it economically dependent upon itself. Politically too, Nehru succeeded in securing a substantial share for the popular leaders in the government immediately and an undertaking from the Ranas that they would introduce democratic reforms, gradually, in Nepal.

## Notes and References

1. Dr. Kirtyanand Singh, *Small Neighbours of Big Powers-India's Attitude Towards Nepal September 1946-March 1963* (Capital Publishing House, Delhi, 1988), p.85.
2. S.K. Jha, "Policy Towards India: Quest for Independence", S.D. Muni, ed., Nepal: *An Assertive Monarchy* (Chetana Publications, New Delhi, 1977), p. 202.
3. *Ibid.,* S.D. Muni, "Political Change: Framework of Analysis," p. 4.
4. Balchandra Sharma, *Nepalko Aitihasik Rooprekha* (Banaras, 1951), p. 375.
5. Girilal Jain, *India Meets China in Nepal* (Bombay, 1959), p. 12.
6. S.K. Jha, *Uneasy partners: India and Nepal in the* Post Colonial Era (Manas Publications, New Delhi, 1975), p. 21.
7. AICC Resolution-V, Jaipur 1948. See N.V. Raj Kumar ed., *The Background of India's Foreign Policy* (Delhi, 1952), pp. 95-97.

8. Richard L. Park, "India's Foreign Policy", Roy C. Macridis, ed., *Foreign Policy in World Politics* (Prentice-Hall, New-Delhi, 1967), pp. 344-45.
9. *The Times* (London), 3 August, 1950.
10. Dorothy Norman, *Nehru: The First Sixty Years* (Bombay, 1965), Vol. 2, p. 269.
11. *Constituent Assembly of India* (Legislative) Debates, Pt.1, Vol. 4, No. 1, 28 November 1949, Col. 9.
12. Leo. E. Rose, *Nepal: Strategy for Survival* (OUP, Delhi, 1973), p.184.
13. Dr. P. Sharan, *Government and Politics of Nepal* (Metropolitan Book Company, New Delhi, 1982), p. 14.
14. Bhola Chatterjee, *A Study of Recent Nepalese Politics* (World Press, Calcutta, 1967), p. 45.
15. India, *Parliamentary Debates*, Pt. 2, Vol. 6, No. 17, 6 December 1950, Cols. 1267-68.
16. A. Gupta. *Politics in Nepal: A Study of Post-Rana Political Development and Party Politics* (Allied Publishers New Delhi, 1964), pp. 32-38.
17. S.D. Muni (ed), *op. cit.,* p. 204.
18. India, *Parliamentary Debates*. Pt 2, Vol. 6, No. 17, 6 December 1950, Cols. 1267-69.
19. *Keesings Contemporary Archives*. November 1950.
20. S.K. Jha. *op. cit.,* pp. 14-20.
21. Ram Manohar Lohia, *India, China and Northern Frontiers* (Hyderabad, 1963), p. 3.
22. See Indian *Constitutional Documents: Munshi Papers* (Bombay, 1967), Vol. 1, p. 178.
23. *The Hindu* (Madras), 15 February, 1950.
24. *Foreign Policy of India-Text of Documents 1947-59* (Lok Sabha Secretariat, New Delhi, 1959, Second edition), pp. 17-19.
25. Tribhuvan Nath, *The Nepalese Dilemma 1960-74* (Sterling Publishers, New Delhi, 1975), pp. 365-66.
26. *The National Herald* (Allahabad), 18 February, 1951.
27. A.S. Bhasin, ed., *Documents on Nepal's Relations with India and China 1949-66* (Delhi, 1970), pp. 32-34.

28. For the text of the letter, see Jawaharlal Nehru, *India's Foreign Policy: Selected Speeches: September 1946-April 1961* (New Delhi), p. 374.
29. For the text of the treaty, see *Foreign Policy of India: Text of Documents: 1947-59* (New Delhi, 1959), pp. 31-33.
30. Rishikesh Shaha, *Nepali Politics: Retrospect and Prospect* (Oxford University Press, Delhi. 1975), pp. 111-12.
31. *Parliamentary Debates*. Pt. 2, Vol. VI, No. 17. 6 December 1950, Cols. 1267-69.
32. Girilal Jain, *op. cit.*, p. 7.
33. *The Rising Nepal* (Kathmandu), 27 May, 1968.
34. Leo E. Rose, *op. cit.,* 180.
35. Ramakant, *Nepal-China and India* (Abhinav Publications, New Delhi, 1976). p. 68.
36. *The Times*, 1 September 1947.
37. Vinod Kumar. "Great Powers and Nepal". *op. cit.,* p. 144.
38. *Keesings Contemporary Archives*, 12-19 July 1947, p. 8712.
39. *Ibid.*, 16-23, August 1947, p. 8778.
40. S.K. Jha, *op. cit.*, pp. 26-27.
41. *The Newyork Times* (Newyork), 5 February, 1950.
42. *Keesings Contemporary Archives*, 17-24 March, 1947, p. 8609.
43. Balchandra Sharma, *op. cit.*, p. 381.
44. D.N. Mallik, *The Development of Non-Alignment in India's Foreign Policy* (Chaitanya Publishing House, Allahabad, 1967), p. 85.

# 4

# SPECIAL RELATIONSHIP (February 1951—March 1955)

## Diplomacy

The coalition Government, which was formed in Nepal, in February 1951 was envisaged as an interim arrangement in the transition from authoritarianism to democracy. It was a "synthesis" of the forces of tradition and modernity. Its constituents were the King, the Ranas and the political party leaders and all of them had committed themselves to the ideals of modernisation. The compromise plan provided for an amnesty for insurgents, the restoration of King Tribhuvan, the inclusion of popular representatives in the cabinet on the bases of parity with the Ranas and the holding of elections to a Constituent Assembly by 1952 on the basis of universal adult suffrage. King Tribhuvan returned to Nepal and issued a proclamation on 18 February 1951, declaring his resolve that his people be governed according to the provisions of a democratic constitution framed by a Constituent Assembly elected by the people on the basis of universal adult suffrage.[1]

Since the Indian government had helped Nepal's new ruling elite to come into power and assured them of support for the establishment of a democratic system, the Nepalese government found in India a friend to be trusted, a philosopher to be consulted and a guide to be relied upon. Whether it touched either the sensitive question of law and order, or the perplexing problem of forming of new ministry of the stupendous tasks of administrative and economic reforms in the country, Kathmandu throughout the early fifties, counted on the aid and advice of New Delhi.[2] In addition Kathmandu's dependence on New Delhi was all the more manifest in the domain of foreign relations and defence. Due to its heavy pre-occupation with domestic issues the Nepalese government could scarcely afford to give serious thought to them. It only echoed the foreign policy pronouncements of Jawaharlal Nehru and literally followed the friendly guidance offered by New Delhi. For example, the Nepalese government did not pay heed to the mounting demand from many political pockets in the country for cultivating relations with China until it received a green signal from New Delhi. The countries even initiated moves for the formal co-ordination in their foreign policies. However, the idea for co-ordination in the field of foreign policy was not new. In reply to a question in parliament in November 1949, Nehru said that he did not know the mind of the Government of Nepal but it would be "desirable for such co-ordination to exist".[4]

But the Interim Government of Nepal ever since its birth, turned out to be a sickly child. Indeed, difficulties in the functioning of the Nepalese coalition cabinet arose at the time of the swearing-in-ceremony itself, which had to be delayed due to a last - minute hitch over the order of precedence among ministers to be sworn-in.[5] A struggle between the Ranas and the modern elites for a higher position in the new power structure followed the "Delhi Settlement". Where as the Ranas tried to maintain their position, the modern elites seemed determined to replace them. This struggle gave rise to mild violence when the Gorkha Dal, a militant group organised by the Ranas, made an attempt on 12 April 1951, to assault Nepali Congress leader and Home Minister, B.P. Koirala. As the struggle between the two groups grew, the Ranas sought the mediation of the Government of India which was a party to the "Delhi Settlement". In May 1951, both the Ranas and the Nepali Congress leaders went to New Delhi where they were again advised to hang on together in the hope that the desired interaction between them will result from their mere physical co-existence. But again a crisis re-appeared in the Rana-Nepali Congress relations in November 1951. B. P. Koirala and his colleagues resigned from the coalition government, forcing the Prime Minister, Mohan Shamsher Rana to resign. The King announced the formation of a new government on 16 November 1951, under the premiership of Matrika Prasad Koirala.

On the other hand, dissensions among the Nepali Congress leaders themselves were occurred. A faction of the Nepalese revolutionaries under Dr. K. I. Singh went much beyond verbal opposition and the situation in western Terai was worse. He refused to heed the ceasefire directive of the President of the party and held aloft the banner of revolt. At the request of the Government of Nepal,[6] the Government of India sent Indian troops in February 1951 to suppress the revolt.[7] In a joint operation of the Nepali State troops and the Indian troops, which lasted for less than a week, Dr. Singh and his armed followers were arrested and the situation was brought under control in that region.[8] But the overall law and order situation in the country remained far from satisfactory and, within two months, once again, the Government of Nepal was forced to seek the assistance of the Indian troops for suppressing the lawless elements in several parts of the country. Even on several subsequent occasions, on the request of the Government of Nepal, the Indian Government sent its troops for administrative and political help.

In the Post-Independence era, Indo-Nepalese relations were essentially based on the treaty of peace and friendship concluded on 31 July 1950, the first of its kind signed by independent India. The treaty among other things, also provided that Nepal would consult India before importing any war equipment from any country other than India but gave the right to Nepal after such consultation to "import from or through the territory of India arms, ammunition or war like material and equipment necessary for the security of Nepal.[9] New Delhi continued to look upon its relationship which was termed as "special" with the Himalayan Kingdom from the angle and substance of this treaty. But the Government of India was criticized for taking an ambivalent attitude, at times supporting the political parties and at other times the King. It was not clear what India really wanted in Nepal: stability or democracy. The same political parties sided with the King or with India, or against the one or the other or both at different times. Instead of building up their strength among the masses, they relied on the King or on the Government of India to attain a position of power or vantage. Disenchantment with the democratic process and increasing apathy towards politics and political parties were the inevitable reactions of the Nepalese People.[10]

The "special" relations between the two countries were exhibited in ways more than one. The civil service machinery inherited from the Ranas was outdated and was not suitable for it. At the "urgent request" of the Government of Nepal, New Delhi lent the services of three experienced civil servants to Kathmandu to help reorganise the administration.[11] Two of them were to function as advisers on administrative reorganisation and the third, Govind Narayan, was to function as a private secretary to King Tribhuvan. These officers of the Government of India prepared administrative rules and instructions for office procedures on the basis of the Indian secretariat manual. They also assisted in the preparation of the Interim Government Act of 1951 which provided the constitutional basis for the new political order.[12] A second team of administrative experts, finalised during the visit of the Nepalese Ministerial delegation to New Delhi in April 1952,[13] was sent to Kathmandu in May 1952 to make a thorough investigation of the administrative machinery of Nepal and make recommendations for its reorganisation and determine the number of the Indian personnel that would be required by Nepal for such a reorganisation.[14] Not only that whenever Nepal needed an experienced man to take charge at the highest level of a department in its secretariat, it sought India's assistance. For instance the first Attorney General of Nepal was an Indian attorney, and the reorganisation of the Nepali Police was for a time entrusted to an Indian Police Officer.[15] King Tribhuvan, his Ministers and high officials frequently visited New Delhi for advice during "periodic political crises".[16]

The collapse of the Rana-Congress coalition in November 1951 and the formation of Nepali Congress Government did not solve the problem of dissensions which reappeared in the Nepali Congress Party even before the formation of the new Government, each of the two Koirala (step) brothers (B. P. Koirala and M. P. Koirala) leading a rival faction. The personal rivalry of the two brothers developed into a conflict and, when it attained crisis proportions, Jaya Prakash Narayan intervened and helped them solved their differences in March 1952.[17]

However, it could not prevent split in the party for long. Serious political differences between the Koirala brothers once again surfaced in the first week of July and inevitably led to a split in the party and to the fall of the Nepali Congress Government in August 1952.[18] When M. P. Koirala submitted resignation he also left the Nepali Congress and formed another party known as the Rashtriya Praja Party. Actually the inter-party and Intra-party rivalry was highly detrimental to Political stability in Nepal. The Government of India always showed keen friendly interest in rendering assistance to deal with this problem, though its role had to be severely limited by considerations of political propriety. Nehru was always sensitive to the charge of interference in Nepal's domestic politics, but at the same time, he was deeply concerned about Nepal's political development. He, therefore, never hesitated in playing a decisive role in the Nepalese politics when asked for but exercised restraint in taking any initiative which might be branded as an imposition on the Nepalese government.[19]

The Koirala ministry was replaced on 14 August 1952 by the Advisory Regime, King Tribhuvan acting as his own Prime Minister assisted by a team of six Royal councillors. He visited New Delhi on September 4-7, 1952 and discussed the situation in Nepal with Nehru. When the situation did not improve, King Tribhuvan again paid "a sudden and secret visit to New Delhi in December 1952, believeably to discuss with the Government of India the issue of replacing his direct rule (Advisory Regime) with a government of Political parlies.[20] The King terminated the Advisory Regime in June 1953 perhaps on Nehru's advice.[21] On the termination of the Advisory Regime, M. P. Koirala was once again appointed Prime Minister. He was also authorised to negotiate with other leaders for the formation of an all-party Government. In the beginning this cabinet included only members of the Rashtriya Praja Party, but later, on 18 February 1954 it was expanded to include representatives of some other parties also, viz, the Praja Parishad, the Jana Congress, and the Nepali National Congress and hence was called the national cabinet. The national cabinet survived till 31 January 1955 when M. P. Koirala submitted his resignation. In fact, besides the governmental instability, the general political conditions in

Nepal were not at all favourable for ushering in democracy. The naked lust for power which characterized the elite-behaviour in the country had not only given birth to numberous political parties—many of which consisted of only half-a-dozen members but also created confusion in the evolution of sound opposition based on ideological conviction.[22]

Although India had to play a decisive role in Nepalese politics throughout the early 1950s, Nepal's heavy dependence on India and the resultant Indian presence in its affairs invited criticism of India's Nepal policy and also endangered suspicion about new Delhi's intentions in some quarters in the Kingdom. The overbearing attitude of the Indian Diplomats, particularly the Indian ambassador, C. P. N. Singh, was sharply resented by many of the prominent Nepali leaders.[23] His meddling with the Nepalese politics strengthened the wide spread notice in that country that India was playing the role of a king maker. Apart from this, many of the Nepalese who could not find a place in the cabinet or who had to quit it for one reason or the other, held India responsible for their fate. They often retaliated by resorting to anti-Indian propaganda and activities. Even at the peak of this relationship when Nehru paid his first visit to Kathmandu in June 1951, a motley group staged a black flag demonstration against the Indian Prime Minister.[24] However, on no occasion, the official attitude of the Nepalese government was in any way expressive of an anti-Indian stance. On the contrary, throughout the early fifties, Kathmandu consistently tried to remove the misgivings about India's objectives towards Nepal and the anti-Indian activities in Nepal.

**Strategy for Security**

The transformation of Tibet into a Chinese military base and the continued movement of Chinese troops to Nepal's northern frontier alarmed India. Nepal now became a frontier state of paramount importance. The threat of India's security also became real because it has open border with Nepal. If China were to draw Nepal under its influence, India's strategic position would be seriously undermined. Nehru declared :

From time immemorial the Himalayas have provided us with magnificent frontier. Of course, they are no longer as impassable as they used to be; but they are fairly effective. The Himalayas lie mostly on the northern border of Nepal. We cannot allow that barrier to be penetrated, for it is also the principal barrier to India. Much as we stand for the independence of Nepal, we cannot allow anything to go wrong in Nepal or permit that barrier to be crossed or weakened, because that would be a risk to our own security.[25]

India responded to the situation by adopting a multi-pronged approach. It moved to strengthen Nepal's political, military and economic capabilities in a number of ways. As *The Times* (London) commented in a leading article, the aim of the Indian policy in Nepal was to keep that country strong so that it remained a bulwark of India's defence on the southern slopes of the Himalayas.[26] At the diplomatic and foreign policy levels, it tried to bring Nepal closer to itself. Finally, perhaps, it also took initiatives to reach an informal understanding with peking to ensure for itself a special position in Nepal.

India-Nepal co-ordination in the field of foreign policy and defence continued. Soon after the conclusion of the treaty of 1950, New Delhi proposed to Kathmandu that checkposts be established along Nepal's Tibetan border for strengthening the border defences of that country as also for strategic and military intelligence purposes.[27] Accordingly, the Government of Nepal established the checkposts in September 1951 and started strengthening its border security system with India's assistance so that it could face the challenge from the north.[28] It was manned jointly by Indian technicians and Nepalese military personnel. Although the Chinese disapproved the setting up of military checkposts in the northern forntier of Nepal, they did not utter a word in public. Nevertheless, they continued to seek ways and means to undermine Indian influence in Nepal and bring the Himalayan Kingdom under their domain.

The modernisation of the Nepalese army was another urgent task for which the Nepalese government sought[29] and obtained India's assistance. In early 1952 after the abortive revolt when the rebels fled to China, Beijing readly granted them asylum and provided them broadcasting facilities to persuade the population to overthrow the "reactionary" rule in the Himalayan

Kingdom and set up a Chinese style "people's democracy. It also offered to provide military assistance to the rebels to "liberate" Nepal and curtly rejected Kathmandu's request to extradite them.[30] On the other hand, the 1952 revolt underlined the desirability of having a reliable[31] and well-disciplined army because the leader of the revolt had taken shelter in Tibet and it was feared that he was possibly plotting for a better organised rebellion.[32] Following a formal request[33] from Kathmandu, the Government of India sent an Indian Military Mission (IMM) to Kathmandu on 27 February 1952.[34] Headed by a Major General, the mission initially had a strength of twenty officers and men. It rose to 197 officers and men by December 1953.[35] The Mission throughly reorganised the Nepalese army which was reduced from 25,000 ill-organised, ill paid and indisciplined soldiers to 6,000 well-equipped and properly trained men[36] India also extended the facilities to Nepal to send selected personnel to the Indian National Defence Academy for training as officers.[37]

Despite domestic political pressure, the Nepalese government continuously evaded the question of cultivating relations with China till 1954. But the conclusion of the Sino-Indian agreement in April 1954 recognising Tibet as an integral part of China changed the entire situation. It gave New Delhi a promise from Peking that it would respect the special position of the former in Nepal before it entered into diplomatic relations with the PRC. After signing the treaty India perhaps secured the Chinese assurance to the effect[38] and it gave Nepal green signal to go a head. The treaty was a Himalayan blunder for India and a great victory for China. It exposed India's weakness, threatened New Delhi's special relations with Nepal, opened the strategically situated Himalayan Kingdom to the world of Chinese communism and gave a new impetus to the Chinese design in the Himalayas. Kathmandu was now feeling a growing pressure for opening diplomatic relations with China. This was a phase when the "Hindi-Chini Bhai-Bhai" tide was at its peak in India. Probably, then only India thought that if it could not help Tibet, it should act post-haste in securing Nepal's entry in the UN so that the new nation might acquire international recognition.[40]

**Exchange of Visits**

The most important visit which took place after the installation of Interim Government in Nepal was Nehru's tour to Kathmandu 16-18 June 1951. He reached Kathmandu on 16 June and received a warm welcome from both the public and the Government though, a handful of persons waved black flags to him at the airport.[41] Nehru, on his part, repeatedly repudiated during the course of his speeches the charge of India's interference in Nepalese affairs and at the same time pointed out the importance of Indo-Nepalese collaboration in the interest of both the countries. On several occasions he referred to the traditional ties between India and Nepal.

The day Nehru reached Kathmandu he addressed a public meeting in which he emphasised that Nepal's freedom was essential to the well-being of India, Nepal and the world. He reminded that Nepal and India were traditional friends through history and many bonds of geography and culture held them together. Therefore, whatever advice he could tender them was as friend and not as India's Prime Minister.[42] During the visit Nehru also gave the first hint at public meeting in Kathmandu, in June 1951 when he said, "If you seek our help in, say, technical or other spheres, we will do our utmost to be useful to you, but we never want to interfere.[43]

Being compelled by the economic and political factors, Nepalese Prime Minister M. P. Koirala visited New Delhi 19-22 July 1953 to discuss with Nehru and other Indian ministers on the issues. During 1952-53 the Government of Nepal had for some time, been faced with financial instability on account of a steep rise in the exchange rate between Nepali and Indian currencies caused "due to the increased demand for Indian rupees for making payments to meet the cost of large imports which the Nepalese traders are making from India.[44] Since Nepal depended mainly on imports from India for its requirements of manufactured goods, both consumers and business community of Nepal were hard hit. There were strong inflationary pressures on Nepal's economy.[45] Politically too, the problem of lawlessness erupted in the country on a very large scale. In New Delhi, in course of the discussion, Koirala told

Nehru that a blueprint for Nepal's first five year plan had already been drawn up and that one of the purposes of his visit was to seek India's "guidance and assistance in its implementation."[46]

However, the financial outcome of Koirala's visit was important. He told a press Conference on 25th July that "Nepal would receive Rs. 10,00,000 as a grant from India for five years under Colombo Plan for use on irrigation projects."[47] He told further that in future the Government of India would transfer to Nepal the excise duty levied in India on Indian and foreign imports to Nepal, increasing the revenue of the Kingdom by Rs. 30,00,000 to 40,00,000.[48] An agreed formula he told, had also been evolved regarding the opening of Nepalese State Bank for co-ordination of exchange facilities.[49] Besides these, on many occasions, high level delegations, for consultation on various matters, visited frequently on both sides.

**Politics**

For a century and a half, a weak China and a strong south had forced on Nepal a policy of accommodation and compliance first towards the British and then towards India. In the fifties the emergence of China as a powerful next-door neighbour re-asserted the balance between south and north and required Nepal to find a policy. At the same time Nepal's situation between Communist China and democratic India, drew the interests of the global powers of that cold war epoch. On the other hand, as quest of identity has been one of the major planks in the foreign policies of small power, Nepal also tried to project its image as an independent sovereign nation on the world political scene. Even a cursory view of its voting behaviour in world forums, such as, in the United Nations would show that Nepal took independent stand on various issues and was not influenced by the stand taken by India, the Western bloc or the Soviet bloc.[50]

The very first objective of US policy in Nepal was to help provide economic assistance for various Rana regimes, to enable them to meet communist threat from within and without. In 1950 when Nepal underwent a major political upheaval, its society reflected a typical specimen of a backward economy. The population was growing at an alarming rate. Agrarian economy, the mainstay of the nation, was primitive, and, other national resources like, forest wealth and hydel power, were till untapped. However, the coalition of political parties in the governments since 1951 at least served to rouse the government's concern for popular welfare. It was soon realised that the welfare of the common man could best be achieved by planned economic development of the country.[51] But infact, following the political changes, progressive ideas had began to stir people's imagination in the Kingdom. This was a period when most of the backward nations were experiencing "a revolution of rising expectations". Responding to its urges, Kathmandu too began to devise plans for raising the living standards of the masses with the object of evolving an egalitarian society, free from exploitation.

In the early fifties to start the process of development, Nepal had knocked at the doors of just two capitals, New- Delhi and Washington. It is important to note here that the overall progress of the "fifties", aided by cold war tension, gave Nepal considerable leverage in securing assistance from both blocs. At the start, US allocations to Nepal remained just an infinitesimal fraction of the American global aid disbursement. With the US, the Government of Nepal signed its first external aid pact, the Point Four Agreement, under which both agreed to co-operate in the interchange of technical knowledge and skills for securing a balanced and integrated development of the country. In 1952 America's first TCM (Technical Assistance Co-operation Mission) office was established in Kathmandu. However, the American assistance to Nepal had been channelled mainly for specific development projects in different sectors. Assistance made available so far by US fell into four distinct categories: cash contribution, commodity contribution, training facilities and free technical advice. The TCM was later renamed as USAID (United States Assistance for International Development) and began its operations in 1954 in two select fields, Health and Education. Americans had since sponsored and financed many projects ranging from village development to construction of the important Kathmandu- Hetauda Ropeway.[53]

Following Chinese occupation of Tibet there were legitimate fears in Kathmandu about Chinese designs as the Chinese maps continued to show the Himalayan Kingdom as a part of China. It strengthened the Chinese position to assert their historic claim on Nepal. In the summer of 1952 the Chinese further demonstrated their assertive attitude towards Nepal and described Mount Everest as "our highest mountain. By 1952 when their all pressures failed to produce the expected results, China began to drop feelers to Kathmandu through New Delhi for opening diplomatic relations with Nepal. Kathmandu felt deeply concerned when New Delhi recognised China's suzerainty over Tibet in 1954. For it India had been criticised in Nepal that it had brought Communist China right up to their door step. The Sino-Indian agreement on Tibet accelerated Nepal's inclination to establish direct relations with China.[54]

In May 1954 the Nepalese government strongly indicated its intention to establish diplomatic relations with Beijing. Foreign Minister D. R. Regmi said if the Chinese "approach us formally, we shall do the right thing at the right moment. For the moment Nepal wanted to be on friendly terms with the Chinese and would not do anything which creates embarassment for either side".[55] In September with Nehru's blessings Nepal began to discuss the question of establishing diplomatic relations with China.[56] China too discussed the question of establishing diplomatic relations with Nehru when he visited Beijing in the autumn of 1954. It succeeded in securing Nehru's agreement for establishing diplomatic relations with Nepal. In return they promised to respect India's special position with Himalayan Kingdom.

The process of establishing diplomatic relations with China received further impetus after the death of King Tribhuvan in March 1955 and King Mahendra's rise to power in his place. It marked a new era in Nepal's international relations in which Nepal moved away from the policy of "special relationship" with India and evolved a policy of equal friendship with New Delhi and Beijing. Further at the Bandung Conference of Afro-Asian countries held in April 1955, Nepalese delegate Subhan Jang and Zhou Enlai discussed the question of the establishment of diplomatic relations with China and laid down the groundwork for serious negotiations. In July 1955 a Chinese delegation arrived in Kathmandu for the final round of discussions. On 31 July an agreement was reached on the establishment of diplomatic relations on the basis of the "five principles of mutual respect for each others territorial integrity and sovereignty, non-aggression, non-interference in each others internal affairs, by any reason of economic, political and ideological character, equality, mutual benefit and peaceful co-existence". Finally on 1 August 1955 Nepal and China signed the agreement providing for the establishment of diplomatic relations between the two countries.

With the signing of the agreement the Chinese were, naturally, pleased with Nepal's growing desire to forge closer relations with Beijing. They described the establishment of diplomatic relations as the "opening of a new page" between Nepal and China, and predicted that "there is every reason to believe that China and Nepal will find new strength" and their friendship will flourish for the "common benefit closer and warmer than at any time in the past".[57] The development between the two countries provided China with the golden opportunity to enter into a strategically vital area in order to challenge India. The Soviet Union too, welcomed the establishment of diplomatic relations between China and Nepal and indicated its own interest to establish similar relations with Kathmandu. A Soviet scholar even predicted that it would open "great perspectives to strengthen traditional co-operation and friendship" between China and Nepal and" "enhance Kathmandu's authority in international arena." It was also described as an "expression" of Nepal's independent foreign policy.[58] A plus point for China was the appointment of Tanka Prasad Acharya, that raised high hopes in Beijing and improved prospects to extend Chinese influence in the Himalayan Kingdom and eliminate India's special relations. Acharya declared, two weeks after appointment that he would revise Nepal's "special relations" even in matters pertaining to aid and trade with India.[59]

**Analysis of the Attitude**

India's Nepal Policy was mainly guided by political motives, important among those being security, strategy control and influence. These motives could be served only if there was political and economic stability in Nepal. Hence it was interested in Nepal's stability also, New Delhi found in Kathmandu a very weak, inexperienced docile and dependent government which frequently looked to it for help and guidance. India regarded Nepal as deserving of its help, sympathy and guidance. However, India's zeal to help the Himalayan Kingdom emerged into a strong and progressive country precisely for two reasons. First, a strong Nepal would be a bulwark against any threat to India from the north and would also frustrate the Chinese design in the Himalayas. Second, Delhi's decisive role in ushering in a new political order in Nepal made it incumbent on the Government of India that the post-Rana government should make a mark in the nation-building activities commensurate with the expectations of the Nepalese intelligentsia.

The "Delhi Settlement" which had paved the way for India's "special relationship with Nepal failed to satisfy all the factions in Nepal. It gave birth to anti-Indian feelings in Nepal and made it apprehensive of its big neighbour. Nepalese people doubted India's motives and future intentions with regard to the sovereign status of their country.[60] They were afraid that they might lose their independence. Related to it was the issue of Nepalese nationalism which, in search of a distinct national identity started emphasising its difference with India. Some of the political parties of Nepal did their best to fan anti-India sentiment in that country. The Rana's, specially conservatives, felt bitterly aggrieved at India's role in the revolution which dethroned them. In their search for political issues, they found "a convenient handle on the question of foreign interference". India, with its close involvement in the initiation of the political change and in the stabilisation of the new system thereafter, became an easy target for political criticisms."[61]

However, on several occasions, Nehru tried to allay Nepalese apprehensions. In June 1951, in course of his visit declared at a public meeting, in Kathmandu that India did not want to interfere in Nepal.[62] Again in March 1952 he said in parliament that his government had "taken very particular care not to deal or interfere in any way with the internal affairs of Nepal."[63] According to Nehru anti-Indianism in Nepal was partly the result of foreign intrigues.[64] But in fact, the Indian diplomats working in Nepal failed to play their part satisfactorily. Their overbearing attitude and style, and the interference by them in the details of Nepalese politics intensified the anti-Indian trend in non-official sections which derived sustenance from many sources. In Kathmandu, the Indian diplomats not only neglected but often offended a section of Nepalese politicians and intelligentsia. It seems that anti-Indianism was basically the manifestation of resentment created in the minds of the Nepalese elite by the overwhelming dependence of their country on India. What perturbed politically conscious Nepal was the impression created by the Indian press and Indian politicians in the post-1950 year that Nepal was some kind of an area of Indian influence and that India must oversee Nepali independence and sovereignty.

## Notes and References

1. Rishikesh Shaha, *Nepali Politics-Retrospect and prospect* (Oxford University Press, Delhi, 1978), p. 115.
2. S.K. Jha. "Policy Towards India: Quest for Independence", S.D. Muni, ed., *Nepal: An Assertive Monarchy* (Chetana Publications, New Delhi), pp. 205-6.
3. S.D. Muni, *Foreign Policy of Nepal* (National Publishing House, New Delhi, 1973), pp. 286-87.
4. *Constituent Assembly of India* (Legislative) Debates, Pt. 1, Vol, 4, No. 1, 28 November 1949, p. 9.
5. *The Hindu* (Madras), 20 February, 1951.
6. India, *Parliamentary Debates*, Pt. 1, Vol. 6, No. 26, 12 March 1951. Cols. 2163-64.
7. See *Ibid.*, Pt. 1, Vol. 8, No. 1, 17 May 1951, Cols. 4358-59.
8. India, *Parliamentary Debates*, Pt.1, Vol. 9, 20 August 1951, Col. 465.
9. S.D. Muni, *op. cit.*, pp. 283-85.
10. Rishikesh Shaha, *op. cit.*, p. 115
11. *The Times* (London), 19 April 1951.
12. B.L. Joshi and L. E. Rose, *Democratic Innovations in Nepal* (University of California Press, Berkeley, 1966) p. 101.
13. India. *Parliamentary Debates*. Ist Session, 1952, Appendix 1, Annexure 27, p. 58.

14. *Ibid.*
15. L.E. Rose, *Nepal: Strategy for Survival* (OUP, Delhi, 1973), p. 198.
16. *Ibid.*
17. *The Statesman* (Calcutta), 6 August 1952.
18. A. Gupta, *Politics in Nepal* (Allied Publishers, Bombay. 1964), p. 76.
19. Shree Krishna Jha, *Uneasy Partners—India and Nepal in the Post-Colonial Era* (Manas Publications, New Delhi, 1975), p. 67.
20. S.D. Muni, *op. cit.,* p.75.
21. *The Hindu*, 6 June 1953.
22. A. Gupta, *op. cit.,* p.68.
23. S.D. Muni, *op. cit.,* pp. 286-87.
24. Tribhuvan Nath, *The Nepalese Dilemma 1960-74* (Sterling Publishers, New Delhi, 1975), p. 368.
25. *Jawaharlal Nehru's Speeches 1949-53* (Publication Division, Government of India, New Delhi, 1954), p.176.
26. *The Times*, 21 April 1951.
27. B.N. Mullick, *The Chinese Betrayal* (New Delhi, 1971), p. 123.
28. A.D. Barnett, *Communist China and Asia* (Eurasia Publishing House, New Delhi), p. 312.
29. India, *Parliamentary Debates*, Pt. 1, Vol. 1, No.15, 27 February 1952, Cols. 374-5.
30. *The Indian Express*, 26 September 1955.
31. *The Times*, 19 April 1951.
32. *The Hindustan Times*, 3 November 1953.
33. India *Parliamentary Debates*, First Session, 1952, Vol. 1, 27 May 1952, Col. 230.
34. In reply to a question from Shri Raghunath Singh in the House of People, Shri Anil Kumar Chanda, the Deputy Minister of External Affairs, said that "the mission was sent in April 1952 at the request of the Government of Nepal". See India, *House of People Report*, Pt.1, Vol. 2, 15 April 1953, Col. 2073.
35. A.S. Bhasin, *Documents on Nepal's Relations with India and China* (New Delhi, 1970, p. 37.

36. Girilal Jain, *India Meets China in Nepal* (Asia Publishing House, Bombay, 1959), p. 95.
37. L.J. Kavic, *India's Quest for Security: Defence Policies 1947-65* (University of California Press, Berkeley, 1967), p. 57.
38. A.S. Bhasin, *op.cit.,* pp. 26-27.
39. Hemen Ray, *China's Strategy in Nepal* (Radiant Publishers, New Delhi, 1983), p. 8.
40. Tribhuvan Nath, *op. cit.,* p. 369.
41. *The Hindu*, 17 June 1951.
42. *Ibid.*
43. *The Statesman*, 17 June 1951.
44. *Lok Sabha Debates*, Pt. 1, Vol. 5, 28 September 1954, Cols. 1743-44.
45. India, *House of People Debates*, Pt. 1, Vol. 2, 29 April 1953, Cols. 2538-39.
46. Joshi and Rose, *op. cit.,* p.111.
47. *Keesings Contemporary Archives*, 12-19 September, 1953 p. 13136.
48. *Ibid.*
49. *Ibid.*
50. Sita Shrestha, *"Nepal in United Nations". op. cit.,* p. 163.
51. Tribhuvan Nath, *op. cit.,* p. 32.
52. *Ibid.,* p.73.
53. *Ibid.,* p.112.
54. *The Times of India*, 23 January 1954.
55. *The Hindu*, 6 May 1954.
56. *The Newyork Times* (Newyork), 27 September 1954.
57. *Rennin Ribao*, 4 August 1955.
58. B. Kudriashchev, *Sovremennie Nepal, Mezhdunarodnaia Zhizn* No. 6, 1958, pp. 102-7.
59. *The Gorkhapatra*, 30 January 1956.
60. Joshi and Rose, *op. cit.,* p. 174.
61. *Ibid.*
62. The Hindu, 17 June 1951.
63. India, *Parliamentary Debates*, Pt. 2, Vol. 2, No. 3, 4 March 1952, Col. 1965.
64. *The Times of India*, 22 February 1952.

# 5

# DEFIANCE OF SPECIAL POSITION (March 1955—1960)

## Diplomacy

The death of King Tribhuvan in March 1955, and accession to the throne of King Mahendra had made a world of diffcrence to India-Nepal ties. The phase of Nepal's "special relationship" with India underwent a significant- change. At the time of accession the King was thirty-five year old and, had spent a greater part of his life in the involuntary seclusion of the Royal Palace under the Ranas. But from the beginning, even as a Crown-Prince he had demonstrated a self-assertive character and a proclivity for experimentation on difficult occasions.[1] However, the changes had been made imperative owing to realignment of forces in Nepal's domestic politics and external milieu. In the domestic political scene the new monarch symbolised the demands for a change in Nepal's foreign policy. He was in no way obliged, like his father King Tribhuvan, to perpetuate India's guidance and leadership over Nepal. To facilitate King Mahendra's innovations in foreign policy, a highly pronounced anti-Indian feeling had also come to exist in a large majority of the Kingdom's political parties and elites. Externally too, the conclusion of the Panchsheel Agreement in April 1954, between India and China under which the former had accepted the latters suzerainty over Tibet had paved the way for the regularisation of diplomatic relations between Nepal and China.[2]

The new King wanted to develop new kind of relationship with India because he felt that India's extensive presence was an obstacle in his way and resented Nehru's patronizing attitude. He was interested in the diversification of Nepal's interaction with other countries and understood that Nepal could no longer remain isolated from international affairs and that it must come out and seek her place in the world on the basis of sovereign equality.[3] At the same time Nepal was effortful to keep India on friendly terms, and King Mahendra's extensive tour to India in November 1955 should be viewed in this background. The main purpose of the visit was to seek information on the concept of direct rule. It is believed that during the course of his discussions with Nehru, he did not make any promise when the former advised him to ask someone to form a cabinet in Nepal in place of Council of Royal Advisers, constituted on 14 April 1955. However, the Government of India realised that the new King would not like the interference of outside powers with day today administration and internal affairs of Nepal. It started making use of every opportunity to appease King Mahendra. Nehru Government did not say anything against the way of functioning of King Mahendra while the direct rule of Nepal was welcomed by the Indian press and the leading newspapers of India in their editorial comments had all praised in one way or the other of King Mahendra.[4] Though the King was aware of the sentiment against the continuance of direct rule, he was hardly reconciled to the prospect of parting with power. As head of the state, he could well have given political parties direction and guidance but he was set on a more ambitious course.

King Mahendra's attitude towards India became quite clear when to the general surprise of all, and more so to the Indian leaders, he announced in January 1956 the formation of a Cabinet headed by Tanka Prasad Acharya. The new Prime Minister was a votary of Marxism, without being a party member. The King wanted to establish diplomatic relations with China and USSR to counter balance the growing influence of democratic countries in Nepal. He considered Acharya to be a suitable person for carrying out a "policy of balance". Three days after his appointment as Prime Minister, T.P. Acharya, held a press conference at Kathmandu on 29th January 1956 to explain the programmes and policies of his government. Addressing the conference he said that his government would follow the foreign policy" in conformity with Nepal's keen desire for stable peace in the world". He emphasised that Nepal would expect co-operation from all friendly countries like India, China, Britain, US and France. He would also accept help from the USSR or other countries, if the "aid is unconditional and without any strings".[5] Thus it was clear from the very first statement of the new Prime Minister that the present Government was not totally anti-Indian in attitude but by establishing close relations with China it was trying to convey India that she would maintain a balance between the two neighbours. Two weeks later Acharya declared that he would revise Nepal's "special relations" even in matters pertaining to aid and trade with India.[6]

The appointment of T.P Acharya as Prime Minister and his pro-China attitude raised high hopes in Beijing and improved prospects to extend Chinese influence in the Himalayan Kingdom and eliminate India's special relations. The Chinese were optimistic that they would be able to bend Acharya to their point of view to develop an intimate relationship between the two countries. Beijing considered the situation in Nepal very encouraging. Many Nepalese politicians were making loud demands for changing their country's policy towards India. In fact, many favourable tendencies were evident in Nepal's domestic and foreign policies which revealed the strengthening of Sino-Nepalese relations and the weakening of Nepal's relations with India.[7]

But from the very beginning, as to Nepal's policy of diversification of relations India had no objection. Even in the phase of special relations it had not stood in the way of Nepal developing its relations with the United States or France. By the time Acharya became the Prime Minister of Nepal, India had completely reconciled itself to such a situation. President Rajendra Prasad gave the hint about the attitude of the Government of India when addressing the National Council of Asian Relations and World Affairs on 22 October 1956, he declared at Kathmandu that in the modern world no country could live in isolation.[8] It was with New Delhi's concurrence that Nepal moved for the establishment of diplomatic relations with the PRC and the former had also supported Nepal's case for admission to the United Nations to which it was admitted in December 1955. Further it welcomed the Sino-Nepalese agreement of August 1955; affirming the Panchsheel principles of co-existence and establishing diplomatic relations between China and Nepal.[9]

Although New Delhi had no reservation with regard to the diversification of Nepal's external relations, it was not unmindful of the implications of the innovations initiated by Acharya in Nepal's relations, particularly in respect of PRC. At the moment it was not difficult to imagine the resentment and annoyance in Delhi on Nepal's blunt defiance of India's established position. Nehru who had all along been opposed to the extension of foreign influence in Nepal was placed in a delicate position. In May 1956 Acharya paid an official visit to Beijing where he indicated Nepal's desire to play the role of a "buffer" between India and China in order to free his country from India's sphere of influence.[10] During the visit he took the opportunity to declare that Nepal would always play the "great role of perpetuating China-India friendship and would always remain a "dependable link" between the two countries.[11] India, on the other hand, disapproved of the Nepalese campaign to turn Nepal into a "buffer" between India and China. But New Delhi was unable to prevent such trends and could do nothing in this respect except to be watchful and vigilant.

Having realised that Nepal had taken some hasty steps in its eagerness to counter balance India in order to develop good relations with China,[12] the King dismissed T.P. Acharya on 14 July 1957 and appointed Dr. K. I. Singh as the new Prime Minister. His appointment came as a great relief to India. *The Times of India*, in its editorial, viewed it as a welcome development for India.[13] The new regime witnessed a pro-India start in the Nepalese foreign policy with the theme of "special relationship with India" dominating Nepal's foreign transactions emphasising upon the inherent closeness of Indo-Nepal relations, he stated that Soviet Union and China would not be allowed to open their embassies and that Nepal would continue to conduct its business with overseas powers through its embassies in New Delhi and London.[14] Unfortunately, Dr. Singh had a very brief tenure. His government which had become a potential threat to the palace was dismissed by the King on 14 November 1957.[15] He was not satisfied with either T. P. Acharya or K. I. Singh, for he was determined to gain for Nepal a greater degree of flexibility and independence in dealing with both of its immediate neighbours. From the dissolution of the K. I. Singh government till the formation of a new government after the general election in 1959, in fact, Nepal remained under direct rule of King Mahendra.

Serious differences between India and China had developed on account of brutal suppression of the Tibetan revolt by China in April 1959. India earned Chinese hostility for sympathising with the Tibetans and for granting asylum to the Dalai Lama. By mid-1959, the two countries involved further in a serious border controversy which deepened the differences and posed a formidable security problem for India by making alive the entire Sino-India border. On the other hand Nepal adopted a policy of neutrality in the Tibetan affair considering it to be an "internal issue" of China. Kathmandu did not support the Tibetan and the Dalai Lama and witnessed the heartless extermination of the Tibetans without any regret. The Chinese appreciated the Nepalese attitude towards the Tibetan uprising and as a "reward" to Nepal, Beijing demonstrated their interest in solving the border issue and other outstanding problems with Kathmandu.

Under the circumstances, the victory of the Nepali Congress and the appointment of B.P. Koirala as the Prime Minister of Nepal was quite reassuring to India. It generated a feeling in India for close relationship with Kathmandu. Soon after the new government assumed charge, Nehru visited the Kingdom for three days and sought its co-operation in guarding the Himalayas. The new regime was no different from a reinstatement of the principles laid down by the King. During his tenure he consistently followed the policy of equal friendship with all countries, especially with Nepal's two neighbours—India and China. On the one hand he was not so much interested in establishing a "special relationship with India but on the other he considered the "equal friendship formula" unworkable in practice, unacceptable in theory and injurious to Nepal's economic interest. Therefore, he preferred to follow a middle course—a close but not overtly dependent relationship with India and friendly but rather formal relations with China.[16] The policies pursued by Koirala were best suited to the national interest of Nepal, and rejected everything that seemed to cast any offensive reflection even remotely, on Nepal's independence and sovereignty. For example, he sharply reacted and objected to the statement of Nehru in 1959 in the Indian Parliament that any aggression on Nepal would be considered as an aggression on India.[17]

As a result of Nehru's visit to Kathmandu in June 1959 and Koirala's return visit to New Delhi in January 1960, the relations between the two countries were further strengthened. Koirala stood for extreme friendliness and extensive co-operation in its relations with India. New Delhi too, began to appreciate Nepal's independent line in foreign policy. With Koirala at the helm of affairs in Nepal, New- Delhi had the psychic satisfaction that he would not at least allow the Chinese to act to the detriment of India's interests in the Kingdom. It resulted in full understanding and co-operation and the two countries signed the new Treaty of Trade and Transit in 1960 whereby Nepal secured the desired facilities for its trade with third countries through Indian ports and territories. Nepal, on the other hand co-operated with India by signing the agreement on the Gandak Project and agreed to give the necessary facilities within its territory for its execution.

Politics in Nepal took a dramatic turn when on 15 December 1960, King Mahendra took over the government by a Royal Proclamation, dissolved Parliament, deposed all ministers including B.P. Koirala, imprisoned the latter along with several other leaders.[18] Actually signs of clash between the King and the Prime Minister began to take shape towards the end of 1959. Provocation was provided by Koirala's assertion at a public meeting in Nepalganj that he derived his authority from a mandate of the electorate, which implied that he could not be thrown out at the pleasure of the King. Mahendra had accepted the statement as a challenge for him. Further the growing power and prestige of Koirala both inside and outside Nepal pained Mahendra. He became a very unhappy man and apprehended the end of the royal power in Nepal. By taking over the government he trampled democracy under his feet and set up a dictatorship to rule Nepal. The event reminded the prophetic words of King Tribhuvan who told Koirala nine years ago." you don't know my son (Mahendra). He is a thorough reactionary ... a diehard Rana supporter ... He will make Nepal, and he will make all of you, weep.[19]

The King's action was not liked by the Government of India and criticised sharply by all shades of people in general. Jawaharlal Nehru commented while replying to the adjournment motion moved by Inderjit Gupta on the issue he said, "it is not for me to criticize the action taken by them but obviously it is a matter for regret for all of us that a democratic experiment or practice that was going on her suffered a setback.[20] At New Delhi, Nehru viewed the King's action as a "complete reversal of the democratic process". The criticism by the Government of India and the way the press and political parties reacted against the Royal take over, the King, his sycophants and some of the Kathmandu-based foreign diplomats frowned that these all amounted to interference in the exercise of sovereignty by Nepal. The King and His men's indignation against New Delhi knew no bounds when they found that thousands of Nepalese political workers, particularly belonging Nepali Congress had escaped to India from where they were preparing to start a wide spread movement. The above factors contributed much for deterioration of India-Nepal relations to a considerable extent, for the coming years. Nehru was worried over the timing of the royal coup because it came at a time when the Sino-Indian relations were at the lowest ebb. On the other hand it served the Chinese objective to destroy the Nepali Congress, eliminate India's influence and secure a dominant position for Beijing.[21]

## Strategy for Security

The main challenge to India's Nepal policy in the late 1950s emanated from Nepal's passionate quest for independence and status in the international society. The most important event of the period was the establishment of diplomatic relations between Nepal and China for which ground work had already been done. On 1 August 1955 Nepal and China signed the agreement providing for the establishment of diplomatic relations between the two countries on the basis of the five principles of mutual respect. The agreement provided China with the golden opportunity to enter into a strategically vital area in order to challenge India. In May 1956, China and Nepal negotiated another agreement under which Kathmandu agreed to give up all privileges and rights it had enjoyed in Tibet under the Treaty of 1856. The minus point for India, at the moment, was the appointment of T.P. Acharya as the new Prime Minister of Nepal who was known for his pro-China and anti-India inclinations. Presumably in India's view, the immediate danger to New Delhi from China came out not so much from its common frontier with China as through the possibility at an extension of Chinese influence in Nepal as the latter was a relatively weak country.[22] In addition, a more serious threat to India's position in Nepal was posed because what started as a Nepalese quest for diversification of foreign relations, aid and status, had later developed into a scramble among the US, the USSR, India and China for spheres of influence, in this tiny but sensitive sub-Himalayan Kingdom.[23]

Now India began to face a complex situation in Nepal because of the shaking foundation of the Sino-Indian friendship on the one hand and the defiant nationalist mood of the Nepalese government on the other. The honeymoon phase of "Hindi-Chini Bhai-Bhai had begun to recede by 1955. Troubles over the MacMahon line had begun. New Delhi was now eager to assure itself that Nepal did not go out of its sphere of influence. India had never been against the normalisation of Sino-Nepalese relations but unconditional Chinese economic aid was regarded as a political move aiming of weaning Nepal away from India.[24] Its anxiety was reflected in the goodwill visit of the Indian President Dr. Rajendra Prasad to Nepal in October 1956 immediately after Nepalese Prime Minister T.P. Acharya's visit to the PRC. President Prasad did not conceal the anxieties of his government. At the royal banquet held in his honour on 22nd October 1956 he said that "any threat to the peace and security of Nepal is as much as a threat to the peace and security of India. Your friends are our friends and our friends yours".[25] However, president Prasad could not succeed in allaying Nepalese misgivings and it touched off a political controversy in Nepal and gave rise to anti-Indian sentiment in some sections.[26]

Dr. Rajendra Prasad's visit was followed by the visit of Nepalese Prime Minister, T. P. Acharya to New Delhi in December 1956. The usual reference of China in Acharya's speeches confirmed his pro-China policy. On Nepal's request the Indian Military Mission was withdrawn on 16 July, 1958, and was reorganised as the Indian Military Training and Advisory Group (IMTAG). As the name suggests, IMTAG advised the Nepalese Army on training and reorganisation and assisted it in filling the vacancies for courses of instruction offered by India and helped in arranging attachments for Nepalese personnel in unit installations and establishments of the Indian Army.[27]

The year 1959 witnessed further deterioration in Sino-Indian relations. In March the Tibetans rose in revolt against the Chinese for the fulfilment of their demand of the regional autonomy. But the Chinese suppressed it with an iron hand. In the meantime, Dalai Lama, the head of the Tibetan government, escaped from Lhasa and took refuge in India. This unhappy development over the Tibetan revolt brought the border dispute between India and China to the forefront. The possibility of armed conflict between the two countries loomed large on the horizon. In the circumstances, the victory of Nepali Congress and appointment of B.P. Koirala as the new Prime Minister of Nepal was quite satisfying for India. Nehru paid a visit to Nepal in June 1959. The return visit was paid by the Nepalese Prime Minister B.P. Koirala in January 1960. The joint communique issued on the occasion was vehemently criticised by pro-China elements, particularly T.P. Acharya who accused the Indian government of having deliberate designs against Nepal's independence and sovereignty. However, in the communique the two Prime Ministers "agreed that their two governments maintained close consultation in matters of common interest"[28] The matters of common interest identified as "freedom, integrity, security and progress".[29]

Apart from all these the Nepalese government was more than cautious on the Tibetan issue as well as on Sino-Indian border dispute so as to leave no room for complaints by India or China. He gave an impression that his government was neutral in the Sino-Indian dispute. During the visit Koirala discreetly avoided any direct reference to the Sino-Indian border dispute in his speeches in India.[30] At the same time, Kathmandu rejected several suggestions pertaining to security put forward by China during Koirala's visit to Beijing in March 1960. In Beijing Koirala signed boundary and economic agreement but before signing the agreement with China he met the Indian Ambassador in Peking.[31] The Treaty of Peace and Friendship was signed between the two countries during Chou-En-Lai's visit to Kathmandu in April 1960, marked the beginning of a new era of association between China and Nepal. Now it was obvious that though China failed to draw Nepal closer to it on security matters, nevertheless it succeeded in weakening the Treaty of Peace and Friendship signed in Kathmandu in 1950 by India and Nepal. The Indo-Nepalese treaty obliged Nepal to consult with New Delhi before concluding a treaty with China, however, Nepal did not do so. The main objective of Sino-Nepalese treaty was to neutralise India's position in the Himalayan Kingdom. It sought to make India realise the growing importance of Nepal in international affairs and appreciate the fact that Kathmandu was able to look after itself without having to invoke the obligations of Indo-Nepalese treaty.[32]

Peking's diplomacy of instigating the Himalayan people against India and also of distorting New Delhi's image in the region received a sudden jolt when on 28th June 1960 the Chinese soldiers intruded into the Nepalese territory, opened fire killing one and capturing 16 Nepalese soldiers.[33] King Mahendra and Nehru discussed in July 1960 the Mustang incident and concentration of Chinese armed forces at many points near the Nepalese border. Again in August 1960, B.P. Koirala broke his Journey at New Delhi en route to Israel, delayed his departure by a day and met Nehru and exchanged views on the developments on the Himalayan border.[34] Thus by the close of the year 1960, India and Nepal stood in an extremely friendly and co-operative mood. However, the royal takeover and dismissal of B.P. Koirala's government on 15 December 1960 relations between the two became tense. Initially the royal machinery tried to impress upon Nehru the need to reconcile with the new regime. Being disappointed from New Delhi, King Mahendra considered it politically advantageous to lean towards China and Pakistan, the two countries hostile to New Delhi.

**Exchange of Visits**

The Government of India accommodated itself to the changed mood of Nepal, particularly after King Mahendra's accession to the throne in March 1955. It realised that the new King would not like the interference of outside powers and hence it used every opportunity to appease King Mahendra. Nehru appreciated the establishment of diplomatic relations with Nepal and China. On the other hand Nepal was preparing a blue-print for an independent foreign policy and in King's opinion it would be a mistake on the part of Nepal, to displease New Delhi. Keeping all these things in view, King Mahendra in response to a special invitation from the President of India paid an official visit to New Delhi 6-18 November 1955. The main purpose of his visit was to seek information on the concept of direct rule as well as in order to win the goodwill of Indian people and government.

During his stay in New Delhi King Mahendra extensively toured of various places in India and repeatedly emphasised and reminded the Indian people the ancient bonds of friendship between the two neighbours.[35] As he was fully aware of the inclination of the Government of India towards the establishment of a democratic system in Nepal, during the course of his visit declared: "We are further striving hard to make democracy in Nepal a reality and thus complete the task which was undertaken by my late lamented father.[36]

On the other hand the Government of India while expressing its willingness to extend full co-operation and help for Nepal's progress and development, deliberately avoided any open reference to the need for the establishment of democracy in Nepal or India's special position in that country. This attitude indicated a slight change in the style of Indian diplomacy vis-a-vis Nepal. New-Delhi had shed off, to a great extent its assertive and paternalistic diplomacy of the earlier period and began to take a cautious and calculated view of the developments in Nepal. Even the Indian spokesman during King Mahendra's visit avoided any direct reference to security, stability and democracy-so much emphasised earlier while discussing India's objectives in the Himalayan Kingdom.

The growing understanding on various issues between Nepal and China was a cause of concern for New Delhi. The successful conclusion of T.P. Acharya's China visit resulted in the signing of an economic agreement between the two countries that signified a dramatic entry by China in an area which had hither to been under Indian influence. The extension of Chinese aid was considered in Indian public opinion as a red alert. Immediately after T.P. Acharya's return from China, India's President Dr. Rajendra Prasad went to Kathmandu on a four-day good will visit in October 1956. The importance of the visit was highlighted by the fact that it was his first trip to a foreign country since assuming office in 1950. Prasad's visit to the Hindu Kingdom of Nepal intended to strengthen emotional attachment of the religious Nepalese people to India.[37] With him India extended an official invitation to the Nepalese Prime Minister to come to Delhi.

Replying to King Mahendra's greetings the President expressed the hope that age-old links based on culture, religions, race, language and other common interests would bind the two countries for ever in perpetual amity and friendship. He offered India's help to Nepal for her First Five Year Plan which envisaged a determined fight against poverty, disease and illiteracy.[38] However, some portions of his speeches for instance that, "any threat to peace and security of Nepal is as much a threat to the peace and security of India,[39] , created some misunderstandings in some sections of Nepal. In nutshell, the impact of the Indian President's visit fell short of Delhi's expectations.

President Prasad's visit was followed by the Nepalese Prime Minister's visit to India for sixteen days in December 1956. In course of the speeches Acharya always gratefully acknowledged India's assistance to Nepal's development, the inspiration that his people while struggling to throw off the autocratic Rana regime drew from India's independence[40] and unbreakable nature of Indo-Nepalese friendship.[41] The main purpose of his visit was to explain his China policy. At New Delhi he was not only treated with honour and courtesy but Nehru perhaps also regretted the "temporary mistakes" that might have been made on India's part, adding that India would learn from your experience and advice.[42] At the banquet given in his honour by Prime Minister Nehru, Acharya said that Nepal considered it her "duty and responsibility to help world peace by the maintenance of Indo-Chinese friendship, co-operation and unity.[43] Further at a civic reception, he elaborated his policy and said: "We in Nepal, situated between India and China, have to make our contribution to the cause of world peace through cementing this friendship and co-operation between the two great countries".[44] Thus, Acharya's speeches and pro-China bias left no doubt that Nepal would follow a policy of equal friendship with both, India and China.

Significantly, while Acharya had made frequent reference to China and Sino-Indian friendship, these issues were altogether absent in the speeches from the Indian side during the visit. But this apart, Nehru showed full respect to the exercise of independence by the Nepalese Prime Minister in pursuing his own course in foreign affairs. Speaking before the Nepalese Prime Minister Nehru openly stated, "India is interested in two things in the context of her relations with Nepal— the freedom and the progress of the country. I am confident that we will be able to help Nepal in her progress and we will consult each other to our mutual benefit".[45]

In fact, what King Mahendra wanted in relation to Nepal's relations with India and China was perhaps a balanced friendship with both. He had already Acharya an ardent supporter of close association with China. This created some doubts in New Delhi about Nepalese intentions. King Mahendra, perhaps to arrest the misunderstandings in New Delhi, dismissed T.P. Acharya's Government on 14 July 1957 and appointed Dr. K. I. Singh as his successor.

The Nepali Congress won the general election held in 1959 and B.P. Koirala was appointed as the new Prime Minister of Nepal in May 1959. In order to achieve a clear understanding and fruitful collaboration with Kathmandu to safeguard the Himalayan fortification of the Indian sub-continent it was imperative for New Delhi to reshape its policy in accordance with the new trends in Nepalese thinking. Within a fortnight after the installation of the Koirala ministry into office, Nehru went on a three-day visit to Nepal on 11 June 1959. Among others, the problem of security of India's northern border was now uppermost in his mind, and as such he reiterated in a very subtle way that the defence of the Himalayas was the joint responsibility of India and Nepal. In the very first speech on arrival at the airfield Nehru said: "The Himalayas are a great force which none can affect. The Himalayas are the old friends of Nepal and India and guard us both. They formed the common link in the poetry, literature, art and religion of our countries.[46] Further during the course of a banquet speech held in his honour by the King and Queen of Nepal on 11 June 1959, Nehru did not fail to remind... "we should remember that the activities of our two countries, like our border, are joined together and they act and react on each other".[47]

Nehru, on his part, during the Kathmandu visit tried to stress the common interest of India and Nepal in the security of the Himalayan frontier and the older and more fundamental character of Indo-Nepal relationship which could not be equated with Nepal's relationship with any other country. At this time Nehru wanted to re-assert India's strategic interests in Nepal without insuring the nationalist feeling of the Nepalese. But, simultaneously he also stated publicly that Nepal as an independent sovereign state had the right to disagree with India.[48]

It was for the first time in the hislory of Indo-Nepalese relations that a joint communique was issued. It stated, "in the course of the talks, a variety of subjects were discussed including the international situation and the developments in Tibet, and social and economic problems which were common to the two countries. There was an identity of views on the policies of the two countries both in the domestic and international spheres being intimated by similar ideals and objectives.[49] This apart, the visit had enabled the Government of India collect the first hand information on the Government of Nepal's view on the Tibetan situation and the Sino-Indian dispute. The Indian Government was at least satisfied to note the similarity of views on the Tibetan issue but the Nepalese stand on the issue was not as bold as the Indians had taken. Perhaps it was because of King's lenient attitude towards China, that Koirala

Government after assuming office dared not to be vocal on the Tibetan issue.

On the invitation of the Government of India a return visit was paid to New Delhi by the Nepalese Prime Minister, B.P. Koirala accompanying his Home Minister, S.P. Upadhyaya 17-31 January 1960. Koirala came to India at a time when he had reasons to be embarrassed by what had happened in Nepal on the signing of the Gandak Agreement and also concern with the security of the country in the face of lurking Chinese threat. The two Nepalese leaders discussed a wide range of subjects with Nehru and other Ministers of the Government of India. With Nehru, Koirala held a secret talks where none other than the Nepalese Home Minister was present. The talk lasted for two hours and ten minutes.[50]

The visit of B.P. Koirala and S.P. Upadhyaya to India resulted in a satisfactory understanding between New Delhi and Kathmandu on the basis of mutual give and take. A joint communique was issued at the end of the visit on 28 January 1960 mentioned in general terms the discussion between the two Prime Ministers on the existing international situation as it affected the two countries and the talks "covered comprehensively the developments on the northern borders of Nepal and India.[51] The two Prime Ministers "recognised that Nepal and India have vital interests in each other's freedom, integrity, security and progress and agreed that the two governments should maintain close consultation in matters of common interest".[52] It indicated clearly Nehru's stand that the defence of India and Nepal was indivisible and was hailed both in India and Nepal by all those who were conscious of the danger to the sub-continent from China. However, there was no doubt that Koirala was moving very consciously on the security matters and at a Press Conference at Chandigarh on 31 January, he disapproved the suggestion of a joint defence between India and Nepal as absolutely unnecessary and termed any military alliance between close friends like India and Nepal as "worse than useless"[53] As Nehru had committed during the visit the revision of the Treaty of Trade and Commerce (1950) as a gesture of goodwill the Government of India concluded with Nepal a new treaty of trade and transit on 11 September 1960.

The treaty aimed at encouraging the collaboration between the two countries in economic development and at facilitating trade with third countries.[54]

**Politics**

In view of diversification of Nepal's international relations 1955 was a year of achievements for Kathmandu. At the Bandung Conference it came closer to China and an understanding reached between the two resulted in the establishment of diplomatic relations. Fortunately Kathmandu was also admitted to the United Nations Organisation as a full fledged member. As Nepal is an independent and sovereign state India had never been against its quest for national identity. However, its growing understanding with a country whose relations with India happened to be tense indicated its strategic and military designs. A noted foreign policy writer and one time Foreign Minister of Nepal, Rishikesh Shaha answers the question what made Nepal to turn China? He wrote, "To the Nepalis, disenchanted with India, China was obvious country to turn to, and wishful thinking attributed to China all the qualities which were found lacking in India. China's response was eager; consequently Nepal-China relations were strengthened, and continue to grow in scope and warmth, although an effort has been made to confine them to the official level. There has been no serious attempt in Nepal to probe Chinese intentions and designs. Obviously, China is judged only by what it does in relalion to Nepal.[55]

T. P. Acharya, the new Prime Minister, who was known for his pro-China indications contributed a lot in distancing away Nepal from India. His visit to Beijing in May 1956 during which he negotiated an agreement, agreeing to give up all privileges and rights it had enjoyed in the Tibet under the treaty of 1856. In Beijing he repeated Nepal's desire to play the role of a "buffer" between China and India. Even before the visit and three days after his appointment, at a Press Conference at Kathmandu explained the programmes and policies of his government that it would follow in international relations those being "equal friendship" with all countries which implied freeing Nepal from "special relations" with India; acceptance of "aid without strings" from all friendly countries, such as, the PRC, India, Britain, the USA, France and the Soviet Union; and the establishment of direct trade relations with other countries instead of conducting them through India by seeking the amendment of Indo-Nepalese trade treaty of 1950.[56]

The concessions given to the Chinese under the premiership of T. P. Acharya made them optimistic that they would be able to bend the present dispensation to their point of view to develop an intimate relationship between the two countries. In fact, many favourable tendencies were evident in Nepal's domestic and foreign policies which revealed the strengthening of Sino-Nepalese relations and the weakening of Nepal's relations with India. Even after the establishment of diplomatic relations, initially China was careful to avoid any blatant and direct challenges to India's pre-eminent position in Nepal. But Chou-En-Lai's five day state visit to Kathmandu in January 1957 marked a significant change in Peking's approach. Peking's main aim was to allay Nepalese fears about China's expansionist designs, to gain the good will of Nepal with a view to consolidate its gain in Tibet, and to get a strong foothold in Nepal's political life. However, at the close of the fifties differences due to Mustang incident and regarding the question of Mount Everest were not resolved. But on all these issues China adopted an extremely conciliatory attitude and ultimately gave Nepal almost all that it wanted from Peking.

The superpowers', policy in Nepal that affected the course of events between New Delhi and Kathmandu are cast in the mould of their broader global strategies rather than formulated with reference to an individual country. The US South Asian policy in Nepal was chiefly determined by this tiny land locked country's location in the Himalayan region. In the fifties, communist China's revolutionary and ideological warfare and the employment of military means for the consolidation of the strategic gains, prompted the American Administration to keep the Himalayan state free from the Chinese expansionism and influence.[57] Nepal's decision for the establishment of diplomatic relations with the Soviet Union was announced in July 1956. The announcement alarmed the United States and it decided to take a more direct interest in Kathmandu to counter the communist bloc forces. Though the US involvement in Nepal in general, and "in the inner workings of the government" in particular, had grown steadily throughout the fifties, yet the Americans felt failure of their diplomacy when King Mahendra visited Soviet Union in June 1958. The visit was marked by growing understanding on various national and international issues between the two countries. Now with the Soviet offer of aid in hand, the Nepalese government began to balance America with Russia much as it had been putting America against India and vice-versa and obtained vastly increased amounts of aid from the US in 1959 in exchange of a concession; *i.e.* to keep the USSR out of education and aviation.[58] It appeared that the Indo-US rivalry in Nepal might be mitigated by the common need to meet the new communist especially Chinese challenge in this sensitive area.

Bilaterally too, Nepal's relations with the US came closer and the King reached an agreement with the United States in January 1958 whereby Nepal and the United States agreed to establish resident embassies in each others capital. Nepal established its resident embassy in Washington in January 1959 and on 29 August, Henry Stebbins was appointed ambassador for Nepal. The United States established its residential embassy at Kathmandu in August 1959 as announced by the Department of State on 5 August 1959, the opening day of its embassy at Kathmandu.[59] The new US ambassador declared Nepal as being within the US defence perimeter, requiring protection against communist imperialism.[60]

The Soviet Union, particularly, during the Stalin's regime continued to look many South Asian countries including Nepal as a stooge of Western Imperialism and consequently Nepal's aspirations for admission to the UN were frustrated by repeated Soviet vetoes. After the death of Stalin, as a part of general shift in Soviet policy towards Asia and Africa it began to take interest in Nepal. Its policy in Nepal at this time was primarily directed against the West. Diplomatic relations between the two were established in the middle of 1956. In a communique issued from Kathmandu and Moscow it was stated that the establishment of diplomatic relations would enhance world peace and co-operation. A statement issued by the Soviet government said that the Soviet interest in establishing diplomatic relations with Nepal was guided by the principle of fostering international peace through developing Soviet relations with such independent countries.[61] One of the factors aiding the commencement of dialogue with the leading Communist bloc power was the presence of T. P. Acharya as Prime Minister and Nara Pratap Thapa as Foreign Secretary, both were known for their pro-camp attitudes. USSR was the second communist with which Nepal forged diplomatic ties.[62] At the time USSR too, faced several criticism in the west over its armed intervention in Hungary, it stood badly in need of moral support from the non-aligned bloc, peopled by small and needy Afro-Asian countries.

Soviet Union became the first among the big powers to invite King Mahendra for an official visit. The King's visit took place in June 1958 was a significant step towards strengthening the relations between the two countries. The joint communique, issued at the end of the visit reaffirmed the faith of both the countries in the principles of peaceful coexistence, disarmament and their general desire to see peace established all over the world. Both stressed the need of China's admission to the UN. The return visit was paid by President Voroshilov in February 1960 when Nepal accepted a Soviet offer of aid. In April 1959 an agreement was signed between the two countries whereby Nepal received $7.5 million worth of economic and technical assistance from the Soviet Union.[63] Even though the Soviet help was quite limited both in scale and scope as compared to that of India and the US, it affected India's position adversely as it was the principal foreign power in Nepal. Russia was willing to undertake a survey of the East-West Highway after its refusal by India and the US. Perhaps by doing so the USSR sought an additional pocket of influence in Nepal, independent of both New Delhi and Peking while retaining the option to lean this way or that, as may be expedient.

## Analysis of the Attitude

The change of guard in Nepal in March 1955 had a far reaching effects on Indo-Nepal relations. The phase of "special relationship established after the "Delhi Settlement" was counting its days. The new King Mahendra was totally against any kind of patronising attitude from India. He viewed Indian guidance and closeness with it as an obstacle in the way of Nepal's development as well as in the diversification of its relations with other countries and great powers of the world. Consequently since the day of his assumption, he tried to equate Indo-Nepal relations with that of Sino-Nepal relations. It was obvious within a year of his office that Nepal desired to treat India and China on an equal footing, chiefly perhaps to lessen its dependence on India, particularly in the field of security and economy. This apart Nepal felt the necessity of balancing Nepal ideologically by forging its relations with communist countries—China and the USSR. Keeping all these in view, and being disappointed over his direct rule in Nepal, during his visit to New Delhi in November 1955, the King appointed T.P. Acharya who was known for his pro-communist attitudes, as the new Prime Minister. During his tenure Nepal not only established diplomatic relations with Peking but made it strong enough by paying a visit to China.

Nepal's growing understanding with China was a cause of concern for the United States. The US began to take active interest in the affairs of Nepal particularly in the field of developmental projects, education, health, sanitation etc. For some time it seemed that the US would co-operate with India to check the Chinese influence in Nepal. However, it was obvious in Nepalese mind that it is not the US but the Beijing which could act as a counter balance against India. Perhaps it was one of the factors leading to the cementing of Sino-Nepalese ties in diverse fields.

In the post-Stalin era the USSR had reshaped its foreign policy preferences particularly towards Asia and Africa. As a result of the new approach it showed goodwill towards Nepal in 1955 by withdrawing its veto in the Security Council on the issue of latter's admission into the UN. The understanding resulted in the establishment of diplomatic relations and further it cemented the bonds of co-operation and friendship between the two countries. Inspite of the Soviet efforts the United States of America remained nearer to Nepal with that of USSR.

By diversifying its foreign relations and distancing away from India, Nepal achieved international stature. However, the scramble for spheres of influence among the superpowers (USA and USSR) and adjacent local powers (India and China) left no option for Nepal but to adopt short-term tactical considerations.

## Notes and Referenccs

1. Bhuwan Lal Joshi and Leo E. Rose, *Democratic Innovations in Nepal: A Case Study of Political Acculturation* (Berkeley, 1960), p. 179.
2. S.D. Muni (ed.), *Nepal: An Assertive Monarchy* (Chetana Publications, New Delhi, 1977), p. 132.
3. Ramakant, *Nepal China and India* (New Delhi, 1976), p. 90.
4. *The Times of India* (ed.), 21 Februrary 1955.
5. *The Statesman*, 30 January 1956.
6. Gorkhapatra, 30 January 1956.
7. Hemen Ray, *China's Strategy in Nepal* (*Radiant* Publishers, New Delhi, 1983), pp. 12-14.
8. *The Hindustan Times*, 23 October 1956.
9. *Lok Sabha Debates*, Pt. 1, Vol. 4, No. 16 August 1955, Col. 3702.
10. *Pravda*, 13 May 1956.
11. *The Times,* 8 October 1956.
12. Government of Nepal, Department of Publicity, *Proclamations, Speeches and Messages of King Mahendra* (Kathmandu), 1967, Vol. 1, p. 94.
13. *The Times of India*, 31 July 1957.
14. *Keesing's Contemporary Archives*, 31 August-7 September 1957, p. 15791.
15. *Gorkhapatra*, 15 November 1957.
16. Shashi Bhushan Prasad, *The China Factor in Indo-Nepalese Relations: 1955-72—A Study of Linkage Phenomenon* (Janaki Prakashan, Patna, 1988), p. 142.
17. S.K. Jha, Policy Towards India: Quest for Independence, S.D. Muni (ed.), *op. cit.*, p. 210.

18. Royal Proclamation, 15 December 1960. H.M. King Mahendra Bir Bikram Shah Dev, *Proclamations Speeches and Messages* (H.M.G/Nepal, 1967), Vol. 2, pp. 1-3.
19. Bhola Chatterji, *Nepal's Experiment with Democracy* (Ankur Publishing House, New Delhi, 1977). p. 17.
20. *Lok Sabha Debates*, Vol. 49, No. 25, 16 December 1960, Col. 5975.
21. Hemen Ray, *op. cit.*, p. 36.
22. *The Times of India* (editorial). 5 July 1960.
23. E.B. Mihaly, *Foreign Aid and Politics in Nepal: A Case Study*. (Oxford. London 1965) p. 104.
24. Ramakant, *op. cit.*, p.104.
25. *Speeches of President Dr. Rajendra Prasad, 1952-56* (Publication Division, Government of India, New Delhi, 1958), pp. 67-68; The Hindu, 23 October 1956.
26. L.E. Rose, *Nepal: Strategy for Survival* (OUP, Bombay, 1973), p. 215.
27. Sangeeta Thapliyal, "Nepal in India's Security Parameters" *Strategic Analysis*, Vol. XVIII, No. 9, December 1995 (Institute for Defence Studies and Analysis, New Delhi, 1995), p.1199.
28. *Foreign Policy of India: Text of Documents 1947-1964* (Lok Sabha Secretariat Government of India, New Delhi, 1966), pp. 343-44
29. *Ibid.*
30. *The Hindustan Times*, 25 January 1960
31. *Ibid.*, 26 March 1960.
32. Hemen Ray, *op. cit.*, p.27.
33. *Naya Samaj*, 1 July 1960.
34. *The Hindustan Times*, 10 August 1960.
35. See, His Majesty King Mahendra Bir Bikram Shah Deva, *Proclamation, Speeches and Messages*, *op. cit.*, pp.19-31.
36. *The Statesman*, 4 March 1955.
37. S.K. Jha, *Uneasy Partners: India and Nepal in the Post-Colonial Era* (Manas Publications, New Delhi, 1975), p. 108.
38. *Asian Recorder*, Vol. 1, No. 96, 27 Octoberand-2 November 1956, pp. 1103-4.

39. *The Statesman*, 24 October 1956.
40. *The Indian Express* (Delhi), 5 December 1956.
41. *Ibid.*
42. S.D. Muni, *Foreign Policy of Nepal* (National Publishing House, Delhi, 1973), p. 101.
43. *The Indian Express*, 5 December, 1956.
44. *Ibid.*
45. *The Times of India*, 5 December 1956.
46. *Asian Recorder*, Vol. 5, No. 27, 1959, p. 2747.
47. *Jawaharlal Nehru's Speeches* Vol. 4 (New Delhi, 1968), p. 270.
48. *Ibid.*
49. *Foreign Affairs Record*, Vol. VI, No. 6, June 1959.
50. *The Hindustan Times*, 28 January 1960.
51. *Ibid.*, 29 January 1960.
52. *Foreign Policy of India: Text of Documents* (New Delhi, 1966), pp. 343-44.
53. *Asian Recorder*, Vol. 6, No.7, 13-19 February 1960, p. 3157.
54. Shashi Bhushan Prasad, *op. cit.*, p. 112.
55. Rishikesh Shaha, *Nepali Politics: Retrospect and Prospect* (Oxford University Press, Delhi, 1978), pp. 121-32.
56. *Gorkhapatra*, 30 January 1956.
57. B.M. Jain, "Role of Superpowers: Security and Strategic Dimensions", Ramakant, B. C. Upreiti (eds.), *Indo-Nepal Relations* (South Asian Publishers, New Delhi, 1992), p. 335.
58. E.B. Mihaly, *op. cit.*, pp. 81-82.
59. *Department of State Bulletin*, Vol. 41 (July-December 1959), p. 270.
60. Mira Sinha, "Nepal's Role in Sino-Indian Relations: 1949-69", *Journal of Institute for Defence Studies and Analysis,* Vol. 2, No. 4, April 1970, pp. 475-76.
61. Illaha Redko, *Soviet Sangh Nepal Mitrata Ko Bato* (Soviet Information Bureau, Naxal, Kathmandu, 1981), p.13.
62. Tribhuvan Nath, *The Nepalese Dilemma 1960-74* (Sterling Publishers, New Delhi, 1975), p. 320.
63. E.B. Mihaly, *op. cit.*, p. 98.

# 6

# SETBACK AND RECONCILIATION (1961—1962)

## Diplomacy

The dismissal of Koirala government and Mahendra's seizure of power had brought about a great deal of strain on Indo-Nepalese relations. It had far-reaching repercussions on India's policy towards Nepal as well as Nepal's policy towards India. New Delhi failed to reconcile the direct rule of King Mahendra and had a soft corner for the workers of Napali Congress residing in the country. King Mahendra, on the other hand, wanted rather needed an assurance from India that the anti-royalist elements, taking refuge in India due to the open border would not be allowed to use Indian soil as a base for their activities to subvert the new regime.[1] New Delhi's unwillingness to give such guarantee brought the King closer to China. He cultivated friendship with China, not because of pro-Chinese proclivities but for popularising his regime at home and in putting diplomatic pressure on India to change its stand on the Nepali Congress activities. The Kathmandu— Kodari road agreement signed with Beijing had, at least enabled Nepal to maintain psychologically a balance between its relations with India on the one hand and China on the other.[2] This double edged diplomacy of King Mahendra went so long as he retained some hope of persuading Nehru to reconcile himself with the new regime. Nehru too, endeavoured to persuade Mahendra to come to some settlement with the Nepali Congress and restore democracy in the country, but having failed India adopted a conciliatory approach in resolving routine matters between the two countries. It continued its massive aid to Nepal and wanted to retain its dominant position.

The course of events that followed the royal takeover, had created a bad blood between the two countries but inspite of that India and Nepal were genuinely in a mood to curb such activities. Rishikesh Shaha, Finance and Planning Minister of the Government of Nepal, acknowledged at a press interview at Kathmandu on 17th January, 1961 that lots of responsible comments had appeared recently in the Nepalese press which were not constructive. He deprecated India-baiting in the Nepalese press and asserted that relations between Nepal and India were too close and valuable to be sacrificed for anything.[3] Dr. Tulsi Giri, the Foreign Minister to the Government of Nepal lamented over the provokating reactions and appealed to both the Governments "to break the vicious circle" harming relations between "two brotherly neighbours". On 12 January, the Government of Nepal appealed to the people and the press in India and Nepal to desist from expression of opinion which might prejudice "ancient and indispensable friendship between the two countries".[5] The Home Ministry also asked official agencies to ensure that anti-Indian matter did not appear in official publications. In this background three-days official visit of Dr. Tulsi Giri, the Nepalese Foreign Minister to New Delhi in January 1961 took place and that too could not succeeded in persuading Nehru of King's viewpoint. India continued to express its concern about the situation in Nepal. But this continued expression of outrage by Nehru and the Indian press against Mahendra gave additional opportunities to the Chinese. The Beijing had supported the monarch with firm determination for the deterioration of Nepal's relations with India that furthered China's policy in eliminating New Delhi's influence and to draw the Himalayan Kingdom under its sphere of influence.

The Indo-Nepal relations were clouded further for the one reason or the other. India's continued concern at the development in Nepal and the adverse comments by governmental and non-governmental agencies made the King feel the urgency of diversifying its relations. The exchange of visits and ideal expression of views bore no fruit. Towards the end of August 1961 King Mahendra had a stop-over at Delhi on way to Belgrade for the conference of non-aligned nations and the air was full of expectations. However, the King's talks with Indian leaders, which had been held without any fixed agenda[6] could not make much improvement in Indo-Nepalese relations except that the King spoke in high sounding phrases about Nepal's friendliness towards India. But that was more a formality than a reflection of the existing reality. The royal regime apart from statements here and there pointing out the desirability of Indo-Nepalese friendship was engaged in fanning hostility towards India. The root cause of its hostile attitude was the presence of some Nepalese political leaders in India, who it feared, would organise themselves against the royal regime with Indian sympathy and support.

Relations with India remaining strained, King Mahendra considered it politically advantageous to lean towards China and Pakistan - the two countries hostile to Delhi. Perhaps the King acted on the logic that India under the circumstances could ill afford losing Nepal to the side of her enemies and that this would compel Nehru to reconcile himself with the new regime and hold the Nepalese rebels under check. On 11 September 1961, while returning from Belgrade the King paid a state visit to Pakistan, the first ever by a Hindu-monarch to an Islamic state. Pakistan, which had so far only nominal relations with Nepal, viewed it as an opportunity to come closer to Kathmandu. President Ayub Khan threw a feeler pointing out the danger to small neighbours from India by stating that a powerful India would be a matter of concern to neighbours like Nepal, Burma and Ceylon.[7] To give another shock to India, King Mahendra in October 1961 went on a state visit to China and reached an understanding on security matters. It was during this visit that an agreement on the construction of a highway linking Kathmandu with China's Tibet region was signed on 15 October 1961. The Road Agreement had dangerous implications for India's defence system, particularly at a time when Sino-India relations had reached the point of no return.

Towards the close of 1961, Indo-Nepalese relations reached the lowest ebb following the movement of Nepali opposition leaders against the royal regime. Although Bharat Shamsher, a prominent leader of the Nepali Congress said that the agitation would be on the Nepalese soil and not from that of India, but it might be directed by the Nepalese leaders in India. He also declared. "I do not think that the Government of India will have any hand in any agitation against the Nepalese government though we know that India would like Nepal to return to democracy".[8] His statement was followed by a declaration of the Minister of External Affairs in which it was said that the Indian government would not encourage or support any movement on the Indian soil directed against a friendly country. However, the news of launching of a movement against the royal regime naturally created concern in the palace and in Kathmandu, and the government machinery was put on alert to meet the situation. From this onwards till the cessation of the movement after the Chinese attack on India in October 1962 the two countries were more or less in a cold war situation. Inspite of India's willingness to improve the relation with Nepal because of the growing tensions on the Sino-Indian border the Government of India viewed political stability and peaceful atmosphere in the Kingdom as vital for Indian security and integrity. On the invitation of Indian Government King Mahendra paid an official visit to New Delhi 18-23 April 1962 which failed to remove the misunderstandings between the two countries and the differences persisted as earlier.

The Sino-Indian border conflict came as a God-send to Nepal in so far as it forced Subarna Bahadur to call off the Nepali Congress movement. The large-scale Chinese attack on Indian military posts on 20 October 1962 and other subsequent advance into the Indian territory constituted a disaster for India and this put New Delhi in a frantic search for security. One thing common in all the three countries, namely, India, China and Nepal was the realisation of the strategic importance of Nepal which prompted India and China to reframe their economic and political policies vis-à-vis Nepal. The Chinese, however, launched a limited war against India had achieved its local military objectives. Nepal was not directly invoked in the hostilities, but the unfavorable results of the brief border war led to basic changes in India's policy throughout the South Asian region that paved the way to the advantage of the royal regime in Nepal.

In the post-1962 period, the Nepalese foreign policy as pursued by King Mahendra, had several features. The most obvious was the blatant utilisation of threat to "turn to China"—which enjoyed a marked superiority over India in military capacity on the Himalayan border, at that time to extract a variety of concessions from India. The first and most important was New Delhi's guarantee that it would not support anti regime Nepalese political forces. The entire opposition movement, still an important if badly divided force in Nepali politics was severely, weakened by this development. As a result of the war Nepal also obtained a number of economic concessions from India. Hence it adopted a neutral attitude in the war towards India and China, counterbalancing the former with the latter and manipulated the triangular politics to its advantage. From now onwards both China and India were eager to provide economic aid to Nepal.[10]

**Strategy for Security**

The timing of the royal coup in Kathmandu was not suited to New Delhi from security's point of view. Sino-Indian relations were reaching on the point of no return. By mid-1959 India and China confronted each other menacingly over the border issue. The situation went on deteriorating further as evidenced by fiery exchanges of strong notes, protests, complaints and allegations of intrusions, and even actual clashes leading twice to the outbreak of hostilities—first in November 1959 and then in October 1962. At a point where India was anxious for its security, the growing estrangement between Kathmandu and New Delhi was deepened by a long chain of events, all connected with the rebel activity of National Congress at Kathmandu and some of the terai towns. King Mahendra just to neutralise India as a factor in Nepal's political calculation tended to downplay the Chinese connection in order to avoid increasing anxieties in India.

India sought to ensure its security by promoting stability in the Kingdom of Nepal. New Delhi had the apprehension, as earlier "that the respect, in which the King's person is held in his country is not a good enough guarantee of internal stability in these revolutionary times."[11] It believed that a measure of people's participation in the Government was essential to make the government of the Kingdom broad-based and stable. As such it wanted certain popular institutions to grow and develop along with the monarchy. Common political values and institutions would give rise to a community of interests between the two countries and ensure the security of both.[12]

On the other hand, King Mahendra who was fully aware of Nepal's strategic significance,[13] turned to China and started wooing it believing that such a step on his part would force New Delhi to withdraw support from the Nepali Congress rebels. New Delhi was not happy with all this, but there was nothing particularly ominous about the "equal friendship formula for Indian security requirements as long as Sino-Indian relations remained friendly. On account of tense Sino-Indian relations by 1961 the Chinese were encouraging, both verbally and through tangible monetary contributions, all forms of anti-Indianism in Nepal. However, the most important step that alarmed India was the signing of an agreement between Nepal and China on 15 October 1961, providing for a road-link between Kathmandu and Kodari, containing dangerous security implications for India. New Delhi felt aggrieved and disturbed at the general drift of a traditionally India oriented towards Peking. The Indian government objected strongly to the signing of the agreement as it viewed that the road would expose Nepal to a new danger from across its northern border. Chinese troops might swoop in along it and the Nepalese army would be able to put up only a token resistance. It would also pose a direct threat to India's security, particularly in view of the fact that there was already a road link, the Tribhuvan Rajpath, connecting Kathmandu with Raxaul. There was also a possibility and wide spread feeling in India that the road would lead to a considerable increase in Chinese influence in Nepal and open up fresh ideological and physical penetration. However, New Delhi welcomed the border agreement, signed during King's visit to Beijing.

Keeping in view the politico-strategic importance of Kathmandu-Kodari road, the news of the agreement "came as a great shock" to Indian public opinion. *The Hindu* appropriately wrote in its editorial that at a time when the Chinese were exerting pressure all along India's northern frontier a road link between Kathmandu and Lhasa would also "strengthen China's strategy in her aggressive moves on the Indian border and weaken India's bargaining strength".[14] The

Government of India expressed its reaction in a restrained way by simply conveying Nehru's precise statement that he was "not satisfied" with the road agreement.[15] On the other hand the Government of Nepal all along the period played down the security and strategic importance of the road and emphasized its economic and commercial aspects.[16] In April 1962 when King Mahendra came to New Delhi Nehru raised the issue and made him fully aware of the risks involved in the road agreement. Later King Mahendra admitted in Kathmandu in an interview given to the National News Agency (Nepalese) that "India seemed to feel that Lhasa-Kathmandu Road might have an adverse military effect on India's defence".[17] There was no doubt that the agreement had strengthened New Delhi's lurking suspicion that Nepal was attempting to play off China against India.[18]

The Mahendra-Nehru talks held during the visit did nothing to arrest a further deterioration in the relations between the two countries. But the tour had perhaps made King Mahendra to realise the futility of confrontation and pressures as an approach towards India because of its counter productive nature. "The more the King used China to pressurise India, the more India used the rebels to pressurise the King".[19] Now the King was in search of an alternative approach and wanted to test the "Quiet Diplomacy" as persistently advocated by Rishikesh Shaha. In July 1962 the King replaced Dr. Giri as Foreign Minister by Rishikesh Shaha, who carried more goodwill in India. The new Foreign Minister was doing his best to put an end to the sorry state of affairs persisting between India and Nepal. Shaha believed that India and Nepal were inevitably bound and must make greater efforts to each others point of view. At his very first press conference after assuming the charge of foreign affairs, Shaha declared:

> Our security and freedom in our opinion depend a large extent on the maintenance of cordiality between India and Nepal..We have never believed in playing one neighbour against another, nor have we ever attempted to exploit the misunderstanding between our two neighbours in order to promote our mean selfish interests.[20]

Inspite of the odds put forward by anti-India elements in Nepal and opponents of the new foreign minister, his visit to New Delhi took place in the first week of September 1962. He met Nehru and other members of his cabinet. Rishikesh Shaha in his talks with Nehru tried to convince the latter of the King's sincerity, nevertheless he failed to secure a clear assurance from Nehru that the movement against the King would be ended. All that he could say was that he would ask the state governments to be more vigilant than before. The "Quiet Diplomacy of Shaha had failed to act on Nehru and it became clear from the Nepalese Foreign Minister's subsequent speeches blaming India. Nehru's stand on the situation particularly in his recent talks with Shaha, became quite clear when on 15 September a spokesman of the External Affairs Ministry categorically stated that it was for the Nepalese authorities to deal with the activities of lawless elements inside Nepal and that the Government of India could only exercise vigilance in their territory.[21] Soon thereafter it was felt that diplomatic confrontation with India, as practised by Giri and Thapa was the only alternative course left to King Mahendra.

However, all efforts to contain the deterioration in the relations between the two countries failed until October 1962 when a common danger arose and seriously threatened the security of both. The Chinese attack badly mauled India, revealed its military weaknesses, made it security scared. Simultaneously, it also revealed the delicacy of Nepal's position in the Himalayan border area. Neutrality was possible for Nepal only as long as the Sino-Indian dispute did not explode into a full-scale war. The conflict brought into sharp focus the need for cordial relations between India and Nepal for their mutual security and integrity. Border raids stopped in Nepal. There was virtually a total cessation of charges and counter-charges that had been exchanged almost daily between the two Governments for the last two years. The Nepali Congress announced the suspension of the agitation against the King's regime. During the conflict Nepal kept an outward form of neutrality,[22] though its sympathy for India was there.[23]

New Delhi in its search for security took the initiative for the normalisation of relations with Nepal. The King too realised that relations with India could not be allowed to continue in a state of semi crisis without adversely affecting the security and integrity of both the countries. He, therefore, accepted New Delhi's offer of "a rapprochement based on acceptance and support of the royal regime.[24] He, on his part, did what he could to expedite restoration of friendly relations. Mahendra agreed not to allow the Chinese to act against India's vital interests in Nepal. However, Nepal also made side by side an attempt to lessen its sole dependence on India in security matters and approached both the USA and the U.K. for arms assistance when Tulsi Giri the Chairman of Nepal's Council of Ministers, visited these countries in 1963.

**Exchange of Visits**

In pursuance of his double edged diplomacy King Mahendra still retained some hope of persuading Nehru to reconcile himself with the new regime. Keeping in view as the main purpose Dr. Tulsi Giri, Foreign Defence and Palace Affairs Minister of Nepal, visited New Delhi 19-22 January 1961. Firstly his visit was aimed to remove misunderstandings from Nehru's mind owing to recent developments in Nepal,[25] and secondly to seek an assurance from Nehru that the Nepali Congress and the Nepalese Communists would not be allowed to use India as a base for their activities to subvert the new order.[26] Giri's discussions held with Indian leaders, mainly with Nehru had covered a wide range of subjects, including the suspension of democracy in Nepal, Nepal's economic development plans and Indo-Nepalese relations.[27] He had secret talks with Nehru for two hours[28] and the only hint about the content of his talks was available from his own statements later on to the press. Contrary to his statements Giri revealed that he had not requested not to permit anti-Nepal activities on Indian soil "as Nehru must have read my statements in this regard in newspapers.[29] Perhaps Giri failed to convince Nehru the circumstances which compelled the King to dismiss Koirala Ministry and that was why he could not even dare to discuss the issue of Nepali political workers with Nehru. Inspite of this he expressed "perfect satisfaction" at the talks on his return to Kathmandu that there was no misunderstanding between Nepal and India, and his talks with Nehru would further consolidate the relations between the two countries.[30]

New Delhi apart from governmental efforts to improve its relations with Nepal made attempts through non-governmental agencies for removing misunderstanding between the two neighbours. In July 1961 Jaya Prakash Narayan visited Kathmandu and impressed upon the King that new royal experiment in Panchayat democracy should be made under normal democratic conditions. He conveyed his anxiety to the King that a democratic experiment could not succeed under undemocratic conditions and "experiment in Panchayati Raj was being made in Nepal under conditions of denial of democratic freedom and suppression of duly constituted democratic institutions.[31] But Narayan failed in his mission was clear from his stated impression that for the time being at least there would be no further change in the political situation of Nepal.[32] In general Nepal's, suspicion that India was aiding the rebel activity was so deeply incensed that the sarvodaya leader was greeted with blackflags when he visited Kathmandu.[33]

Amidst the atmosphere of misunderstanding and mutual suspicion India took the initiative for the normalisation of Indo-Nepal relations owing to the growing tensions on the Sino-Indian border. In that situation political stability and peaceful atmosphere on the Kingdom was vital for Indian security and integrity. In response to New Delhi's invitation, King Mahendra visited India 18-23 April 1962 and discussed with Nehru all the problems which had created a wedge between India and Nepal. Even before the visit he declared in Kathmandu: "I go to Delhi with confidence and hope, I am sure that a great statesman of Nehru's vision will understand our difficulties and problems."[34] But the King came to New Delhi with full of bitterness against India that were evident from the speeches, wherein he implicitly charged India with the violation of the UN Charter.[35]

In New Delhi although "a wide range of subjects covering relations between the countries were discussed[36] detailed discussions took place on specific issues. The first of these was the question of the Nepalese rebel activity in India. It was by far, the most important issue from the King Mahendra's point of view and he raised it. Prime Minister Nehru tried to dispel King's suspicion of Indian assistance to the rebels and also gave the assurance that India had no desire or plan to foment troubles in Nepal. But the Indian side failed to satisfy the King that it had taken all necessary measures to prevent the exiled Nepalese Congress leaders from organizing violence from India and that any further restrictions on them were practicable.[37] In fact, the King wanted that the Nepalese rebels functioning in India should be arrested and deported.[38] But the Government of India's stand was that since Nepalese subjects enjoyed full civil rights in India under the Indo-Nepalese Treaty of 1950 it could not prevent peaceful political agitation by the exiled Nepali Congress leaders living in India.[39] The second was relating to the shape of democracy in Nepal. India had keen interest in it and this issue was perhaps raised by Nehru. But in view of the known strong views of the King[40] on this issue, Nehru limited himself to offering a suggestion to the King that it was "important to give the people a sense of participation in activities connected with the country's development.[41] Evidently India was not satisfied with what had been done until then in that direction.

Contrast to the aggressive mood of King Mahendra the Indian side was marked by friendly and cordial tone. Indian president Rajendra Prasad in his speeches on the occasion, reiterated the Government of India's oft-repeated stand not to interfere in the internal affairs of Nepal.[42] Commenting on the current troubles in Indo-Nepalese relations he set an optimistic tone saying. "These difficulties should not be allowed to make us oblivious of the fact that our common basic interests are identical and that security, independence and territorial integrity of each is of vital interest to the other."[43] But King Mahendra during the visit maintained a complete silence on the security and defence aspects of Nepal-India relations. This marked a break from King's state visit to India in 1960.

The Joint Communique issued at the end of the visit on 23 April 1962, stated that Nehru had "assured King Mahendra that India was vitally interested in Nepal's stability and prosperity and, that while freedom of expression was permitted in India the Government of India were against all violent or unlawful activities of any kind". They had agreed that India and Nepal had a vital interest in each other's sovereignty, independence and territorial integrity and had reaffirmed their intention of consulting together an appropriate measures of mutual assistance. They had also agreed that "propagandist publications led to misunderstandings. Such misunderstandings should be removed and differences of opinion between the two governments concerning facts should be settled when necessary, by joint informal inquiries carried out by senior officials designated by the two governments......"[44]

However, King Mahendra's visit to Delhi brought no immediate change in Indo-Nepalese relations. For a very brief period "a lessening of tension was visible in the atmosphere"[45] but ultimately it proved to be a lull before the storm. The cause of this relaxation was that, following King Mahendra's visit to New Delhi, the Nepali rebels perhaps adopted for some time a policy of "wait and see" if there was any liberal change in the policy.[46] In general, India and Nepal appeared to be moving cautiously.

As the Mahendra-Nehru talks, held in New Delhi did nothing to arrest a further deterioration in the relations between the two countries Nepal took another important step for rapprochement with India. King Mahendra sent his new Foreign Minister Rishikesh Shaha in September 1962 because he wanted to test Shaha's technique of "quiet diplomacy" and see how far that worked with New Delhi. Shaha tried to create a friendly atmosphere for frank talks with Nehru and, therefore, contrary to what Giri had alleged, he told newsmen at Kathmandu on the eve of his visit that India was implementing the joint statement issued by King Mahendra and Nehru in April 1962.[47] The Nepalese Foreign Minister had a clear mandate from the King to convey to Nehru that Nepal would restore civil liberty, establish a democratic system within two months and release all Nepali Congress leaders in detention if the violent movement going on was ended.[48] He had a series of talks with Prime Minister Nehru and other senior members of his cabinet. But he failed to convince Nehru of the King's sincerity in the proposal. Perhaps Nehru was sore because nothing had been done in Nepal since the King had visited New Delhi in April to give people "a sense of participation" as the Prime Minister had then urged him. It was not surprising, therefore, that on 29th September, Nehru told a Press Conference at London that Nepali Congress exiles could not be denied the right of peaceful agitation in India and that he had advised the King to improve situation through friendly negotiations with the Nepali Congress leaders.[49] Indo-Nepalese tension got a new height on 29 September 1962 on the issue of border incidents between the two at Raxaul, which led to the disruption of trade at Raxaul causing immense inconvenience to the Nepalese people and their Government. However, a new friendlier chapter in Indo-Nepalese relations commenced with the visit of Lal Bahadur Shastri India's Home Minister to Kathmandu in March 1963.

**Politics**

Following the royal coup Indo-Nepalese relations for various reasons deteriorated to a considerable extent. Kathmandu was indignant over the Indians "connivance" of rebel activity. As the anti-India sentiment ran high at Kathmandu, the King turned his face against New Delhi and looked for friends beyond India. He speeded up, particularly after takeover, the process of establishing diplomatic relations with as many as six countries.[50] However, New Delhi's concern was limited, in security terms, only to China and Pakistan which were likely to affect India's defence adversely and hence became a cause of worry for India.

One major factor which strengthened Nepal's relations with many countries including China, USA, USSR, Pakistan etc. was their support either directly or indirectly to the royal takeover. A few days after the royal coup, China voiced its support for Mahendra and hailed his action as a "supreme example of neighbourliness. The Chinese Communist embraced the royal dictatorship at the expense of the democratic forces for their national interest. Unlike the Chinese the American and Soviet reaction to the takeover at the time was sober and their support to King Mahendra was indirect. The United States viewed Mahendra's coup as an "internal affair". President Kennedy assured Kathmandu that friendly relations between the United States and Nepal would be "preserved."[51] The Soviet reaction to the royal coup was at first non-commital. The Soviet press reported the dismissal of the Koirala government and the arrests of the Congress, Communist leaders without any comment.[52] But the release of the communists in early 1961 was welcomed by the Soviets and they adopted a pro-Monarch attitude, praised his policy of neutrality in international affairs and applauded the development of friendly relations between Nepal and communist nations.[53]

In 1961, King Mahendra made an extensive foreign tour to exploit its differences with India. Right from the beginning of the King's rule both China and Pakistan showed extreme friendliness towards him. Peking, in particular, geared its diplomacy to exploit the situation to the detriment of India, with whom it had now a direct confrontation in the Himalayas. Taking a lenient view of its boundary claims Peking showed a friendly gesture with Nepal and not long after the trouble between the two started it was announced in Peking on 6 February, 1961 that agreement on general delineation of the border between Nepal and China had been reached.[54] This tempo of goodwill and understanding continued. China announced further the acceptance of report of the joint Sino-Nepalese border committee that the Mustang shooting in 1960 had taken place within the Nepalese territory as claimed then by the Government of Nepal.[55] It was also announced on 12 June that the Chinese had agreed to bear almost the entire cost of the project they had promised to execute in Nepal under the Rs. 14 crore assistance programme. In July 1961 the two countries posted their first resident ambassador in each others capital. On 5 September 1961, China signed an Aid protocol in Kathmandu under which it agreed to offer Nepal a cash grant worth Rs. one crore commodities worth Rs. 2.5 crore in Nepalese currency as a gift.[57]

The most important event of Sino-Nepal relations was King Mahendra's visit to Peking from 28 September to 15 October 1961. The visit was marked by the signing of an agreement on the construction of a highway which had an immense strategic value. The Chinese on their part, meticulously exploited every opportunity to strengthen Mahendra's anti-India policy. Chairman Liu Shaoqi congratulated the King for opposing "foreign aggression and pressure" and said that "the heroic

Nepalese people have remained firm and unyielding and always maintained the independence and dignity.[58] Actually the King wanted to use Sino-Nepalese friendship as a counter weight to the "threat" from National Congress forces operating from India. An opportunity now lay open before China to ensure that its security interests were watched on Tibet's Southern border by Nepal without the latter being made to feel that it was a vassal or satellite of China.[59] But the drift in Indo-Nepal relations continued and in that process Nepal continuously tried in an undisguised, even crude manner to play off China against India.

At the moment both the super powers were trying tirelessly to keep Nepal at a distance from China. The USA and USSR together with India, concerned with the power imbalance in the Himalayas, decided to outbid the Chinese for influence in Nepal by increasing the cost of competition for the latter. Nepal naturally benefited from the aid giving spree which followed. In regard to Indo-Nepal relations America was facing a dilemma. If it had became tough on India and pressurise New Delhi to mend fences with Kathmandu, Indo-American relations were likely to get a setback. Unlike Pakistan, America's marginal influence on India was also questionable. India had demonstrated in the past as well, that it was not prepared to be duped by America. Implicitly, America should not venture to ask India to a particular thing. In case of Nepal, America was sensitive to the monarch's sensibilities that an open succour to the revivalism and restoration of democratic institutions in Nepal might be looked upon by the King with suspicion and might be interpreted as an act of interference in its domestic affairs. Though in principle America had been pleading for "regional demoralisation" in practice it was not easy task for the US government to work vigorously and support openly for the restoration of democratic institutions in Nepal.[60]

From the beginning the US strategy of both pressurising and counselling India to exercise restraint in dealing with smaller states of the region under the pretext of maintaining regional peace and stability was aimed at keeping India in a low profile and neutralizing the Soviet influence in the subcontinent. The main tenets of the US policy are:

(i) to decrease Nepalese dependence on India;

(ii) to keep India in a low profile in the region;

(iii) to checkmate India's over-arching and over-extensive strategic reach and beyond the region;

(iv) to help maintain independence and autonomy for Nepal and also extend oblique support to the democratic process in Nepal;

(v) to prevent China from exploiting the situation in its favour by exacerbating tensions between India and Nepal.[61]

Thus, the primary consideration for the US in Nepal was China and USSR. It extended full support to the new regime. Immediately following the takeover, a spokesman of the US State Department, while answering press questions, said that the takeover had nothing to do either with the Russians or the Chinese and that being so there was nothing to worry about.[62] To the general surprise of democratic elements in Nepal, the United States, also began to give full support to the newly declared Panchayat System. The US embassy in Kathmandu evinced keen interest in offering its guidance to panchayat members. In his address at the opening of the first district Panchayal Development Conference, held on 29 May 1963, in Kathmandu the US Ambassador Henry Stebbins called upon the "district leaders" to mobilise all their resources for nation-building activity. However, despite the criticism the US seemed to have felt no trouble by any such considerations. Its aid programme in Nepal was more ambitious and complex, designed as it was to boost the existing regime "until Panchayat System produced results". It was aimed not only against China but also against the USSR and India. It appeared that a sustained bid was being made by the US to increase its influence in Nepal at India's expense. New-Delhi's stock in Nepal, particularly after the Sino-Indian border clash was at an all time low. India's own vulnerability against the Chinese and its consequent dependence upon the West and the USSR had increased.

The delayed establishment of Nepal-Soviet relations was further cemented by the visits of the important leaders on both the sides. The USSR, in contrast to India appeared to work with the King's new regime which followed the royal takeover of 15

December 1960. The first and foremost reason of USSR taking interest was its widening rift with the Chinese which is an adjacent power in Nepal. India's increasing collaboration with the USSR had also compelled the latter to have its influence expanded in Nepal owing to the mounting tension in Sino-Indian relations which culminated in the border war of October-November 1962. All these factors made USSR moderate in relation to Nepalese developments and it had no objection in working with the new dispensation so long as it kept a power distance from the Chinese. Consequently the Soviets discouraged opposition to the King by the communist party of Nepal. The Soviet Union was happy that there had not been a communist takeover in Nepal because it would be undesirable for USSR, for a communist regime in Nepal would most likely come under Chinese influence. The Soviets, therefore, had a vested interest in maintaining in power in Kathmandu, a neutralist non-communist government.[63]

The Soviet aim was to check the Chinese influence over the Kingdom. But the Chinese were playing the same game. In order to secure his newly established regime King turned towards China and, in 1961 the Kathmandu-Kodari Road agreement was signed and that alarmed the Russians. However the Soviet aid programme in Nepal was exclusively directed against China. The Soviets made no attempt to compete against India or the US. The initial Soviet success in Nepal was probably due to the Chinese unwillingness and, inability to enter the race seriously. Since the Soviets interests in Nepal were relatively limited, they considered it futile to play with such high stakes against China. The Soviets might not have further liked to complicate their cordial relations with India by increasing their role in Nepal beyond a certain point.

**Analysis of the Attitude**

The level of understanding that Indo-Nepal relations had gained during the first elected government of B. P. Koirala, suffered a setback by the royal takeover of 15 December 1960. India refused to accept the event and reacted sharply though, with restraint. Nehru expressed his regret over the situation making it repeatedly clear that it was a domestic issue of Nepal and he did not want to interfere. However, he made no overt or covert attempt to pressurize King Mahendra perhaps realising the danger of antagonising the Nepalese government when the Sino-Indian relations were in such a deplorable condition. But he did not hesitate at all to allow the Nepalese political victims of the King's takeover to take shelter in India and also to organize and express themselves freely and peacefully within the limits of the law of the land. In fact this permission and Nehru's adverse comments on royal takeover became the main irritant of Indo-Nepal relations for coming days.

While dealing with Nepal the growing Chinese economic influence was a cause of concern for New Delhi and it strenghened its resolve not only to continue but to broaden and deepen it further. India applied two mind—one for Royal Government and the other for the Nepalese people. It had no love or sympathy for the King's absolutist regime. But it continued to be friendly and sympathetic to the Nepalese people at large.[64] Following the Kathmandu-Kodari road agreement it started viewing the Government in Kathmandu as tended to be unfriendly. It exercised pressures for the restoration of democracy in Nepal.

Following the royal takeover, quite for some time King Mahendra tried to have terms with New Delhi but Nehru was not prepared to yield. His twice visit to India failed to convince Indian people in general and the Government of India in particular. Being disappointed from India Nepal turned its face for the support and help for the royal regime. At the point China got an opportunity and exploited Indo-Nepal drift to a large extent. China openly supported the royal takeover, while the reactions of USA and USSR were mild and sober. Having found known support for the new Kingdom Nepal started whipping up anti-Indianism and New Delhi, in response, started exercising mild pressures not only to stop it but also to make it relent. India increased all sorts of diplomatic, political and economic pressures upon the King to restore democracy. The Nepalese relations with China grew in diverse fields, including security, while the other powers, such as, USA and USSR for their own reasons were trying to distance away Nepal from the Chinese influence.

However, the Sino-Indian armed conflict of October 1962 was a turning point in Indo-Nepal relations. It came as a boon to King Mahendra. The immediate response of the royal regime to the conflict must have been one of relief for New Delhi and, it hastened to make fundamental changes in its Nepal Policy. The unofficial economic blockade was lifted and, trade began to flow across the border again. The Nepali Congress leaders, perhaps on the advice of the Government of India suspended their agitation in November 1962 and the circumstances helped King Mahendra in achieving what he had long desired to achieve. Now security became the primary concern of India. Having opened India's eyes in respect of its military weaknesses compelled it to go for a frantic search for security. Nepal too began to respond positively and a new era of Indo-Nepal relations commenced thereafter.

## Notes and References

1. N. Ghildial, "Indo-Nepal Relations and China", Ramakant and B.C. Upreiti (eds.), *Indo–Nepal Relations* (South Asian Publishers, New Delhi, 1992), pp. 322-323.
2. *Ibid.*
3. *The Statesman*, 8 January 1961.
4. *The Hindustan Times*, 9 January 1961.
5. *The Times of India*, 13 January 1961.
6. *The Indian Express*, 1 Jun 1961.
7. *The National Herald* (Delhi), 18 August 1961.
8. *The Statesman*, 14 November 1961.
9. *The Hindustan Times*, 15 November, 1961.
10. T. R. Ghoble, *China-Nepal Relations and India* (Deep and Deep Publications. New Delhi, 1986). pp. 50-51.
11. Durga Das, "Indo-Nepal Relations", The Indian Express. 10 October 1961.
12. Ramakant, *Nepal-China and India* (Abhinav Publications, New Delhi, 1976), p. 163.
13. S.K. Jha, *The Uneasy Partners : India and Nepal in the Post-Colonial Era* (Manas, New Delhi, 1975), p. 205.
14. Editorial, The Hindu, 26 April 1962.

15. *Rajya Sabha Debates*, Vol. 36, No. 1, 27 November 1961, Cols. 23-6.
16. *The Indian Express*, 23 January 1962.
17. *The Hindustan Times*, 24 April 1962.
18. *The Guardian* (Manchester), 4 May 1962.
19. Ramakant, *op. cit.*, pp.194-5.
20. *The Gorkhapatra*, 18 July 1962.
21. *The Hindu*. 17 September 1962.
22. A. S. Bhasin. *Documents on Nepal's Relations with India and China 1949-1966* (Bombay, 1970), 238.
23. R.S. Chauhan, "Smaller Powers and Neutrality", S.P. Verma and K.P. Mishra. (eds). *Foreign Policies in South Asia* (Orient Longman), New Delhi. 1969). pp. 271-3.
24. L. E. Rose, *Nepal : Strategy for Survival* (OUP, Delhi, 1973), p. 250.
25. *The Statesman,* 23 January, 1961.
26. The Times of India, 15 January 1961.
27. *Ibid.,* 20 January 1961.
28. *Kalpana*, 21 January 1961.
29. *Ibid.*
30. *Ibid.,* 23 January 1961.
31. *The National Herald*, 20 July 1961.
32. *Ibid.*
33. Tribhuvan Nath, *The Nepalese Dilemma 1960-74* (Sterling Publishers, New Delhi, 1975), pp. 372-73.
34. *The Indian Express*, 12 April 1962.
35. King Mahendra, *Pages of History*, Series 2, pp. 132-34.
36. See the Joint Communique issued at the end of King Mahendra's visit to India, 23 April 1962, *Foreign Policy of India : Text of Documents 1947-1964* (Lok Sabha Secretariat, Government of India, New Delhi, 1966), pp. 345-46.
37. *The Statesman*, 22 April 1962.
38. *The Hindu*, 21 April 1962.
39. *The Times of India*, 21 and 23 April 1963.

40. *The Newyork Times*, 21 April 1962.
41. See the Joint Communique in Foreign Policy of India : Text of Documents 1947-1964, *op.cit.*, pp. 345-46.
42. *Foreign Affairs Record* (Delhi), Vol. 8, No. 4, April 1962, p. 96.
43. *Ibid.*
44. *Ibid.*
45. A.T. Chandra Mohan, "Indo-Nepalese Ties Show Improvements", *The Indian Express*, 14 May 1962.
46. *The Sunday Standard*, 24 June 1962.
47. *The Gorkhapatra*, 4 September 1962.
48. S.K. Jha, *op. cit.*, p. 200.
49. *Naya Samaj*, 10 September 1962.
50. *The Dawn* (Karachi), 11 April 1962.
51. *The Hindu*, 17 December 1960.
52. *The Pravda*, 16 and 17 December 1960.
53. *Izvestia*, 19 February 1961.
54. *The Times of India*, 7 February 1961.
55. *The Hindu*, 12 March 1961.
56. *The Gorkhapatra*, 13 June 1961.
57. *Ibid.*, 6 September 1961.
58. *Xinhua*, 29 September 1961.
59. Tribhuvan Nath, *op. cit.*, p. 338.
60. B.M. Jain. "Role of Superpowers : Security and Strategic Dimensions," Ramakant and B.C. Upreiti (eds.), *op.cit.*, p. 337.
61. *Ibid.*, p. 335.
62. *The Hindu*, 17 December, 1960.
63. E. B. Mihaly, *Foreign Aid and Politics in Nepal : A Case Study* (OUP, London, 1965), p. 162.
64. Dr. Kirtyanand Singh, *Small Neighbours of Big Powers : India's Attitude Towards Nepal—September 1946-March 1963* (Capital Publishing House, Delhi, 1988), p. 207.

# 7

# DEPRESSION AND EXPLOITATION (1963—1971)

## Diplomacy

The armed conflict of October 1962 had a far-reaching effects on Indo-Nepal relations. It weakened India's position in the region on the one hand and disturbed Nepal over the acute imbalance in the Indian and the Chinese military strength in the Himalayan area on the other. India's world image was tarnished and created doubt about her capacity to defend the small states of Himalayan region against the Chinese and so New Delhi was reduced to a low profile in international politics. The other small powers of the area—Nepal, Burma and Ceylon though maintained strict neutrality in the Sino-Indian confrontation also shared this rejoicing to some extent, for any reduction in the capacity of India in the power-structure of this region in which she had so far an almost unchallenged position would necessarily enhance their status and manoeuvrability.[1] This apart, China's strategic presence in Nepal, superpower's increased interest in the region and King Mahendra's diplomacy of diversification provided Nepal an upper hand to bargain with India and New Delhi had to play into Nepal's hands.

The Chinese sympathy and promises for Kathmandu's industrialization was at its height in the phase of Sino-Indian armed conflict. As the war was certainly not an unmixed blessing, King Mahendra felt that any further weakening of Indian position was not to his advantage. The theme of his policy of preserving Nepal's security was based on the maintenance of a balanced relationship between the two giant neighbours. The doubtful credibility of the Chinese assurances and the unpredictability of Mao's moves could not have been completely unnoticed in the Himalayan Kingdom. The aggression had tilted King Mahendra into a sense of reality with regard to Nepal's relations with India. By the time Nepal discovered that it had gained nothing from its intimate relations with China except verbal promises. The abandonment of almost all economic projects by China on "technical grounds" dismayed the Nepalese. The newspaper *Daily Nepal*, even reproached China for holding out "false hopes about assisting Nepal in its industrialization programme" and said that the "talk of Nepal's industrialization through Chinese assistance is like a strange labyrinth".[2]

In the changed atmosphere King Mahendra endeavoured to assert his country's independence in international affairs in an attempt to secure greater economic aid from India and other countries. The immediate problem for Kathmandu was to agree that despite different political setups, coexistence between Nepal and India in the new situation could only pave the way for their salvation. Relations with India could not be allowed to continue in a state of tension without adversely affected the security and integrity of both countries. The process of negotiations between the two started with the visit of Tulsi Giri to New- Delhi in early December 1962, who on his return to Kathmandu told the newsmen on 12 December that no fundamental differences existed between Nepal and India. Giri also disclosed that he had invited the Indian Home Minister Lal Bahadur Shastri, to visit Kathmandu.[3] Shastri's visit to Kathmandu took place in March 1963 with which things seemed to have changed for the better and a steady improvement in the Indian approach towards Nepal was clearly in sight. He also succeeded in assuaging all fears and suspicions that Nepal had so far harboured against India.[4]

However, the growing of understanding between India and Nepal in the post-aggression phase was unpalatable to both Pakistan and China who were interested in reducing the power and influence of New Delhi in the region. As the chances of Indo-Nepal friendship became visible both the countries geared up its diplomacy to keep Nepal away from Indian influence. It was in this background that Ayub Khan, Pakistani President with his Foreign Minister Z. A. Bhutto came to Kathmandu in May 1963, the first-ever by an Islamic head of state to the Hindu

Kingdom. Similar developments took place in Sino-Nepalese relations too. Peking showed various friendly gestures to bring Kathmandu nearer to itself and the latter responded favourably with a view to increasing its bargaining position vis-a-vis New Delhi. On 14 January 1963 Nepal signed with China the Road Protocol for the construction of a road by the Chinese between Kathmandu and Kodari according to the agreement already arrived at.[5] On 20 January the Nepalese Foreign Minister visited Peking and signed the Boundary Protocol.[6] King Mahendra, being aware of all these facts sensed New Delhi's delicate position and exploited the situation to his advantage. As the king said :

> The present situation is so advantageous and, in fact, provides such a golden opportunity to us that if we fail to make good use of it, not only the present generation of Nepalese, but also generations to come will have to repent at leisure.[7]

At the time Nepal blatantly utilised the threat to turn to China which enjoyed a marked superiority over India in military matters on the Himalayan border. By doing so he extracted several concessions from India. But despite this the Nepalese government continued unabated with the policy to reduce its dependence on India. Although New- Delhi increased economic assistance to Nepal, it also made determined efforts to have maximum economic contacts with other countries particularly China and Pakistan. Kathmandu consolidated its friendship with China and widened its relations with Pakistan with an obvious intent to use them as a political lever in its relations with New Delhi.[8]

The signs of improved relations between India and Nepal was marked by the increased frequency of visits by the dignitaries of the two countries in order to maintain regular political contacts. In August, 1963 King Mahendra came to India on his four-day official visit. During the tour the Government of India made efforts to remove many of the irritants in the relations between the two countries. Firstly, it modified significantly its stand on King Mahendra's undemocratic rule. Radhakrishnan, the Indian President, while welcoming King Mahendra on his arrival, referred to the recent land reforms and social reforms introduced in Nepal and said it a "great step towards the emancipation of the people". Later on, when the Indian president paid a return visit to Kathmandu same year in November, he termed the new model of Panchayat System, introduced in Nepal recently as "an experiment in democracy."[9]

In 1963 the new constitution which envisaged King Mahendra's Panchayat System came into force that at least in theory, designed to combine the merits of both the Parliamentary and Communist system in such a way as to prevent the people of Nepal to be swayed in the direction of either India or China. Even Nepal's concept of non-alignment apparently acquired a new dimension. In Algiers meeting of Foreign Ministers, for instance, while Nepalese Foreign Minister, Kirtinidhi Bista pleaded for exclusion of Russia in Afro-Asian Conference, India moved heaven and earth to get Russia admitted into the Afro-Asian family. Again India for the first time supported the General Assembly resolution condemning China for suppression of human rights in Tibet, Nepal opposed it.[10] By the time Nepal had begun to receive foreign aid from many sources. Although it was a new phenomenon which was now seen making inroads into an area so far dominated by India. Yet having increased its political contacts with Kathmandu New- Delhi avoided any expression of its views on the issues, involving the two countries that might incite Nepal's hostile attitude. Despite Kathmandu's increasing approchements with Beijing India made every effort to keep Nepal on friendly terms. Swarn Singh, the External Affairs Minister of India, leavened the efforts by signing five development aid agreements during his visit to Kathmandu in August 1964. He reminded Nepal the common security dangers and said, "Nepal and India are sailing in the same boat and their safety lies in keeping together. Weakening of one implies the weakening of the other."[11] Nevertheless, later on when the signs of improvement in Nepal's relations with China were visible it no longer felt the urgency of appeasing Kathmandu. India gave up the patronising behaviour and displayed a more restrained and less assertive attitude towards Nepal. It refrained from making any effort to introduce Parliamentary System in Nepal but reconciled to the King and his panchayat system.

Lack of willingness on the part of New Delhi to commend openly and in unequivocal terms the prevailing political system in Nepal, the Government of India signed in January 1965 an arms assistance agreement with Nepal. When India was passing through a conflict with Pakistan in 1965, King Mahendra paid a state visit to New Delhi. At the moment Indian leaders wanted the King's support on Kashmir issue and on the persuasion of New Delhi King Mahendra agreed to add a sentence in the joint communique that the principle of self determination can only apply to dependent and trust territories and cannot be extended to integral parts of sovereign states.[12] Nepal also foiled Pakistani attempt during the war, to create misunderstandings between the two countries by announcing that Nepal had asked India not to employ the Gurkha-troops in Kashmir against Pakistan. But the Nepalese Government despite its friendly relations with Pakistan, denied the report and adhered to its previous commitment to India.[13]

The outbreak of armed conflict between India and Pakistan in last quarter of 1965 had affected New Delhi-Kathmandu relations. Nepal realised the futility of its policy of using China against India. The most critical and unexpected development of the failure of China to do anything effectively to support its ally Pakistan and there was the distant possibility that China might be ready to intervene forcefully in support of Kathmandu in the event India moved against King Mahendra's regime. Even China's ultimatum to India during the war and concentration of Chinese troops along the border of Sikkim, temporarily dampened Nepalese enthusiasm for Beijing and caused considerable uneasiness about China's objectives in Nepal. In an editorial *Samaj* expressed its concern and said that the Chinese ultimatum had "stunned" the whole world and urged Beijing to withdraw it and respond to India's proposal for a peaceful settlement of the border problems rather than resort to pressure tactics. Otherwise the world would be forced to suspect that a plan had been hatched earlier for a "joint action by China and Pakistan.[14]

Evidently worried by demonstration of Chinese military power, King Mahendra decided to further ameliorate his relations with India. He came to India in December 1965 and met President Radhakrishnan, Prime Minister Shastri and other leaders. In the banquets and public receptions arranged in his honour with a view to improve Indo-Nepal relations, the King addressed Indian leaders affectionately as "brothers" and praised the Indian people for their "abundance of goodwill" towards Nepal."[15] This spirit of amity and cordiality continued when Surya Bahadur Thapa arrived in India in April 1966 and said that the friendship between Nepal and India was a "sacred trust" left to them by their ancestors, and should be nourished in an "objective manner" at the social, economic and intelligentsia levels.[16] However, Nepal's objective in seeking to improve relations with India had been motivated by the desire to draw away from China's intimate embrace before it was too late, especially at a time when it was in the grip of Great Proletarian Revolution.[17]

The year 1967, which was the high point of the cultural revolution in China, witnessed a few unusual incidents in the relationship between Nepal and China. With the completion of Kathmandu-Kodari Highway and Soviet attempts to join influence in Nepal, a change in Chinese attitude towards the Himalayan Kingdom was obvious. The expression of gratitude to Beijing for its support by the Nepalese leaders convinced to regard Nepal as their satellite in the Himalayas and Mahendra as an obsequious follower were determined to handle them accordingly. China's response towards Nepal took turn of an imperial power towards a dependent territory. But the Nepalese press reacted sharply when on 24 February 1967, *Peking Review* published a picture of some Nepalese peasants and children saluting the portrait of Mao. *The Motherland*, a daily newspaper from Kathmandu remarked that the photograph had exposed "China's narrow thinking..... For the Nepalese the Mao philosophy is meaningless since for them the Mao thought are far from reality and workable only in Ghengiskhan period", while *Daily Samachar* said that "the Nepalese cannot tolerate the insult". Inspite of the Nepalese reactions China continued their propaganda to popularize Maozedong's thought in the Himalayan Kingdom. Further objectionable matters causing harm to Nepalese sentiments were published in successive months. In addition due to lack of courage, the royal government did not do anything to stop these activities. Mahendra's acquiescence encouraged the Chinese to treat him as a ruler of a dependent state and gave new impetus to the Chinese determination to spread Mao Zedong thought in Nepal. On 14 June 1967, some 400 jeering Chinese led by their ambassador in Nepal demonstrated at the airport against "Indian reactionaries", "US imperialists" and "Soviet revisionist". They also insulted everyone, who did not raise abusive slogans against India, United States and the Soviet Union.

Reacting over the incident, Kirtinidhi Bista, the Nepalese Prime Minister said that he found "nothing objectionable" in the Chinese vandalism. But a few Nepalese newspapers resented the Chinese demonstrations against India, United States and the Soviet Union and talked of "equal status" of Nepal and "misuse of diplomatic privileges by the Chinese".[20] Being deeply disturbed by the Chinese demonstrations and its campaign to propagate Mao thought, a group of students, on 1 July 1967, perhaps in retaliation, showing anti-China slogans demonstrated in front of the Chinese pavillion at Mahendra's birth day exhibition, smashed glass panes of Chinese cars and removed Mao's portrait. The Chinese became furious over the happening and threatened Nepal with "dire consequences" unless anti-China activities were immediately stopped. The threat caused considerable fear and concern in Nepal[21] and it quickly expressed its "disapproval of the anti-China demonstration, apologised and closed the exhibition.[22] But the Chinese were not appeased and as long as the cultural revolution lasted, China did not allow Nepal to relax. It kept Nepal on its toes by means of its pressure tactics. Officials of the Chinese Embassy alternately attended and boycotted state function in Kathmandu.

Even the good created after the successful visit of Lal Bahadur Shastri, Indian Prime Minister, in 1965 and Mrs. Gandhi during her visit in 1966 failed to remove the differences between the two countries in matters of trade and transit. Politically too, the Indian policy did not succeed in its long-term objective of arresting the increasing influences of China and Pakistan in the Himalayan Kingdom. Towards the close of the sixties Nepal had certain issues on which it wanted a favourable deal with India. Apart from problems relating to trade and transit it had some border disputes which it wanted to settle to its advantage. Kathmandu's Trade and Transit Treaty of 1960 with India was to expire in October 1970 and Nepal was campaigning for inclusion of favourable terms in the new treaty. However, a more serious issue of psychological and political nature was that B. P. Koirala who was released in November 1968, in early 1969 came to India and started criticizing the panchayat democracy in Nepal. Hence, King Mahendra's posture towards India at this stage was aimed to preserve his political system and he calculated that having raised a storm with India he might have relieved from the growing oppositional strains on the system, by diverting the people's attention, at least, for the time being. On the other hand, India saw Nepal's pro-China game and was determined to assert its leadership in the Himalayan Kingdom. New Delhi revised its earlier policy of accommodation and adopted a stiff attitude to make Nepal realise that India was not to be bullied. India during the visit of Dinesh Singh, India's Minister for External Affairs, tried to assert its pre-eminent position in June 1969 but accused of having "big brotherly and uncompromising attitude" towards Nepal.[23]

In the circumstances, Kirtinidhi Bista, the Nepalese Prime Minister, came out with a diplomatic bombshell against India. In a remarkable and untypical interview with *The Rising Nepal* on 24 June 1969, Bista questioned some basic aspect of the Indo-Nepalese relations. He charged India with having failed to inform Nepal, as envisaged in the 1950 Treaty about important developments in its relations with the US, USSR, Pakistan and China. He challenged the validity of existing mutual security arrangements between the two countries. He also expressed resentment at the term "special relationship and stressed that Nepal "could not compromise its sovereignty for India's so called security."[24] Bista's statement was supported by almost all the newspapers of Nepal, China and Pakistan but India took no notice of Bista's blistering interview. *The Gorkhapatra* declared that "Nepal cannot compromise sovereignty for the sake of India's security nor will it accept limited sovereignty."[25] *Renmin Ribao*, a daily newspaper of China, praised Nepal's "toughness" towards India and reiterated China's verbal promise that Beijing would "safeguard Nepalese sovereignty and integrity."[26] While *The Dawn* (Karachi) said that "the presence of the Indian military group in Nepal becomes dangerous as soon as it disregards Nepal's national interests flagrantly interferes in Nepal's internal affairs and comes out subversion against the Nepalese government."[27]

King Mahendra first, to divert the attention of Nepalese people from the dissatisfaction of its Panchayat System and then to pressurise New Delhi to accept favourable terms in the new treaty of trade and transit had adopted this posture. His obvious strategy was to separate the political from the economic issue but India believed that the two were inter-related and refuged to budge. The lapse of the treaty led to an impass and hardships to the Nepalese people as they solely depended on India for many of the essential items of their daily lives. Although the Government of India took some unilateral steps to prevent such hardships and allowed basic facilities to Nepal from 1 January 1971, yet in general, it showed a stiff attitude in respect of the trade and transit treaty. Simultaneously, apart from launching a pre-planned campaign for immediate compliance of India on the issues raised by Bista, the Nepalese Government tried to lobby international support. The governments of various countries were approached for pleading Nepal's case as a land locked country and for putting pressure on India.

But all this was of no avail. Mahendra soon saw the limitation of his pressure tactics. The economic situation of the country continued to deteriorate and the people began to blame the government for its failure to conclude a new trade treaty with India. By the time the emerging crisis of East Bengal also required better rapport between India and Nepal. Ultimately a new Treaty of Trade and Transit valid for 5 years was signed in Kathmandu on 13 August 1971. However, Mahendra did not accept the failure of his anti-India posture. He continued to conspire with the Chinese and Pakistani against India. He opposed India's policy towards the freedom struggle in Bangladesh and justified Pakistani repression of the people of Bangladesh for self- determination.[28]

In August 1971 the conclusion of Indo-Soviet Treaty of Peace and Friendship had a profound impact on Nepal. Kathmandu had viewed India so far as a weak neighbour. It could now visualised that the balance of power in the region was changing with the growing Soviet interest in the sub-continent. As a result of 14-day India-Pakistan war of December 1971, Pakistan disintegrated and out of it, emerged a new nation named Bangladesh. The disappearance of old and unified Pakistan as a balancing power against India reduced to some extent the bargaining position of Nepal vis-a-vis New Delhi. On the other hand, the emergence of a confident, strident and pre-eminent India in the new geo-political realities in South Asia created apprehensions both in Kathmandu and Beijing. Nepal viewed India's determined effort to help the people of Bangladesh as an ominous signal by the Nepalese monarchy because one aspect of this development was the growing strength of the democratic camp on the sub-continent. The Chinese too, adopted a cautious attitude towards Nepal and did not indulge in encouraging the monarchy and their supporters to undertake any thing that could be used as a pretext by India to intervene in the similar way it had done earlier in Bangladesh.

The war opened the Nepalese eyes and it was clear that China connection had lost much of its utility for Kathmandu. If China would do nothing to protect Pakistan, a far more friendly power in South Asia it was unrealistic to assume that it would do for Nepal under a similar set of circumstances.[29] Hence Nepal began to assert friendly relations and traditional ties between New Delhi and Kathmandu. King's willingness to seek co-operation and understanding with India[30] generated hope in India and uncertainty in China.

## Strategy for Security

Following the India-China war of October 1962 India became security scared. Defence assumed the top priority in the country and Nehru, who had all along been opposed to the idea of taking military assistance from foreign countries, had to redefine his non-alignment and acquiesce in accepting such assistance from the foreign powers in order to safeguard country's territorial integrity. Kathmandu too, in the post-war phase adjusted its policy to the new circumstances in South Asia in which it ignored its "special relations" with any country. However, the switch over necessitated an exercise in tight rope walking in the conduct of relations with both India and China. A beneficial aspect of this neutral policy lay in the fact that it provided Nepal a device to counter the political influence of the National Congress rebels. It created the impression that in the event of any pressure from the south, there will immediately be ready a force from the north to protect country's sovereignty.[31] In 1963 soon after the war the IMTAG was again reorganised as the Indian Military Liaison Group (IMLG). The group consisted 23 officials. The two countries also have some understanding in defence matters and Chief of the Indian Army, General J. N. Choudhary, was accorded a very warm welcome during his visit to Kathmandu in July 1963. He also held discussions with King Mahendra and other military officials of Nepal on "matters of common military interest.[32] New Delhi felt the security dangers equally and further Swarn Singh, India's Minister for External Affairs, in course of his visit to Kathmandu in August 1964 referred to the common security stakes and said that their safety lies in getting together.

Apart from having terms on defence matters with New-Delhi, King Mahendra explored the possibility of securing military assistance from the countries other than India but had succeeded in obtaining merely a limited quantity of military assistance from Britain and the United States on a short term basis. The delivery of "limited arms supplies" by US and UK was a disturbing factor for Peking. However, King Mahendra in line with determined efforts to find a counter-weight to the risk of the security of his Kingdom allowed the Chinese to build the Kathmandu-Lhasa Highway. It was not based on the theory that Nepal lay within the Indian sphere of influence. But perhaps King Mahendra, being not fully satisfied with the security dealings with US, UK and China signed with New Delhi an arms assistance agreement in January 1965 whereby it was decided that the arms aid from the United States and the United Kingdom would be supplemented by India. It was also reaffirmed that Nepal would get arms from other sources (with the exception of China) only when India would not be in a position to supply the necessary equipments. Further Nepal agreed to the Indian proposal in April 1965 for getting various strategic roads and airfields constructed through Indian co-operation, acceeded to India's request for not allowing the Chinese to undertake any project in the Terai area of Nepal[35] and cancelled the agreement with China whereby the latter had undertaken to construct a portion of Nepal's East-West Highway and handed it over to India.[36] Nepal also supported although having persuaded by the Indian leaders, New Delhi's claim over Kashmir after the Indo-Pak war when King Mahendra visited India in December 1965.[37]

King Mahendra was fortunate in the sense that the Chinese were generally co-operative with the King even on those occasions when they were less than happy with some Nepalese foreign policy decisions.[38] China's objectives in Nepal was primarily directed at complicating India's relationship with neighbouring states in order to limit New- Delhi's ability to take effective action outside the South Asia region. The Chinese presence in Nepal expanded considerably after 1962, but not to the point where it might have been reasonably viewed as dominated by New Delhi[39] or threatened by Kathmandu. From the beginning of 1966 Kathmandu began to be shadowed by the propaganda of Maoism among the Nepalese people. China at the time, was in the grip of Great Proletarian Cultural Revolution and wanted to mobilise the Nepalese people for China's new revolution. However, the propaganda among the Nepalese did not go unnoticed and King Mahendra continued to improve his relations with Beijing's enemies—India, Israel, Yugoslavia and the Soviet Union. In early November 1966, he sent Giri Prasad Budathoki, Nepal's Defence Minister, to New Delhi for the purpose of securing arms from India. He sent Royal Army personnel to Israel for training as para troopers in the face of a strong protest by China.[41] Nepal's trade, economic and cultural relations were improved considerably with Yugoslavia and the Soviet Union.

China was not happy with this development in Nepalese foreign policy and was worried particularly on the Soviet attempt to gain influence in the country. Although India had no objection for Nepal being close to other countries specially the Chinese. It was conceded by Prime Minister Mrs. Gandhi after her return from Kathmandu in October 1966. She said "China is a neighbour of Nepal and naturally they would like to remain friends of China also".[12] However, this hopeful stance did not last long and aberrations were seen in Nepal's relations with China on the one hand and with India on the other.

In May 1967, King Mahendra inaugurated the Chinese built Kathmandu-Kodari road. The opening of the Highway, as viewed generally in India, posed a serious threat to India's security and that India could not afford to be complacent about it. Whether or not China would actually use the road for an attack on India, the potential danger had been created and, in any case, India's defence perspective could never be the same again. M. C. Chagla, the then Minister for External Affairs, assured the anxious Lok Sabha on 3 July 1967 that India was prepared to meet any threat posed by the road. Even before the opening when it was reported that the road was strong enough to carry out the tank and as such some members of Parliament suspected the real motive behind it as Nepal was having very cordial relations with China. Mrs. Indira Gandhi, the Indian Prime Minister, had to clarify her government's thinking about it, though unwillingly in the Rajya Sabha on 22 November 1966. She said :

> We do know about the road, but there is nothing much we can do about this except to point out to our Nepalese friends the threat which China is posing to us here, as the honourable member pointed out, in collusion with Pakistan. But China is a sovereign country and Nepal is sovereign country and their dealing with each other is not something in which we can interfere.[43]

India lodged a strong protest on 26 July 1967 with the Nepalese Government against the repeated anti-Indian demonstrations by the Chinese at Kathmandu, particularly after the opening of the Highway. Nepal in reply to New- Delhi's protest note maintained that the road was nothing but an economic measure, intended to provide with an additional outlet to Nepal's expanding trade and commerce without detriment to any. The Nepalese newspapers had welcomed the opening and even declared :

Now we do not need to pass through India while visiting any part of the world. Our dream has now been realised by our Chinese friends .... China earns our eternal gratitude .... The highway will endure for centuries as a road of friendship, peace and co-operation between Nepal and China.[45]

But the Chinese viewed the Highway as a way to arrive at the Nepalese capital within a shortest possible time. They hoped that the road would bring "Maozedong's thought" to Nepal to make the Nepalese China-conscious. As the construction of the Kathmandu-Kodari Highway being over, the Chinese behaviour with the Nepalese no longer remained as polite as it was at the beginning of the sixties. This became perceptible during the peak of the cultural revolution and at the ceremonial function of the road when Liu Hai-Yun, the visiting Chinese Minister of International Trade, after praising the Nepalese workmen for accomplishing the "difficult task of building a road across the Himalayas" he said" The Chinese people sincerely hope that the Nepalese people will constantly 'achieve fresh successes in their lofty cause of opposing imperialism, colonialism and building up their motherland. On the other hand Kathmandu was conscious enough to meet the pressures which it experienced from the Chinese side during 1967-68. It adopted a two-pronged approach. One, the issues involved were localised and bilaterally with China. They were not allowed to affect other aspects of the Sino-Nepalese relations. Two, Nepal maintained close contacts and understanding with India and explored the possibilities of meeting the situation if the Chinese pressures were to acquire a dangerous proportion.[47] But Peking remained effortful to impress on Kathmandu that it was China's presence to the north that had proved to be the best guarantee for the maintenance of Nepal's independence and sovereignty against a hostile and threatening neighbour like India.

Apart from this both the superpowers (USA and USSR) had considered the road as of immense strategic importance. Soon after King Mahendra's visit to the United States an American Army General T. Z. Conway, visited Nepal in November 1967 where he inspected the Kathmandu-Kodari highway and the Mustang region. The visit was significant in view of the prevailing apprehensions regarding the strategic significance of the highway constructed with Chinese assistance ostensibly for commercial purposes. Soviet Union was alert to the road developments and on 13 July 1967 *The Soviet Journal Literaturnava Gazeta* underlined the great military and strategic importance to China of the 67-mile long mountain road from Tibet to Kathmandu and warned against its inherent threat to Nepal.[49]

New Delhi's policy towards Nepal was strongly influenced by the new-found confidence with which the Indians now viewed their relationship with both China and Pakistan. Kirtinidhi Bista, the Nepalese Prime Minister was well known for his pro-China sentiment and it was not a secret that the Chinese regarded him as their man in the Himalayan Kingdom. India considered the pro- China game of Bista as a danger to Indo-Nepal relations. In early June 1969, Dinesh Singh, India's Minister for External Affairs, visited Kathmandu with a view to assert India's pre-eminent position in Nepal. On 5 June he told the Nepalese that "Nepal and India are bound together by defence relations". King Mahendra was not satisfied with the progress of discussion between the two countries on the terms of the treaty of trade and transit, Prime Minister Bista and the Chinese were enraged and resented India's refusal to accept Nepal's conditions.

A few days after the visit of India's Foreign Minister, Bista started a new campaign against India, supported by the Chinese, the pro-Chinese groups in Nepal and Pakistan. In a typical and even surprising press interview to the English Daily *Rising Nepal* Bista said on 24 June 1969 that the work of both the Indian Military personnel and Indian Military Group had been completed in Nepal and "they can and should therefore, be withdrawn". While replying to a question regarding their mutual obligation under the 1950 Treaty of Peace and Friendship between Nepal and India Bista maintained that since the treaty was signed several military developments of great importance had taken place in India's relations with the Soviet Union and the United States on the one hand and with Pakistan and China on the other. Referring to the Indian personnel on Nepal's checkposts and the presence of the Indian Military Group in the Kingdom he declared : "To connect their presence in Nepal with any treaty or with any overall relation between the two countries is not correct. Such an attempt provides ground for misinterpretation of India's intentions towards Nepal by interested parties.[51] The statement created a furore in both Nepal and India.

On 25 July 1969, Nepal officially conveyed through its Ambassador in New Delhi the demand for withdrawal to the Government of India.[52] This was accompanied by the approval of a private resolution by the Rashtriya Panchayat asking the Government to make arrangements for the withdrawal of Indian personnel from the northern check- posts and of the Indian Military Mission Group.[53] Nepalese demand created a sensation and the matter was thoroughly discussed in both Houses of Parliament through "calling attention" motion. The then Minister for External Affairs announced in the Lok Sabha on 29 July that India had informed the Nepalese authorities that it had no objection in principle to acceding to their request in this regard. The Indian side, in its talks with Nepalese-authorities held on the issue in the first week of September, expressed New-Delhi's desire to accept the Nepalese demand provided Indian security interests were safeguarded through alternative arrangements. But these conditions were not acceptable to the Nepalese government. Even before Bista's statement of 24 June, India's Minister for External affairs Dinesh Singh during his visit to Nepal discussed the question of the withdrawal of Indian personnel from checkposts in Nepal's northern frontier and the Indian Military Group from Kathmandu. But his talks with the Nepalese Prime Minister Bista did not lead to any concrete results.

Nepal took a step further in this regard and on 1 January 1970, it replaced the Indians on their northern checkposts. Following this development India's Minister for External Affairs went to Nepal in February on a five-day unofficial visit. He discussed with the King and Nepalese ministers on the question of alternative security arrangements though their discussions were not made public. Finally, on 18 August 1970 the Indian Military Liaison Group was also wound up in Kathmandu.[58] Later on from King Mahendra's interview to *The Times of India* on 19 October it became clear that Nepal and India had arrived at a full understanding on exchange of "military information" on developments harmful to either country and added that Nepal had agreed to Indian proposal for stationing senior military personnel at the Indian Embassy in Kathmandu "for the agreed period and job".[59] Although the storm over the checkposts issue was over it nevertheless left clouds of misunderstandings in Indo-Nepalese relations. Having secured the victory over the checkpost issue the Nepalese government now concentrated on the realisation of its terms on trade and transit from India. During this relatively low-key but sustained confrontation the China factor proved to be of limited utility to Kathmandu. The Royal government approached the Chinese on the occasion but found nothing more than comforting words. Kathmandu also contacted several countries for help and to pressurise India to come to Nepalese terms. But all went in vain and in August 1971 the two countries signed a new Treaty of Trade and Transit, although less favourable from the Nepalese point of view. Perhaps one major factor behind the signing was the freedom movement, going on in the East Bengal.

The tidc of Indo-Nepalese relations turned towards the close of 1971. Till now Kathmandu's politics with Pakistan had generated so much heat and it abruptly came to an end with the disintegration of Pakistan out of which emerged a new nation of Bangladesh. India's role both militarily and diplomatic in the process of the emergence of Bangladesh demonstrated its credibility and capability as a dominant power in the region. During the Indo-Pak war of 1971 King Mahendra apart from supporting Yahya Khan and branding India as an "aggressor", hoped that the Chinese would demonstrate its military might in favour of Pakistan because a victory for India would change the balance of power in South Asia. Hence Nepal realised its manoeuvr-ability in the new politico-military realities in the sub-continent and the royal regime formally recognised the Republic of Bangladesh on 15 January 1972 disregarding China's aggressive and negative approach.

**Exchange of Visits**

In the post-phase of Sino-Indian war of 1962 India and Nepal for their own reasons wanted to come close to each other.

The conflict forced New Delhi to look for reconciliation with Kathmandu on the terms the latter has been demanding for the last two years—the acceptance of the royal regime, prevention of the use of Indian territories for rebel activities in Nepal and above all, the acceptance of Nepal's right to decide for itself the type of government that it should have. In response to the invitation extended by Nepalese Foreign Minister Tulsi Giri during his last unofficial visit to India in December 1962, India's Minister of Home Affairs Lal Bahadur Shastri paid a visit to Kathmandu 2-5 March 1963. Kathmandu viewed the four as an opportunity to extract further concessions from New Delhi and hence continued its pressure tactics. Just on the eve of Shastri's visit the Nepalese government made a request to India for improved transit facilities for her trade, as well as for permission to construct a road linking Bhadrapur (East Nepal) with the East Pakistan border.[60] It also provided King Mahendra an occasion to raise Nepalese stakes and it spared no effort in piling up complaints galore against the Indian Embassy and Indian Aid Mission officials to blame them for the deterioration in Nepal-India relations. Shastri too, in course of a series of talks held with the King, Tulsi Giri and U. B. Thapa sympathised with Kingdom's difficulty and explained India's position with sincerity and straight forwardness.

Things seemed to have changed for the better with the visit of Shastri and a steady improvement in the Indian approach was clearly in sight. The visiting Home Minister, while addressing at a reception given in his honour by the Nepal-India Friendship Association, impressed the Nepalese by talking plain facts without indulging in philosophical and idealistic preachings. He made no reservation in expressing the fact that the traditional friendship between India and Nepal had "suffered somewhat recently" but at the sometime very confidently declared that the apprehension in the minds of the Nepalese would be set at right quickly and without difficulty and that he expected a revolutionary change in the existing situation as a result of exchange of good will visits and mutual understanding of problems.[61]

The Joint Communique issued at the end of Shastri's visit on 5 March 1963, noted the mutual satisfaction of the two countries "at the outcome of the talks which were marked by friendliness and sincerity" and expressed the hope that "in view of their basic unity and friendship ...... small differences could be discussed and settled by frank discussions.[62] It also emphasised that both India and Nepal were sovereign nations and India had no desire other than to have "the friendliest relations" with Nepal. The communique reiterated that Nepal and India are bound by unbreakable ties of geography, culture and traditions and have a vital interest in each others well being". It in addition, contained an assurance that the Government of India was anxious for the speedy implementation of the joint economic programme in Nepal.[63]

It was clear from the contents of the Communique that Shastri's visit was primarily aimed to remove the elements of bitterness and hostility between the two. Following the visit India and Nepal were able to make adjustment in a spirit of mutual give and take. Kathmandu was happy over tacitly accepting of King's rule by the Nehru government. Even during the visit, Tulsi Giri said on 4 March that he was satisfied that honest efforts were being made by both sides to lay "a new basis for permanent friendly relations" to remove once for all every source of misunderstanding between the two countries. Undoubtedly, Shastri succeeded in laying the foundation of a new friendlier chapter in Indo-Nepalese relations. On his return from Kathmandu Shastri told the Lok Sabha on 7th March 1963 :

Nepal is a small country with a small population and small resources. But during my brief stay in Kathmandu attempted to make it clear beyond any doubt that we in India are not given to thinking of ourselves far less acting—in the way of a big brother.[64]

Later on, in June 1963 King Mahendra expressed satisfaction that "today friendly India too has shown a proper understanding of our stainless objectives and a concordant change in the direction of friendship and cordiality towards us."[65]

In the background of successful tour of Shastri, a return visit was paid by King Mahendra and Queen Ratna, accompanied by Tulsi Giri to New Delhi 27-30 August 1963. He discussed with Nehru, president Radhakrishnan and other Indian leaders matters of mutual interest. King Mahendra, on his behalf assured the Indian government that Nepal was not being drawn towards China. In a joint communique issued on 30 August 1963, the King assured that Nepal's efforts to establish trade relations with other countries were in no way aimed at against India's interest. King Mahendra's visit to India produced an air of satisfaction in New Delhi. The impressions gained ground that friendship between the two countries had its root too deep in history and culture to be blown by passing winds and that temporary strains in relations, instead of leaving a bitter trail of memories, had rather helped both countries to appreciate each others difficulties a little better.

The royal visit was soon returned by the Indian President Radhakrishnan's four-day visit to Kathmandu in the first week of November same year. During the visit, the Indian President had informal discussions with King Mahendra and Tulsi Giri. A joint communique was issued at the end of the visit on 8 November 1963, said that "Nepal and India have a vital interest in each other's well-being, independence and integrity", and that personal contacts at different levels should be maintained with a view to strengthening the traditional bonds of friendship between them. In a farewell broadcast President Radhakrishnan praised the far reaching social reforms introduced by King Mahendra. He termed Nepal's National Panchayat as "an experiment in democracy".[69]

India in the post-Nehru era, under the Premiership of Lal Bahadur Shastri and Mrs. Indira Gandhi, continued the policy of exchanging visits. In response to King Mahendra's visit of June 1964, India's Minister for External Affairs Swarn Singh paid a visit to Nepal in August 1964. It was significant to note that this was Swarn Singh's first visit to a foreign country after assumption of office. Now, New Delhi began to patch up its policy towards Nepal and gave up its patronising behaviour and displayed a more restrained and less assertive attitude towards Nepal. Attempts were on to keep Kathmandu pleased and satisfied. On 25 August 1964 Swarn Singh told a news conference in Kathmandu :

We are of the view that the system of government is essentially the concern and responsibility of the country concerned and we as a Government have always looked with sympathy and understanding at the system of government that prevails here.[70]

The relations between the two countries were further strengthened through the visits of Shastri in 1965 and Mrs. Gandhi in October 1966. Referring directly to the Nepalese political system, she remarked : India is watching with interest the evolution of Panchayat system in Nepal.[71] Moreover, while she was in Kathmandu, announced that the Indian Aid Mission would be renamed "to convey the idea that will co-operate with Nepal."[72] Later, when Morarji Desai, the Deputy Prime Minister of India, during his visit to Nepal in 1967 was straightway asked to comment on Nepal's Panchayat system, he evaded the question by a general remark. Every country has the right to evolve its own system."[73] Previously in November 1965 King Mahendra was on tour to India when Indo-Pak war was passing through, expressed the view in the joint communique that principles of self-determination can apply only to a dependent and trust territories and can not be extended to integral parts of a sovereign state.[74]

On the invitation of the Government of India, Gehendra Bahadur Rajbhandari, the Nepalese Foreign Minister, visited New Delhi in May 1969. He had fruitful discussions with the Government of India. Expressing satisfaction over his talks in New Delhi, Rajbhandari disclosed that Nepal and India had agreed to set up Boundary Commission to conduct joint surveys for demarcating the entire boundary between the two countries so that no border dispute might arise in future.[75]

To continue the unfinished dialogue, Dinesh Singh, India's Minister for External Affairs, went on a four-day goodwill visit to Kathmandu on 5 June 1969. His visit was aimed to persuade HMG " to harmonise its trading policy with India. G. B. Rajbhandari, the Foreign Minister of Nepal at a banquet in honour of his visiting counterpart said that Nepal wanted trade rather than aid. He insisted on a "free flow of goods between two countries. In reply to the toast Dinesh Singh said, "We live south of the Himalayas and our destinies have been tied together. He reminded that the two countries have special relations which neither has with any other country. This special relationship could neither be undermined nor neutralised by other countries because this is good to the people of both India and Nepal". However, the main purpose of the tour was that if Nepal wanted to avail of the facilities offered under the Friendship and Trade Treaties, it must honour its obligations in terms of the Trade Treaty failing which New Delhi shall have no option but to make an overall review of the bilateral relations forfeited because Nepal posed a counter threat to checkmate India's move to end the open border facility. The Nepalese side look determined to take maximum advantages from India under the threat of removal of the Indian wireless operators posted on Tibet border and the IMLG based at Kathmandu.

During his stay in Kathmandu India's Foreign Minister described the Indo-Nepalese relations as "special" and the concept received sharp reaction among the Nepalese leaders. Reacting to the statement, K. N. Bista the Nepalese Prime Minister, who was known for his pro-China inclinations said later on in June 1969 at Kathmandu,".... to our way of thinking it is not possible that Nepal should compromise its sovereignty or accept, what may be called limited sovereignty for India's so called security". He also maintained that "the theory of special relations for Nepal outside geographical, social and economic realities is out of step with modern developments in our relations. He did not see any relation in the withdrawal of Indian personnel in the checkposts, the IMLG and the Treaty between Nepal and India as desired by the Indian side. Failure of talks on the bilateral issues led to take Nepal the actions which would please Peking. Denunciation of India, open disavowal of Nepal-India "special relations" and the staging of anti-India demonstrations were essential items on Bista's programme for pleasing Peking.

In the further talks held between the two countries New Delhi agreed to arrange a phased withdrawal of the IMLG and the Indian wireless operators on the one hand and left Kathmandu free to take its course on the other. As agreed earlier the withdrawals of the Indian personnel were finally completed on 18 August 1970. Nepal took it as its victory and started a new campaign against India in the country and tried to internationalise the issue. On several successive occasions it raised the issue to pressurise India with a view to have a new trade treaty in its favour.

V.V. Giri, the President of India went to Kathmandu on 28 February 1970 mainly to attend the marriage ceremony of Prince Birendra. However, King Mahendra took the opportunity to raise the issue in a thanks giving ceremony organised after the wedding while addressing the foreign guests. He remarked :

Nepal seeks nothing more than usual trade and transit facilities in accordance with the customary international practices in a spirit of good neighbourliness. We like to be frank and friendly with our friends and neighbours. We will appreciate if they are likewise frank and friendly with us.[79].

New Delhi was not prepared for the shock on the occasion when delegations from over fifty countries were assembled. President Giri perhaps in cold anger rose abruptly just after the King concluded his address, offered his "thanks" to the host and left the royal palace accompanied by the Indian Ambassador, Raj Bahadur. Apart from the regular and official visits of high dignitaries from both the sides, several delegations headed by relevant ministers visited time to time and discussed the matters in dispute.

## Politics

The efforts of Indian Prime Minister Lal Bahadur Shastri to reconcile Nepal during his visit to Kathmandu in March 1963 with Nehru's consent encouraged Nepalese to believe that India was now apologetic. Particularly after the Sino-India war of October 1962 India felt the need of rapproach with Nepal and assured the King that the anti-royal elements would not be allowed to continue their activities from the Indian soil and consequently the anti- regime agitation was suspended. This assurance on the part of Government of India came as a great relief for King Mahendra. In response, King Mahendra said that Nepal would not promote Chinese interests at India's cost. However, Nepal did not stop anti-Indianism in totality and keeping in view New Delhi's delicate position Kathmandu began to exploit the situation to its advantage.

The most famous threat on the part of Nepal was to turn to China which had a greater military strength in the region. Not only that China too adopted a liberal attitude towards Nepal even on those occasions when they were less than happy with some foreign policy decisions. By the time many of the Nepalese leaders appealed to Mahendra to seek Chinese "active support to deter India.[80] On the otherhand Nepal's vilification of India came as a windfall to China and Beijing decided to exploit it. Earlier on the eve of Sino-Indian war China had expressed its readyness to help Nepal in the event of foreign aggression and also declared that "the Nepalese people can count on the resolute support of the 650 million Chinese people".[81] At the time Chinese main objective of Peking's people support to King Mahendra was to encourage Nepal to nullify its Treaty of Peace and Friendship with India and take Nepal in its sphere of influence. China had taken the responsibility of the continuation of royal regime in Nepal maintain status quo and served a notice to New Delhi in this regard. But King Mahendra while praising the Chinese for its protection of royal regime, was not certain about China's long-term goals in Nepal. Kathmandu's instinct of survival with sovereignty prevented it to fall into the Chinese trap and to annul the Indo-Nepalese Treaty of July 1950. The two countries signed a Boundary Protocol on 21 January 1963 was hailed by *People's Daily* editorial as marking the final and complete settlement of the boundary question between Nepal and China.

When India made some fruitful efforts to improve its relations with Kathmandu both China and Pakistan felt uneasiness. They tried their best to keep Nepal away from India and have some friendly terms with the Himalayan Kingdom. King Mahendra perhaps in order to have a favourable deal from New Delhi accelerated the process of growing friendship with Pakistan. Apart from exchange of a trade delegation between the two countries, President Ayub Khan accompanied by his Foreign Minister Z. A. Bhutto, came on a four-day state visit to Nepal 9-13 May 1963. However the Nepalese were doubtful enough about Chinese motives, particularly after the Sino-Indian war of October 1962. For instance, Nepal exercised utmost caution in ratifying the 1964 Nuclear Disarmament Treaty because Peking was then engaged in exploding nuclear devices. Inspite of the fact that Kathmandu had already signed the treaty at Moscow, Washington and London it took months to ratify it at Kathmandu. It required the efforts of the two ambassadors Henry Stebbin (USA) and E. Zebrodin (USSR) to get the Treaty ratified as "King Mahendra's Government was opposed to blasting of nuclear devices anywhere in the world." But the Nepalese who were well acquinted with the Chinese military strength never wanted to displease Peking in chain. Nepal collaborated with China at the Algiers preparatory meeting for the Afro-Asian Summit Conference. It was represented by K. N. Bista, Nepalese Deputy Prime Minister and Foreign Minister who opposed India's proposal for USSR's admission in the proposed conference. Bilaterally too, Peking and Kathmandu came closer and several treaties and agreements of mutual interest were signed between the two countries.

A temporary setback to Sino-Indian relations appeared after the inauguration of Kathmandu-Kodari Highway in May 1967. Chinese attitude towards Nepal changed and Peking began to view Kathmandu as its satellite. China, during the days of cultural revolution tried to propagate Maoism that led to misunderstanding and slogans were raised against India, USA and USSR by the pro-China elements. The above three powers registered their strong protest to Kathmandu and made it alert of the Chinese designs. By the time Nepal sought to improve its relations with India being motivated by the desire to draw away from China's intimate embrace before it was too late. However, Peking took the incident seriously which happened in Nepal in July 1967, warned Kathmandu and a protest note presented, declared :

Since the beginning of the Great Proletarian Cultural Revolution the reactionary forces in Nepal have become frantic and unbrilled in their anti-China activities. The Nepalese press have also carried large number of anti-China articles viciously attacking China's great cultural revolution and brazenly insutling chairman Mao ..... what is particularly intolerant is that the Nepalese government openly encouraged the hooligans to insult our great leader Mao .... thereby committing grave anti-China outrage .... the Chinese people solemnly pointout once again the great Socialist China is not to be bullied .... and whoever trails behind revisionism, imperialism and reaction will surely eat the bitter fruit of their own making .....[82]

King Mahendra and his royal regime was not in a position to challenge the abusive denunciations because China had given verbal guarantee to protect his royal regime. The Nepal-China alliance was fruitful as an effective counter-weight to India. In order to enjoy this privilege HMG was willing to swallow Chinese arrogance. In the successive years Nepal showed its accommodative gestures to China, although there were occasions when Kathmandu felt distressed with Chinese behaviour.[83] The Chinese were perhaps determined to prevent Nepal not only to rejoin their enemies, but also bind the royal regime more tightly to their chariot.'

In an apparent attempt to soothe Chinese anger. King Mahendra dispatched his pro-China Deputy Prime Minister Kirtinidhi Bista to Beijing. Soon after Bista arrived Chin Yi reminded him of China's "greatness" and asked him to be careful of attempts by imperialism, revisionism and reaction to slander and vilify China.[84] Bista too, forgetting the recent insult praised Chinese leaders for their "correct and friendly attitude" towards his country. During the visit Bista had an opportunity to "renew" his personal contacts with the Chinese leaders and met the great leader of China Mao Zedong, where he reiterated Nepal's sincere gratitude" for China's help and promised" not to abandon China's friendship for India."[85]

Inspite of the Nepalese expectations, China failed to provide Kathmandu the basic needs when a deadlock with India arose on the treaty of trade and transit at the close of the sixties decade. The tactic of rousing popular feeling against India did not prove to much of its use and people began to blame HMG for the failure of the talks with India. Being compelled the Government of Nepal signed with India a less favourable treaty on 13 August 1971. Another incident of immense significance was India-Pakistan war of 1971 which resulted in the creation of Bangladesh as a new sovereign state on the one hand and emergence of India as a regional power on the other. At the moment China did not help Pakistan beyond verbal assurance and blaming India for imposing a war. Appropriate adjustments in the operating principles of Nepal's foreign policy seemed essential and were in the process while King Mahendra died in January 1972.

In the first part of the sixties USA increased its influence in Nepal at India's cost. It enhanced the volume of aid and took active interest to consolidate the newly established order and for that purpose adopted all kinds of measures. At the moment Nepal wanted to lessen its sole dependence in defence matters on India and China. The USA was suspicious over the growing Chinese influence in the region and in the circumstances in February 1964 USA agreed for the first time to a Nepalese request for military assistance to be given directly. The Great powers together with India, concerned with the power imbalance in the Himalayas and decided to outbid the Chinese for influence in Nepal by increasing the cost of competition for the latter. However, inspite of the huge aid funds donated by Washington Nepalese policy of non-alignment could not be pressurised and it took an independent view of the American role in the Vietnam conflict. In 1966 the Rashtriya Panchayat adopted a resolution condemning the "inhuman bombing" by US forces in Vietnam. Apart from this left-oriented students staged heavy demonstrations in front of the American library and they delivered a memorandum to the US embassy which stated that the US actions in Vietnam were opposed to humanity and demanded an immediate withdrawal of US forces from that country.[87]

1967 was a less happier year for Sino-Nepalese relations. During the phase of Cultural Revolution pro-China elements in Nepal became active and raised slogans against India, USA and USSR. Kathmandu while facing difficulties with China cultivated the global dimensions of its foreign policy and contacts with the superpowers were maintained at the highest level. In the wake of these developments, there were two situations. One was growing criticism of US bombing in North Vietnam coinciding with its troubles from China and the other King Mahendra, on the invitation of President Johnson, was paying his second official visit to the United States in November 1967.

King Mahendra and Queen Ratna accompanied by Kirtinidhi Bista, Deputy Prime Minister and Foreign Minister of Nepal visited United States of America in November 1967. In Washington during the exchange of views the King hoped to build a new Nepal and the Americans shared his vision and hope, and considered that it was hard for a nation to be torn from the cacoon of its past to be catapulted forward almost overnight, into the twentieth century. The visit offered King Mahendra and President Johnson an opportunity to become acquinted with each other and to discuss matters of mutual interest and concern. The personal rapport and mutual esteem, esteeming from the talks bore frankness and friendship which characterised the relations between the United States and Nepal. On the conclusion of the visit a joint communique was issued on 1 November 1967, noted that the King had explained to the president the efforts made in Nepal to secure better standard of living for the people under the Panchayat system and the measure of success achieved in that direction. The President was impressed with the progress made in Nepal under His Majesty's leadership and praised Nepal's emphasis on increasing agricultural production and the increased self help measures taken by Nepal. President assured the King of the continuing deep interest of the United States government and people in supporting Nepal's efforts to reach its goal. Their friendly exchange of views reflected mutual respect and equality. It reinforced the already strong bonds of friendship which had characterised Nepalese-American relations since their inception in 1947 and made more meaningful their common quest for peace, justice and progress. In the same month Army General of the United States of America, T.Z. Conway, visited Nepal where he inspected the Kathmandu-Kodari highway and the Mustang region.

Aimed at explaining the Nixon Doctrine of the President, the US. Vice President Spiro T. Agnew paid an eighteen hour visit to Nepal on 5-6 January 1970. The visit served to enhance the prestige of King Mahendra at home. As disclosed by Agnew he found in King Mahendra an encouraging response to the Nixon Doctrine. He also expressed appreciation of the royal efforts "to broaden the political base in the establishment of greater powers of local government". He suggested Nepal to play a mediator's role. It was difficult to say whether Nepal was willing to involve itself in the role envisaged by US but it was surely a new evaluation of Nepal's diplomatic potential. In early 1971 the long-strained relationship between China and the United States began to normalise and they had started their secrect talks through various channels. In that context a Nepali weekly reported that the diplomatic officials of the United States were not holding their talks in Warsaw only but also in Kathmandu.[89] Bista expressed his wholehearted welcome at the time when the White House announced the proposed visit of US President Nixon to China. Following the Sino-American rapprochement and the growing Indo- Soviet collaboration since the conclusion of the Treaty of Peace and Friendship between them in August 1971, Nepal's significance for superpowers has further declined. Soon after the emergence of Bangladesh as an independent sovereign power it became clear that while Nepal wishes to maintain its close and fruitful relations with India, it was not likely to close or even weaken its other policy options.

The widening of rift between China and the Soviet Union provided Nepal a golden opportunity to have further good relations with Moscow. Soviet support for the royal regime and Nepalese identity of views with Moscow on Peaceful Co-existence and Partial Nuclear Test Ban Treaty made the two to understand each other better. Kathmandu, even despite Chinese ill will towards Moscow praised Soviet Union for its policy towards Nepal. In an interview with *Pravda*, Giri extended his "warm" support to the Soviet policy of peaceful co-existence and paid tribute to Khrushchev for resolving the Cuban crisis. Although Nepal's endorsement of Soviet policies was not liked by China, particularly on partial test ban treaty when Zhou En-Lai in a letter to Tulsi Giri asked not to support the test ban treaty. But in his reply Giri explained that Nepal considered the treaty as a "step in the right direction." On 26 August 1963 Nepal signed the controversial treaty to demonstrate that "we do not toe anybody's line."[93] The Soviet Union welcomed the adherence of Nepal to the nuclear test ban treaty and regarded it as

Kathmandu's demonstration of its "independent foreign policy." Tulsi Giri, during his visit to Moscow in October 1963 thanked Moscow for its economic assistance. He also revealed that Nepal was getting more aid from the Soviet Union than China.[95] Praising the Soviet Union's policy towards Nepal King Mahendra said that he had found in Moscow a "dear friend" always ready to co-operate" in the interests of progress and happiness of humanity.[96] However, Moscow, despite the cordial and friendly relations with Kathmandu was alert in relation to the Kathmandu-Kodari road which was assisted by the Chinese and had immense strategic significance.

The cementing of Kathmandu-Soviet relations were against the Chinese interests in Nepal and Peking launched a campaign to discredit Soviet economic aid to Nepal with an attempt to boost its own image among the Nepalese people. Responding to the Chinese gesture the royal regime in early 1964 took several steps to improve its relations with China. On the other hand Nepal-Soviet relations witnessed some strain when in 1968, the Soviet Union had militarily intervened in Czechoslovakia and Kathmandu had condemned the action.

Brezhnev's declaration at an international Conference of Communist and Workers' Parties, held in June 1969 that the Soviet Union intended to create a new collective security system in Asia was not welcomed in Nepal. Kathmandu was of the opinion that an alliance of Asian countries would serve no purpose because an alliance with one group would cause an immediate reaction in the other group. Chinese reaction to the new Soviet system was acute and they claimed that Moscow's drive for Asian collective security was directed against China. In June 1971 Mahendra visited Soviet Union and conducted negotiations in an atmosphere of friendship and mutual understanding. In the joint communique issued at the end of the visit both sides noted with satisfaction the successful development of bilateral friendly relations. Both confirmed their desire to strengthen further the existing relations and, in particular agreed to expand economic co-operation on a mutually advantageous basis to promote and consolidate Nepal's national economy.

**Analysis of the Attitude**

India after the war of October 1962 changed its attitude towards Nepal. A new era in Indo-Nepal relations started with the visit of Lal Bahadur Shastri, India's Home Minister, to Kathmandu which to a large extent succeeded in removing the misunderstandings between the two. In the changed circumstances China was a military power and its influences in Nepal expanded considerably. New Delhi was worried over the Kathmandu's growing relations with Peking and it assured Nepal that India would not allow the Nepali Congress workers to continue their anti-Royal activities from the Indian soil. In return King Mahendra assured Nehru that he would not allow the Chinese influence to grow at India's cost. In pursuance of the assurance King Mahendra cancelled the agreement with China where the latter had undertaken to construct a portion of Nepal's East-West highway and handed it over to India.

When some signs of improvement in Indo-Nepalese relations became obvious both Peking and Pindi became liberal to the Kingdom in order to keep Kathmandu away from Indian influence. Although India tried its level best in the first half of the sixties to have a friendly terms with Kathmandu. But when later on the signs of improvement in Nepal's relations with China were visible it (New Delhi) no longer felt the urgency of appeasing Nepal. In the meantime, Nepal expanded its contacts with two superpowers because, it viewed both China as well as India with suspicions. It took maximum benefits from the widening gap of Sino-US relations on the one hand and rivalry between the two superpowers on the other. At the close of the sixties the economic relations between India and Nepal strained and New Delhi was not in a mood to sign any new agreement on Kathmandu's term. The Himalayan Kingdom on its part, made it an international issue and tried to mobilise the world opinion in its favour. But all went in vain and it signed a less favourable treaty with India.

At the close of the sixties the differences between China and United States were narrowed down and signs of improvement were in sight. On the other hand, Soviet interest in Nepal also declined due to its increasing relations with India and Moscow never wanted to improve its relations with Kathmandu at New Delhi's stake. 1971 was an important year for the region as it changed the balance of power in India's favour. The emergence of Bangladesh and India's role in its liberation, opened the Nepalese eyes and a shift in policy preferences were imminent. Nepal was stunned at China's inaction in Indo-Pak war of 1971 and learnt a lesson that China could be of no more use to him than it was to Pakistan. New geo-politico realities were to take its visible shape when King Mahendra died in January 1972.

## Notes and References

1. S.K. Jha, *Uneasy partners : India and Nepal in Post-Colonial Era* (Manas Publications, New Delhi, 1975), p. 212.
2. *Daily Nepal*, 11 January 1964.
3. *The Statesman*, 16 January 1963.
4. Shashi Bhushan Prasad, *The China Factor in Indo-Nepalese Relations 1955-72* (Janaki Prakashan, Patna, 1988), p. 121.
5. *Asian Recorder*, Vol. 9, 12-18 February 1963, p. 5045.
6. Ibid., 19-25 February 1963, p. 5050.
7. Tribhuvan Nath, *The Nepalese Dilemma 1960-74* (Sterling Publishers, New Delhi, 1975), p. 377.
8. S.K. Jha, "Policy Towards India : Quest for Independence", S.D. Muni (ed), Nepal. *An Assertive Monarchy* (Chetana Publications, New Delhi, 1977), p. 213.
9. *The Statesman*, 6 November 1963.
10. Progress of Nepal-India Co-operation programme, p.12.
11. Address to Nepal-India Friendship Association, Kathmandu.
12. A. S. Bhasin, *Documents on India's Relations with Nepal and China 1949-66* (Academic Book, Bombay, 1970), pp. 107-8.
13. Murlidhar Dharamdasani, *Indian Diplomacy in Nepal* (Aalekh Publishers, Jaipur, 1976), p. 83.
14. *Samaj*, 21 September 1965.
15. *The Hindustan Times*, 21 December 1965.
16. Hemen Roy, *China's Strategy in Nepal* (Radiant Publishers, New Delhi, 1983), p. 66.

17. *Ibid.*
18. *The Patriot*, 3 May 1967.
19. *The Times of India*, 14 July 1967.
20. *The Motherland*, 26 June 1967 and *The Samachar*, 9 July 1967.
21. *Nepal Times*, 8 July 1967.
22. *The Statesman*, 13 July 1967.
23. *Nepal Times*, 9 June 1969,
24. *Rising Nepal*, 25 June 1969.
25. *Gorkhapatra*, 26 June 1969.
26. *Renmin Ribao*, 29 June 1969.
27. *Dawn*, 29 June 1969.
28. Hemen Roy, *op.cit.,* p. 97.
29. Shashi Bhushan Prasad, *op.cit.,* p. 153
30. *The Statesman*, 20 February 1972.
31. Tribhuvan Nath, *op. cit.,* p. 376.
32. *Asian Recorder*, Vol. 9, 1963, p. 5357.
33. Tribhuvan Nath, *op.cit.,* p. 379.
34. Dillip Mukherjee, "Signs of the Times", *Far Eastern Economic Review* (July-September 1969), pp. 126-28.
35. *Sunday Standard*, 2 April 1965.
36. *The Hindustan Times*, 20 December 1966.
37. A.S. Bhasin, *op. cit.,* p.107.
38. Leo. E. Rose, "King Mahendra's China Policy", S.D. Muni (ed), *op.cit.,* p.234.
39. *Ibid.*
40. *Indian Express*, 3 November 1966.
41. *Arab Observer*, 21 February 1965.
42. *Amrita Bazar Patrika*, 22 November 1966.
43. India, *Rajya Sabha Debates*, Pt. 1. Vol. 58, No.11, 22 November 1966. Col. 2304.
44. *Gorkhapatra*, 16 October 1961.
45. *Nepal Bhasa*, 26 May 1967.
46. Tribhuvan Nath, *op.cit.,* p.349.

47. S. D. Muni, "The Dynamics of Foreign Policy" *op.cit.*, p.133.
48. *Ibid.*, p.137.
49. *Asian Recorder*, Vol. 13 (1967), p.7864.
50. *Gorkhapatra*, 6 June 1969.
51. *Rising Nepal*, 25 June 1969.
52. *The Statesman*, 2 July 1969.
53. *The Times of India*, 26 and 27 July 1969.
54. India, *Lok Sabha Debates*, series 4, Vol. 30, No.1, 21 July, 1969, Cols 230-44 and Rajya Sabha Debates, Pt.1, Vol. 69, No.1, 21 July 1969 Cols 117-32.
55. *Ibid.*
56. *Rising Nepal*, 10 June 1969.
57. *The Times of India*, 2 January 1970.
58. *Gorkhapatra*, 17 August 1970.
59. *The Times of India* 21 October 1970.
60. *Samaj*, 26 February 1963.
61. *The Hindustan Times*, 5 March 1963.
62. *Foreign Policy of India* : *Text of Documents* : 1947-1964 (New Delhi, 1966), pp. 347-48.
63. *Ibid.*
64. *The Hindu*, 9 March 1963.
65. Tribhuvan Nath, *op.cit.*, p.377.
66. *Foreign Policy of India : Text of Documents 1947-64* (Lok Sabha Secretariat, New Delhi, 1966), p. 350.
67. *Eastern Economist, 6 September* 1963, p. 446.
68. *The Times of India*, 30 August 1963.
69. *The Statesman*, 6 November 1963.
70. *The Hindustan Times*, 26 August 1964.
71. *The Times of India*, 6 October 1966.
72. *Ibid.*, 8 October 1967.
73. *Ibid.*, 25 October 1967.
74. A. S. Bhasin *op.cit.*, pp. 107-8.
75. *Gorkhapatra*, 8 May 1969.

76. Tribhuvan Nath, *op.cit.,* p. 386.
77. *Ibid.*
78. *Gorkhapatra*, 17 August 1970.
79. *Rising Nepal*, 3 March 1970.
80. *The Indian Express*, 8 October 1962.
81. *Xinhua*, 23 November 1962.
82. *Ibid.,* 21 July 1967.
83. Tribhuvan Nath *op.cit.,* p.355.
84. *Xinhua*, 25 May 1968.
85. *Ibid.*
86. Vinod Kumar, "Great Powers and Nepal", S.D. Muni (ed.) *op.cit.,* p.156.
87. *Samaya*, 12 July 1966.
88. *Department of State Bulletin*, Vol. 57 (1967) p. 109.
89. *Samiksha*, 8 January 1970.
90. *Ibid.,* 9 March 1971.
91. *Pravda*, 28 April 1963.
92. *The Indian Express*, 23 August 1963.
93. *The Statesman*, 28 August 1963.
94. *Pravda*, 27 August 1963.
95. *Ibid.,* 24 and 25 October 1963.
96. *Ibid.,* 18 February 1963.

# 8

# READJUSTMENTS OF POLICY (1972—1976)

## Diplomacy

The Indo-Pak war of December 1971 and re-emergence of India as a potential regional power had affected the course of New Delhi-Kathmandu relations in ways more than one. The end of the war in India's favour, China's failure to come to the rescue of Pakistan in late 1971 exposed the limited economic, diplomatic and military capability of Peking, south of the Himalayas. The rise of Bangladesh as an independent state in the face of China's determined—if only vocal—opposition is indicative of China's inability to directly challenge the major influence of India backed by the Soviet Union.[1] At the moment India seemed to enjoy Russian's support as a counter to China's influence in South Asia, while the United States was making assiduous efforts to normalise relations with China and maintaining a low key profile for India in South Asia. As Scalapino had clarified, "Gone is the time when India-Pakistan seemed sufficiently matched in power to warrant external effort at sustaining the peace via military equilibrium between these two states. In any case India is the dominant power of the subcontinent today and for the foreseeable future".[2] In the post-war phase with the weakening of Pakistan, Nepal's foreign policy options became a little circumscribed. Even though it no longer deferred the recognition of Bangladesh. Nepal declared that it did not mean that its relations were less friendly with Pakistan. It was proclaiming its friendship with Islamabad in a laboured attempt to assert the independence of its foreign policy from the Indian hegemony. In this context it became apparent to Nepal that it may not be in position to play the peripheral powers against India in its efforts to fulfil its own national interest. The very change in the sub-continental power equation compelled Nepal not to play its well-tried policy of blow hot and blow cold in the context of India.

The "change of guard" in Nepal and Birendra's accession to the throne came as a welcome relief to political lobbyists suffocating under the weight of his father's authoritarianism. With the change of leadership it was hoped in diplomatic circles that Prince Birendra considered a liberal democrat, would bring substantial change in the political system, policy projections and foreign relations. However, in the case of Indo-Nepalese bilateral relations, the new King preferred to follow the policies of his father with a slight shift perhaps, keeping in view the changing sub-continental environs. The Nepalese policy planners well conceived the fact that Kathmandu was not in a position to face a hostile Delhi. Therefore, the political exigencies demanded that Kathmandu must rapport with New Delhi and at the very outset of the decade the Nepalese Prime Minister, Kirtinidhi Bista visited India in April 1972 for mending the damaged fences of relationship and talking about reactivisation of the letters of exchange, Treaty of Friendship of 1950, with the comment that there exists an "identity of approach" between the two countries. But on the other, he was not hesitant in raising an accusing finger at India on the functional incompatibility of Indian aided projects in Nepal by commenting that Nepalese were quite concerned about projects like the Kosi and Gandak and that Nepal has been cheated. Thus, King Birendra initiated a policy of continuity than change in relations with India.

In line with the top level visits of the heads of government to improve further relations a return visit was paid by Mrs. Indira Gandhi, Indian Prime Minister to Kathmandu in February 1973. During her stay in Kathmandu she assured the Nepalese leaders that India was not extending any assistance to rebel activity against the Nepalese Government.[6] Her visit was followed by King Birendra's visit to India in October 1973. Despite the goodwill created by these visits Kathmandu has not abstained from airing out its resentment against India nor has it restrained itself from taking decisions affecting India's interest. Some irritants in their relationship were built in and some came in the wake of the development of time. Domestically, the stagnant national economy was creating legitimate grievances for the burgeoning middle class. In this backdrop if the external global and regional environments were compelling the King to be more close to India, to pacify the domestic unrest he started to blame India for Nepalese failures. The Nepalese authorities continued to believe in their rights as a landlocked state and that Nepal had peculiar dissatisfaction over the provisions of the supply of development goods. Kathmandu demanded faster flow of goods, fulfilment of the stipulated targets, simplification of formalities and an agreed diversion of even those goods which were, in short supply, in India.[7]

Despite the expression of goodwill by both sides on various occasions the anti-India activities of Nepal and its insistence on more concessions from New Delhi made Indian attitude firm. The new Indian posture created fears in the royal coterie. Birendra intensified his efforts to gain India's acceptance of his neutral foreign policy of equal friendship with India and China. In May 1973 he told a Norwegain reporter that Nepal wanted "equal friendship with India and China and denied that he sided with one neighbour against the other at different times.[8] Even earlier by the summer of 1972 Nepal and China were convinced that India had no intention to give armed support to the Nepali opposition to restore democracy, King Birendra described Nepal's relations with China as "cordial and traditional" characterized by warmth of friendship and mutual trust".[9] King Birendra also sent K. N. Bista to Beijing to assure the Chinese leaders that Nepal would continue its policy of friendship towards China. After returning home Bista declared his visit as "satisfactory, beneficial, and pleasant". However, the Nepalese fear was strengthened further in the integration of Sikkim into the Indian Union. The developments in Sikkim provided both Peking and Kathmandu an opportunity to inaugurate a new campaign of velification against India. Following the Chinese lead Nepal protested against granting of the status of an Associate State to Sikkim. G. P. Karki, the Nepalese Foreign Minister, denounced India and declared that, "it is our irrevocable policy that there should be no outside interference in the internal affairs of any nation. Sikkim's interest lies in unity and mutual co-operation of her people.[11] The Nepalese press charged India with imperialist designs.[12] While the royal government organized anti-India demonstration.[13]

Above all, the Nepalese perceived the change in Sikkim as a threat to the Nepalese monarchy. It heightened the Nepalese fears that Koirala's followers, though debarred from functioning from the Indian border, may now start operating from the Nepal-Sikkim border. The Nepalese were also contacted on behalf of the Chogyal against whose domination a revolt was made in Sikkim, to raise the Sikkim issue at the UN. Even an unofficial Sikkimese delegation paid a visit to Nepal and established liaison with the locally based foreign embassies.[14]

Nepalese view on the Sikkim issue clouded Indo-Nepal relations and New Delhi adopted a firm and assertive attitude towards Kathmandu. India questioned the legitimacy of the Nepalese government to express its "concern" for India-Sikkim relations and warned that "we will reply to friendship with greater friendship, but we also know to deal with hostility.[15] Nepal responded quickly to the Indian threat and declared that "We should" not allow Sikkim affair to cloud the totality of Indo-Nepalese relations .... The totality of Indo-Nepalese relations is much too important to be restricted to the issue relating to Sikkim.[16] Soon thereafter Nepal sent his Prime Minister Nagendra Prasad Rajal to New Delhi for "free and frank" discussions and to remove "misunderstandings". His visit succeeded in removing mutual suspicion and misgivings between the two countries. Nepalese press now stopped its anti-India comments. There were also no further demonstrations against India. But Peking endeavoured to maintain Nepal's anti-India posture over Sikkim and declared that Nepal was the "next target" of India's "expansionism" and cited the presence of opposition leaders of Nepal in India.

On 9 May 1974 India successfully conducted a nuclear explosion at Pokhran in Rajasthan. It was neither officially welcomed nor denounced by Nepal. A Government spokesman said that there was no reason why we should not believe Mrs. Gandhi's statement that India was firmly committed to the peaceful uses of nuclear energy. However, it maintained that as a signatory of the Partial Test Ban Treaty (1963) and the Nuclear Non-proliferation Treaty (1968), Nepal was opposed to any testing and development of nuclear devices. It added further that it wanted "a complete international ban on the testing and development of nuclear weapons in the interests of world peace". But its relations differed with another neighbour who had been demanding a nuclear free zone on the subcontinent.

Still, Kathmandu was restless to have an international guarantee, more or less on the Swiss model, of Nepal's independence, sovereignty and neutrality in the event of war in the region. The origin of the idea of declaring Nepal a Zone of Peace may be traced back to King Birendra's statement at the Non-aligned Summit in Algeria in 1973[18] in which he said, "Nepal, situated between two of the most populous countries in the world, which within her frontiers, to be enveloped in a Zone of peace.[19] Although it was not pronounced on that occasion for one reason or the other the authorities seemed deliberately intended to retain at least for domestic compulsion, the reference to the Zone of peace proposal in the official newspapers.[20] But it was actually mooted on 25 February 1975 at the coronation ceremony of King Birendra.[21] In his historic address, which was attended by many foreign dignitaries the King expressed his wish that all friendly powers and the neighbouring states in particular, would recognize Nepal as a Zone of peace :

> And if today peace is an overriding concern with us, it is only because our people genuinely desire peace in our country, in our region and everywhere in the world. It is with this earnest desire to institutionalize peace that I stand to make this proposition—a proposition that my country, Nepal, be declared a Zone of peace.[22]

Perhaps the Indian rebuff and a straight forward mood in pursuing a realistic policy with New Delhi compelled Kathmandu to think in terms of finding some way out so as to keep itself inaccessible from any prospective Indian interference. As a result of this thinking, King Birendra revived his father's concept of equidistance in the form of a 'Zone of peace' which has become one of the main planks of Nepalese foreign policy.

Meanwhile, King Birendra intensified his effort to gain India's acceptance of his policy of equal friendship with India and China. He pleaded that the idea of zone of peace would remove his country as an area of contention between India and China. Although he disavowed any intention of using Beijing to counter New Delhi—the main feature of his father's foreign policy[23] but in the same month the King made his 'zone of peace' proposal public and the two countries signed a new economic agreement providing China to build the 407-kilometre Pokhara-Surkhat road in western Nepal. The signing occasion was also used as initiation of a new campaign of insinuation against India as Tao Chih, head of the Chinese economic delegation, hoped that China's economic assistance would "help bolster Nepal's strength to retain its national sovereignty, territorial integrity and economic independence against foreign interference."[24]

Despite King Birendra's desire and welcome of the proposal of declaring Nepal a Zone of peace by many countries of the world including China, Pakistan, USA and others, India did not support the idea because it ignored the geopolitical realities. In its view Indo-Nepal relations could not be equated with those of Nepal-China relations. India's presence in the Himalayan Kingdom does not threaten China's interest, while China's presence in Nepal is detrimental to India. On the other, the leadership, policy planners and intellectuals of Nepal are of the opinion that the concept of 'Zone of peace' is significant for Nepal as it may not only provide perpetual peace to the country but create an environment of peace in the region and further on the globe. They felt that once Nepal is declared a 'Zone of Peace' it may attain political stability which would put its economy on a sound footing by increasing revenue surplus, providing stability in construction work, improving the supply of construction material; making the economy capable of absorbing more resources and mobilising manpower for development. For them the concept is an anti-thesis of global lawlessness.[25]

Apparently, Kathmandu did not seem to be satisfied with its own logic. Even in an attempt to bring pressure on India Nepal sought and readily obtained verbal endorsement by some major powers in the world. But unless the proposal is accepted by India it would have no significance in practical terms.

Because of the geopolitical and economic reality which faces Nepal, India's acceptance of the proposal is crucial to the attainment of whatever aims Nepal may have in putting it forward.

On 26 June 1975, Mrs. Indira Gandhi declared emergency rule in India. Palace circles in Kathmandu expressed satisfaction at the similarity between Mrs. Gandhi's arguments in support of her resort to Emergency powers and late King Mahendra's justification of his abolition of Nepal's Parliamentary System. In the circumstances Tulsi Giri, the new Prime Minister of Nepal, visited New Delhi first in December 1975 and then in April 1976. Giri seemed to have tried his best to gain the confidence of the Indian government by expressing its full faith in its verbal assurance that it would not help the efforts of B. P. Koirala and other Nepali leaders in exile to restore democracy in Nepal.[26] During the visit the Nepalese Prime Minister while referring to his country's policy of "equal friendship" with India and China, admitted that there was a "definite tilt" towards India in "Nepal's bilateral relations".[27] There were definitely some "special factors" Indo-Nepal relations and cited Kathmandu's 90 per cent in trade with India and the recruitment of Gurkhas in the Indian Army. The Indian response to the visit was also encouraging.

Whenever, a distant possibility of rapprochement between India and Nepal was in sight the Chinese became active to keep the two countries apart. India was emphasising its special relationship with the Himalayan Kingdom, the Chinese continued to encourage Nepal to internationalize Birendra's proposal of a "Zone of peace" in order to pressurize India. In May 1976 Hua Kuo-feng speaking at a banquet in honour of Bhutto declared: "We firmly support the firm stand of His Majesty of Nepal in declaring Nepal a Zone of peace. We are ready to assume appropriate commitment arising therefrom.[28] In course of his visit to Beijing in June 1976 King Birendra expressed Nepalese gratitude to the Chinese leaders for their "prompt support" to his proposal of "Zone of Peace.[29] Kathmandu also planned to seek Soviet support for the proposal and exert pressure on India. The King went to the Soviet Union in November 1976, but failed to convince the Soviet leaders of its utility. Actually the Soviets saw no need to support his plan against India and advised him to abandon it and work for strengthening relations with New Delhi. Birendra reacted sharply to the Soviet view and soon after returning home perhaps, in retaliation, imposed several restrictions on Indian nationals and in response New Delhi banned free movement of Nepali citizens across the border in some designated areas. However, the defeat of Mrs. Gandhi and victory of the Janata Party in the general elections of 1977 viewed in Kathmandu as the end of India's firm attitude and the beginning of an era of more concessions.

**Strategy for Security**

King Mahendra died in January 1972 when readjustments in Nepal's foreign relations were under active consideration in accordance with the new strategic environment, emerged after the Indo-Pak war of 1971. King Birendra who ascended the throne of Nepal carried forward his father's task of following the policy of distancing Kathmandu from New Delhi with added vigour, enthusiasm and determination. He refused to abide by the basic doctrine governing the 1950 treaty and reinterpreted the Nepalese security in such a manner as to disentangle Nepal from its mutual obligation vis-a-vis India, Birendra pursued the concept of balanced neutrality between the two giant neighbours as enunciated by the late King Prithivi Narayan Shah in 1769 and attempted to introduce uncertainty in the prevailing strategic proximity between Nepal and India on the one hand and China on the other. In the circumstances he even went to the extent of redefining Nepal's geo-strategic location. Rejecting the idea of a "buffer state" as being "outmoded" he said that "Nepal is not a part of Asia which touches both China and India. Our historical experience is that we maintain friendly relations with both these countries."[30] However the changed circumstances in the regional balance of power in which India had an upper- hand, compelled Kathmandu to change its earlier line of policy towards New Delhi. A perceptible change in Nepalese attitude was apparent and just on the eve of his visit to India Kirtinidhi Bista, the Prime Minister of Nepal, at a press interview on 16 April 1972 ruled out the necessity of signing a friendship treaty of the kind Bangladesh and the Soviet Union had concluded with India. Instead he emphatically declared; "Our relations with India are so extensive and intimate that I do not see any need of any measure in addition to what we already have". Explaining Nepal's relations with India and China he observed that Nepal has always maintained good relations with both India and China. But taking into account the geographical realities it had always to be "more oriented towards India" in trade and other matters.[31] Soon thereafter during the visit he even agreed to reactivate the 1950 treaty in his talks with the Indian leaders in New Delhi.[32]

Despite India's good gesture of goodwill for Nepal as displayed during Mrs. Gandhi's visit to Nepal and successful talks with high power economic delegation, headed by D. P. Dhar in April-May 1973, the Nepalese government remained meticulously cautious on regular basis. In pursuance of his father's style of diplomacy he did not show any neglect of its northern neighbour and King Birendra sent his Prime Minister and later went himself to the People's Republic of China soon after visiting India.[33] Kathmandu had not abstained from airing out its resentment against India nor has it restrained itself from taking decisions that affected India adversely. On a number of occasions Kathmandu had raised the difficulties of a land locked country from international forums. Such a line of diplomacy very nearer to the desire of maintaining equal friendship with both India and China, perhaps with a tilt depending on the need of the hour had been followed by late Mahendra and was being kept intact by King Birendra.

The new monarch, King Birendra was not satisfied with the poor state of Nepalese security, sandwiched between the two giant neighbours India and China. He was effortful and sincerely desired to keep Nepal away from the periodical ups and downs in the relations between these two and against the possibility of the ultimate breakdown of those relations, and therefore, internationalised Kathmandu's security concerns. On the day of his coronation in his historic address, he expressed his wish that all friendly countries and the neighbouring countries in particular would recognize Nepal as a Zone of peace. Whatever may be compulsions—domestic or external, the idea received a universal coverage and promptly supported by the major regional as well as global powers, although they had their own interest in doing so.

Amid the views, the proposal was made public, its endorsement by India was crucial to the attainment of whatever aims Nepal may have in putting it forward. In Indian opinion the King had tried to undermine the significance of 1950 treaty while securing international commitment in favour of the prevailing order. The proposal of a "Zone of peace" had ignored the geopolitical realities and its relations with Nepal could not be equated with that of China. Once the proposal is accepted by India its significant presence in Nepal would diminish automatically and the decks would be cleared for China. This fact was clear from the explanation submitted by the Nepalese authorities to India that reads that Nepal will continue to honour the obligations of all existing Treaties which it has concluded with other countries so long as they remain valid. The sentence "...... so long as they remain valid" seemed to be written in the Indian context. The moment India accepts the 'Zone of Peace proposal what would be the guarantee that Nepal would not play down the Peace and Friendship Treaty of 1950 the main irritant of Nepal since long and put the Indian security in jeopardy. This could prove a suicidal act on India's part and taking into account the free access of China in Nepal and India's 1800 kms. long open northern frontier, spread along the state borders of Bihar, Uttar Pradesh, Bengal and Sikkim.[36]

There were other questions to be answered. Even on the part of Kathmandu as to what actually they want? Whether a complete neutralization[37] or a non-aligned posture. Whether the issue is limited to its neighbour or the world at large? If it is limited to the neighbour, there is no guarantee that the global powers would not use Nepal as their base in the coming years. If a world consent is required it should be brought before the world organization. And if only the genuine non-aligned idea is there behind the proposal, who could prevent Nepal from adhering to the same? Because in the past Nepal had not hesitated in raising up these postures at the international forums.[38]

King Birendra's proposal for declaring Nepal a 'Zone of Peace' dominated the Indo-Nepal relations for over a decade.

Kathmandu's persistent plea for acceptance of its proposal was discussed with the Indian leaders when Tulsi Giri, Nepalese Prime Minister, came to India in April 1976. But Giri failed to secure Indian support for King Birendra's proposal for a Zone of Peace. Even before the visit, Sunanda K. Dutt in an article in *The Statesman* explained the complexities the proposal involved. He wrote :

> There is no reason to suppose that Nepal's geopolitical importance to India is greater than it is to China. Sino-Indian relations are hardly of a kind to permit Peking and New Delhi to set aside their differences and agree to underwrite Nepal's peace. The kind of rapprochement that would permit an encouraging joint venture would surely wipe out the raison a' etre for King Mahendra's proposal: It hardly makes sense to suggest a Zone of peace sandwiched between the two friendly countries.[39]

The Nepalese on the other, were pretty adamant and refused to accept the geopolitical reality as represented by the above view. The disagreement relating to the issue was not only on interpretation but also on the facts themselves as was evident from an editorial in *The Rising Nepal* of 23 February, 1976 :

> Much of the hesitancy is due to the feeling that the proposal ignores the so called reality that **Nepal** lies south of the Himalayas and that Nepal's geopolitical importance can not be the same to India and China. But since Nepal's territory lies both to the north and south of the Himalayas, there is no reason to suppose that Nepal's geopolitical importance to India is greater than it is to China. Prospects of institutionalising peace in this region can not certainly be less appreciable to our than to the other. In other words, there is certainly no cause for alarm or misunderstanding over the implications of Nepal's proposal for a Zone of Peace.[40]

Whenever we come to redefine the relations between close neighbours like India and Nepal the countries of their power equilibrium can not be ignored. The policy makers in Nepal were obviously aware of the changing strategic context in the sub continent where China and Pakistan may not be unduly excited about jumping into the Indo-Nepalese brawl as they did during the 1960s. Even the Americans were keen on keeping India in good humour for better returns in the larger strategic issues concerning Asia. But despite these facts Nepal continued to raise the issue, although with the active support of the Chinese in several international forums. It resulted in the hardening of New- Delhi's attitude towards Nepal by the end of the year 1976.

**Exchange of Visits**

The Indo-Pak war of 1971 and strengthening of its relations with USSR and Bangladesh made the Nepalese leaders uncertain of India's mood. The new King Birendra and his Prime Minister Kirtinidhi Bista felt the need to have a more amicable relations with India without any fundamental change in Nepal-China relations. In his first public speech Birendra obliquely acknowledged India's role in the 1950 revolution which ended the autocratic rule of the Ranas and led to the formation of a common front by his grand father King Tribhuvan and the Nepalese people. He also demonstrated his willingness to seek co-operation and understanding with India.[41] On the other, the new King disappointed those who stood for liberal democracy in Nepal and soon they were disillusioned to find that the fundamentals of his policy were no different from those of his father. And it was not unlikely to let out the long suppressed desires of the Nepalese for freedom in their political system. Thus the political exigencies too, demanded that Kathmandu must establish rapport with New Delhi in order to evade possible danger to its internal political system particularly from the Nepalese Congress exiled in India.

Kirtinidhi Bista, the Nepalese Prime Minister paid a 16-day visit to India in April 1972. His visit was aimed to assure New Delhi that "taking into account the geographical reality, Nepal has always to be more oriented towards India." Bista, at a Press Conference in New Delhi also conceded that the Indo- Nepalese Treaty of 1950 was still in force and rejected any need for entering into a new treaty with India, like the one, India has entered with the Soviet Union and Bangladesh. Instead he declared: "Our relations with India are so extensive and intimate that I do not see any need of any measure in addition to what we already have."[42] The main purpose of his visit as he stated was not to discuss with India any disputed issue but to thank Mrs. Gandhi for the "generous assistance" for the economic development of Nepal. During the stay in New Delhi he took meticulous care to explain that Nepal really wanted "best relations" with India.

Although New Delhi accorded a warm reception to the Nepalese Prime Minister, no joint communique was issued at the end of the visit nor it did any promise of aid follow from India despite Kathmandu's belated clearance to the construction of Kosi Western Canal. Probably it had come to New Delhi's notice that a few days before proceeding to India, Bista and the Kathmandu based Chinese Ambassador were together at Muglingtar had settled between themselves the aid projects that would be assigned to China in Nepal's Fifth Plan. Bista, immediately after his return from India paid a visit to China in the autumn to assure the Chinese leaders that Nepal would continue its policy of friendship towards China. In Beijing Bista sought as revealed by Zhou Enlai, his country's firm commitment to Nepal in the event of an Indian intervention on behalf of the rebels, but Beijing did not make any commitment, either direct or implicit, to protect monarchy in the event of a very real prospect of India's intervention.[44] However, the visit certainly indicated that King Birendra was following the policy of seeking a balanced relationship between India and China.[45]

A goodwill visit was paid to Kathmandu by Mrs. Indira Gandhi, Indian Prime Minister, 7-11 February 1973. Her visit accelerated the pace of developing amity between the two countries. In her talks with the King and the Nepalese Prime Minister, Mrs. Gandhi repeatedly assured them that India intended no interference in the internal affairs of Nepal and that she would not permit or encourage the Nepali Congress insurgents to indulge in hostile activities from the Indian soil.[46] The Prime Minister of India also succeeded in revitalising the provisions of the 1950 treaty.[47] She told the royal government that under the provisions of the treaty "we have to appraise each other of important developments" and asked Bista to inform her about his visit to China in previous November. After initial hesitation, Bista informed Mrs. Gandhi of his visit to China under the provisions of the treaty, thus formally putting a seal on the resurrection of the treaty at the highest level.[48]

Nepal responded favourably to the good gesture of Indian Prime Minister during her official visit and Bista also assured that his country wanted the "best relations" with India. He said that Indo-Nepalese relations were now placed on an "even keel" and Mrs. Gandhi's visit had been a "key contributing factor in the process of Nepal's consistent desire to maintain and strengthen best relations with India"[49]. Birendra also held the view that Mrs. Gandhi's visit had enhanced "mutual understanding" and enlarged" the area of co-operation so happily exists between the two countries."[50] But at the same time, Bista left no doubt that Nepal did not envisage to return under New Delhi's sphere of influence. Nepal would continue its relations with China on the basis of "good will, mutual understanding and mutual confidence." Although India was not opposed to Sino-Indian relations as long as it was not directed against New Delhi.

Accompanied by the Queen, the Nepalese King along with his Foreign Minister came to India on a state visit in October 1973. During the visit, the King spoke warmly about traditional ties of race, language, religion and culture between the two countries and at the same time emphasised the need for co-operation between them in trade and economic development, with a plea for special consideration of the inherent difficulties of Nepal as a landlocked country.[52] He talked of remodelling Indo-Nepal relations on a more "mature and sober basis and also of "revitalizing" their old ties".[53] Welcoming King Birendra Indian President V.V. Giri described his visit as a "historic opportunity" to discuss questions of bilateral and international importance. He also expressed the hope that "together we can perhaps review our faith in the common destiny of India and Nepal which is not only decreed by geography and history, but also the facts of contemporary life". He saw the royal visit as yet another "reaffirmation of our resolve to work together to the mutual benefit of our people".[54] Despite the gesture of goodwill expressed by both the sides, King Birendra was not unmindful of its relations with China and, at a civic reception he declared that "while we need India as a friendly nation, we also need the understanding and assistance of China" and asked India to support his policy of "equal friendship" with New Delhi and Beijing.

The Joint Communique issued at the end of the visit, stated that the talks between the King and Indian leaders covered a wide range of subjects of bilateral and international importance and "were held in an atmosphere of extreme cordiality and mutual understanding highlighted by the community of approach. All these developments were pointers to a healthy change in Indo- Nepal relations for sometimes after the accession of the new monarch. Subsequently King Birendra said in an interview with correspondents on 1 March 1974 that there was much more understanding now between India and Nepal and that the two countries had improved relations after the exchange of visits between the leaders of the two countries.

Indo-Nepal relations received a jolt during 1974-75 on account of India's successful conduct of nuclear explosion devices on 9 May 1974, integration of Sikkim into the Indian Union on the one hand and New Delhi's cold response towards King Birendra's proposal of declaring Nepal a 'Zone of Peace' on the other. In the circumstances, Y.B. Chavan, India's Minister for External Affairs, went to Kathmandu in January 1976 and a return visit was paid by Tulsi Giri, the Nepalese Prime Minister to New Delhi in April 1976. He held an extensive discussions with Indian Government leaders. The visiting Prime Minister stressed the importance of the relationship between India and Nepal were not of the same kind as relations with other countries and, recommended that the Himalayan Kingdom should not take India for granted. She told Giri that Indo-Nepalese relations were different from those with such countries as China and the Soviet Union.[58]

After his return to Kathmandu Tulsi Giri in June 1976, claimed complete success for his mission to India when he said to the press "My main purpose was to lay the policy framework for durable Nepal-India relations through free and frank discussions with the Indian leaders. This purpose has been achieved". Although Nepalese press did not consider his visit to New Delhi as a success and commented: "we have not, apparently been successful in securing India's support for the Peace Zone Proposal. Similarly, Indian press comments do not indicate that India had endorsed Nepal's proposal to separate politics from economics.[60]

**Politics**

In the Post-Mahendra era the new monarch Birendra had to face a world around him in which India was a dominant power. Nepalese dilemma regarding its foreign relations remained as earlier. King Birendra and his officials feared the possibility of Indian intervention, particularly after the signing of Indo-Soviet Treaty in August 1971. Although Nepal had used its China connection to counter balance its relations with India yet it became apparent that in the changed circumstances China could not go beyond the verbal assurance in case of actual intervention by New Delhi. After all, the only alternative left for the new King was to follow his father's diplomacy. He again emphasised social, economic, religious and cultural ties with India on the one hand and tried to keep China in good humour making it clear that Nepal had not divorced the policy of equidistance in its relations with the giant neighbours on the other. He initiated a policy of continuity than change in its relations with India. Related to all these were the changed concept of superpowers. In the 1970s, India's pre-eminent position in South Asia, as was evident from India's role in the emergence of Bangladesh in 1971, its peaceful nuclear explosion in 1974 and the merger of Sikkim in the Indian federation had a cumulative impact on the US strategic thinking and proded the Administration to deploy combined means to checkmate India's growing power projection in the region. The United States used the strategy of both pressurising and counselling India to exercise restraint in dealing with smaller states of the region under the pretext of maintaining regional peace and stability but chiefly to keep India in a low profile and neutralizing the Soviet influence in the subcontinent. So far as Indo- Nepal relations were concerned, Soviet Union did not want that their relations should reach a breaking point, because it would not only deteriorate security environment in the region but it would also encourage China to exploit the situation in its favour.

The year 1972 saw a relaxation in tension in the Far- East following Nixon's visit to Peking in February 1972, China's attitude to South East Asian countries still remained enigmatic. The Nepalese undertook their probe mission to Peking to ascertain whether a relaxation in tension was in the offing between Peking and New Delhi. Any lessening in the Chinese truculence towards India was likely to have an impact on the Nepalese foreign policy which showed a tilt to China to proclaim its independence from the Indian dominance on the subcontinent. China was never found wanting throughout 1972 in its efforts for "safeguarding Nepal's just struggle in its efforts to maintain its sovereignty and independence. China's attitude to its neighbours, south of the Himalayas, was conditioned mainly by the nature of its relations with India.

The Chinese seemed to recognise that the situation in South Asia had undergone a radical change and it adopted a cautious attitude towards Nepal. Initially it did not indulge in encouraging monarchy and its supporters against India. They also felt that they would have to play their cards carefully if they wanted to preserve their interests in Nepal and at the same time prevent an overbearing presence of India in that country. But by the mid-1972 Nepal and China were convinced that India did not desire to intervene in Nepal to restore democracy in the way it had done in Bangladesh. Although Nepal did not expect too much from the Chinese against India, yet its friendship with Beijing had immense significance. In September 1972 while receiving the new Chinese envoy TasoChih, Birendra described Nepal's relations with China as "cordial and traditional characterized by "warmth of friendship and mutual trust."[62] The same year in November he also sent Kirtinidhi Bista to Beijing to assure the Chinese leaders that Nepal would continue its policy of friendship towards China. As a result of the visit the two countries signed a bilateral trade agreement and promise of more grants in aid. Being encouraged by the Birendra's assurance Zhou Enlai reiterated China's "resolute support to the Nepalese people in their "just struggle" against foreign interference and praised Bircndra for his ability to preserve the policy of non-alignment, independence and neutrality.[63] In succession King Birendra paid a visit to China in December 1973 in order to renew the assurances of Chinese support against the hegemony of a group of nations" and found that it had counter balanced the growing Indo-Soviet influence in the region.

King Birendra gave Nepalese security a world-wide base while declaring his desire on 25 February 1975 that all friendly powers and the neighbouring countries in particular, would recognise Nepal a Zone of Peace. He denied any intention of using Beijing to counter New Delhi—the main feature of his father's foreign policy.[64] The Chinese naturally welcomed the proposal because "for years Nepal has given China powerful support in international affairs" and "has always tried to be friendly to China. China's support for the proposal was expressed in June 1976 when King Birendra visited Sichuan. Hua Keofeng on the occasion declared: "The proposal to declare Nepal a Zone of Peace reflects the strong desire of the people of Nepal to safeguard their national independence and state sovereignty. The Chinese government firmly support this just proposition". He also promised that "the Chinese people will always stand together with you in your struggle against hegemonism and expansionism".[66] Perhaps Nepal feared India's progress in the scientific and strategic fields and draw a conclusion that neither China nor Pakistan, or Bangladesh, or any other power would come to its rescue if it picked up a conflict with India. Therefcre, just to defend itself from the superior military might of India and China some way out should be traced and obviously that is the Zone of Peace Proposal. However, it could hardly be treated as a practical approach as *The Hindustan Times*, in its editorial mentioned that "Nepal's purpose will be better served by regulating its dealings with its neighbours on a pragmatic basis rather than by seeking to institutionalize a theoretical concept.[67]

The changed balance of power in the region in which India became a dominant power compelled the superpowers to take alive interest the area. The superpowers perception and policies were impinging upon Indo-Nepal relations especially in contextual parameters of their security and strategic concerns. The strategic thinking germanes to the superpower policies towards India and Nepal essentially stemmed from their geopolitical contest in the South Asia region. For the United States of America it was not possible to ignore a region that offers markets, raw material and highly skilled human resources that in the long run contribute to American strength and prosperity. Strategically too, the region offers a promising opportunity to promote its vital security interests in the Gulf, in the Indian Ocean and in the Mediterranean.

As a part of US strategy in the region the process of normalisation of Sino-American relations started by the Nixon-Kissinger team in the early 1970s. President Nixon visited Peking in February 1972 and the joint communique issued at the end stated that both the countries would work towards eventual normalisation of their relations on a full scale. That brought a sudden flight from the policy of containment to the policy of detente between the two countries. Since then Kathmandu became a meeting place for the high ranking diplomats of China and the United States. The American Ambassador stationed at Kathmandu, Carol C. Laise, had played prominent role in that connection and she was described as "not only America's envoy to Nepal, but also Kathmandu's effective ambassador in Washington.[68] Nepal's viewpoints were sympathetically and immediately received in the United States during that period. The relationship changed from "timidity and speculation to that of intimacy"[69] The visit of the US Deputy Secretary of State, Kenneth Rush to Kathmandu took place in 1973 who assured Kathmandu that America's relations with Nepal would in no way be guided by its relations with any Nepal's neighbours and that Nepal stood on its own significant. The obvious reference was to the detente with communist China and the prevailing cold relations between New Delhi and Washington.[70]

India's expansionist posture demonstrated in the successful explosion of nuclear devices in 1974 and integration of Sikkim in the Indian federation. These added speed to the normalisation of Sino-American relations had made other small nations of the region conscious of their stakes. In that kind of situation King Birendra declared on 25 February 1975, the day of coronation his wish to declare Nepal a Zone of Peace. The United States was interested a good deal in Nepal's proposal and the full text of the King's speech was published in the United States Congressional records. David Cox, the Chief of the South Asia desk in the US State Department in an interview with a journalist said that the USA was interested in the King's idea of Peace Zone and further stated that proposal was timely and clearly reflected Nepal's foreign policy. However, in general the United States was not satisfied with the role played by third world countries in the United Nations and Nepal was ranged in that category due to shared social and economic problems and "not because it was opposed to any body, certainly not to the US nor because it was guided by bloc spirit"'.[72] But, later on, Kathmandu felt a delicacy in its relations with US when Jimmy Carter became President and laid special emphasis on human rights.

Although Nepal fall into Indo-Soviet equation by recognising the Government of Bangladesh in early 1972, it was very conscious, based as it was on two factors. First in the Nepalese outlook, the Soviet Union's interest in the Kingdom had declined as a natural consequence of the Soviet efforts to expand and deepen its relations with India. Secondly, there was an uncanny suspicion in the Kingdom that the Soviet Union might ignore Nepal's basic national interest in the process of strengthening its position in the subcontinent. The suspicion was expressed by Y.N. Khanal in the Seminar on "Foreign Policy" in CEDA Kirtipur, in 1973:

Nepal-Soviet relations call for a vigorous effort based on a realistic appraisal of mutual interest. In the course of such renewed efforts, it is essential for our diplomacy to impress upon the Soviet Union that it should continue to refuge to be a party to any attempt from any quarter to decide or compromise Nepal's future, behind its back, as an independent sovereign member of the international community. This vigilance is necessary because, historically speaking, trade-off third countries have taken place at the time of either extreme friendship or of extreme hostility between major powers.[73]

Nepal wanted to keep "equidistance between India and China and, with that spirit reorientation in the foreign policy was given by the King. He proposed that Nepal be declared a 'Zone of Peace' on the occasion of his coronation ceremony on 25 February 1975. Initial response to the proposal was positive and Turabai Kulatov, Deputy Chairman of the presidium of the Supreme Soviet of the USSR, who led the Soviet delegation to the ceremony welcomed the proposal in the statement read out at a meeting organised by the Nepal-Soviet Friendship Society in his honour. However, Soviet enthusiasm about the Zone of Peace seemed to suffer a subsequent decline and the Soviet Ambassador K.B. Udumyan, at a press conference on 5 March 1976, interpreted the initial gesture merely as Soviet support of Nepal's policy of positive non-alignment and of the King's desire not to allow Nepal to be an area of tension and a centre for hostilities against other countries.[75]

The Soviet Union was optimistic that Nepal as an Asian country would give objective consideration to its proposal for an Asian Collective Security System. Although observers were of the view that the Soviet-sponsored move was unlikely to find much favour in Nepal because some Asian countries, notably China, seemed irrevocably opposed to it yet as a small power of South Asia, Nepal saw no harm in supporting this security system. Nor did its endorsement entail grave security implications for the country. The Nepalese Foreign Minister during his visit to the Soviet Union discussed Asian Collective Security System. In Kathmandu too, Soviet ambassador Udumyan, made persuasive plea before the Nepal Council of World Affairs that the people of all Asian nations should sit together and discuss problems of peace and security in Asia on the pattern of the Helsinki declaration for European countries.[76] He further maintained that his country fully supported Nepal's foreign policy of positive non-alignment as it would bring peace and security in the region and in Asia as a whole. The two countries discussed in detail various national and international issues relating to their security and various dimensions thereof when King Birendra accompanied by his Foreign Minister Krishna Raj Aryal went on a week-long visit to the Soviet Union in November 1976.

**Analysis of the Attitude**

In substance, the new King Birendra continued his father's policies in regard to its foreign relations. Although he had to face a new situation owing to the emergence of Bangladesh as a sovereign, independent nation in which India was evidently an influential power in the region. The event had reduced, to some extent, the bargaining position of Nepal. It became more difficult for Kathmandu to ignore geopolitical realities and, therefore, it recognised the new state of Bangladesh and tried its level best to readjust its policies with India. The changed regional balance of power compelled the superpowers to take active interest in the area. The USSR was neither willing nor thinks it proper, from its strategic point of view, to please Nepal at India's cost. But the United States of America was anxious enough to reduce Soviet influence in the region and wanted to keep India in a low-profile. For this, US started normalisation of its relations with China in order to prevent Peking from exploiting the situation in its favour by exacerbating tensions between India and Nepal.

Nepalese attitudes towards India was further influenced by its successful conduct of nuclear explosion devices in 1974 and integration of Sikkim into the Indian Union. It became more suspicious of India's motives and to have an international commitment to its security, King Birendra, declared on 25 February his wish to recognise Nepal as a 'Zone of Peace' and requested the immediate neighbours to endorse it. As the proposal was against the Indian fear and influences, its approval by India was crucial to the attainment of its primary objectives. Although the proposal received verbal endorsement by several countries of the world, China and the US took special interest. India, as it understood the real motive behind the proposal did not support the idea of declaring Nepal a 'Zone of Peace' saying that it ignored the geopolitical realities of the region and Nepalese aim could be achieved by adopting a practical approach rather than by institutionalising it.

Despite the dominant position, New Delhi gained in the post-war phase India never intended to use it against Nepalese national interest. Nepal's growing intimacy with the Chinese was a cause of concern for New Delhi and India was opposed to use China against India, in any form. India's nuclear explosion, integration of Sikkim in the Indian federation was not to threaten Kathmandu as it was aimed to enhance New Delhi's image and potentiality on global basis. India also did not like Nepal's effort to internationalise its security concept by declaring the idea of 'Zone of Peace'. Because it would go in favour of China and against Indian interests, New Delhi did not endorse it. Apart from all these India was effortful to have a fruitful relations with Nepal and took genuine interest in its economic development. However, normalisation of relations between China and USA and their joint venture to reduce Indo-Soviet influence in Nepal had hardened Indian attitude on matters, relating to Kathmandu interests.

## Notes and References

1. Rishikesh Shaha *Nepali Politics: Retrospect and Prospect* (Oxford University Press, New Delhi, 1978), p. 182.
2. Robert A. Scalapino, *Asia and the Road Ahead: Issues for the Major Powers* (University of California Press, Berkeley, 1974), p. 20.
3. Tribhuvan Nath, *The Nepalese Dilemma 1960-74* (Sterling Publishers, New Delhi, 1975), p. 471.
4. S.K. Chaturvedi, "Indo-Nepal Relations: Tension Areas", *Foregin Affairs Report*, Vol. XXX VIII, No.5, May 1989 (Indian Council of World Affairs, New Delhi, 1989), p. 67.
5. *Ibid.*
6. *Asian Recorder*, 2-8 April, 1973, p. 13319.
7. S. Viswam, "Political Community-the View from Kathmandu", *The Statesman*, 12 October 1973.
8. *The Statesman*, 25 May 1973.
9. *Rising Nepal*, 29 September 1972.
10. *The Statesman*, 18 February 1973.
11. *Rising Nepal*, 11 August 1974.
12. *The Motherland*, 2 September 1974.
13. *The Times of India*, 5 September 1974.
14. Tribhuvan Nath, *op. cit.*, p. 477.
15. *The Hindustan Times*, 29 November 1974.

16. *The Times of India*, 3 November 1974.
17. *The Statesman*, 12 December 1974.
18. S.K. Chaturvedi, *op. cit.,* p. 69.
19. *Rising Nepal*, 9 September 1973.
20. *Ibid.*
21. Gorkhapatra, 26 February 1975.
22. A Souvenir Birthday Issue of the *Journal of the Nepal Council of World Affairs*, 1975, pp. 3-4
23. *Rising Nepal*, 26 February 1975.
24. *Xinhua*, 3 February 1975.
25. Govind R. Agrawal, Rajeshwar Acharya and Pustam Pradhan (eds.): *Fundamentals of Nepalese Foreign Policy*, CEDA, Kathmandu (Nepal), pp. 11-53.
26. Rishikesh Shaha, *op. cit.,* p. 173.
27. *The Hindustan Times*, 8 April 1976.
28. *The Statesman*, 18 February 1973.
29. *Xinhua*, 2 June 1976.
30. S.K. Jha, "Nepal's India Policy", *Foreign Affairs Report*, Vol. XXV, No.11, November 1976.
31. *The Hindu*, 17 April 1972.
32. *The Hindustan Times*, (editorial) 6 May 1972.
33. Shree Krishna Jha, *Uneasy Partners: India and Nepal in the Post-Colonial Era* (Manas Publishers, New Delhi, 1975), p. 311.
34. *The Times of India,* 23 April 1989.
35. S.K. Chaturvedi, *Bharat-Nepal Sambandh* (New Delhi, 1983), p. 183.
36. S.K. Chaturvedi, *op. cit.*, p. 70.
37. *The Motherland*, 27 February 1975.
38. *Nepal Times*, 27 February 1975.
39. *The Weekly Mirror*, 10 March 1976.
40. *Rising Nepal*, 23 February 1976.
41. *The Statesman*, 20 February 1972.
42. *The Hindu*, 17 April 1972.
43. *The Times of India*, 19 April 1972.
44. *Xinhua*, 18 and 19 November 1972.

45. Rishikesh Shaha, *op. cit.,* p. 135.
46. *The Times of India*, 9 February 1973.
47. *The Hindu* (editorial), 12 February 1973.
48. *The Hindustan Times*, 15 February 1973.
49. *Ibid.,* 18 February 1973.
50. *The Statesman*, 23 July 1973.
51. *Xinhua*, 4 May 1973.
52. Rishikesh Shaha. *Op. cit.,* p. 135.
53. *The Times of India*, 9 February 1973.
54. Hemen Roy, *China's Strategy in Nepal* (Radiant Publishers, New Delhi, 1983), p. 106.
55. *Gorkhapatra*, 13 October 1973.
56. *Asian Recorder*, 15-21 January 1974, p. 11797.
57. *Ibid.,* 17-22 April, 1974, p. 11971.
58. *Statesman Weekly*, 10 April 1976.
59. *Gorkhapatra*, 15 June 1976.
60. *The Rising Nepal*, 17 April 1976.
61. Tribhuvan Nath, *op. cit.,* p. 479.
62. *Rising Nepal*, 29 September 1972.
63. *Xinhua*, 15 November 1972.
64. *Rising Nepal*, 26 February 1975.
65. *Renmin Ribao*, 1 August 1975.
66. *Xinhua*, 2 June 1976.
67. *The Hindustan Times*, 13 February 1982.
68. *Himali Bela*, 27 May 1973.
69. *The Motherland*, 4 June 1973.
70. *The Hindustan Times*, 26 April 1973.
71. *The Rising Nepal*, 30 March 1950.
72. *The Times of India*, 26 September 1975.
73. Yadunath Khanal, *Nepal Transition From Isolationism* (Sajha Prakashan, Kathmandu, 1977), p. 84.
74. *The Times of India*, 27 February 1975.
75. *Gorkhapatra*, 5 March 1976.
76. *The Times of India*, 19 October 1975.

# 9

# BALANCED RELATIONSHIP (1977—1984)

## Diplomacy

The change of government in New Delhi in March 1977 witnessed India's slow return to realism in its relations with the small neighbours in general and Nepal in particular. India's relations with the neighbours were more relaxed than ever since independence and Janata Government's new diplomacy met with far greater initial success in the neighbourhood. The new regime under the premiership of Morarji Desai was hailed by the two leading newspapers of Nepal. *The Rising Nepal* and *The Gorkhapatra*, in their editorials, congratulated Desai on his assumption of the office and hoped that this would facilitate the opening of a new chapter in the close and meaningful relations between the two people and Governments of the two countries.[1]

The Janata Government in India appeared to have largely succeeded in "winning the confidence and trust of the authorities in Kathmandu through a process of give and take"[2] Kathmandu appeared to have shed its earlier prejudices to co-operate with India in a big way. But Nepal did not give up the stance of viewing itself as a buffer state between India and China, notwithstanding the qualitative improvement in the relations between the two countries which was now characterized by trust and confidence. Bista gave expression to this anxiety of Nepal when, in his address to Indian Council of World Affairs on 16 April 1978, said that in the situation when it became difficult for India and China to strike for peaceful coexistence, a small country like Nepal could not influence the course of events by taking side in such a situation.[3] Kathmandu's efforts to seek the involvement of China in the affairs of the subcontinent under the guise of regulating the use of the eastern rivers also betrayed the same anxiety.[4] Nor did it gave up the idea of a Zone of peace which was based, as Bista said on its realisation that it could not seek comfort by walking on a razor's edge all the time for avoiding involvement in conflicts of big power interests working at cross purposes.[5]

The performance of the new regime was not up to the Nepalese expectations and Kathmandu was surprised to know that the Janata Government was not willing to alter the bilateral relationship with Nepal, established by Mrs. Gandhi's government. During his visit to Kathmandu, Atal Bihari Vajpayee, the Minister for External Affairs, under the new dispensation in July 1977 rejected Birendra's proposal that Nepal be declared a "Zone of Peace". This position was reiterated by Prime Minister Morarji Desai when he went to Kathmandu in December 1977. Desai also rejected King Birendra's appeal for economic co-operation between Nepal, India and China because China did not "belong to this region and therefore, could not be a participant in any affairs of South Asia. However, he advocated increased co-operation between Nepal and India—the two countries located south of the Himalayas. The Indian Prime Minister also made it clear that the Treaty of 1950 continued to be a valid basis for Indo-Nepalese relations.[6]

Kathmandu, despite its honeymoon with the Chinese tried to balance its relationship with bordering neighbours (India and China) and described it as "very good". Answering to a question K. B. Shahi, Nepalese Foreign Minister in the Rashtriya Panchayat said that Nepal had all along looked at the progress and achievements of both China and India as our own. He declared that Nepal's relations with India "transcended" the efforts of minor incidents taking place at times owing to open border stretching thousands of miles and various levels of contacts between the people of the two countries.[7] Shahi was optimistic on Nepalese Peace Zone Proposal and referred to the support extended by many countries including China, Pakistan and Bangladesh and said that the Indian viewpoint was "gradually coming favourable to the reality of the proposal". He informed the members that the talks designed to seek Indian support to the Peace Zone proposal were underway and would continue at various levels. The main thrust of Nepal's foreign policy had been to safeguard and promote her independence and sovereignty, maintain friendly relations with all countrics of the globe, the neighbouring countries in particular, and contribute to world peace. However, a desire on the part of Nepal to invite big power intervention in its dealings with India and New Delhi's opposition to such moves, eroded unfortunately. For the reasons, the then government in New Delhi refused to accept Nepalese proposal that it be declared a "Zone of Peace", guaranteed by the two superpowers and the Chinese. Nepal knew well enough the havoc of big power intervention in South Asia in support of Pakistan, had caused in the past and might cause in future, given the current flurry over Afghanistan. King Birendra, cvcn tried during his recent visit to Sri Lanka to drum up support for the Zone of peace idea. But Sri Lankan President J. R. Jayawardene, presumably because of his awareness of the Indian reservations, had given the Nepalese proposal only vague and ambiguous endorsement.[10]

The approach of the Janata Government towards Nepal was less assertive and was characterized by greater co-operation and accommodation. But the victory of Mrs. Gandhi in the general elections of 1980 frightened the Nepalese monarchy and the vested interests. They saw the return of Mrs. Gandhi to power as a special problem for their country. She was a critic of Janata Government's foreign-policy and more forthright in asserting India's politico-strategic interests in the Himalayan Kingdom. Hence, Kathmandu with the active support of Peking tried to prevent Mrs. Gandhi from putting new pressures on Nepal. Although in view of the danger in its southern forntier and the Soviet presence in Afghanistan, the Chinese were unwilling to give an open encouragement to the Nepalese vehemence against India. Yet the world-wide criticism of the Soviet action in Afghanistan provided a convenient tool for the Nepalese monarchy to exploit the crisis to pressurise India. However, India felt unhappy with King's activities to mobilise small Asian states to present a united stand under New Delhi's leadership. Actually, New Delhi wanted the South Asian countries to evolve a united stand on their approach to the Afghan question, but Birendra torpedoed it.[12] Soon after the assumption of power by Mrs. Indira

Gandhi, King Birendra paid an official visit to India in March 1980 and the discussions held between them covered bilateral relations including the political, economic and technical matters. It was agreed that Nepal-India relations were characterized by mutual trust and confidence. They further agreed that every effort should be made to increase contacts between the two countries at all levels to expand co-operation in mutually beneficial spheres.[13]

Two important dignitaries of the Government of India P. V. Narasimha Rao and Neelam Sanjiva Reddy, Minister for External Affairs as well as President of the Indian Republic respectively went to Kathmandu and discussed with Nepalese leaders matters of mutual interest. In the banquet speech Reddy noted with satisfaction that in recent months there had been a realisation on both sides of the need to co-operate purposefully in harnessing all available water resources to mutual benefit. He declared, "India attaches highest priority to our relations with friendly Nepal, which arc multifaceted and extensive. I am confident that these relations based as they are on mutual respect and understanding will continue to grow in a spirit of trust and goodwill. In reply, King Birendra pointed out that it seemed ironic that despite the rich potentials in resources and means, Nepal and India had not yet been able to liberate themselves from the clutches of poverty.[14] But in a close look of India-Nepal relations, Kathmandu was not sure of what its "giant" neighbour was up to and India in its turn was not sure whether Nepal had not only slowly but surely been drifting away from the sort of relationship that shared history, culture and tradition had shaped. India was legitimately worried over Nepalese idea of Zone of peace that not only imply an international agreement on Nepal but also provided third countries with an opportunity to interfere in the affairs of the subcontinent. Apart from all these, the proposal would dilute the Indo-Nepalese Treaty of Peace and Friendship of 1950 which declared that there should be perpetual peace between the two countries.[16]

Surya Bahadur Thapa, the Nepalese Prime Minister, during his visit to India in February 1983 expressed his wish to launch a new phase of diplomacy and said that as friendly neighbours are on an equal footing the two countries could make much head way by mutual co-operation. Despite the differences on sensitive issues like Kampuchea or Afghanistan both are firmly committed to non-alignment. He requested New Delhi not to misunderstand Nepal for its relations with China or its move to declare its territory as a Zone of Peace.[17] The main objection that the New Delhi had as regards Kathmandu was its intimate and evergrowing relations with the Peking at India's cost. On most of the issues Nepalese views had not been similar to India's. Whether it is Kashmir or Kampuchea, Sikkim or Afghanistan, Nepal had been seeking a line of thinking virtually opposed to India's.[18] Further, in the same year their relations came under in explicable stresses owing to arrest of 35 Nepalese nationals by the Indian authorities in Siliguri.[19] It seemed that Nepal took offence at this and rounded up some small traders of Indian origin in Kathmandu and took them to Raxaul to push them across the boundary into Indian territory.[20] Kathmandu also charged allegations against Indian police personnel and said that the Indians had committed crimes against Nepalese citizens.[21] However, India expressed surprise at Nepal lodging a protest over a "purely local" incident involving criminals and raising to a political level to give it the dimension of a border incident.[22]

The happenings of Siliguri and Raxaul had strained Indo-Nepal relations. A section of the ruling circles in Kathmandu feared that their country may face in the fertile Terai region the same situation as Sri Lanka did in northern Jaffna. As revealed later it was only a small part of the unfolding mystery why a powerful section was too keen to spoil relations with India. Kirtinidhi Bista, five times Prime Minister of Nepal visited Peking where he sought assurances against India creating another "Sri Lanka" in the Terai. As reported, Bista sought Chinese help to involve the USA in the issue.[23] At the moment New Delhi occupied a profile next to the Chinese in Nepal's foreign policy as indicated by King Birendra in a interview given to a foreign daily. He said that Nepal "has close and warm relations with China and ties with others "were guided by the principles of non-aligned movement". India if interested to note is the most prominent in the category of "others".[24]

Just to check the downward slide in Indo-Nepal relations Asian Study Circle organized a day long seminar on current issues in "People to people Relations" between the two countries. Inaugurating the Seminar, Balram Bhagat, former Lok Sabha speaker said that although India was like an elephant in size compared to Nepal "this elephant is vegetarian and peace-loving". Nepal had therefore, nothing to fear from India. In this complex situation Rishikesh Shaha, former Foreign Minister of Nepal also felt the need for revitalisation of Indo-Nepal relations. He was not in favour of closing the border of the two sides. However, he suggested that the border must be controlled not to prevent the free movement of the people across it but to stop smuggling to keep track of the flow of Nepali and Indian currency and to collect data about the flow of Indians into Nepal and the flow of Nepalese into India.[25] It appeared that on the issue the Nepalese Government faced a dilemma. If it did not restrict the flow of Indians into Nepal, Kathmandu would be gradually drawn into the Indian economic sphere, regardless of whatever, political changes might take place. On the other hand, if the Government restricts the flow of Indians by tightening up citizenship requirements on all kinds of activities then the government might have invited Indian retaliation.[26]

In that kind of situation the Nepalese Government thought for the implementation of Gurung Report[27] and it caused serious concerns at New Delhi. The said report had come to assume an omnious significance from India's point of view following the attempt made in the previous year to round up some destitutes in Kathmandu and deport them to India by labelling them as illegal immigrants though in theory. The Nepalese Government had appointed a co-ordination committee to suggest ways and means of implementing the Gurung report. Although the implementation of the report was discussed in detail by P. V. Narasimha Rao, India's Minister for External Affairs, and General Padma Bahadur Khatri, the Nepalese Foreign Minister along with other irritants in Indo-Nepal relations. Yet the Government of India was not satisfied with the assurance and was seeking adequate guarantees against any discrimination of its citizens of Indian origin, specially those settled in the Terai region. Despite this problem and some differences about transit facilities to Indian ports for Nepalese goods[29] Padma Bahadur Khatri claimed his recent visit to India as "very satisfying".[30]

**Strategy for Security**

The assumption of Janata Party's Government in March 1977 posed no new threat to the security of Nepal. The atmosphere of mutual suspicion regarding each other's motives and designs as prevailed earlier had been removed to a large extent and the two countries felt a more amicable era of their relations, particularly on bilateral issues. But even the new regime that followed the policy of "Good- Neighbourliness" and "Beneficial Bilateralism" was not going to compromise on the issues which were against New Delhi's interest. As its predecessors the present dispensation was opposed to involve any third country in the affairs of the region. Both Morarji Desai and Atal Bihari Vajpayee, Prime Minister and Minister for External Affairs respectively, on several occasions, outrightly rejected Nepal's Proposal for declaring it a "Zone of Peace. Sensing India's mood on the issue King Birendra discussed the issue with Deng Xiaoping when the latter visited Kathmandu in February 1978 and endeavoured to secure a Chinese firm commitment against India's involvement in Nepal.[31]

For its security sake Nepal criticized Soviet aggressive posture in Kampuchea and their invasion of Afghanistan and following Sino-American line demanded the immediate withdrawal of the Soviet troops from that country. The first statement issued by the Nepalese Foreign Minister on 1 January 1980 stated that the HMG had been watching events in Afghanistan with increased concern. Recent developments, including the large foreign military presence, in that non-aligned sovereign country, had deeply aggravated Nepal's concern since they posed a danger to peace and stability, HMG believed in the inviolability of the sovereignty, independence and territorial integrity of all small states and their right to determine and chart their destiny themselves without foreign interference, Nepal opposed foreign intervention wherever it might occur.[32] As against India which did not vote on that issue in the UN, Nepal voted in favour of the resolution concerning the immediate withdrawal of the foreign troops from Afghanistan.[33]

However, a pro-Moscow weekly came out with the view that the Nepalese Government's policy had totally abandoned the national interest of Nepal. It was not through mistake but deliberately that Nepal had thrust itself into the Sino-American axis and Nepal would never be able to escape from the diverse consequences of that step. In view of the fact that the new government of India had not only adopted an attitude totally opposed to that of Nepal, China, USA and Pakistan concerning the Afghan incidents, but had even regarded their conspiracies as dangerous for the independence and stability of the subcontinent. The Nepalese foreign policy development had thus pursued a path contrary to that of India and for that matter, to its own interests, on major international issues.[34]

Despite all these the Government of India agreed with the Nepalese view that a new danger had been posed to peace and stability in the region with the Soviet intervention in Afghanistan. This indication was given by Neelam Sanjiva Reddy, Indian President, in a banquet speech organized in honour of King Birendra on 6 March 1980. He referred although indirectly to Afghan crisis and said, "In the recent past, our region, which has so far remained peaceful, has become an area of tension resulting from the likely induction of massive arms into it. Your Majesty has recently referred to the "shadows of cold war" which have "over taken" the region in our "neighbourhood" and the dangers inherent in the "call of arms". We fully share your Majesty's concern and are happy to note that both India and Nepal agree that it is not conducive to peace and stability in our area".[35] In the changed circumstances Kathmandu laid emphasis on strengthening of its ties with friendly neighbours like India and China. King Birendra while addressing the 32 session of the elected Rashtriya Panchayat referred to his visits to Britain, Egypt, Pakistan, Cyprus, Belgium, Yugoslavia and Baharain which had further strengthened Nepal's relations with them.[36] The Himalayan Kingdom, at the same time, sent senior Nepali Military officials for training in the Pakistani and the Chinese military institutions since the early 1980s'. India reacted sharply to this because, in India Nepali officials not only occupy important ranks in the Indian army but those from Nepal army were also admitted into special and exclusive military training establishments dealing with high mountain warfare and counter insurgency operations.[37]

Apart from all these Kathmandu continued its policy of using China card against India and weakened its defence proximity with New Delhi. It was implied in the equal relationship aspect of the Zone of Peace proposal and it had taken measures to do so. In an important move Nepal's Zone of peace proposal after the Third Amendment found a place in the Directive Principles of the constitution, extended further the regional idea and her support for the South Asian Summit proposal put forward by Bangladesh, as a next step in the same direction.[38] This step showed Nepalese growing feeling of insecurity and in all his public statements, Nepalese Prime Minister Surya Bahadur Thapa had consistently emphasised regional co-operation and had maintained that recognition of the Zone of peace reflected the aspirations of the Nepalese people. In the light of developments in Afghanistan and reports that the Soviets have established a sophisticated electronic listening post in their embassy in Kathmandu to monitor Chinese nuclear and missile activities in Tibet, it required no reading between the lines to understand why Nepal wanted India's formal consent to the Zone of Peace proposal.[39]

But the two neighbours-India and China were fundamentally differed on the approach that had a sensitive geo-political affect in the region. Narasimha Rao, India's Minister for External Affairs, in his recent visit to Kathmandu, in the last week of November 1981, discussed the issue and as earlier, India had been firm in retaining the greater flexibility of bilateral agreements with its northern neighbours, even, as it emphasised regional security, in the Indian Ocean area in the south. Nepal had little choice. In a diplomatic statement Rao reminded, "None of the countries of the region stand to gain anything by India being weakened or embarrassed in any way.[40] In course of a banquet speech reply at Kathmandu, Rao specifically said that Nepal would not be a Zone of peace in isolation. He maintained that success of all peace initiatives could be brought about in the context of harmony and amity "globally generally and in our region in particular". All around them in the region there was a rapid escalation of tensions and aimed at destroying the harmony and tranquillity of our area", "under no pretext, therefore, most countries in our region become a catspaw in the game of great powers".[41] However, the Indian and Nepalese spokesman said that Rao and Thapa had decided that in view of the critical and insecure international situation, it was necessary for the countries of the subcontinent to remain in touch with each other and evolve an atmosphere of co-operation and understanding to deal with the difficult security environment in the subcontinent.[42] Further during the three-day secretary level talk of the two governments, India had promised Nepal that it would try to "understand" its proposal for the Himalayan Kingdom being declared a Zone of peace but maintained that there should be efforts to make the entire South Asian region a Zone of Peace.[43]

The Nepalese proposal continued to be an irritant in Indo-Nepal relations. Inspired apparently by the West which wanted a decade ago to deflect the world focus on the Indian Ocean being declared as a Zone of peace, elements not friendly to India drew a red herring across the trial. China was quick to endorse Nepalese demands realising that India's loss was China's gain.[44] the National Pancha convention went a step further in this direction and adopted a resolution asking the government to take all possible measures at the diplomatic level to obtain maximum support for the proposal that Nepal be declared a Zone of Peace. R. D. Sathe, Indian Foreign Secretary during his five-day official visit to Nepal discussed the Nepalese plan in detail and describing his talks as "useful" conveyed that India needed more exercise on the Peace Zone proposal.[45] Kathmandu had a grievance that New Delhi had showed cold response towards its proposal and at a time when India was itself mending her fences with the Peking, Nepal felt uneasiness and wanted to avoid any direct conflict of interests with India. It tried to renew its effort to strengthen traditional relations in the bilateral sphere. The visit of Surya Bahadur Thapa, the Nepalese Prime Minister along with Padma Bahadur Khatri, Nepalese Foreign Minister in early 1983 should be viewed in this context.[47]

Above all, as claimed by official sources, Kathmandu did not see any threat from India or China now or later but they felt that Nepal would get a psychological boost if its proposal finds multilateral support. If Nepal is declared a Zone of peace they said it would contribute to the cause of peace and stability in the region, inject a new meaning and hope into the principles of non-alignment and help Nepal to focus entirely on economic development.[48] Side by side, Kathmandu began to take active interest in the meetings and deliberations of the South Asian Regional Co-operation.[49] It should be noted here that since the emergence of this regional organisation the insistence of Nepal in respect of "Zone of Peace had diminished considerably.

**Exchange of Visits**

In the first week of April 1977 King Birendra paid an unofficial visit to India to attend the World Conference on Religion, Philosophy and Culture. He was anxious to be assured of the attitude and policies of the new Indian government.[50] He stopped over for a day (2 April) in New Delhi and used the opportunity to hold wide ranging discussions with Morarji Desai, the new Prime Minister, Atal Bihari Vajpayee, the new Minister for External Affairs and Jagjivan Ram on various issues of mutual interest, including the need to conclude a new treaty of trade and transit as soon as possible and to conduct negotiations to that end.[51] At this time Desai's Government was only a week old and the King's visit to New Delhi happened to be the first visit of any head of the state since the Janata Party's assumption of power.

The King returned reassured that the relations between India and Nepal would continue to be friendly. Krishna Raj Aryal, Nepalese Foreign Minister who accompanied the King, termed the visit as "successful" and said the new administration in India was looking forward to having "very good relations with Nepal" and that was what Nepal wanted.[52]

Atal Bihari Vajpayee, India's new Minister for External Affairs paid a visit to Nepal 14-16 July 1977. Nepal had a lingering suspicion, further strengthened by the controversy over the release of Koirala, that the new Government in New Delhi, like its predecessors would take it for granted and have an overbearing attitude towards it. Vajpayee tried to remove misunderstandings and reinforce trust and confidence between the two neighbours. He showed ample awareness to the sensibility and psychology of India's small neighbours which had been keen for the recognition of its distinct identity and personality and for being treated on equal footing. Vajpayee in his speeches in Nepal repeatedly referred to Nepal's independent status in the comity of nations, disavowed, on India's part, any interest to interfere in its affairs, conveyed India's desire to have friendship on the basis of equality, and showed interest in Nepal's economic development and mutual beneficial co-operation.

Vajpayee discussed with his Nepalese counterpart all matters pertaining to India-Nepal relations in friendly and cordial atmosphere. However, two of them require special mention because of their overriding significance. The first of these was Nepalese proposal that it be declared a Zone of peace. Vajpayee clarified his Government's stand in this regard which was that the entire subcontinent should be an area of peace. He informed the Nepalese side that his government was taking steps to improve relations with all of India's neighbours. As far as Nepal was concerned, he indicated that, in keeping with the friendly relations between the two countries, India would consider any suggestion from the Government of Nepal with an open mind.[53] At the same time he also affirmed that there was a Treaty of Peace and Friendship between India and Nepal which accepted that both countries would live in perpetual peace and that this Treaty and India's subsequent actions fully reaffirmed the independence, sovereignty and territorial integrity of Nepal.[54]

With his eloquence characterized by frankness and sensibility alike and with his willingness for pragmatic accommodation, Vajpayee succeeded in removing misunderstandings and in reinforcing trust and confidence between the two countries. Nepal welcomed the change of style in New Delhi of which Vajpayee gave ample proof.[55] Even before Vajpayee left for Kathmandu both sides were aware that many of the problems had been blown out of proportion resulting in mutual suspicion.[56]

Vajpayee's visit to Kathmandu was followed by Desai's visit in December 1977. Desai was accompanied by his Foreign

Minister, Vajpayee. On his arrival in Kathmandu Desai said India's relations with Nepal go on getting strengthened not only for mutual advantage but for the good of the whole neighbourhood. In reply to a question from a press reporter he said in his characteristic style that there was going to be complete co-operation between the two countries. There was no question of discussions about it.[57] He conveyed to the Government and people of Nepal that India cherished friendship with them and sought to promote relationship in a manner which respected the independence of both, advanced mutual interests and brought benefit to both.[58] Wide ranging discussions were held and mutually advantageous agreements reached which had earlier been settled between Vajpayee and Nepalese leaders.

The Joint Communique, issued at the end of Desai's visit noted that the measures of identity of their views led the two Prime Ministers to believe that based on goodwill and trust a new chapter could be opened in relation between the two countries. They recognised the need to strengthen their economic co-operation on the basis of equality and mutual benefit. Desai affirmed India's determination to continue to participate fully in the developmental programmes of the Himalayan Kingdom. It was in this spirit of understanding that they agreed to give priority to project on the rivers linking the two countries for multiple benefits and the Devighat power project to which the Government of Nepal attached great importance.[59]

The two sides felt the necessity to remove bottlenecks in the execution of pending projects and agreed upon specific measures to set in motion the process of expeditiously executing four projects on the rivers Karnali, Mahakali, Rapti and Trishuli.[60]

On his return from Kathmandu, Desai told the Parliament, in a statement on 12 December 1977, that the decision to have two treaties and a separate agreement was a reflection of the spirit of respect of each others independence as well as sensitivity that each country's economic policies did not harm the other.[61]

Kirtinidhi Bista, the Prime Minister of Nepal visited India 15-20 April 1978. It was evident that the climate of relations between the two countries had considerably improved since the formation of the Janata Government in India. Bista appeared to be assured of India's goodwill for Nepal. Wide ranging and encompassing discussions were held between the two sides which were marked by complete understanding and shared perception on both bilateral and international issues.

A notable area of discussion was the economic technical and ecological aspects of the various river projects for harnessing the waters of the tributaries of the Ganges in Nepal with Indian assistance. These discussions related to the progress of the projects that were already under construction with Indian collaboration and others that were now under active consideration. The talks reflected the keenness of the two sides for a periodic review of the ongoing projects and an early commencement of the feasibility studies of the others to draw up a time bound programme for their completion.[62]

In a joint communique, issued on 17 April 1978, the Prime Ministers of the two countries expressed their hope that the draft agreement on the Devighat hydro-electric project would be signed soon. Bista, on his part, expressed his happiness at India's decision to increase its commitment for the renovation of Chandra Canal, construction of pumped canal and the distribution system of the western Kosi canal in Nepal.[63]

Bista stressed Nepal's policy of self-reliance in economic development. Desai pledged India's continued assistance in various fields of Nepal's scientific, technical and infrastructural development. Both expressed that India's contribution had been beneficial to the development of Nepal.

India's Minister for Industry, George Fernandes, paid a visit to Kathmandu 24-26 September 1978 for as he said, "formalizing" the understanding and discussions arrived at earlier in giving shape to bilateral discussions during the past few months, particularly, in respect of joint industrial ventures. Ground had already been cleared during the official level talks ten days earlier in New Delhi in respect of a large cement factory and a large paper factory with Indian collaboration and minority equity participation.[64]

Fernandes utilised the opportunity to discuss the problem of the control of floods and the plans to use river water resources for irrigation and power generation. He found the Nepalese response to the Indian viewpoint of joint control of floods "very positive" and was appreciative of Nepal's gesture of help and sympathy towards flood victims in India. It emerged from the discussions that the members of the planning commissions of both the countries should hold a meeting with the energy experts to formulate the plans to use river water resources for irrigation, power generation and flood control. Fernandes was satisfied with the discussions and said that a deep understanding had been reached.

The return of Mrs. Gandhi in power, at New Delhi, in January 1980 had changed the circumstances. King Birendra visited New Delhi with a view to study the mood of the new regime. Neelam Sanjiva Reddy welcomed King Birendra at a banquet speech on 6 March 1980 and expressed happiness that no major irritants existed in our relations and we must now seriously consider embarking upon programmes of exploring the wealth westowed by nature, to translate into action our mutual desire for the prosperity of our peoples. He also expressed the hope that these combined efforts would be in the best interests of our two countries. King Birendra, on the occasion in a banquet speech reply praised Indian efforts made in the development of Nepal.

In New Delhi, Birendra met Mrs. Gandhi, India's Prime Minister, on 7 March 1980 and had a 90-minute exchange of views with her. At the later stage K. B. Shahi, Foreign Minister of Nepal and his Indian counterpart, P.V. Narasimha Rao also joined the talks. They discussed in detail international situation as well as situation obtaining in this region of Asia. They agreed that all efforts should be made by all the countries of the region as well as others to reduce tension in the area. As per the joint statement, issued at the end of the visit of King Birendra to New Delhi on 8 March, 1980 the discussions also covered bilateral relations including the political, economic and technical matters. It was agreed that Nepal-India relations were characterized by mutual trust and confidence.[66] They further agreed that every effort should be made to increase contacts between the two countries at all levels to expand co-operation in mutually beneficial spheres. King Birendra during the visit availed the opportunity of renewing his acquaintances with several leading personalities of India, known in the field of politics, art and culture.

A return visit was paid by P. V. Narasimha Rao, India's Minister for External Affairs to Nepal. The three-day official visit beginning from 27 November 1981 was described by both sides as goodwill mission.[67] Although there was no structured agenda for the talks in Kathmandu, the whole gamut of India-Nepal relations were expected to come up for discussion with special focus on Nepal's proposal of zone of peace and the utilisation of Kathmandu's vast water resources. Curiosity on both sides prevailed on the eve of Rao's visit to Nepal because it would be first visit of a senior member of Mrs. Gandhi's cabinet since she assumed power in January 1980 as well as after the elections in Nepal.[68] Later at a dinner, hosted in honour of the visiting guest Nava Raj Subedi, Minister of Panchayat, Local Government and Health, HMG, recalled the age-old relationship with the India and said, "our bond of friendship, nurtured over centuries by facts of geography, history culture and economics, has been strengthened further in recent years by our mutual trust and understanding and our common aspirations of peace and development.[69] Rao too, in his reply speech cautioned Nepal against the forces of destabilization and against elements of both in internal and external which tried to disrupt Indo-Nepal friendship.[70]

According to the Indian spokesman the talks between Surya Bahadur Thapa and P. V Narasimha Rao covered a wide range of international issues and some of the more important aspects of bilateral relations, prospects of regional economic co-operation with special emphasis on Indo-Nepalese bilateral economic ties were gone into at some length.[71] During the visit Rao also met King Birendra which lasted for half an hour and was described by the latter as "satisfactory". He hoped that the high level "useful contacts" between the two close and friendly neighbours should continue to forge.[72] On 29 November Rao had opportunity to address the prestigious Nepal Council of World Affairs with distinguished gathering of intellectuals, academics and other eminent people. In his address Rao reiterated India's commitment to bilateralism and maintained that India and

Nepal instinctively understood that perpetual peace and friendship should prevail among them. He reminded Nepal that peace was one of the most important objectives of India, which was fundamental to its foreign policy, was that it wanted to live in peace with its neighbour.[73]

However, Rao's assertion in Kathmandu that Nepal could not be recognised as a zone of peace in isolation and the entire South Asia region be declared a zone of peace pained Kathmandu much and, as a result India-baiters became active in Nepal. The Himalayan Kingdom did not see any hurdle in recognising the proposal when China, Bangladesh and Pakistan had already expressed their readiness to accept the proposal. So, the Nepalese continued to keep up the anti-India chant. It was despite the fact that country's water resources minister agreed that the two had much to gain through bilateral co-operation in exploiting the rich potential of joint rivers. Elements sympathetic to this country attributed the hysterial campaign against India's failure to accept the peace Zone proposal to the strong "vested interest which the ruling elite had developed in sustaining hatred for India.[74]

In response to an invitation of King Birendra, Neelam Sanjiva Reddy paid a four-day state visit to Nepal in December 1981. As the Indian Head of the State was visiting in over a decade and a half, a great deal of significance was attached.[75] The two dignitaries after their first meeting expressed the view that the time had come to make more meaningful the existing bond of co-operation between the two countries.[76] Speaking at a banquet in his honour by King Birendra, Reddy said although India faced a difficult economic situation" our commitment to Nepal's development and our concern for the welfare of the Nepali people remain as firm as ever". He also expressed satisfaction that in recent months there had been a realisation on both sides of the need to co-operate purposefully in harnessing all available water resources to mutual benefit. Although Reddy did not refer to Nepalese proposal for declaring the country a Zone of peace on his part yet when it was raised by Surya Bahadur Thapa, Nepalese Prime Minister, he was believed to have said that the proposal should be seen in the light of the 1950 Treaty of Peace and Friendship between the two countries. President Reddy invited King Birendra and the Nepalese Prime Minister to come to New Delhi for discussions on the said proposal. However, the Indian President as he crossed the Nepalese air space thanked King Birendra for the "warm hospitality and affection of the Government and people of Nepal. In a message Reddy said," My visit has reinforced my faith in the future of our relationship and convinced me more than ever before that the friendship between our two countries will grow even further in the years to come".[79]

In the background of the successful visit of R. D. Sathe, India's Foreign Secretary, to Nepal on the one hand and narrowing down of India's differences with Peking on the other, Nepalese Prime Minister Surya Bahadur Thapa and Padma Bahadur Khatri, Nepal's Foreign Minister paid an official visit to New Delhi in early February 1983. The visit was aimed to discuss the various aspects of Indo-Nepal relations.[80] Speaking at a dinner hosted in honour of the Nepalese Prime Minister Mrs. Gandhi said that Thapa's visit would pave the way for utilising their water resources more profitably and that economic co-operation between India and Nepal would be further expanded and diversified. In reply Thapa expressed his country's appreciation for the generous co-operation India had been extending to Nepal in her economic development despite being pre-occupied with her own development.[81] As a major breakthrough in economic co-operation India and Nepal agreed upon joint execution of three major multipurpose river valley projects for harnessing the water resources for irrigation and power generation for the benefit of both the countries.[82] The Indian spokesman said that Thapa's visit had given a new impetus to friendly relations between the two countries. The talks were held in a cordial atmosphere and had contributed to strengthening their ties.[83] *The Hindustan Times*, editorially welcomed the visit and wrote that Nepal, freed of its inferiority complex, the feelings of insecurity, had launched a new phase of diplomacy as the visit was termed as "successful mission" to New Delhi.[84]

At a later stage Indo-Nepal relations deteriorated on account of Siliguri-Raxaul happenings and Nepal thinking of implementation of Gurung report, which would deprive a large number of Indian origins in Nepal from the citizenship facility. In this tense situation, Padma Bahadur Khatri, Nepalese Foreign Minister came to New Delhi on three day official visit 12-14 September 1984. Khatri, in New Delhi, discussed in detail the implementation of Gurung report with his Indian counterpart P. V. Narasimha Rao. During the talks the Indian side had taken up the question of hostile propaganda, refusal to repatriate known criminals seeking refuge in Nepal and other issues like double taxation, exchange of VIP visits and increased cultural co-operation.[85] Ram Niwas Mirdha, the Minister of State in the Ministry of External Affairs, in reply to a question in Lok Sabha on 22 August 1984 said that the Foreign Ministers of India and Nepal held two rounds of talks during which some of the projects in which India was assisting Nepal as well as matters pertaining to the latest rounds of secretary level meetings on the Karnali and the Pancheshwar Projects were discussed. Khatri was satisfied with his three day visit to India as he told reporters at the Kathmandu airport. He said that he and Rao finalised the establishment of a joint communication to oversee and co-ordinate all activities and projects of the two countries.[86]

## Politics

For the Nepalese the change of guard in New Delhi, in March 1977 made no difference as was evident at the end of the year when Morarji Desai, the new Prime Minister along with Atal Bihari Vajpayee, the Minister for External, Affairs, visited Kathmandu. Despite a definite increase in mutual confidence there was no gain on issues which had clouded Indo-Nepal relations. It was made clear on the part of the Government of India that it was opposed to any move of involving third country in the affairs of the region so far as the proposal for zone of peace was concerned, not only Nepal but the entire South Asia region be declared a Zone of Peace. The new declarations were not favourable for Kathmandu so, as earlier it continued the policy of internationalising several issues including the idea of Zone of peace. India, on the other knew it well that Kathmandu was less believable internationally and it did politics sometimes to harm and tease New Delhi and sometimes to enhance its stature.

Peking too, was anxious to know the new regime's policy towards Kathmandu. In February 1978 Deng Xiaoping visited Nepal and King Birendra assiduously endeavoured to secure a firm Chinese commitment against, India's involvement in Nepal. Deng, at Kathmandu, endorsed Birendra's proposal of Zone of peace and praised his efforts to "safeguard" Nepal's independence and sovereignty against India, but he did not commit to give a slight increase in economic aid. At the same time he also rejected Birendra's suggestion that China should be a participant in the proposed Ganges-Brahmputra River development Project to the disappontment of royal regime and the vested interest in Nepal.[87] However, King Birendra sensing the conscious attitude of the Chinese, expressed gratitude for Peking's support and declared that Kathmandu would never change its policy of friendship towards Beijing for India. King Birendra paid a visit to Beijing in May 1978 and in reply to a banquet speech on 14 May recalled that the relations between our two countries are good and marked by growing spirit of understanding and co-operation. In succession K. N. Bista, the Nepalese Prime Minister visited China in September 1978 and reaffirmed Kathmandu's policy of non-alignment, peaceful co-existence, non-interference in the internal affairs of our countries and mutual respect for sovereignty and territorial integrity which were directed towards the promotion of friendship with all countries and particularly with our neighbours.[88]

Still not satisfied and assured with the Chinese nature of help, King Birendra planned to visit Peking in August 1979. *People's Daily* welcomed the tour editorially and praised Nepal for its adherence of the principle of maintaining independence and state sovereignty. King Birendra, during the visit, sought China's firm commitment against India and as a gesture supported the Chinese policy towards Kampuchea and Vietnam. But the Chinese leaders did not demonstrate any inclination to make a firm commitment to protect monarchy. Instead, Peking expressed its intention to improve relations with India. Suddenly Kathmandu got an opportunity to exploit the situation arising from the Soviet intervention in Afghanistan in December 1979 and Mrs. Indira Gandhi's return to power, in New Delhi, in January, 1980.

Although in view of the danger in its southern frontier and the Soviet presence in Afghanistan, the Chinese were unwilling to give an open encouragement to the Nepalese vehemence against India. The Soviet action was criticized world over and Kathmandu had an opportunity to exploit it. On the occasion Birendra supported the Chinese and Pakistani as well as arms aid to Pakistan by the Beijing and the United States. He set out on a tour to Bangladesh, Sri Lanka, Singapore and Burma to mobilise them as a leverage against India. Even Foreign Minister K.B. Shahi went on to describe the US decision to rearm Pakistan as a "bilateral affair.[91]

Nepal under Birendra, had continued to play the role of a plaint client state. It was anxious to follow the Chinese lead as a device to counteract India's apprehended pressure to follow New Delhi's line. India, of course, expected Nepal to continue the policy of non-alignment. It could do business just as well with a ruling King as with a Prime Minister responsible to an elected legislature. The Nepalese tactics of playing one power against the other might work for a while but not all the time. In the long run it would not be a productive policy.[92] But just to gain sympathy the Monarch referred to his Zone of Peace proposal when he hosted a banquet to the French President Mitterrand recently and, 'President Zia of Pakistan visited Nepal in May 1983. Despite Nepalese preferences for the Peking King Birendra said that Nepal had always good bilateral relations with India and China and had never played off one against the other. While answering questions at a National Press Club at Washington, he declared, "We do not think so. This is a very short sighted approach. We will have good relations with all our neighbours".[93]

Initially Kathmandu was psychologically disturbed specially after election of Jimmy Carter as the US President. The new President was the champion of human rights and Nepal feared of cuts in US economic assistance as it was kept quite at low profile. Perhaps in response, Nepal released several political prisoners from imprisonment by the year 1978-79 to the satisfaction of Carter Administration and in a most drastic step the King announced a National referendum to be held on 24

May 1980 through which the existing Panchayat System was put on trial-to choose either reformed Panchayat system or multi-party system. Now the Americans too, had every reason to be satisfied since Carter's human rights policy was considered to be gaining ground in Nepal. Apart from this, the US had strategic importance too. Speaking at the Nepal Council of World Affairs on 9 November 1981, US ambassador Carleton Coon stated that Nepal's stability and the preservation of national integrity were as important to the US as its progress. He added that the US perceived a strategic significance in Nepal's continued internal stability and its continued regional role as a moderating, balancing and restraining influence.

By the end of 1982 Peking expressed its desire to have its relations normal with New Delhi and hence started taking less interest in anti-India activities of the Himalayan Kingdom. On the other at the moment Indo-Nepal relations deteriorated owing to dispute over citizenship issue and implementation of the Gurung report. It was in this background that Surya Bahadur Thapa, Nepalese Prime Minister, went to the United States in February 1983. George Schults, the US Secretary of State, hosted a launcheon in honour of the visiting guest in which he praised a constructive role played by Nepal towards the cause of world peace. Thapa, on his part, explained Nepalese position and added: We believe that by declaring Nepal a Zone of Peace we would be contributing to the establishment of stable peace and a conducive atmosphere for the development of not only our country but also of the region and the world as well.[94] However, Kathmandu had a definite gain during King Birendra's visit to the United- States 7-12 December 1983 when the latter had endorsed Nepalese proposal for Zone of Peace. Later the outgoing US ambassador to Nepal Carleton Coon, said at a dinner hosted in his honour by Padma Bahadur Khatri, Nepalese Foreign Minister on 1 August 1984, that relations between Nepal and the United States were based on the spirit of friendship and goodwill and both countries had been sharing common perceptions on important global issues like peace and development.[95]

Nepal-USSR relations were at the disappointing note and the Palace viewed pro-Soviet elements, as hostile to the existing regime. In the middle of 1978, a former Prime Minister Matrika Prasad Koirala, highlighted the Nepal-Soviet friendship and said that Soviet Union shared Nepalese yearning for world peace as articulated through the Zone of Peace proposition.[96] The USSR intensified its activities in Nepal during the student's stir against the existing order while pro-Moscow Communists of the Kingdom were of the view that Nepal should enter into some kind of a friendship treaty with Russia. But the King doubted Soviet intentions and turned down the proposal of pro-Russian elements. Further King Birendra even warned the Nepalese people after the return from Havana in September 1979 that we are facing a situation, similar to a cold war and hence advised the people to refrain from involving with any of the country on the basis of ideology. The Soviet Union too was not happy with the Nepalese welcoming Sino-Japanese treaty. The relations between the two countries deteriorated to a considerable extent after the Soviet intervention in Afghanistan that posed a fresh threat to the security of the region. However, the Joint Communique issued on 15 December 1981 at the end of Vasioli V.Kujnetsov, the first Vice-President of the USSR's visit to Nepal, both sides agreed that the friendship of the two nations was based on mutual respect of each other's national sovereignty and non-interference in the internal affairs of each.[97]

China's improving relations with the United States of America was a cause of concern for Kathmandu. President Reagan's visit to Beijing in 1984 strengthened the level of understanding between the two. On the other hand, despite Chinese objections to the massive Soviet armed presence along the long Sino-Soviet border, a talk for normalisation of relations was going on between the Soviets and the Chinese. In the meantime the visit of the Secretary General of the Soviet Ministry of Foreign Affairs, Yuri Fokin took place in August 1984, who expressed satisfaction over the talks he had with the Nepalese officials. He also said that he was returning home with better understanding of the Nepalese points of view on various matters.[98]

**Analysis of the Attitude**

The new regime that took reigns of administration in New

Delhi in March 1977 had no intention, as earlier, to harm Nepal's national interest in any way. It adopted a liberal attitude with India's immediate neighbours in general and Nepal in particular because for the first time it was a non-Congress Government who had nourished a soft corner towards the Socialists of Nepal. Going a step further and in response to Nepalese long-pending demands the two countries signed two treaties in March 1978 relating to the trade and transit. However, India's consistent position on international matters, such as, involving third country in the affairs of South Asia and Nepalese proposal for declaring it a Zone of Peace-an attempt on the part of Kathmandu to internationalise these issues were vehemently opposed. New Delhi, on several occasions made it crystal clear that India would oppose any such move. This unchanged Indian mood disappointed Nepalese and on these issues, positions remained unyielding. Even after the Soviet intervention in Afghanistan at the close of 1979 that posed a new threat to the security of the region Nepal, contrary to India adopted Sino-American line and lost the goodwill that Indo-USSR had for Kathmandu. The Himalayan Kingdom in collaboration with Pakistan tried to make a front against New Delhi that clouded their relations to a large extent. For a while during 1982-83 the problem of Indian origins in Nepal came to the floor but soon it became a matter of the past.

For the Nepalese the proposal for declaring their country a Zone of Peace had become a matter of sentiment rather than of security. In the name of Peace Zone proposal Nepal wanted to involve maximum countries of the world, so that it might be safe from the Indian threat. The Nepalese monarchy, in particular doubted Indian motives that it might help democratic forces in the Kingdom. Despite liberal economic attitude of the Government of India towards Kathmandu it was not satisfied on the political issues. The return of Mrs. Gandhi to power had added Nepalese fears and anxieties. King Birendra was in a hurry to have a Chinese commitment that it would protect Nepalese monarchy in the event of Indian intervention. Thus, as earlier, Nepal continued to follow the Chinese lead as a device to counteract India's apprehended pressure to follow New Delhi's line. The Indo-phobia had become a irreducible posture of the Nepalese monarchy.

## Notes and References

1. *The Times of India* 28 March 1977.
2. *Ibid*, 30 September 1978.
3. *The Hindu*, 17 April 1978.
4. *Ibid.*
5. *Ibid.*
6. *India News*, 26 December 1977.
7. *The Hindustan Times*, 1 September 1980.
8. Ibid.
9. Inder Malhotra, "Relations with Nepal: Slow Return to Realism", *The Times of India*, 6 March 1980.
10. *Ibid.*
11. *The Rising Nepal,* 5 January 1980.
12. *The Gorkhapatra*, 9 March 1980.
13. Avtar Singh Bhasin (ed.), Nepal's Relations with India and China: Documents 1947-1992, Vol.1, (Siba Exim., Delhi, 1994), p. 390.
14. *The Indian Express*. 8 December 1981.
15. *The Statesman*, 10 December 1981.
16. *Ibid.*
17. *The Hindustan Times*, 7 February 1983.
18. *The Times of India*, 5 August 1983.
19. *The Tribune*, 1 September 1983.
20. *The Patriot*, 10 September 1983.
21. *The Statesman*, 27 September 1983.
22. *The Tribune*, 27 September 1983.
23. *Ibid.,* 12 October 1983.
24. *Ibid.*
25. *The Times of India*, 1 January 1984.
26. *Ibid.*
27. The Nepalese Government had appointed a one man committee in 1982 consisting of Harka Bahadur Gurung, a former Minister of Commerce, Industry and Planning to go into the question of alleged Indian influx into the Kingdom and suggest remedial measures to control it. In a voluminous

report he submitted, he suggested many drastic measures which would amount to virtually taking away the citizenship or severally restricting the rights of many million persons of Indian origins settled there. *The Hindu*, 13 July, 1983.

28. *Ibid.*
29. *The Hindustan Times*, 16 July 1984.
30. *The Times of India*, 16 July 1984.
31. *Xinhua*, 5, 6 and 7 February 1978.
32. *The Rising Nepal*, 2 January 1980.
33. *Ibid.*, 16 January, 1980.
34. *Samiksha*, 18 January 1980.
35. Avtar Singh Bhasin (ed.), *op. cit.*, p. 388.
36. *The Patriot*, 26 June 1981.
37. Nalineet Ghildial, "Indo-Nepal Relations and China", Ramakant, B C. Upreiti (eds.), *Indo-Nepal Relations*, (South Asian Publishers, New Delhi, 1992), p. 324.
38. S. Sahay, "A Close Look-Indo-Nepal Relations", *The Statesman*, 10 December 1981.
39. *The Hindustan Times*, 1 December 1981.
40. *Ibid.*
41. *The Statesman*, 28 November 1981.
42. *The Hindustan Times*, 30 November 1981.
43. *The Times of India*, 30 November 1981.
44. *Ibid.*, 5 August 1983.
45. *The Hindustan Times*, 12 April 1982.
46. *The Statesman*, 26 April 1982.
47. *The Hindu*, 23 January 1983.
48. *The Times of India*, 16 July 1983.
49. *Ibid.*, 15 July 1984.
50. *The Indian Express*, 4 April 1977.
51. *The Hindu*, 4 April, 1977.
52. *Ibid.*
53. *Ibid.*, 17 July 1977.
54. S.C. Gangal, *Indian Foreign Policy-A Documentary Study of India's Foreign Policy Since the Installation of the Janata*

*Government of 24 March 1977* (Young Asia Publishers, New Delhi, 1980), p. 281.

55. L.S. Baral, "India and Nepal", Bimal Prasad (ed.), *India's Foreign Policy-Studies in Continuity and Change* (Vikas Publishing House, New Delhi, 1979), p. 187.
56. Aruna Asaf Ali, ed., *Link*, Vol. 19, No. 50, 24 July 1977, p. 1.
57. *The Hindu*, 10 December 1977.
58. S.C. Gangal, *op. cit.*, p. 283.
59. *Ibid.*
60. *Ibid.*, p. 284.
61. *Ibid.*
62. See the Joint Communiqué in *Asian Recorder*, 21-27 May 1978, p. 14318.
63. *Ibid.*
64. *The Times of India*, 28 September 1978.
65. *Ibid.*
66. Avtar Singh Bhasin, *op. cit.*, p. 390.
67. *The Statesman*, 26 November 1981.
68. *The Times of India*, 27 November 1981.
69. Avtar Singh Bhasin, *op. cit.*, p. 395.
70. *Ibid.*
71. *The Statesman*, 28 November 1981.
72. *The Hindustan Times*, 30 November 1981.
73. *Ibid.*
74. *The National Herald*, 6 December 1981.
75. *The Hindustan Times*, 9 December 1981.
76. *Ibid.*
77. *The Indian Express*, 8 December 1981.
78. *Ibid.*
79. *The Hindustan Times*, 11 December 1981.
80. *The Hindu*, 23 January 1983.
81. *The Statesman*, 4 February 1983.
82. *The Times of India*, 5 February 1983.
83. *The Naitonal Herald*, 5 February 1983.

84. *The Hindustan Times*, 7 February 1983.
85. *The Hindu*, 13 July 1984.
86. *The Times of India*, 15 July 1984.
87. *Die Welt*, 9 February 1978.
88. R.K. Jain (ed), *China-South Asian Relations 1947-1980* (Radiant Publishers, New Delhi, 1981), p. 431.
89. *Ibid.*
90. *The Rising Nepal*, 29 August 1979.
91. *Ibid.*, 5 January 1980.
92. *The National Herald,* 6 December 1981.
93. *The Tribune,* 10 October 1983.
94. *The Rising Nepal,* 16 February 1983.
95. *Ibid.*, 2 August 1984.
96. *Ibid.*, 20 July 1978.
97. *Barhdo Nepal-Soviet Maitri* (Soviet Information Bureau, Naxal, Kathmandu, 1982), pp. 9-11.
98. *The Rising Nepal*, 31 August 1984.

# 10

# DOMINANCE OF DEADLOCKS (October 1984—June 1991)

## Diplomacy

The brutal assassination of Mrs. Indira Gandhi on 31 October 1984 was followed by the quick succession of her elder son Rajiv Gandhi as the new Prime Minister of India. In contrast to domestic political affairs, foreign policy was a sphere where the new Prime Minister had been able to draw upon experienced and astute counsel in understanding a strategy that had proved, in broad terms, realistic, independent, rooted to the ground and successful in keeping India's flag aloft.[1] The new Prime Minister in a broadcast to the nation, elaborated his government's foreign policy and declared, "Jawaharlal Nehru bequeathed to us a foreign policy which Indira Gandhi so creatively enriched. I shall carry it forward. We want to develop closer relations with each of our immediate neighbours in a spirit of peace, friendship and co-operation. We have always believed that non-interference, peaceful co-existence and non-alignment should be the guiding principles of our relationship.[2]

Within a week of the oath of Rajiv Gandhi, Lokendra Bahadur Chand, Nepalese Prime Minister, met with his Indian counterpart at New Delhi on 4 November 1984 and discussed the matters of mutual interest. Further, Nepalese Foreign Secretary Biswa Pradhan in April 1985 during the visit of Romesh Bhandari, India's Foreign Secretary to Kathmandu appreciated the policy pursued by the new regime and said that Rajiv Gandhi's policy of strengthening its relations particularly with neighbouring countries was encouraging. The Indian Foreign Secretary in a dinner speech reply said that the new government gave top priority in the Indian foreign policy scheme to the objective of improving the country's relations with its neighbours. Nepal, he said, is an important neighbour with which India wanted to have improved relations. However, the issue of extremists clouded Indo-Nepal relations at the moment. It is a known fact that extremists and unsocial elements find it easy to slip into the contiguous territory in an effort to evade arrests. Consequently the governments of both the countries had developed a disbelief towards each other[3] to the extent that even honest assurances of the leadership fail to generate confidence. The bomb blast of June 1985 in the Nepalese capital[4] and earlier terriorist acts in the different parts of the country[5] were not the outcome of India's support, but a projection of the socio-economic and political discontent simmering beneath the surface due to the rising graph of poverty, unemployment and exploitation. It was the hightime that the leaders of both the countries should evolve a co-operative mechanism to discourage such activities in the sub-region. The incidents followed a letter from the Indian Prime Minister Rajiv Gandhi delivered by his special envoy Shiv Shankar to King Birendra on 5 July, 1985, assuring him that India was committed to co-operating with all countries in curbing "the growing menace of terrorism". The message was in the light of the reports that those suspected of being responsible for the series of explosions in Nepal on 20 June 1985 were based in India.[6] When King Birendra visited New Delhi in September 1985, Indian President Zail Singh also reiterated India's clear and consistent policy towards its neighbours. He said, "It is based on panchsheel, the principles of non-alignment and those enshrined in the UN Charter. We are convinced that an atmosphere of peace and stability in our region, free from terrorism, violence and conflict is essential for economic development and prosperity."[7] A return visit was paid by Zail Singh, Indian President to Kathmandu in July 1986.

But the problems in Indo-Nepal relations appeared on surface following India's role in Sri Lanka and Maldives and at a later stage differences between the two countries on the renewal of trade and transit treaty signed in March 1978. In June 1987 when India supplied food to Sri Lankan Tamils by a military aircrafts, Nepal had deplored the event and expressed grave concern "because Nepal has always and everywhere condemned any violation of the territorial integrity of sovereign states."[8] Kathmandu also objected the use of Gorkha troops by the Indian Peace-Keeping Force (IPKF) in Sri Lanka. India was surprised to see the reports that the Nepalese authorities viewed the IPKF role in Sri Lanka's communal terms; on the basis of a specific clauses (Annexure III para 3) of the Tripartite Treaty of 1947 between India, Nepal and Britain which said,. "Gorkha troops shall not be used against Hindu or any other unarmed mob."[9]

Perhaps, keeping in view the recent developments in Indo-Sri Lanka relations, Kathmandu had apprehended Indian motives and felt insecured. King Birendra directed the Nepali negotiators in March 1988 to finalise a deal with the Chinese. In June July 1988 hundreds of trucks, carrying sensitive cargoes reached Nepal through Kodari-Kathmandu highway. The Nepalese purchase of arms was against the Indo-Nepal Friendship Treaty of 1950 and negation of the 1965 agreement on import of arms between the two countries. Although Nepal pleaded that the purchased arms were defensive weapons,[10] but the treaty of 1950, in Nepalese perception, was itself embodied "unequal" relationship and Kathmandu wanted to take care of its own security. It had no wish to find itself entangled in Indian security webs woven by Indians. The King of Nepal wanted his Kingdom to be "non-aligned" between India and China. It was an old wish, now brought to reality. Even the responsible Nepalese treated the 1950 treaty as an old world's treaty. So much had happened in the world in the last four decades. Nothing of that reflected in the Indo-Nepalese Treaty.[11]

In addition, unfortunately, the vision of 1950 treaty had been eroded and that too, became a cause of serious concern for New Delhi. According to Articles six and seven both the countries will provide national treatment to the citizens of the other country in territory with regard to participation in industrial and economic development of such territory and grant concessions and contracts relating to such development. Further they will be granted same privileges in the matter of residence, ownership of property, participation in trade and commerce in the country concerned.[12] In violation of the above articles and despite the fact that a large number of Nepalese continue to enjoy all the rights, stringent restrictions had been placed on ownership of property by Indians in Nepal. In April 1987 something much more serious happened and the Government of Nepal included Indians in the category of foreigners requiring work permits for employment in any organised sector. The work permit system was initially for three districts but in September 1988 it extended to the whole of the country. As the news of this effect were flashed in newspapers that the work permit and identity cards, introduced by His Majesty's Government in organised sector on a limited scale, had deprived many Indian nationals of employment opportunities in Nepal, the chief spokesman of his Majesty's Government Radhey Shyam Bista termed the report as "false and misleading". He said "The provision of work permit and identity card is neither aimed against the Indian nationals nor against the SAARC objectives".[13] However, it was certain that the new system had been introduced to the disadvantage of the Indian migrant workers in Nepal. They had been treated improperly and in many cases humiliated. With such a partisan attitude the bilateral relationship was bound to come into the ambit of the question mark.

The purchase of arms from China and Kathmandu's descriminating attitude towards the Indian migrants in Nepal naturally hardened Indian attitude on the treaty of trade and transit. On 23 March 1978 India-Nepal signed two separate treaties on trade and transit. Before the signing of the treaty there were only two transit points that as a result increased to fifteen. Doubtless, Morarji Desai, the then Prime Minister of India, did so in the sincere belief that generosity to a small neighbour would engender goodwill and perhaps gratitude. But what it produced instead was blatant and reckless increase in the smuggling into India of third country consumer goods, imported under the transit treaty for Nepal's own use. This was so because, over the years, the ruling establishment in Kathmandu had gone out of its way to erode and damage the special relationship between India and Nepal born of extremely close ties of geography, history, economics, culture and religion.[15]

The Treaty of Trade and Transit which was signed in 1978 continued until 1988 and was extended twice for the period of six months each, continuing till 23 March 1989. Now the Transit Treaty had actually expired and it brought bilateral trade relations to a grinding halt, putting the Nepalese to great inconvenience. The closure of transit points further affected adversely, interests of those who were engaged in trade business in Nepal. Growing tensions in the Indo-Nepal relations surfaced and no solution seemed in sight. Both began to blame each other for the non-renewal of the transit treaty. The present crisis had energised an internal political debate in the Kingdom, particularly so because the ordinary Nepalese had been hit hard economically, for no fault of theirs. It exihibited the extent of the gap that existed between Nepal's social needs and state priorities.[16] Kathmandu wanted to renew the transit treaty in the existing form whereas New Delhi desired to discuss the whole gamut of Indo- Nepal relations in accordance with the changed circumstances and was in a mood to sign single unified treaty in place of the two. Although Nepal was ready to sign the treaty and King Birendra, in a new year's message to the nation said, "it is indeed unfortunate that at a time when all our energies were being directed to fulfilling the minimum basic needs of our people, we have been exposed to hardships imposed on us by our geography as a landlocked country. As is known to all my government is ever ready to settle this problem through friendly dialogue and negotiations."[17] However, the heart of the deadlock was referred by Kirtinidhi Bista, former Prime Minister of Nepal, in course of an interview when he said that India should respect and understand Nepal's legitimate aspirations for a resolution to the problem. Nepal should also strive to lessen India's doubts and apprehensions "instead of adding to its perplexities".[18] As the events moved faster, the policies of the royal establishment left no option for the Government of Rajiv Gandhi but to look to its own country's interest first. Nepal should have been wise enough to know that India would not sit idle seeking its security interest jeopardised. No government worth the name would allow that to happen.[19]

Although, even at this crucial juncture Nepal failed to arouse sympathy in the Indian public, foreign policy makers of New Delhi had to face a strong criticism for its handling of its relations with Nepal. But P. V. Narasimha Rao, Minister for

External Affairs, told the Parliamentary Consultative Committee on External Affairs that India will take into account its paramount security interests while formulating its Nepal policy. They added further that India would also take into account the interest of its citizens and the people of Indian origin living in Nepal.[20] However, at the same time they reiterated India's desire to have friendly relations with Nepal and indeed with all its neighbours. India had all the goodwill towards the people of Nepal and wished them well.[21] Thus, the message conveyed to the palace was clear that India would not compromise with Kathmandu where issues concerning its security and interests of Indians residing or working in Nepal were concerned. On trade it was for Nepal to decide whether it wished to continue with its post-March 23 decision of Most Favoured Nation (MFN) basis of trade or on the previous arrangement with some modifications. New Delhi was equally firm in safeguarding its bilateral interests.[22]

Sensing India's unyielding attitude on the issue and, as crisis within the monarchy-ruled country began to deepen, some positive signals for restoring the stalled Indo-Nepalese dialogue were emerged from Kathmandu. Initially the King of Nepal seemed to have determined to show that in the present day world the small is not entirely at the mercy of the big.[23] Kathmandu's efforts to internationalise the issue to mobilise public opinion at home and gain positive support from the donor countries for its cause but by way of assistance it could neither get petroleum products to run the wheels of industry and transport running nor monetary assistance to save economy from collapse. On the other hand, New Delhi had already conveyed Kathmandu that if it wanted to resolve the problem sincerely, it must stop internationalising the issue- and its anti-India propaganda war through its official media.[24] In the circumstances, P. V. Narasimha Rao, India's Minister for External Affairs, in a major breakthrough to resolve the stalemate in Indo-Nepal relations went to Kathmandu on a two-day visit 25-26 August 1989. Useful discussions were held with the King and his Nepalese counterpart, Shailendra Kumar Upadhyaya.[25] The conversation was "marked by cordiality and understanding in the true tradition of Indo-Nepal friendship. The much awaited Summit between Rajiv Gandhi, India's Prime Minister and the Nepalese King Birendra also succeeded in removing misunderstandings on certain issues and Nepalese Foreign Minister termed the meetings as "very useful."[26]

Rajiv Gandhi's foreign policy was said to be a "muscular policy." In that perspective New Delhi's attitude towards the neighbour was of an arrogant big brother rather than that of a co-operative friend. Consequently, India not only sought to bargain from a position of strength but even indulge in teaching a lesson to them, if the need arose.[27]

As a result of the general elections held in November 1989, with the support of the Bharatiya Janata Party and the Left Front, Vishwanath Pratap Singh became the new Prime Minister of India. Although the election was fought on domestic issues, the Indo-Nepal relations received adequate publicity in the speeches of the political leaders. The National Front manifesto had referred to India's relations with Nepal and stated that "negotiations will be started on all issues of contention to find an amicable solution" and also help" strengthen the economy of Nepal and honour her self-respect.[28] V. P. Singh, the Prime Minister of India, after taking over the office expressed his government's keenness to take all possible steps to improve its relations with Nepal.[29] On 2 December 1989, in an interview he said that an "undue shock was given to Nepal, and the trauma, which Nepal had to undergo due to the deadlock in Nepal-India trade and transit relations, is quite unnecessary."

Kathmandu too, welcomed the change of guard in New Delhi. Prime Minister Marich Man Singh Shrestha, in his message of congratulations to the new Indian Prime Minister, said that he was encouraged by the latter's reported statement to improve relations with Nepal and assured his full co-operation and support towards improving the traditional, close and friendly relations between Nepal and India to the mutual benefit of the peoples of both countries. *The Rising Nepal* in its editorial, while welcoming the new dispensation stated that everyone was wishing V.P. Singh's success in his endeavours, hoping that Nepal's position in favour of a dialogue to end the unfortunate stalemate in Nepal-India relations would be reciprocated and that definite steps would be taken earlier towards improving the bilateral relations.[30]

But as far as the basic content and substance of the foreign policy was concerned, V. P. Singh soon realised that there was no scope for a sharp divergence or major departure, while answering a question he conceded that foreign policy is not partisan. It meant that it does not belong to a single party. It is dictated by geo-political considerations.[31] He elaborated this idea in course of an interview to a foreign media when he said that in relation to Nepal security issue between the two countries needed to be settled early. The National Front Government did not bring about a drastic change in India's Nepal policy. In the circumstances, Shailendra Kumar Upadhyaya, the Nepalese Foreign Minister, visited New Delhi 2-5 January 1990 for talks on the Indo-Nepal trade and transit dispute.[32] The talks were held, according to a foreign policy spokesman, in cordial and friendly atmosphere, covered the entire gamut of relations and were aimed at achieving understanding on broad components of bilateral relationship.[33] However, no breakthrough came as a result of these negotiations. Despite the fact that New Delhi was willing to accommodate Nepal, it was not willing to surrender its security and other concerns, while negotiating with Nepal. India was not prepared to give security a back seat while talking to Nepal. Hence it belied the hopes of several people, particularly in Nepal, that with the change in government, things would get normalised. The strategic perceptions of the government were not substantially different from their predecessors.[34] As a follow up of this visit, official level talks were held in New Delhi 3-5 February 1990 between delegations led by the Foreign Secretaries of the two countries.

The success of V. P. Singh in building an anti-Congress front in India in 1989 showed that centrist and leftist parties could join hands politically for a clear-cut objective. The year also witnessed a common objective for the Nepali Congress and the leftist parties in the Himalayan Kingdom. This common approach was to have a multi-party political system in Nepal in place of the partyless panchayat system. Thus, a new political grouping was intended to organise a political struggle for democracy. In the new system King Birendra was bound to appoint the leader of the majority party as his Prime Minister. On 18 February 1990 the movement for democracy started. Ultimately the revolution celebrated its victory on 19 April 1990 by the swearing-in- of a new ministry with Krishna Prasad Bhattarai as the Prime Minister. Bhattarai, in a letter to the Prime Minister of India on 30 April 1990 said, "I am deeply grateful for your friendly sentiments and encouraged by your expression of desire to resolve Nepal-India relationship and strengthen it in all areas. 1 fully reciprocate your friendship and wish to assure you of my whole-hearted effort to that end.[35] He also proposed a meeting at the highest level with India for a political settlement and added that for him there was no prestige issue on such a vital matter which was affecting the entire Nepalese people and also the Indian people living on the other side of the border.[36]

As the Interim Government in Nepal led by Bhattarai was more responsive to Indian initiatives and sensitivities, Inder Kumar Gujral, India's Minister for External Affairs, said in an interview with *The Rising Nepal*, a Government- owned English daily, that India was willing to accommodate the economic aspirations of the Nepalese people.[37] He hinted that India was disturbed about "security concerns" and descrimination of Indian nationals in Nepal. "If these two things are sorted out there will hardly be anything which can keep us away from co-operation.[38] It was an opportune moment and in a bid to minimize the economic problems of the people of Nepal as well as widen his political support, Bhattarai came to India and negotiated with it in June 1990. The understanding reached between the two governments brought an end to almost a year long stalemate. Governments of India's agreement to open all the traditional points of transit for trade purposes and a few more to allow foreign tourists to visit Nepal had indeed been widely acclaimed in Nepal.[39] The acrimony and suspicion that marked Indo-Nepal relations during the past two years or so had given way to a new phase of mutual understanding and goodwill.[40] As a follow up, the accord implementation was reviewed in August 1990 when Inder Kumar Gujral paid a three-day official visit to Kathmandu.[41] The Indian Foreign Minister also met King Birendra, who expressed the desire that India should play a major role in the regional development of South Asia through SAARC. The situation on both the sides became favourable to a point that Kathmandu turned to India for expert advice and friendly consultations for Constitution Recommendation Committee and, New Delhi, in response, made available the services of Dr. Laxmi Mall Singhvi, eminent constitutional expert and Jurist together with Bombay based leading lawyer and writer on constitutional issues A. G. Noorani.[42]

In November 1990, the Bharatiya Janata Party had withdrawn its support from the National Front Government and Chandra Shekhar succeeded V. P. Singh as the new Prime Minister of India. The first country, the new premier choose to visit was Nepal in February 1991 at a time when Nepalese were going to embark on the great democratic exercise of universal adult franchise with a view to institutionalising parliamentary democracy. In Kathmandu Chandra Shekhar discussed with Bhattarai, his Nepalese counterpart, in an cordial atmosphere. He sought to dispel misconceptions in Nepal that India being much bigger in size would try to dominate Nepal's economy but suggesting that the two economies were characterized by a relationship of interdependence rather than of dependence.[43] The multi-party elections under the new constitution were held on 12 May, 1991 and Chandra Shekhar, the Indian Prime Minister, sent the warmest felicitations and goodwishes to Girija Prasad Koirala on assumption of Prime Minister's office of the Himalayan Kingdom.[44]

**Strategy for Security**

With the formation of South Asian Association for Regional Co-operation (SAARC) Nepalese interest and efforts for declaring the Kingdom as a Zone of peace had diminished to a large extent. Kathmandu viewed this regional association as a substitute for Nepalese concept of security against the big powers. As the international situation was marked by complexities and confusion, King Birendra was worried about the independent survival of small states of the region in particular. On 2 May 1985 when the President of Maldives visited Nepal, King Birendra at a banquet referred to the drama how the strong, the powerful and big meddle into the affairs of the small and the weak countries by the use of or rather the abuse of ideas, the media and even arms covertly or overtly. It was against this dismal world order that the poor and developing countries faced an unprecedented challenge to their dignity and independence. It was in line with this policy that Nepal attached great importance to SAARC as it provided a forum for increased contacts and co-operation among the countries of this region.[45] At the moment Nepalese security perception was significantly influenced by the development in Sri Lanka and New Delhi's soft corner for the Indian settlers there. Randhir Subha, Nepalese Foreign Minister, in a defying mood said, "India's perception of her security has to change. The Nepalis feel that they have a right to think of their security".[46]

India's interference in the trouble-torn Sri Lanka's Tamil problems made Nepal apprehensive and, feared of creating another Jaffna in the Terai region of Nepal. Kathmandu understood the desire of India to help the Sri Lankan Tamils on humanitarian grounds but at the same time it had deplored the air dropping of food materials in Jaffna in 1987 without prior consultation with Colombo. On the other, Peking had made it clear that gone are the days when General Chen Yi promised of "two bullets for one" fired from the Indian side. Hence, Nepal could not count on China's armed support in any confrontation with India brought about by Nepal's own actions. King Birendra's other friends like the UK, the USA and Japan were too far away to be of much help because of geographical separation from the landlocked Kingdom of Nepal.

In the circumstances, King Birendra had decided to buy ground to air missiles and other hardware from China. The purchase of arms was not merely against the Article 5, 6 and 7 of the Treaty of Peace and Friendship as provision under five of the treaty says: "The Government of Nepal shall be free to import from or through the territory of India, arms, ammunition or warlike material and equipment necessary for the security of Nepal. The procedure for giving effect to this arrangement shall be worked out by the two governments acting in consultations".[48] Other than this, the deal with China was a negation of the 1965 agreement on import of arms, between India and Nepal, which had made India the major arms trade partner of Nepal.[49] By violating these two, Kathmandu seemed to have a step further in its search for strategic diversification and distancing from India..[50] New Delhi's main concern was that by doing so Nepal had violated the basic understanding between the two countries in matters of security, because Kathmandu had neither consulted nor informed India before entering into such a deal. The palace, perhaps, was aware of this fact and soon after the guns had been ordered King Birendra was told with the utmost deference that the order would badly hurt Indo-Nepal relations. The cost he was told, would be far more than the loss if the deal were cancelled. The King's response was that it was too late.[51]

In July 1988, about 500 trucks with the Chinese arms rolled on the Chinese built Kodari-Kathmandu road to the airport to deliver military supplies reportedly included anti-aircraft guns, medium range missiles A. K. 47 rifles, huge quantities of ammunition and uniforms, etc. The deal was kept such a close guarded secret in the palace that even the Prime Minister and his cabinet colleagues did not know about it until it was fully executed.[52] The fact that Nepal used China as a counter balancing force against India was denied by Marich Man Singh Shreshtha, the Prime Minister of Nepal. Replying to a discussion on the Nepalese government's policies in the Rashtriya Panchayat, he maintained that Nepal had done nothing against India and had no intention of doing such thing in future. Nepal did not believe in playing one friend against the other, Nor did it believe in improving its ties with one at the cost of the other.[53] Perhaps, in favour of the Chinese arms deal he said, "our defence arrangements are related only to our internal security. Therefore, the question of any threat to neighbours does not arise." As for Nepal "We do not feel any threat from anyone."[54]

At this juncture, New Delhi began to feel that it was unnecessarily needled. The Indian military establishment also resented Nepal's overtures to China. The Indian line was that there was a point beyond which it would not tolerate free wheeling and security was that sticking point. Nepal's buying of arms from China was therefore, unpardonable. India also wanted to know from Nepal what it would like the framework of the relationship to be. If the Treaty of Friendship of 1950 was in a number of ways irrelevant now, then what should be new guidelines be.[55] Even in Nepal, the majority of the people, as elaborated by G.P. Koirala, leader of the Nepali Congress, were not in favour of the arms deal with China. He criticized the royal government that on the one hand Nepal had been advocating the cause of establishing a Peace Zone and on the other it is buying arms from China that too, at the cost antagonising one of its major trading partner-India who accounted 50% of Nepal's trade.[56] It had indeed cost us on the diplomatic front, was very dear as it affected adversely the Indo-Nepal relations which had always been cordial.[57] These were a general feeling in Nepal that it had not been paying due regard to India's security concerns.[58] It was in this background and dispute over the work permit issue, New Delhi hardened its attitude on the renewal of the treaty of trade and transit that led to a lot of miseries for the Nepalese People.

When on 1 December 1990. Vishwanath Pratap Singh succeeded Rajiv Gandhi as the Prime Minister of India the hopes were raised in Nepal that the trade and transit treaty would be reviewed. But the situation improved only when in April 1990 an Interim Government was formed under the premiership of Krishna Prasad Bhattarai. The new Prime Minister paid an official visit to New Delhi in June 1990 during which India agreed to maintain status quo in regards to treaty of trade and transit. Bhattarai, in response, gave a categorical assurance that his country would take care of Indian suspectibilities on security matters and would not allow Nepal to be a base for any anti-Indian activity.[59] The joint communique, issued at the end of the visit said, "India and Nepal agree to respect each others security concerns. The two countries shall have prior consultations with a view to reaching mutual agreement on such defence related matters which in the view of either, could pose a threat to its security."[60] By accepting the security concerns of India an implicit assurance was elicited from Nepal that it would not use a policy of equi-distance, violating Indian security interests, and this included not granting the Chinese projects in the Terai and importing arms from China.[61] The new Indian Government reiterated its stand to respect Nepal's sovereignty and an assurance of non-interference in the way the Nepalese want to conduct their affairs. Inder Kumar Gujral, the Minister for External Affairs, during his visit to Kathmandu in August 1990, said, "There will be no interference in politics, as we have found that interference has never paid."[62]

In place of V. P. Singh, Chandra Shekhar became the Prime Minister of India in November 1990. He appointed Dr. Bimal Prasad as India's ambassador to Nepal who accepted Nepalese relations with Peking. Dr. Prasad added further that geographically China held a key position, north of Nepal. Hence it is essential for Nepali leaders to maintain good relations with China and we should understand this point.[63] The security matters and Nepal's relations with Beijing were also discussed between Bhattarai and Chandra Shekhar when the latter took a visit to Nepal in February 1991. In course of the formal talks, the Nepalese Prime Minister had asked for India's help in raising two more mountain divisions for his army. With the Indian response, being cautious in view of the forthcoming elections in Nepal, Bhattarai appeared to have suggested that Nepal might have to seek China's assistance if India demurred. More or less, Candra Shekhar followed the wise policy of the National Front government towards Nepal.

**Exchange of Visits**

King Birendra of Nepal visited New Delhi in September 1985. At New Delhi he met several political leaders including Rajiv Gandhi, India's Prime Minister and the discussions held between them, covered a broad spectrum of subjects relating to bilateral and international relations. In course of the talks the King's proposal of Nepal being declared as a 'Zone of Peace' also figured. Indian President Zail Singh hosted a banquet in honour of the visiting King on 18 September 1985 and said that Nepal is more than a neighbour for us. India is determined to expand and enrich our contacts with our neighbours. Many initiatives have already been taken by us. He also took the opportunity to reiterate common traditions and historical experiences, that the two countries shared.[64] King Birendra in a reply speech felt the need of not only a renewal of old contacts but also the beginning of a new friendship that understands and appreciates our aspirations and difficulties. He expressed gratitude once again to the people and Government of India for their gesture towards Nepal. In the past three decades something in the building of infrastructure in Nepal has been achieved. Fortunately, the government and people of India have not merely been sympathetic, but have positively contributed to the cause of economic development in Nepal.[65]

In July 1986, President Zail Singh paid a visit to Kathmandu and discussed with King Birendra the matters of mutual benefit. Speaking at a banquet King Birendra welcomed Indian President on behalf of the government and people of Nepal and sought for India's more co-operation to secure the basic needs of her people. He expressed the hope that with abiding goodwill and a common desire to build our destiny together we look forward to a steady growth in mutual co-operation. As a matter of fact, we have been impressed by the sense of purpose and commitment shown by the leadership in India towards the promotion of understanding and co-operation in the region.[66] The Indian President in reply, reaffirmed India's commitment to the maintenance of friendly relations with all countries based on the time tested principles of Panchsheela and on the recognition of the need for interdependence, co-existence and co-operation for mutual benefit. Regional co-operation among the nations of South Asia has taken root and become a well established concept which has been welcomed by all the countries of the region. It is only by strengthening the framework of co-operation among the SAARC nations that we shall be able to speed up the process of economic development and provide a brighter future for our peoples.[67]

Rajiv Gandhi too. viewed this regional institution as of great significance while, improving India's relations with the neighbours. He had aptly made use of personal diplomacy and the extension of economic and technical assistance. Speaking at the SAARC Summit in Kathmandu, on 2 November 1987, the Indian Prime Minister spoke about, "the multi-faceted co-operation" evolved under the Association; and, envisaged "development comprising much more than economic growth".[68] He emphasised that "people should be kept at the core of the development process. King Birendra came New Delhi on 29 September 1988, primarily in his capacity as Chairman of

SAARC and discussed measures to further develop areas of mutual co-operation. There was special emphasis on areas of special interest to the common man in all the SAARC countries, such as, housing, environment and food security. The bilateral matters between India and Nepal were also reviewed in depth.[69]

Nepal had started flouting the security clause of the Treaty with India and purchased anticraft guns from China. Events came to a head when the Treaty lapsed on 23 March 1989. Nepal wanted that trade and transit should be covered in a separate treaty. India's plea for the continuance of a unified treaty was disregarded. Nepal had refused to come forward for negotiations and instead dragged the issue of the abrogation of the treaty to the United Nations and other world fora like the World Bank and the IMF.[70] In this background of Indo-Nepal relations, P. V Narasimha Rao, Minister for External Affairs, visited Nepal 25-26 August 1989 to initiate the process of discussions. It was in keeping with India's position of wanting normal relations with Nepal despite the problems that could not be wished away. The discussions with Nepalese Foreign Minister Shailendra Kumar Upadhyaya would be on the basis of mutual respect and common benefit.[71] Diplomatic circles felt that India had timed it well so as to prepare a good meeting ground for Prime Minister Rajiv Gandhi and King Birendra at Belgrade during the NAM Summit in September 1989.[72]

On 25 August 1989 Rao was called on King Birendra and the meeting was described as the centre piece of the current bilateral dialogue. Both sides attached considerable significance to the discussion, the first of its type since the two countries began their drift in March this year. But Rao's meeting with Nepalese leaders including the King was an indication that he was in Kathmandu for purely preparatory works and not meant for discussions on substantive issue.[73] The only achievement despite this was that a basis had been established to continue the-discussions.[74] Rao told newsmen at the Tribhuvan international airport that he was "very satisfied with the discussions. It was good successful and hopeful." When he was asked about the outcome of the discussions Rao smilingly said, "We have agreed to agree."[75] In a major breakthrough to resolve the five month old stalemate in Indo-Nepal relations, Prime

Minister Rajiv Gandhi and King Birendra of Nepal have agreed to have a summit meeting at Belgrade on September 4 during the forthcoming non-aligned Summit.[76]

The new government, which took over in New Delhi on 1 December 1989 under the premiership of Vishwanath Pratap Singh, inherited a strained Indo-Nepal relations. The new government expressed keenness to take all possible steps to improve its relations with Nepal. Kathmandu too, was willing with the change of government in New Delhi to resolve through meaningful negotiations, its dispute with India.[77] In this positive and hopeful background Shailendra Kumar Upadhyaya, the Foreign Minister of Nepal visited New Delhi 2-5 January 1990 for talks on Indo-Nepal trade and transit disputes.[78] The discussions, held between the Foreign Ministers of the two countries on the first day was seen as the beginning of a new bilateral chapter. According to a Foreign office spokesman the two sides agreed to work for the opening of a new chapter, notwithstanding what had happened in the past to lead to strains and tensions. They underlined the importance of friendly relations between the two countries like India and Nepal with a long history of amity and good neighbourliness to regional co-operation as a whole and to the activities of the SAARC in particular.[79]

Though no immediate solution emerged at the end of two day's talks, the mist of obstacles, suspicions and misunderstanding that characterized the relations between the two countries in the past year had been cleared.[80] At the same time, the approach of the new government, as evidenced during the talks, seemed intended to convey to Nepal that India harboured no ill will towards its neighbours and that all its problems would receive sympathetic consideration. The joint statement, issued at the end of the visit on 5 January 1990 at New Delhi said that the discussions took place in an atmosphere of great warmth, sincerity and cordiality. They resulted in great mutual understanding of each other's interests and concerns and of the problems affecting their bilateral relations that needed early solution. As per the decision during this visit, a Nepalese official delegation led by Foreign Secretary N. B. Shahi came to New Delhi 19-22 February 1990. The talks held between them contributed to greater mutual understanding of each other's serious concerns and sensitivities. They registered progress towards a comprehensive solution of all outstanding problems.[81]

As a result of the mass movement led by the pro-democratic elements in April 1990, an Interim Government was sworn-in with K. P. Bhattarai as the Prime Minister of Nepal. Soon after the assumption of office, Bhattarai proposed a meeting at the highest level with India for a political settlement to the year long impass in the relations between the two countries.[82] Inder Kumar Gujral, India's Minister for External Affairs, in an interview expressed India's readyness to respond positively to the economic aspirations of the people of Nepal.[83] In this friendly and cordial atmosphere K. P. Bhattarai paid a three-day visit to New Delhi in June 1990. Bhattarai was to discuss with the Indian leaders the entire gamut of bilateral relations, trade and security issues would get special attention.[84] The Interim Government, on its part, as a gesture of goodwill and to accommodate India's susceptibilities on security matters; postponed the purchase of the last consignment of arms from China.[85]

The Indian Prime Minister V. P. Singh hosted a dinner in honour of the visiting dignitary on 8 June 1990 and said, "We attach high priority to improving relations with our neighbours. In this Nepal has pride of place. India and Nepal shared ties that go back to the beginning of recorded history". He added, "I am confident that through our mutual friendship, we will find a common way out for a unanimous solution to our problems which will be fair and effective to both the sides.[86] Responding to the speech Nepalese Prime Minister said that he was impressed by the depth and intensity of the care and feeling with which India wanted to improve bilateral relations.[87] At New Delhi Bhattarai was happy over the talks that covered all aspects of bilateral relations which came under a severe strain following a trade and transit row after the expiry of bilateral treaties in March 1989.[88] According to an offical spokesman the discussions were marked by "particular warmth and cordiality. The talks went beyond the schedule and the full delegation level discussions could not take place.[89]

The Joint Communique signed at the end of the visit on 10 June 1990 said that the trade and transit ties would be restored by 1 July 1990. It stated "The two leaders declared their solemn intention to usher in a new era of co-operation between the two countries, particularly in the sphere of industrial and human resource development, for the harnessing of the waters of the common rivers for the benefit of the two peoples and for the protection and management of the environment.[90] The biggest achievement is the faith restored and Bhattarai's visit will mark a watershed. As he himself admitted the problem was confusion "partly on our side, partly on the Indian side too that has gone."[91] Soon after his arrival in Nepal Bhattarai told the newsmen that his talks with his Indian counterpart V. P. Singh had helped remove all misgivings. Both the countries would now work with mutual trust and confidence. For him it was a big political economic triumph. His government could now resonably devote all attention to the framing of a new democratic constitution and the holding of elections.[92] King Birendra also understood to have expressed his happiness at the accord between the Prime Ministers of India and Nepal.[93]

In an encouraging and hopeful atmosphere, Inder Kumar Gujral, India's Minister for External Affairs, went to Nepal on a three-day visit 5-7 August 1990. According to the competent sources, the main purpose of the visit was to review the implementation of the accord signed by V. P. Singh and K. P. Bhattarai in June this year.[94] By the tour Gujral looked forward for further strengthening of relations between the two countries.[95] In his talks with the Nepalese counterpart, assured Nepalese leaders of India's support to build a new prosperous democratic Nepal. He also agreed to a Nepalese request to open up three additional entry points for non-Indian tourists along Nepal's border with Uttar Pradesh.[96] King Birendra expressed the desire that India should play a major role in the regional development of South Asia through the SAARC when Gujral met with him in course of the visit on 6 August which lasted for half an hour.[97] The Indian Foreign Minister had also an opportunity on 5 and 6 August to address Nepal Chamber of Commerce and Nepal Council of World Affairs respectively, in which he reaffirmed India's policy towards neighbours. *The*

*Rising Nepal*, in its editorial on 9 August concluded that the visit had reaffirmed the deep bonds of friendship and understanding between the two countries. It added further that the prevailing rapport should be maintained for mutual benefit, without compromising the national interests of either side.[98]

Chandra Shekhar, the new Prime Minister of India who assumed office in November 1990 was scheduled to visit Kathmandu in February 1991. The timing of the visit was viewed variously in political circles here as it came just a couple of months before the Himalayan Kingdom's first multi-party elections after the restoration of democracy.[99] But there were others who took a more "balanced and realistic view of Indo-Nepal relationship. This school of thought claimed that Chandra Shekhar was visiting Nepal only to keep his own words. Soon after assuming office of the Prime Minister he had said that his first "official visit would be to Nepal, a close and friendly neighbour with whom India's relations have indeed been varied and wide ranging from time immemorial."[100] The three-day visit of the Indian Prime Minister was expected to review the impact of various tariff concessions and other facilities given to Nepal on trade with India.[101] In Kathmandu, according to the spokesman Chandra Shekhar would have a heavy schedule, apart from his engagements with the King and the Nepalese Prime Minister, he will met a wide cross section of political leaders and attend several public functions.[102]

In course of the visit the two governments had several fruitful discussions, benefitting the two countries. According to a decision the joint Sub-Commission on Water Resources would meet from April 15-17 in the Indian capital at the level of Secretaries. The meeting would review the entire range of co-operation and, would also finalise matters concerning future plans. India would help Nepal in expanding the Bir Hospital by adding 200 beds to those existing, and it would also consider a Nepalese proposal for setting up another hospital at Birganj.[103] However, the visit failed to disguise the fact that the Indo-Nepal relations had not yet emerged from the woods of suspicion. This was reflected in both the banquet speech of the Nepal's Prime Minister K. P. Bhattarai and in the talks between the two Heads of Governments which the Indian spokesman said was marked by frankness, cordiality and warmth.[104] In the banquet speech on 13 February, Bhattarai pointedly stated that Indo-Nepal relations had to be based on the principles of sovereign equality, territorial integrity and non-interference in one anothers internal matters. During the one to one formal talks differences between the two came to the surface on security matters.[105]

**Politics**

Initially, under the Premiership of Rajiv Gandhi the Nepalese viewed no threat for their security. Kathmandu's rigidity for declaring Nepal a Zone of peace was diminished later due to the emergence of a regional institution namely South Asian Association for Regional Co-operation (SAARC) comprising India, Nepal, Bangladesh, Sri Lanka, Pakistan, Bhutan and Maldives. But the security perception of the Himalayan Kingdom began to change with the Tamil problems in Sri Lanka. A large number of people of Indian origin were residing in the Terai region of Nepal and it was natural for them to be apprehensive of the same problem in their country. It deplored Indian handling of the issue and dropping of food materials for the Tamils without the consent of the Sri Lankan Government.

On the other, the growing Sino-Nepalese interaction in economic and political field was a part of a broader Chinese strategy and had vital security implications for India. Several scholars believed that unless China asserts itself as a power to be reckoned within the Asian region, global aspirations would simply be meaningless, but in this regard, it seemed to perceive an Indian threat to its role. Almost certainly, China could hardly play a significant role in South-East Asia where American strategic and recently Japanese economic interests are predominantly and hence, Peking had no choice but to play a role in South Asia region.[106] Perceiving an Indian threat to its role in the area, it thus, attempted to enter the region in a big by feeding anti-Indian diet to the small nations neighbouring India. Consequently it had tried always to improve relations with other countries at India's cost.[107]

Perhaps being fearful from the developments in Sri Lanka, Kathmandu decided in early 1988 to have a security deal with Beijing. This step was taken by Nepal at a time when there was already some tension in its relations with India in the wake of the expiry of the trade and transit treaties of 1978. The actual expiry of the treaty on 23 March 1989 led to the untold sufferings for the Nepalese people. The attitude of the Government of India became stiff on the issue because, in utter violation of the Peace and Friendship Treaty of 1950, Kathmandu had grew its defence understandings with China. Secondly, Kathmandu had imposed several restrictions unilaterally in its trade dealings with New Delhi and began to discriminate Indian settlers there. Perhaps, in the circumstances Rajiv Gandhi, the Prime Minister of India, visited China in December 1988 and received a major breakthrough. During his stay in Beijing the two countries had signed a cultural agreement. A joint working group was formed to oversee India-China relations, generally and, to maintain peace and tranquillity in the border areas specially.[108]

The deadlock over the trade and transit issue had affected adversely the economy of Nepal and internal politics as well. The Indian Prime Minister declared that India would not sign trade and transit treaty separately and would be happy to discuss even the Treaty of Peace and Friendship, if so desired by Nepal. But the Nepalese leadership, at one point, declared that it was not willing to continue its trade links with India and liked to have transit facilities to clamour that India had imposed an economic blockade on the borders.[109] Although a section of the Nepalese people expected India to make continue concessions that are not normally extended by one government to another except on grounds of close friendship. But friendship was the last thing that Nepal's power elite seemed willing to display towards New Delhi.[110]

To add insult to the injury, Nepal tried to internationalise this issue by propagating against India and dispatched envoys to China, USA, Pakistan, Bangladesh, South-East Asian countries and to the United Nations Organization. A delegation of Nepali legislators under the leadership of the President of the National Assembly was first to raise its voice at its joint meeting with members of the European parliament in Brussels against the no treaty regime allegedly imposed by India against Nepal. Thereafter at the Asian Development Bank Meeting in Beijing the Nepalese Finance Minister talked about the enormous economic losses likely to be sustained by Nepal as a result of India's action in restricting the supply of essential commodities. Finally, at the ministerial meeting of the Coordinating Bureau of Non-aligned countries, the Nepalese Foreign Minister himself, in disregard of the convention of not discussing bilateral differences at the non-aligned meeting publicly accused India of straining relations with Nepal, in a manner quite incompatible with the spirit of non-aligned countries to promote co-operation between themselves.[111]

However, China, USA and Pakistan had suggested Nepal not to internationalise the issue but to sort out the same amicably because these powers knew perfectly that there was no economic blockade whatsoever on the borders as propagated by Nepal.[112] At the moment Nepalese calculation of China fell flat. Kathmandu had envisaged solid moral and financial support from China. But Peking had made it clear to the Nepalese ministers its inability to commit and extend any solid assistance to the landlocked country.[113] In a significant development, Nepal was further disappointed when the Chinese Premier Li Peng's visit to Nepal took place in November 1989. In contrast to the Nepalese expectations, the premier expressed his government's incapability to provide greater economic and political support for Nepal, as in his opinion, Beijing was already confronted with the problems both at home and abroad.[114] At the same time he reaffirmed China's policy to develop good neighbourly and friendly relations with every country in South Asia big or small. He also referred to the vast improvement in Sino-Indian relations since Rajiv Gandhi visited China. After Premier Li Peng's visit it appeared that Nepal would not be able to play the China card against India. However, the premier was not happy on India's insistence that Nepal should clearly specify its stand on the security perception.[115]

For the United States of America Nepal's balanced economic development was crucial for the subcontinental peace and stability. Perhaps, it was this thinking that prompted the Bush Administration to urge India to break the impass on trade and transit treaty. Although the US had no doubt that Nepalese economic dependence on India cannot be abandoned. At best it could be moderately reduced. The US Officials, however, argued that American aid to Nepal is designed to support its economic development and to continue the role for regional equilibrium. Howard Schaffer, US Deputy Assistant Secretary of State for the Near East and South Asia, on 27 February 1989 justified the concept before the House Foreign affairs sub-committee and said :

> "Demonstrating our support for Nepal's sovereignty, our aid programme is designed to support Nepal's own efforts to achieve balanced economic and political development".[116]

In the wake of the Indo-Nepal stalemate over the trade and transit treaty the Government of the United States had categorised the trade stand off largely "a bilateral dispute and called for mutual settlement; while many Congressional insiders criticized India's trade blockade of Nepal as "an explicit show of muscle"[117] As the impass prolonged the US Congress had threatened "stronger responses" if India continued to be "indifferent" to the misery of the Nepalese people. Just before the 101st Congress adjourned, Representative Richard Durbin personally delivered to Indian Ambassador Karan Singh a petition signed by 49 legislators. The petition asked New Delhi to "actively pursue a quick negotiated settlement" of the disagreements between the two countries. It assailed the blockade saying that it represented "an astonishing indifference to the economic misery and spiritual suffering of the Nepalese people.[118]

However, the officials of the US maintained that it had no intention to pressurize India but urge it to "end the perception that it is pulling undue pressure on a small neighbour.[119] A US State Department spokesman stated that India's good gesture will make a major contribution to the regional stability and good-neighbourliness".[120] In fact, the US was urging in this matter to take a "liberal and humanitarian view of the problem in the larger interest of the region.[121] Acting on its long term strategy in Nepal the United States continued to extend financial support to the Himalayan Kingdom. In the financial year 1990, the Bush Administration recommended a total aid of 12.6 million dollars to Nepal, including a development assistance of

$ 12 million.[122] In April 1990 an Interim Government under the premiership of K. P. Bhattarai was formed, the stalemate ceased to exist two months later. In the changed situation as claimed by Stephen Solarz, Chairman of the US House of Representatives Sub-Committee on the South Asia and Pacific, India was keen to reach an agreement with Nepal and that "the establishment of democracy in the Himalayan Kingdom has created the basis for close relationship between the two neighbouring countries.[123]

The Soviet Union was a well wisher of New Delhi and hence did not want to change the regional balance that might undermine Indian influence. It realised that strained Indo-Nepalese relations might be encashed by India's adversaries like Pakistan and Sri Lanka. Since India and USSR had converged on strategic and security perceptions, the strategic equilibrium would be disturbed if intra-regional problems become more perturbing and external forces make strategic thrust into the regional affairs. Keeping these facts in view and due to its strategic concerns, the Soviet Union was in favour of an early resolution of bilateral problems between India and Nepal. When after 23 March 1989, India stopped supplies of essential commodities it (the USSR) immediately agreed to review the agreement on the supply of petroleum products to Nepal. K. U. Kuimatov, the Soviet Ambassador to Nepal, reiterated that his government was willing to supply petroleum and oil products to save Nepal from economic hardships.[124] Thus the Soviet Union wanted to prevent the situation from taking an ugly turn sought to allay Nepalese fears that Soviets would postpone or refuge supplies of petroleum and oil products. This stance of the Soviet Union made it amply clear that India would continue to receive their full co-operation and succour despite regional realignments or global strategic shifts.[125]

**Analysis of the Attitude**

As earlier, Nepalese quest for its security either in the concept of declaring Nepal a Zone of Peace or strengthening and widening of South Asian Association for Regional Co-operation (SAARC) was continued. In no way the foreign policy of Rajiv Gandhi was differ to that of Indira Gandhi that made the

Himalayan Kingdom fearful particularly after the developments in Sri Lanka's Tamil problem. Apart from finalising a defence deal with Peking Kathmandu began to alienate the Indian settlers in Nepal and introduced Permit System that deprieved a lot of Indians from their livelihood. Although Nepal had done it to avoid Sri Lanka type situation in the country, it pained New Delhi to a considerable extent. When the treaty of trade and transit expired on 23 March, 1989 India refused to renew it or continue it in the present form. As a result the Nepalese people had to face a lot of difficulties and, on the other his Majesty's Government tried to internationalise the issue by specifying it as the economic blockade against Nepal, but in vain. A time came when the people of Nepal began to blame their own government for the hardships and internal political problems increased. Following the change of guard in New Delhi in December 1989 an Interim Government was formed in Kathmandu in April 1990. The two freshers came out with a conciliatory attitude and a status no was restored in June 1990. Except some reservations on security matters, Kathmandu remained co-operative with New Delhi.

On the other, India had resented from the beginning for making any bilateral issue a international one. In the initial years of Rajiv Gandhi's premiership there was no surfaced problem between the two countries. But New Delhi's soft attitude towards the Tamils in Sri Lanka made Kathmandu apprehensive of its motives. Two issues-Nepalese purchase of arms from the Beijing and introduction of work permit system in regards to Indian settlers there made Indian attitude stiff over the renewal of trade and transit treaty in the present form and hence allowed to expire. Nepalese made efforts to raise the issue in various international gatherings but India adopted a wait and watch policy towards the developments. Actually, India wanted to discuss with Nepal the whole gamut of its relations and needed some clarifications on defence deal with Beijing and rules which were anti-Indian in trade transaction. In the meantime, change of guards in both the countries created favourable circumstances and a status quo was restored. With the establishment of democracy in Nepal it was hoped that the relations between the two countries would be strengthened in coming years.

## Notes and References

1. B.K. Ahluwalia and Shashi Ahluwalia, *Rajiv Gandhi—A Profile in Courage* (International Publishing House, New, Delhi, 1985), pp. 81-82.
2. *Ibid.*, pp. 74-77.
3. *The Times of India*, 26 September 1985.
4. *Ibid.*, 29 August 1972.
5. *Ibid.*, 22 June 1985.
6. Keesings Contemporary Archives, August, 1985, *op. cit.*, p. 33784.
7. Avtar Singh Bhasin (ed.), *Nepal's Relations with India and China, Documents 1947-1992*, Vol. 1 (Siba Exim, Delhi, 1994), p. 424.
8. *Ibid.*, pp. 434-35.
9. *The Hindu*, 8 July 1989.
10. Chanchal Sarkar, "Some Irritants-Indo-Nepal Relations", *The Hindustan Times*, 10 April 1989.
11. Bhabani Sen Gupta, "India and Nepal-End of Special Ties" *Ibid.*, 24 May 1989.
12. S.K. Chaturvedi, "Indo-Nepal Relations : Tension Areas", *Foreign Affairs Reports*, Vol. XXXVIII, No. 5, May, 1989 (Indian Council of World Affairs, New Delhi, 1989), p. 76.
13. Avtar Singh Bhasin, *op. cit.*, p. 437.
14. Inder Malhotra, "Political Commentary : State of Play with Nepal", *The Times of India*, 27 April 1989.
15. *Ibid.*
16. S.D. Muni, "A Common Destiny", *Ibid.*, 23 April 1989.
17. *Ibid.*, 14 April 1989.
18. A.G. Noorani, "India-Nepal Relations : The Heart of the Matter", *The Indian Express*, 11 April 1989.
19. A.N. Dar, "Mr. Bhattarai Plays it Right", *The National Herald*, 16 June 1990.
20. *The Times of India*, 6 May 1989.
21. *Ibid.*
22. *The Hindustan Times*, 14 June 1989.
23. *Ibid.*, 26 May 1989.

24. *Ibid.*, 14 June 1989.
25. *The National Herald*, 27 August 1989.
26. *The Times of India*, 13 September 1989.
27. Pradip Bose and G.S. Bhargava, "India and Her Neighbours", G.S. Bhargava (ed.), *Perestroika in India : V.P. Singh's Prime Ministership* (New Delhi, 1990), p. 130.
28. Manorama Kohli, "Foreign Policy Initiatives of the National Front Government in India" Ramakant (ed.), *South Asian Studies*, Vol. 25 No. 1 and 2 January-December 1990 (South Asian Studies Centre, Jaipur, 1990), p. 139.
29. *The Times of India*, 13 December 1989.
30. *The Rising Nepal*, 4 December 1989.
31. *The Times of India*, 16 December 1989.
32. *The Hindustan Times*, 1 January 1990.
33. *The Hindu*, 4 January 1990.
34. *The Times of India*, 13 December 1989.
35. Avtar Singh Bhasin, *op. cit.*, p. 471.
36. *The Times of India*, 23 April 1990.
37. *Ibid.*, 2 June 1990.
38. *Ibid.*
39. Jagat S. Mehta, "Blazing a New Trail", *The Indian Express*, 31 August 1990.
40. *The Patriot*, 12 June 1990.
41. *The Times of India*, 4 August 1990.
42. *The Hindustan Times*, 10 August 1990.
43. *The Hindu*, 14 February 1991.
44. Avtar Singh Bhasin, *op. cit.*, p. 515.
45. *Ibid.*, pp. 421-22.
46. *The Indian Express*, 11 April 1989.
47. *The Front Line*, April 28, May 11, 1990.
48. A.S. Bhasin, *Documents on Nepal's Relations with India and China, 1949-66,* (Academic Book, New Delhi, 1970), pp. 254-55.
49. *The Statesman*, 27 May 1989.

50. S.D. Muni, "Chinese Arms Pour into Nepal". *The Times of India*, 1 September 1988.
51. *The Hindustan Times*, 10 April 1989.
52. *The Times of India*, 1 September, 1988.
53. *Ibid.*, 11 July 1989.
54. *Ibid.*
55. Chanchal Sarkar, "Cornered Kingdom", *The Indian Express*, 2 September 1989.
56. *The Hindustan Times*, 1 January, 1990.
57. *Ibid.*
58. S.K. Jha, "Nepal's India Policy", *Foreign Affairs Report*, Vol. XXV, No. 11, November, 1976.
59. *The Times of India*, 11 June 1990.
60. *Ibid.*
61. Sangeeta Thapliyal, "Nepal in India's Security Parameters", *Strategic Analysis*, Vol. XVIII, No. 9, December 1995 (Institute for Defence Studies and Analysis, New Delhi, 1995), p. 1201.
62. *The Statesman*, 23 August 1990.
63. *The National Herald*, 6 January 1991.
64. Avtar Singh Bhasin, *op. cit.*, pp. 423-24.
65. *Ibid.*
66. *Ibid.*, pp. 429-30.
67. *Ibid.*, pp. 430-32.
68. Adish C. Aggarwala, *Rajiv Gandhi : An Assessment* (Amish Publications, New Delhi, 1993), pp. 65-66.
69. Avtar Singh Bhasin, *op. cit.*, p. 435.
70. Adish C. Aggarwala, *op. cit.*, p. 67.
71. *The Hindu*, 24 August 1989.
72. *The Hindustan Times*, 25 August 1989.
73. *The Hindu*, 26 August 1989.
74. *Ibid.*, 27 August 1989.
75. *The National Herald*, 27 April 1989.
76. *Ibid.*
77. *The Hindustan Times*, 9 December 1989.

78. *Ibid.*, 1 January 1990.
79. *The Hindu*, 4 January 1990.
80. *The Statesman*, 6 January 1990.
81. Avtar Singh Bhasin, *op. cit.*, p. 467.
82. *The Times of India*, 23 April 1990.
84. *Ibid.*, 2 June 1990.
84. *The Hindu*, 8 June 1990.
85. *The Times of India*, 8 June 1990.
86. Avtar Singh Bhasin, *op. cit.*, p. 473.
87. *The Statesman*, 9 June 1990.
88. *The Hindu*, 11 June 1990.
89. *Ibid.*
90. Avtar Singh Bhasin, *op. cit.*, p. 485.
91. *The Statesman*, 11 June 1990.
92. *The Hindustan Times*, 11 June 1990.
93. *The Times of India*, 15 June 1990.
94. *Ibid.*, 4 August 1990.
95. *The Tribune*, 5 August 1990.
96. *The Indian Express*, 6 August 1990.
97. *The Hindustan Times*, 7 August 1990.
98. *The Rising Nepal*, 10 August 1990.
99. *The Patriot*, 11 February 1991.
100. *The Times of India*, 11 February 1991.
101. *Ibid.*, 12 February 1991.
102. *Ibid.*
103. Avtar Singh Bhasin, *op. cit.*, pp. 513-14.
104. *The Hindu*, 14 February 1991.
105. *Ibid.*
106. Nalineet Ghildial, "Indo-Nepal Relations and China", Ramakant, B.C. Upreiti (eds.), *Indo-Nepal Relations*, (South Asian Publishers, New Delhi, 1992), p. 327.
107. *Ibid.*
108. Adish C. Aggarwala, *op. cit.*, p. 65.

109. S.K. Chaturvedi, *op. cit.,* p. 78.
110. *The Statesman* (editorial) 29 August 1989.
111. Rishikesh Shaha, "The Nepal-India Imbroglio", *The Indian Express*, 24 June 1989.
112. S.K. Chaturvedi, *op. cit.,* p. 78.
113. *The Patriot*, 26 May 1989.
114. Nalineet Ghildial, *op. cit.,* p. 327.
115. *The Hindustan Times*, 21 December 1989.
116. *US Official Text*, 28 February 1989, p. 13.
117. *The National Herald*, 15 April, 1989.
118. *The Hindustan Times*, 5 December 1989.
119. *The Times of India*, 28 May 1989.
120. *Ibid.*
121. *Nepal News*, 1 May 1989.
122. *US Official Text*, p. 116.
123. *The Patriot*, 3 June 1990.
124. B.M. Jain, "Role of Super Powers : Security and Strategic Dimensions", Ramakant, B. C. Upreiti (eds.) *op. cit.,* p. 340.
125. *Ibid.*

# 11

# POSITIVE POSTURES
## (June 1991—December 1997)

### Diplomacy

In the general elections held in India, Congress Party voted to power and, its leader P.V. Narasimha Rao assumed the office of Prime Minister on 21 June 1991. Soon after the taking over his office, despite lack of considerable interest among a cross section of the Nepalese intelligentsia, Kirtinidhi Bista, the former Prime Minister of Nepal described Rao as a "niceman, a man of understanding" under whose stewardship the relations between Nepal and India are likely to improve and the principle of "mutual benefit and co-operation is expected to thrive to the satisfaction of both the countries.[1] King Birendra and Girija Prasad Koirala, in the Nepalese Parliament referred to the inseparable ties with India and said that Nepal would continue its efforts towards signing trade and transit treaties and agreement on co-operation to control unauthorised trade with India.[2] But Kathmandu was less than happy for the new Prime Minister can not said to have maintained a "personal rapport" which his predecessors with the possible exception of V. P. Singh had with the Nepalese leaders.[3] People from various walks of life including Man Mohan Adhikari, President of the United Communist Party and leader of the opposition in the Nepalese Parliament, wanted to have an amicable relationship with India because of the open border, cultural heritage, religious, social intercourse and also economic factor.[4]

In a cordial and co-operative atmosphere and as a follow up of the decision during Chandra Shekhar's visit to Nepal in February 1991, the two countries conducted three successful meetings of the Indo-Nepal task force in August, September and

October. After the end of the second meeting the two sides expressed satisfaction that they had been able to evolve a comprehensive framework in the area of trade and commerce and three hydro-electric projects.[5] It had explored this field of great length. The Joint Commissions's meeting was expected to touch some of their proposals and a number of initial agreements on the subject may be signed during G. P. Koirala's visit to India in the first week of December 1991. In course of the visit the discussions between the two countries were held in an atmosphere of the utmost warm friendship and sincerity. A number of key decisions were taken with a view to deepening and expanding mutually beneficial co-operation.[6] With the series of agreements signed during the visit India and Nepal once again began to build their economic and cultural relations within a framework of treaties that had been damaged in pursuance of misconceived politics.[7] A return visit was paid by P. V. Narasimha Rao, the Indian Prime Minister, to Kathmandu in October 1992, which marked a substantial improvement in trade sector, in particular.[8] Nepalese intimate relations with India was an important in Kathmandu's foreign policy as 619-member ruling National Congress General Council (Mahasamiti) in its recently presented report noted the need for extensive economic and political ties between the two neighbours.[9] In sequence Koirala too, had said that Nepal had "very good" relations with India and he wanted to further strengthen these cordial ties.[10] He even claimed that if some issues came up both countries were now in a position to sit together and resolve them amicably.[11]

However, all these did not mean that relations between India and Nepal had come so perfect and intimate that all kinds of differences had been evaporated. True, the problems were not intense at the moment but their existence was unquestionable.[12] Prime Minister G. P. Koirala was under a fair amount of pressure. He faced attacks not only from the United Marxist Leninist opposition, but also from within his own party. In September 1992 the General Secretary of the Party questioned the award of a contract to India to extend the Tribhuvan international airport and not to China. Relations with the Government of India and the King of Nepal had not been smooth. King Birendra's proposal for declaring Nepal a "Zone of peace" was specially irksome to New Delhi which was interpreted a means to give equal status to China and India.[13] Although both the King and the Nepalese Prime Minister had been emphasising equally important its friendship with both the neighbours. G. P. Koirala, in reply to a question said that Nepal had good relations with its northern neighbour China and described it as an index to the success of Nepal's foreign policy and added that both the countries India and China were cordial, friendly and sympathetic to Nepal.[14]

The relations between the two countries were strained when in March 1994 Delhi Police raided two houses in Kathmandu, in search of a person allegedly involved in a murder case in New Delhi. As a mark of protest, the Nepalese Government called the Indian Ambassador to Nepal Dr. Bimal Prasad to its Foreign Office and handed over a protest letter to him pertaining to the raids on 27 March 1994. All MP's strongly criticized India for interfering in sovereignty and integrity of Nepal.[15] But the Government of India done well in promptly assuaging the feelings of Nepal over the unfortunate incident. Expressing "great regret" over the incident New Delhi reiterated its policy of "strict respect and scruplous adherance to the principle of non-interference in the internal affairs of Nepal and respect to its territorial integrity and sovereignty.[16] Considering the present upbeat mood in Indo-Nepal relations, Minister of State in the PM's office Bhuvanesh Chaturvedi paid a two-day visit to Nepal as Rao's special emissary. In Kathmandu he reaffirmed India's desire to forge closer economic and commercial relations with the landlocked Himalayan Kingdom.[17]

The Government of India was unfortunate in the sense that despite heavy investment in Nepalese economy with the motive of helping the poor people of the country, in return it had to face humiliation at the hands of the communists in the Himalayan Kingdom. The Communists were always in search of some excuse which could provide them an opportunity to start an anti-India tirade. On the other, the Chinese were fortunate that they had cultivated good friends in Nepalese press who always portrayed Peking as a good friend of the Kingdom where as India is projected as a devil who wants to engulf Nepal. It was a fact that the Indian foreign policy towards Nepal had never been up to mark, otherwise steps could have been initiated well on time to counter anti-India propaganda in Kathmandu.[18] In a landmark judgement the Supreme Court of Nepal made it obligatory for foreigners including Indians to obtain work permit or in technical term "Permission from the Labour Ministry via their employer if skilled persons wanted to work in Nepal. The judgement had been operative from 15 May 1994 and surprisingly the court had not consider it necessary to refer to the Indo-Nepal Treaty of Peace and Friendship of 1950.[19]

Indo-Nepal relations were passing through a tense phase and expected to remain so. The Communists who had a pro-China and anti-India inclinations, emerged as the single largest party in the elections held in November 1994. It rode to power on the anti-India, G. P. Koirala wave which was primarily against his pro-Indian image.[20] One of the promises made by Prime Minister Man Mohan Adhikari before the polls was to seek the review of Nepal's 1950 treaty with India. Adhikari campaigned against the treaty because it proved convenient to him in an atmosphere which was anti-India.[21] The new Prime Minister found a tilt in India's favour and declared it to be reviewed.[22] He also refused to accept Indian security umbrella and expressed the desire to have free trade with both Pakistan and Bangladesh.[23] At the moment New Delhi was watching new Nepal which had turned red recently[24] but at the same time on its side, great care should be experienced in not giving any impression of big brotherliness. Efforts had to be intensified to increase cultural and other contacts between Nepal and India.[25] In the circumstances King Birendra of Nepal came to New Delhi and expressed the hope that Indo-Nepal relations would further strengthen in all fields in the months to come.[26] In the same month, Nepalese King, the constitutional head, in his address to a joint sitting of both houses of parliament, on the policies and programme of the newly formed government said that Nepal would balance its ties with India and China on the basis of non-alignment, the five principles of peaceful coexistence and mutual respect and interests.[27] However, the two countries discussed the entire gamut of Indo-Nepal relations in a spirit of friendship and understanding which characterised by mutual respect for the complete sovereignty, territorial integrity and independence of each other.[28] The two countries also held a fruitful discussions of mutual interest when a Nepalese delegation led by Foreign Secretary Kedar Bhakta Shrestha visited New Delhi in June 1995.[29]

Nothing substantial was done in India-Nepal relations during the Premiership of Atal Bihari Vajpayee, who took the oath of the office on 16 May 1996 and had to resign on 28 May 1996 because he could not manage to get the support of the required members in the Lok Sabha. H. D. Deve Gowda succeeded him as a leader of the thirteen political party's United Front on 1 June 1996. Under the new dispensation Inder Kumar Gujral became the Minister for External Affairs. In July 1996, the Communists, in particular, became critical in Nepal inside and outside parliament over the news that India had encroached Nepalese territory in the east. On 3 July the border officials of the two countries after an understanding decided to identify boundary pillars, construct reference pillars and erect the damaged boundary pillars on the basis of the old map of 1874. The agitation in Kathmandu was pertaining to the controversial Junge pillar built across Mechi river in 1818. Although the Indian embassy in Nepal, in a strongly worded press release on 25 July said, "There is no question of boundary pillar being manipulated to the advantage of either Nepal or India. For less are the possibilities of forcible alteration of any of the border lines.[30] Prakash Chandra Lohani, the Nepalese Foreign Minister said, "The newly built markers in Jhapa are in line with the 1816 Sugauli Treaty and they were constructed only on being approved by the joint field team representing both Nepal and India."

For the last several years, Nepal had been facing the problem of Bhutani refugees of the Nepali origin who were driven out by Bhutan and were now attempting to cross the border from the Indian side. In the two-day meeting of Nepalese Foreign Minister P. C. Lohani with Indian leaders in August 1996, Kathmandu sought India's direct intervention in the matter because Bhutan and Nepal had held eight round of talks on the issue, but without success. The Government of India viewed it a bilateral issue and the dispute should be resolved between Kathmandu and Thimpu. Inder Kumar Gujral, India's

Minister for External Affairs, made it clear that both Bhutan and Nepal continue to be India's good neighbour. New Delhi would not like to get involved in any controversy between the two.[31] Apart from this, Lohani said that India had agreed in principle to allow Nepal alternative transit routes through Kakar Bhitta, Phulbari and Bangla bandh points to take its goods to Bangladesh. He also disclosed that on the Indo-Nepalese treaty, both sides have agreed to review it at the "appropriate" level and time.[32] It went to the credit of the coalition Government in Nepal to have the Mahakali treaty ratified on 20 September l996, by an overwhelming majority in the Joint Session of Parliament. The ratification had paved the way for foreign investment in Nepal. Had the treaty been rejected in parliament it would have led to a serious crisis in the government.[33]

In a significant political development in India, Inder Kumar Gujral succeeded H. D. Deve Gowda as country's Prime Minister on 21 April 1997. The new Prime Minister went to Nepal in June 1997 and discussed the matters of mutual interest in a cordial and co-operative atmosphere. The two sides took a number of decisions and as a follow up senior officials from the Home Department of the two countries held their first meeting at Kathmandu in July 1997 which continued for three days. At the end of the talk it was stated that the two sides have agreed to evolve a mechanism to enhance co-operation to check the infiltration of terrorists, smuggling of arms and ammunition, trafficking of girls and crime on both sides of the 1750 kms. open border.[34] Man Mohan Adhikari, as a gesture of goodwill, congratulated the people of India, President of India and Prime Minister on the Golden Jubilee celebration of India's independence and referred to the fact that several Nepalese politicians made their contribution in the freedom struggle.[35]

With the visit of Indian Prime Minister to Kathmandu most of the suspicions existed between the two countries had been evaporated. In the two-day talks between India and Nepal at the Foreign Secretary level concluded in August 1997, in which both sides agreed that a final decision on granting long term transit trade rights to Nepal would be taken after India examined its security concerns.[36] In the discussion the main focus was on the 1950 Treaty of peace and Friendship, which was found as a bedrock of a "special relationship" binding the two countries. Of course, Nepal had been particularly keen to see the treaty changed and had raised the issue time and again. The Indian side made it clear that New Delhi's attitude on the treaty issue had been marked by a certain hesitancy in the past, partly because Kathmandu, while pressing for change did not appear quite clear about the content of such change. It would certainly help the officials of the two sides if the political parties in themselves were persuaded to evolve some kind of a consensus on the issue.[37]

In the first week of October 1997 the six month old coalition government was voted out of power in Nepal and in place of Lokendra Bahadur Chand, Surya Bahadur Thapa became the new Prime Minister of the country. Like many Nepali Congress stalwarts, 69-year old Thapa had graduated from the Allahabad University had done several stints as minister under different governments.[38] In an interview given to *The Hindustan Times* he admitted that India is our close neighbour and none can change this geography. Keeping in view the problem of mass poverty in Nepal he laid emphasis to take advantage of the proximity with India,[39] and execute the hydel projects to advance on the path of progress. Under Mahakali Treaty signed in June this year India and Nepal would jointly execute Pancheshwar project and in pursuance of the decision taken by the high level delegations from India and Nepal made reasonable progress in sorting out the irritants to finalise the detailed project report (DPR) of pancheshwar hydel project.[40] However, at the close of the year a reported reference, the Jain Commission interim report said quoting Research and Analysis Wing's (RAW) letter stating that "the Queen of Nepal has asked major General Aditya Shamsher Jang Bahadur, an honorary aide-decamp to King Birendra, to arrange for the assassination of Rajiv Gandhi" for which Rs.10 crore would be made available.[41] As the news came the Nepalese authorities have taken strong exception to the unsubstantiated references to Queen Aishwarya in the Jain Commission report. India regretted aspersions cast on Nepalese royalty and described it as "groundless and misguided. The External Affairs Ministry spokesman said, "India holds their Majesties the King and

Queen of Nepal in the highest esteem and deeply cherishes her traditional friendly relations with Nepal."[42] In the meantime, on the Jain Commission's controversy between United Front and the Congress, Gujral Government resigned. Because Political parties failed to form viable combination, on 4 December 1997, Indian President K. R. Narayanan dissolved 11th Lok Sabha and the new House was to be constituted by 15th March 1998.

**Strategy for Security**

The concept of security is not static.[43] Human nature being dynamic, society is also ever-changing and so is the concept of security which has to be adjusted in order to promote human development. The concept of security has undergone a change. It is no longer confined to the military or territorial threats to a state but also considers non-military threats. The emphasis has now shifted on the internal source of threats emanating from within the boundaries of the state. The contemporary approach to security takes into consideration the non-military threats, such as, coercive diplomacy, economic and psychological warfare, political subversion, defamatory propaganda, terrorism and political violence.[44]

Though India's relations with its neighbours did not remain untouched by the changing global politics, its security perceptions remained unchanged. The disintegration of the Soviet Union and the end of the cold war shifted the focus of international actors from geo-economics in which no particular nation asserts supremacy. India and China have opened their doors to foreign investors and globalised their economies and responded favourably to each other to improve their relationship. Bilateral negotiations took place in 1988 and 1992 when Prime Minister Rajiv Gandhi and President R. Venkatraman visited China respectively and in 1992 when Li Peng visited India. As a step to normalise their relationship, both governments agreed for Army-to-Army contacts such as exchange of information regarding troop movements and reduction of troops posted along the border.[45] Hence, the conventional threat from China to the Indian security does not exist at the moment, but this does not diminish the strategic importance of Nepal mainly because geo-politics cannot be negated for the sake of geo-economics.

Perhaps, considering the changing international politics and a thaw in Sino-Indian relations, Nepal tried to redefine its security concerns. Commenting on Nepal's security concerns, Koirala said, "The very concept of security is undergoing a radical change. It is no longer limited to the traditional security systems. It is and will be equally determined by economic, socio-humanitarian scientific, technological and environmental factors."[46] Prime Minister Koirala was criticized for having pro-India inclinations but he denied the charge and told the Pratinidhi Sabha in July 1991 that any reference to the "inseparable ties with India" in various fields constitutes only a statement of realities and does not in any way, signal a leaning towards that country.[47] But at the same time he also declared, "As far as our ties with two great neighbours, India and China are concerned, we wish to further strengthen mutual trust and friendship and give them a practical orientation based on ground realities.[48] Despite this, in an important declaration during his visit to New Delhi in December 1991 he said that "in future" Nepal would not depend on arms purchase from China. It was a good news for New Delhi but what was more important was the openness that marked the Nepali premier's approach towards the question, the lack of which in Kathmandu had once clouded its relations with India.[49]

The terrorism in India roped in Nepal. The terrorists and criminals from India started taking refuge on the Nepalese soil. Besides the Kashmiri and Sikh militants, other insurgent groups such as the Bodos and the United Liberation Front of Assam (ULFA) have also been reported to use Nepal as a sanctuary, often with the help of Pakistan Embassy.[50] Although the possibility of Nepal becoming a transit route for drugs is enormous due to its proximity to the Golden Gescent in Central Asia and Golden Triangle in South East Asia.[51] The use of brown suger and synthetic drugs is on the rise in Nepal which finds its way either through the air or land route.[52] Despite the fact that the arms, drugs, and money nexus is not alarming in Nepal, it can become a security threat if left unchecked as through the open border arms can be transported to the terrorists, insurgents or the underworld.

India and Nepal have recognised terrorism and drug trafficking as a new emerging threat to their security and have discussed it at various levels. In 1992 on his visit to Nepal the Indian Prime Minister P. V. Narasimha Rao, had expressed his concern over the issue on which Nepalese Prime Minister G. P. Koirala had assured his government's co-operation to resist terrorism and to deter terrorists from using Nepal as a transit camp.[53] Similar sentiments were reiterated by Man Mohan Adhikari during his visit to India in April 1995. He said that anti-India activities would not be allowed from Nepal's soil. On Kashmiri terrorists taking shelter in Nepal, he said, "we will crack down and put them behind bars.[54]

During the premiership of H. D. Deve Gowda controversy between the two countries arose regarding the pillars built on the border but was settled by the border officials of India and Nepal.[55] India had also increased its co-operation in security and anti terrorism. After H. D. Deve Gowda, Inder Kumar Gujral became the new Prime Minister in April 1997. He took a visit to Nepal in June 1997 and discussed with Nepalese leaders the problems related to security. The two-day talks at the Foreign Secretary level held at New Delhi, in August 1997, had included security discussions. Both sides agreed that the easy trans-border access provided under the provisions of the 1950 treaty had at times been used by terrorists, arms smugglers and other outlaws as an escape route. They also felt the need to redefine the "special relationship" in terms of current realities and the security concerns.[56] For instance, with the patronage of the politicians and connivance of the custom officials about five hundred trucks cross the Raxaul border every day and majority of them carry goods from Calcutta port to Nepal.[57] On both sides of the open border, smuggling activities are on high. Early in October 1997, Surya Bahadur Thapa, the new Prime Minister of Nepal, in an interview commented on the 1950 treaty and said, "Instead of raising a hue and cry in the public, we should have clarity about our requirements. Senior bureaucrats from India and Nepal should thrash out the technical details which should be followed by political commitment to solve the problems."[58]

At present Nepal is facing serious threat from Maoist who have killed more than 150 people and they are reportedly having links with LTTE and ULFA. In this changed circumstances Kathmandu proposed to purchase arms from India when India's Chief of Army Staff, General V. P. Malik went to Nepal in November 1997, on his six-day official visit. General Malik discussed with his Nepalese counterpart about the common problem of terrorism faced by India and Nepal and there was unanimity over the enhancement of co-operation to tackle such problem. He also said that Indian army was ready to impart the training to Nepalese officials to deal with terrorism.[59] Following the discussion, Nepalese Foreign Minister Kamal Thapa told the newsmen in Calcutta, where he came to attend Indo-US investment summit, that it would not allow any subversive activity on its soil against India and called for a fresh Indo-Nepal treaty in the present day context.[60]

**Exchange of Visits**

At the invitation of P. V Narasimha Rao, the Prime Minister of Nepal Girija Prasad Koirala paid a state visit to India 5-10 December 1991. His visit to India was an acute realisation that though it was hard to establish democracy, it is going to be much harder to stabilise and strengthen it.[61] Koirala is also aware that his government cannot meet popular expectations without assistance from friendly countries. India is the only country that Nepal can count upon for genuine and substantial help in strengthening the democratic process.[62] In addition, the visit was preceded by the second meeting of the Indo-Nepal Joint Commission on 4 December, 1991. The joint commission meeting had been preceded by three meetings of Indo-Nepal High Level Task Force, with the mandate preparing a comprehensive programme of bilateral co-operation between Nepal and India for mutual benefit.[63]

During the visit Koirala met his Indian counterpart, P. V. Narasimha Rao, President R. Venkataraman and the Vice-President S. D. Sharma. The Indian Prime Minister assured Koirala of his government's continued commitment to the industrialisation and economic growth of the Himalayan Kingdom and announced further concessions regarding tariff and a substantial relation of the access regime for Nepalese exports to India.[64] The two hour long talks between them had broken the more than 30 year-old deadlock in respect of exploitation of water resources of the Nepalese Himalayas for the common benefit of both the countries and they decided that work of several multi-purpose schemes would be proceeded with. A significant achievement was the agreement between the two Prime Ministers on curbing terrorist activities on the border areas of the two countries. They agreed to deem it their duty to curb all such activities.[65]

The joint statement issued at the end of the visit on 6 December 1991 stated that a number of key decisions were taken with a view to deepening and expanding mutually beneficial co-operation between Nepal and India. These decisions were taken in a spirit of deep friendship, marked by mutual trust and confidence, and were imbued by the shared desire to usher in a new era in bilateral co-operation in a wide variety of fields which would bring direct and substantial benefits to the people of both countries.[66] The successful visit of the Nepalese Prime Minister to India is a happy reminder of the fact that it is never beyond well meaning neighbours to resolve bilateral issues if they display the necessary political will.[67] *The Indian Express*, in its editorial, termed the visit as "fruitful" and hoped that the democratic dispensation in Kathmandu should logically be conducive to ensuring that the sensitive security issue arising from Nepal's location between India and China no longer creates serious strains in Indo-Nepalese ties.[68] In fact the goodwill and spirit of co-operation achieved from the visit should be utilised to further strengthen all kinds of ties to the mutual advantage of both. This is not only desirable, but also essential.[69]

In response to the visit of G. P. Koirala, India's Prime Minister P. V. Narasimha Rao, paid an official tour to Nepal 19-21 October 1992. He was accompanied by R. L. Bhatia, Minister of State for External Affairs. In Kathmandu the discussions were held in an atmosphere of warmth, friendship and sincerity, which marked the extremely close relationship between Nepal and India. Narasimha Rao met with his Nepalese counterpart G. P. Koirala, King Birendra and other leaders which resulted in a number of decisions and step finalised in order to further strengthen and expand bilateral co-operation. The Nepalese

Prime Minister hosted a banquet in honour of the visiting guest on 19 October 1992 and hoped that the exchange of views on many matters of co-operation would be discussed. India's co-operative interest in Nepal's development has been continuous and have covered many important areas of our national life.[70] In a reply speech, Rao stated that our goal should be to create a truly era in bilateral co-operation that will directly benefit our peoples. He also expressed happiness that the two countries have put behind the unfortunate aberration of the last few years and have restored the mutual trust and confidence. We have learnt a new how important our traditional relation is to us both.[71] On the basis of the discussions held between the two governments it was agreed to improve and simplify the regime for export of Nepalese goods to India. These changes marked a watershed in the trade relations between Nepal and India, and should contribute significantly to enhancing Nepalese export to India. The number of other issues relating to India-Nepal trade have also been resolved, which would further facilitate Nepalese exports to India.[72] The Indian Prime Minister, in reply to a question, put forward by a Nepal TV reporter said that the present visit would be remembered for the process we have started and this process is full of goodwill, full of determination, full of certain confidence both between us and also in each country's own strength and plus points in order to push through this programme. So the atmosphere is a new one.[73]

Madhav Nepal, the Deputy Prime Minister and Minister for Foreign Affairs and Defence of Nepal paid a goodwill visit to India 6-10 February 1995 which provided an opportunity for both countries to jointly discuss bilateral issues, the further development of India-Nepal relations, the situation in Indian subcontinent, and other questions of mutual interest.[74] But actually it was a exploratory tour for the coming visit of Man Mohan Adhikari, Nepalese Prime Minister, to New Delhi which took place from April 10 to 14, 1995. It was his first visit to India after assuming office in November 1994. He was held in high esteem by the people of India because he had participated in the quit India movement in 1942 and had also been in the forefront of the democratic movement in Nepal. Hence the visit would significantly contribute to the friendship and multi-faceted ties between the two countries.

During the visit the Nepalese Prime Minister met Indian President and his Indian counterpart P. V. Narasimha Rao. The Indian and the Nepalese delegations led by the two Prime Ministers also met for detailed discussions on issues of common interest. The discussions were marked by the sincerity, friendship and understanding which characterized the close relations between India and Nepal and by mutual respect for the complete sovereignty, territorial integrity and independence of each other.[75] Both India and Nepal reiterated to respect and understand each other's security concerns. Neither side will allow activities on its territory, prejudicial to the security of the other. In succession, Kedar Bhakta Shrestha, Foreign Secretary of Nepal visited India 9-10 June 1995. The two delegations led by the respective Foreign Secretaries had expressed satisfaction on the progress in the implementation of the various projects. They had also useful discussions on the 1950 Treaty of Peace and Friendship, on which contacts would continue. The visits took place at the secretary level were part of a regular and continuing interaction between the two countries on all relevant issues of bilateral interest.[76] When the change of government took place in New Delhi in June 1996, Nepalese Foreign Minister Prakash Chandra Lohani visited India and had useful discussions with Indian leaders.

In a swift political development Inder Kumar Gujral replaced H. D. Deve Gowda as Prime Minister of India on 21 April 1997. He took an important visit to Nepal in June 1997 which marked a significant step towards the strengthening of Indo-Nepal relations. During the visit Gujral and Nepalese Prime Minister had agreed to direct the officials from the Home Ministries to discuss the security matters within one month and as a follow up senior officials of the two countries met in July 1997.[77] The decision to open the phulbari route was taken by India and Nepal and accordingly on 1 September 1997 New Delhi allowed an alternative transit route through phulbari to connect Nepal with Bangladesh.[78] In course of the visit, as a major give-aways the two countries signed Mahakali treaty under which India and Nepal would jointly execute Pancheshwar Project and estimated cost may be about Rs. 20,000 crores. It was decided to finalise the parameters of the detailed project report (DPR) within six months. In pursuance of the decision, the high level delegations from India and Nepal met in the middle of November and made 'reasonable' progress in sorting out the irritants to finalise the DPR.[79] However, despite the new spirit of the Gujral doctrine ushered into Nepal during the visit of Indian Prime Minister, it is the overhang of the ugly Indian complex which continues to shape or rather distort the political discourse on India and Nepal in Kathmandu. What is most striking for a visitor from India, is the undercurrent of passionate resentment ever ready to boil over, be it over the phobia about Nepal being overrun by Biharis or India's inflation imported into Nepal and the flight of Nepali capital across that open border. It is rooted in the insecurity about Nepal's identity and independence.[80]

**Politics**

The Nepalese authorities on several occasions reiterated its policy that it wanted to consolidate the strong bonds of friendship and mutual trust with both the neighbours—India and China.[81] Even Girija Prasad Koirala who was known for his pro-India attitudes, gave an impression that he was prepared to take a few necessary extra strides to obtain the support and goodwill of the current Chinese leadership. At a function of the Nepal-China Friendship Association he declared, "I have no misgiving or confusion about the relationship between Nepal and China."[82] He referred to his talks with the Chinese ambassador in which he assured that Nepal would never go against the national interests of China. The year 1991 also witnessed Koirala's talks with the Chinese leaders on the occasion had helped further develop and strengthen the mutual understanding and friendly relations subsisting between the two countries. During the visit both sides expressed their satisfaction at the various aspects of the bilateral relations between them. Both agreed to further expand the areas of economic co-operation. The two countries also signed an Agreement on Economic and Technical Co-operation to formalize the Grant Assistance of 500 million as a part of peking's co-operation in Nepal's economic development. The joint communique, issued after the agreement arrived at by both sides during the visit to China, was another testimony of Nepal's view of Tibet. Nepal had recognised Tibet as the Autonomous Region of China as declared by China itself.[83]

Perhaps, due to the improvement in Sino-Indian relations, Peking became less assertive on New Delhi-Kathmandu matters and abandoning its earlier attitude, had publicly advised Nepal to maintain cordial and co-operative relations with India. In September 1993, the Chinese Ambassador to Nepal Shao Jiong Chu, said in course of an interview that historically, culturally, socially and in religion Nepal was closer to India, "We are realistic and think it right for Nepal to maintain very close relations with the southern neighbour. It is good for your economic development".[84] However, despite several rounds of talks to ease tensions between India and China, Peking seemed to be in no hurry to improve relations with India. China's support to Pakistan and Myanmar sponsored threats to India remain intact. The Haingyi naval base in Mayanmar which is being constructed with Chinese help, may bring a formidable Chinese naval presence on India's doorstep. At a time when external naval presence in the Indian Ocean is winding down, this development may pose a serious challenge to the Indian Navy. India has to devise its defence strategy in the face of not so friendly world developments as well as low-intensity threats across north eastern and northwestern borders.[85] But in the final analysis Tibet remains China's main strategic concern in the region, not in the military sense but the exigency of keeping outside interference under watch in countering Tibetan insurgency. Officially India and Nepal have reassured the Chinese that they consider Tibet to be an integral part of China.[86]

Kathmandu displayed more inclinalions towards Beijing when in November 1994 the Communist Party of Nepal emerged as the single largest party in the general elections and Man Mohan Adhikari became the new Prime Minister of the country. He charged his predecessor G. P. Koirala's government as having pro-India tilt and declared that he would maintain a balanced relationship. At the moment New Delhi felt that great care had to be exercised in not giving any impression of big brotherliness. There should be no room for misunderstanding on the Nepalese side that we consider ourselves in any way inferior to the Chinese or that we regard ourselves as a guilty party just because we happen to be a far bigger and more developed country than our neighbour. [87]

In the third quarter of 1996 counsellor of the Chinese embassy Zhu Min Cai, visited Nepal Chamber of Commerce and bilateral talks held with the Chamber officials in Kathmandu. The discussion mainly focussed on the bilateral trade between Nepal and China. Regarding the growing trade deficit of Nepal with China, the discussion emphasised on enhancing joint ventures and Nepalese export of China.[88] In 1997 China's relations with USA and India improved considerably. In October Chinese President Jiang Zemin visited the United States of America. Although, his summit with the counterpart represented an unequal bargain, the net gain for the Beijing was respect, acceptance of China's global status and the lifting of a 12-year-old ban on the transfer of US nuclear technology to China. For the US China has a huge potential market "for everything from Fords to French fries".[89] The two countries may soon hold joint military exercise in what is seen as improving ties between the most powerful and most populous countries in the world.[90] In December 1997, Prime Minister Inder Kumar Gujral and the visiting member of the Standing Committee of the Political Bureau of the Communist Party of China (CPC) We X Jiang ring decided to speed up the implementation of the confidence-building measures (CBM), which are mainly concerned with the Indo-Chinese border, its militarisation and ways and means of lessening tension and normalising relations.[91]

In recent years, the American vision of world order had been dominated by non-proliferation of weapons of mass destruction. The visit of key US officials Robin Raphel and Strobe Talbott to South Asia was to promote a institutionalised mechanism to liquidate the nuclear and Pmissile capabilities of India and Pakistan.[92] At a time when there are officials in the State Department and Pentagon with known predilections in favour of Pakistan and against India, New Delhi needs to formulate its response to the US with great care in the post-cold war international dispensation. As a part of its strategy the US did not want to affect Nepal's export and in May 1996 it sent a textile delegation led by chief textile negotiator Rita Hayes. The delegation had discussion on Nepal's readymade garment export to the US with Nepalese Minister for Commerce Fatteh Singh Tharu. The US delegation gave assurance that the present economic condition of Nepal and the problem faced in export trade would be considered sympathetically.[93] US ambassador Sandra Vogellgesang said that export of garment is a significant for Nepal adding that trade is key to economic development of country. The bilateral trade between the two countries had gone in the fiscal year 1994-95 worth US $ 103.3. Major exportable items were garments, carpet and silver ornaments.[94]

In 1997 the unfolding of the so called "Gujral Doctrine" is building up the spirit of good neighbourliness in South Asia has also required considerable gumption, again a quality not likely to be found in a weak and endangered Government. In a flurry of positive actions India, corrected its relations with many countries including Nepal.[95] For the Americans the Gujral Doctrine seems to have resolved the enigma of India in a way that even Gujral could not have anticipated. It has shown the regional pre-eminence that India wants, is not of a kind that is threatening to its neighbour. It has also shown that India's foreign policy concerns are no longer mired in the past. The rapid consolidation of SAARC, economically and politically within the framework of the open economy reflects on the contrary a determined bid to take the whole of South Asia into the inter-dependent world of the future.[96]

The most important event for the development of South Asia was the disappearance of the counter-vailing force (USSR) in world politics which has been present for centuries in some form or the other. The world had become so much used to the post war bipolar balance because it helped nations to execute their long term strategies. Indian attempts to define key international issues along a North-South axis, as evidenced in multilateral negotiations on environment and trade issues, have not proved to be of much success. India is still trying to grapple with the new situation. With no Soviet Union and China to support the strategy of non-alignment, things can not be taken for granted any more. The last visit of Boris Yeltsin to India in March 1993 has established that Russia's future dealings will be more business-like and they can no more be expected to behave like the former Soviet Union. Despite the streamling of the rupee-rouble transaction the prospects of collaboration in some areas, Russia has sent clear signal that its behaviour would be tough on India's nuclear policy and a number of other issues.[97] However, Yeltsin included India in his list of global players despite the objection placed by Chinese President Jiang Zemin during his visit to Moscow.[98]

**Analysis of the Attitude**

The Nepalese were less than happy over the assumption of power by P. V. Narasimha Rao because they found no change in its attitude towards Kathmandu. Several developments took place such as, disappearance of Soviet Union as a counter-balancing force, improving US relations with the Chinese on the one hand and Beijing's mending of fences with New Delhi on the other. Establishment of democracy with King as a constitutional head was itself a development of immense significance. The reigns of administration in Kathmandu when dominated by the Napali Congress seemed more oriented towards India. The lessening of tension between Beijing and New Delhi was a cause of concern for Nepal because, in contrast to earlier now Peking was unwilling to be involved between the two. It often advised Kathmandu to maintain a cordial relations with India and admitted the need of Nepalese proximity with India. In the circumstances, it became difficult for Kathmandu to use China-card against India.

The changes, occured in international arena had shaped India's attitude towards Nepal. New Delhi attempted to improve its relations with Beijing on the one hand and the United States of America on the other. Both New Delhi and Kathmandu laid emphasis to strengthen the South Asian Association for Regional Co-operation (SAARC) because its expansion in several aspects would pave the way for more co-operation among the member-states. New Delhi was happy over the victory of democratic forces in Nepal and adopted, to a large extent, an accommodative attitude towards the bilateral issues, pending with the two countries. With the coming of non-Congress Government in India, Nepal expressed happiness and hoped an era of more amicable and co-operative relationship between the two countries. Except on matters of security India remained helpful for Nepal particularly in the economic development of the Himalayan Kingdom.

## Notes and References

1. *The Times of India*, 22 June 1991.
2. *The Indian Express*, 2 July 1991.
3. *The Times of India*, 22 June 1991.
4. *The National Herald*, 29 July 1991.
5. *The Statesman*, 4 September 1991.
6. Avtar Singh Bhasin (ed.), *Nepal's Relations with India and China, Documents 1947-1992*, Vol. 1 (Siba Exim, Delhi, 1994), p. 525.
7. *The Hindustan Times*, 9 December 1991.
8. Avtar Singh Bhasin, *op. cit.*, p. 537.
9. *The Patriot*, 5 February 1993.
10. *Ibid.*, 2 March 1993.
11. *Ibid.*
12. *The Statesman*, 17 December 1991.
13. Sagarika Ghose, "Nepal: The Politics of Accommodation", *The Times of India*, 1 December 1992.
14. *The Patriot*, 2 March 1993.
15. *The Hindustan Times*, 30 March 1994.
16. *The National Herald*, 31 March 1994.
17. *The Hindustan Times*, 17 June 1994.
18. *Ibid.*, 28 August 1994.
19. *Ibid.*
20. Kuldip Nayar, "Estranged Neighbour : The Arrogant India", *The Indian Express*, 12 December 1994.
21. *Ibid.*
22. *The Times of India*, 21 November 1994.
23. *The Indian Express*, 22 November 1994.
24. *The Hindu*, 22 November 1994.
25. *The National Herald*, 10 December 1994.
26. *The Hindustan Times*, 14 December 1994.
27. *The Hindu*, 24 December 1994.

28. *Foreign Affairs Record*, Vol. XLI, No. 4, April 1995 (External Publicity Division, Ministry of External Affairs, Government of India, New Delhi, 1995), p. 100.
29. *Ibid.*, No. 6, June, 1995, p. 153.
30. *Indian Recorder*, Vol. III No. 39, September 23-29, 1996, p. 2279.
31. *Ibid.*
32. *Ibid.*
33. *Ibid.*
34. *The Hindustan Times*, 22 July 1997.
35. *Ibid.*, 18 August 1997.
36. *Ibid.*, 7 September 1997.
37. *Ibid.*, editorial, 24 August 1997.
38. *Ibid.*, 7 October 1997.
39. *Ibid.*, 12 October 1997.
40. *Ibid.*, 15 November 1997.
41. *Ibid.*, 5 December 1997.
42. *Ibid.*
43. Dietrich Fischer, *Non-Military Aspects of Security: A System Approach* (UNIDIR, 1993), p. 7.
44. R.S. Sharma. "Process for Formulation and Execution of National Security and Defence Policies in the 1990", Kouser J. Azam ed., *India's Defence Policy for the 1990s* (New Delhi, 1992) p. 27.
45. *The Hindustan Times*, 21 August 1995.
46. Sangeeta Thapliyal, "Nepal in India's Security Parameters", *Strategic Analysis*, Vol. XVIII, No. 9, December 1995 (Institute for Defence Studies and Analysis, New Delhi, 1995), p. 1202.
47. *The Times of India*. 11 July 1991.
48. *Ibid.*
49. *The Hindustan Times*, (editorial), 9 December 1991.
50. Sangeeta Thapliyal, *op. cit.*, p.1202.
51. *Kathmandu Post*, 23 April 1993.
52. S.K. Ghosh, *The Traffic in Narcotics and Drug Addiction* (New Delhi, 1987), p.33,
53. *The Telegraph*, 20 October 1992.

54. *Asian Age*, 11 April 1995.
55. *Indian Recorder, op. cit.*, p. 2279.
56. *The Hindustan Times*, 24 August 1997.
57. *Ibid.,* 22 November 1997.
58. *Ibid.,* 12 October 1997.
59. *Ibid.,* 28 November 1997.
60. *Ibid.,* 13 December 1997.
61. *The Times of India*, 4 December 1991.
62. *Ibid.*
63. Avtar Singh Bhasin, op. cit., pp. 524-25.
64. *The Hindustan Times*, 6 December 1991.
65. *Ibid.*
66. Avtar Singh Bhasin, *op. cit.,* p.525.
67. *The Hindustan Times*, 9 December 1991.
68. *The Indian Express*, 7 December 1991.
69. *The Statesman*, 17 December 1991.
70. Avtar Singh Bhasin. *op. cit.,* p. 531.
71. *Ibid.,* pp. 532-33.
72. *Ibid.,* p. 538.
73. *Ibid.,* pp. 542-43.
74. *Foreign Affairs Record*, No. 2, February, 1995, *op. cit.,* p. 39.
75. *Ibid.*
76. *Ibid.*, June 1995, p.153.
77. *The Hindustan Times*, 22 July 1997.
78. *Ibid.,* 3 September 1997.
79. *Ibid.,* 15 November 1997.
80. Rita Manchanda, "The Ugly Indian Image Remains", *Ibid.,* 28 July 1997.
81. *The Indian Express*, 2 July 1991.
82. *The Times of India*, 5 August 1991.
83. Avtar Singh Bhasin, *op. cit.,* pp. 528-29.
84. T. Karki Hussain, "China Changes Stance". *The Hindustan Times*, 28 February, 1994.
85. *USI Journal*, Vol. C XXIV, No. 516, April-June, 1994, p. 207.

86. *The Hindustan Times*, 28 February 1994.
87. *The National Herald*, 10 December 1994.
88. *SAARC News*, Vol. 1, No.12, August 16-2 September, 1996 (Anindya Narayan Chatterjee, Calcutta, 1996). p. 25.
89. N.C. Menon, "An Unequal Bargain", *The Hindustan Times*, 3 November 1997.
90. *Ibid.*, 13 December 1997.
91. *Ibid.*, 17 December 1997.
92. Muchkund Dubey, "Ugly American Again", *The Times of India*, 12 April 1994.
93. *SAARC News*, *op. cit.*, p. 25.
94. *Ibid.*
95. *The Hindustan Times*, 30 November 1997.
96. *Ibid.*, 7 October 1997.
97. *USI Journal*, *op. cit.*, p. 206.
98. Rakshat Puri, "Delhi's Kowtowing to Beijing", *The Hindustan Times*, 12 November 1997.

# 12

# A PHASE OF TRANSITION AND CHANGE (January 1998—December 2008)

## Diplomacy

At the beginning of the year change of government and premiership took place simultaneously at New Delhi and Kathmandu. The result of the general elections held in India in March 1998 went in favour of Bharatiya Janata Party and it emerged as the single largest party in the Lok Sabha. An alliance of eighteen political parties under the premiership of Atal Bihari Vajpayee formed the government at the centre who took the oath of office on 19 March 1998. In sequence a change of premiership took place in Nepal and a new coalition led by Nepali Congress president Girija Prasad Koirala succeeded Surya Bahadur Thapa in April 1998. The new Indian regime, in its foreign policy pronouncements said that it would emphasise the importance of bilateral diplomacy and because it happens to be the larger country it would be all the more responsive to the aspirations and needs of small neighbours.

Unlike India, Nepal proved itself a fast-changing nation even at the start of the Nineties. In 1990, the partyless Panchayat System was abandoned in favour of Parliamentary democracy. A fresh Constitution was enacted which paved the way for competitive party politics. Earlier during the last five decades, Nepal had been hopping between monarchy and democracy, the two competing with each other for supremacy.[1] Now King Birendra agreed to the demands of the people for putting an end to the partyless Panchayat system and agreed to a new constitutional arrangement in which he would continue to be head of the state but the governance would be the responsibility of a cabinet answerable to Parliament. Since a constitutional monarchy was put in place, Nepal's democratic experience has yielded at best mixed results. The changes had climaxed the 30-year-long pro-democracy movement and raised popular expectations.[2]

In addition to this Nepal has been a hot bed of Maoism since the launch of the so-called Jana Andolan in the mid-1990s. Probably revolution was due in Nepal. In an era of rampant globalization, monarchy seems to be obsolete and the Maoist demanded nothing less than the abolition of monarchy. This put the whole system under tremendous pressure. In a society like Nepal where agrarian economy is predominant without any proper semblance of industrialization, revolution can indeed take the extract from Maoism, especially when the legacy of Chairman Mao is breathing so close; the demography of the country not-withstanding.[3] Apart from the economic backwardness of the country and Kathmandu's strong political relations with the Beijing, no less important role was played by the internal dissension of the Nepali Congress which not only made Maoism a strong force in Nepal but emerged as the single largest party in the general elections held in November 1994 and also formed the government but was force to step down and the NC-RPP-NSP coalition came to power in 1995.

Mere establishment of constitutional monarchy was not enough as the nation lacked political stability on account of dissensions among the leaders of Nepali Congress and rising power of Maoism. Economic and social backwardness of Nepal added fuel to the fire and a large section of the people began to lean towards the Marxist ideology. Gradually Nepal was moving towards a phase of lawlessness. It gave birth to Maoist insurgency which disliked the king and the political system equally.[4] In fact, the deteriorating condition of Nepal was a failure of the political system itself. The parliamentary system has been failed miserably in managing popular aspirations of economic well-being and social justice. Political leaders and elected representatives of the people gave priority to their preoccupations with power and pelf rather than to the concerns of their wider social constituencies. The king himself played a significant role in deserting the political system and did not hesitate to quietly patronize the unfolding Maoist rebellion in coming years.

In between the smooth sailing of Indo-Nepal relations, a new factor arose when India and Pakistan exploded its nuclear devices respectively in May 1998. Kathmandu criticized both New Delhi and Islamabad for nuclear testings and held the view that it would increase arms race in the region. In the same month K.R. Narayanan, the President of India, paid a visit to Nepal and pointed out India's nuclear policy since independence. Further in August 1998 Girija Prasad Koirala, the Prime Minister of Nepal, raised the issue of Kalapani in reference to Article 5 of the Sugauli Treaty (1815) when he met his Indian counterpart Atal Bihari Vajpayee at Colombo on the eve of 10th Summit of the South Asian Association for Regional Cooperation. Referring to the occasion Koirala said in Kathmandu that he told Vajpayee to settle the Kalapani border issue as early as possible on the basis of historical documents and other valid papers. He also added that unless India could come up with new valid papers or valid documents proof about Kalapani, it belongs to Nepal.[5] For the present Nepal adhered strictly to the issue and in a 25-point programme signed by the ruling Nepali Congress President and Prime Minister Girija Prasad Koirala and Sahana Prashan, CPN(ML) President, a new found partner-in-governance, the two parties expressed their commitment to ending the border dispute through dialogue while reaffiring that the Kalapani area belonged to Nepal and Indian troops should vacate it. Differences over the issue continued when King Birendra visited New Delhi in January 1999.

The Kingdom of Nepal witnessed a general elections on May 3 and 17, 1999 which gave a clear majority to Nepali Congress party and a 75-year old leader Krishna Prasad Bhattarai was administered the oath as the new Prime Minister of the country on 31 May 1999. A few months later the Bhattarai, while talking to correspondent to *The Times of India* at Kathmandu also spoke on Indo-Nepal relations and said that relations between them are closer than any two independent countries which are neighbours can hope to have. Under these circumstances, he explained, the old issues where there is a difference of perception can be sorted out through quiet discussions. These include the border dispute in the Kalapani area and on the origins of Mahakali river.[6] He expressed satisfaction on the position of India-Nepal trade treaty which allows anything manufactured in Nepal, regardless of the local content, to be exported to India. Transit facilities provided by India through the Chicken's Neck to reach Bangladesh despite the security problems involved are also appreciated.[7] He, however, became philosophical when asked to comment on the recent developments in Kargil and said that a practical solution would have to be found to settle the outstanding disputes between India and Pakistan. He was also optimistic about the international atmosphere which was rapidly changing in favour of peace and prosperity.

In the background of tense India-Pakistan relation on account of nuclear explosions New Delhi, on its part, remained conscious on Islamabad's activities in Nepal. The trans-border smuggling from Nepal to Bihar has assumed alarming proportions. It has been learnt from the reliable sources that the ISI (Pakistan's Intelligence Agency) is desperately trying to broaden its base along the Bihar-Nepal border areas following the near decimation of its network by the Indian security forces in Jammu and Kashmir and Punjab. The sources claimed that the ISI has been supplying sophisticated weapons to the outlaws and private armies operating in different parts of the state. The matter of ISI activities raised when King Birendra visited New Delhi in January 1999. It followed the Nepalese assurance that it would not allow its territory for activities inimical of India's interest. Jaswant Singh, India's Minister for External Affairs under Vajpayee dispensation assured the Rajya Sabha in a written reply that the centre is engaged in a dialogue with the Nepalese government following reports about ISI of Pakistan misusing Nepalese territory against India's interest. He also said that suitable mechanism, such as, the joint working group on border management and regular home secretary-level interactions between India and Nepal have been put in place to prevent misuse of the open border between the two countries.[8] As part of a collaborative efforts, India and Nepal in March 1999 had agreed to link trans-border protected areas through eco-corridors to help provide genetic continuity for animals across the border. It followed a declaration signed after a two-day trans-border meeting of wild-life experts from India and Nepal, it had been decided to set up and maintain linkages between Royal Bardia National Park in Nepal and Katarniaghat Wildlife Sonetuary in Uttar Pradesh.[9]

Indian opinion about ISI's role in anti-Indian activities on Nepalese soil was strengthened further when the hijackers of an Indian Airlines plane IC-814 landed safely in Kandahar enroute to Kathmandu airport. The incident was a major security lapse on the part of Kathmandu despite its oft-repeated promise of checking anti-Indian activities. Around the time a member of the Pakistan Embassy was also arrested in Kathmandu on charge of circulating fake Indian currency notes served to reinforce the Indian argument against Nepal's alleged laxity in ensuring security and curbing anti-Indian activities of Pakistan's Inter Services Intelligence in the country. In the aftermath of hijacking the Indian Airlines plane Indian Prime Minister Atal Bihari Vajpayee wrote a letter to his Nepalese counterpart and expressed India's unhappiness over the security lapses.[10] Indian security agencies have long been warning of ISI activity in Nepal which started operations there during the Punjab crisis.

In Nineties a large number of criminals and terrorists wanted in India had been arrested in Nepal as its cause needs no explanation. It is an open border. And the moment you cross over, you can literally cock a snook at pursuing security officers because they are the ones who can not cross without permission, disclosed a senior police officer. However, on being witness of several cases, India took its first diplomatic initiative only in 1997 when the Prime Minsiters of the two countries met and an Indo-Nepal joint working group was established.

On the bloody night of June 1, 2001, the century old dynasty of Nepal virtually eliminated plunging the country into existential crisis. The Crown Prince Dipendra gunned down 10 members of the royal family including the much beloved King Birendra and Queen Aishwarya. India expressed shock at the tragic and untimely demise of Nepal's king and the queen and declared a three-day state mourning across the country. In a resolution passed at an emergency Cabinet meeting convened by the Indian Prime Minister, the Government of India termed the demise as a very great tragedy and an irreparable loss to Nepal and its people'. It stated that as a neighbour and close friend, we share the feelings of immense sorrow and pray that the mouning nation and its citizens are bestowed the strength and courage to bear this irreparable loss.[11]

After the death of Birendra, his younger brother Gyanendra became the King of Nepal. About dealing with the new king the Indian government remained in a dilemma—what it should or should not do? At the juncture the Indian government was not worried about King Gyanendra's record of hostility towards New Delhi, it, however, caught in the cleft of a legitimacy crisis. In view of king's rejection by the mob the greater fear expressed by India was that there would be no government at all. If the new king failed to win the confidence of the people Nepal's fragile democracy would not survive. The polity then will polarized between a military autarch and urban mobs backed by Maoist guerillas. Thus, New Delhi was keeping a low profile about the developments in Nepal.

In fact Gyanendra's coronation was marked by popular protests and it was believed that the king would rely heavily on the Army to contain public hostility. Both needed each other in this hour of crisis—King Gyanendra would need the Army to consolidate his position and the Army would depend on the palace to hold together a socially diverse country. On the other the elected government had mobilised the Army against Maoist insurgents. Hence, as said by a senior Marxist-Leninist leader, it is going to be a tightrope walk for the new king'. Although containing the Maoist revolt remained a top priority of the new king, many of us including Lok Raj Baral, professor of Political Science at Kathmandu's Tribhuvan University, held the view, 'Gyanendra is mature and shrewd. He will try to adjust to the situation. India remained conscious about the current situation because one of the central planks of the Maoists is to break Nepal's close ties with India. In post-massacre periods the Maoist rebellion had gained a considerable social support and self-confidence to challenge the kingdom's armed forces. The primary target of the Maoist continued to be monarchy, but to tap nationalist sentiment, they also inveighed against Indian 'hegemonists' who allegedly prop up the oppressive system.[12]

In the chain of normal diplomatic relations in February 2002 the protocol to the India-Nepal Treaty of Trade was renewed which strengthened further relations between the two countries. All 12 Articles of the Treaty had been renewed unchanged. As per terms continued access was provided to the Indian market for Nepalese manufactured goods on non-reciprocal preferential, duty-free basis. In its revised form the treaty is proving to be an effective instrument in providing a strong impetus to industrial growth and economic development in Nepal and in expanding bilateral trade ties with India. In the year 2001-02, 60.7% of Nepal's overall exports were to India and 42.5% of Nepal's imports were from India. Despite hectic developments in Nepal relations between the two continued as earlier.

Once again the Government of India faced a delicate position in its relations with the Himalayan Kingdom as the history of dismissing an elected government was repeated on 1 February 2005 when King Gyanendra sacked Nepal's coalition government of Sher Bahadur Deuba and declared emergency in Nepal. The King in an address on nationwide television said, 'I have exercised the rights given to the Crown under the present constitution and dissolved the Government in the larger interest of the people. For the larger interest of the Nepalese general public, the nation and democracy and people's fundamental rights, we have decided to form a new government under my own chairmanship.'[13] On the prevailing situation in the country the king also added in the telecast, 'Innocent children were found massacred and the government could not achieve any important and effective results. The Crown traditionally is held responsible for the protection of national sovereignty, democracy and people's right to live peacefully. It is the duty of the Crown to protect all these segments of society.[14]

The emerging picture of King Gyanendra holding control over Kathmandu with the rest of Nepal in a state of lawlessness, a collapsed economy and rising unemployment was a total failure of expectations that the king would stabilise the country following the 2001 palace massacre. The new change had brought the king face to face with all the popular political forces of Nepal, the armed Maoists and political parties. The event had also isolated him from his erstwhile supporters in the international community, particularly India, the US, the European Union and Britain. Instead of becoming a force for stability and moderation, the monarchy is displaying the very wayward ways that brought Nepal to this sorry pass.[15] Following the declaration mainstream political leaders were arrested and the king assumed absolute power. He did the all in the name of establishing a true democracy but in the context of Nepal, democratization could mean expanding and deepening democracy by reforming the polity to include traditionally excluded groups and extending civil liberties accountable and responsive to people's aspirations. In the words of Robert Dahl; democratization occurs as more people participate in the polity'.

On the development in Nepal India's Cabinet Committee on Security (CCS) discussed the latest situation under the chairmanship of Prime Minister Manmohan Singh and decided that New Delhi would continue to support the restoration of political stability and economic prosperity in Nepal, a process which required reliance on the forces of democracy and the support of the people there. Assumption of direct control by the King Gyanendra had confronted India with the most acute foreign policy dilemma that it had ever faced: to back the king in what was bound to become an all out conflict with the Maoists; or to back away from him and let Nepal slip out of India's sphere of influence. King's action hàd left India with Hobson's choice. If it backs the king in a direct conflict with the Maoists, it will find itself embroiled in a low intensity conflict that cannot be won. As the conflict intensifies, the stakes for India in the king's victory will rise and it will find itself sucked ever deeper into the war. What starts as a supply of sophisticated arms to the Royal Nepal Army (RNA) could end by sucking Indian troops into the conflict.[16] That is why New Delhi has temporised by agreeing to send the arms that are already in the pipeline, but defering a decision on agreements that have not as yet been signed.

India's immediate condemnation of King Gyanendra's action could be looked like a knee-jerk defence of the principle of democracy. In fact the Indian government had been aware of King Gyanendra's increasing restiveness, and had been counselling patience for some time. King's growing frustration was easy to understand. The Maoist insurgency had been going on for nine years. A succession of elected governments had failed both to crush the movement and to bring the Maoist into the political mainstream. A ceasefire had been painstakingly negotiated in January 2003. But endless rounds of talks had brought the Maoists no closer to accepting the constitution.[17] On the other hand, New- Delhi also believes that a democratically elected government is the best bet to solve the problems with the Maoist rebels, who nurse a deep hatred against the monarchy. If the hands of King Gyanendra are strengthened, India expects the Maoists to link up with radical leftist groups in India. The latter are the biggest cause of law-and-order problems in the northern Indian states of Bihar, Uttar Pradesh and West Bengal, as well as the southern states of Andhra Pradesh, Jharkhand and Chhatisgarh. Inspite of these all it was widely believed in the country and outside particularly in the Himalayan Kingdom that New Delhi's decision had totally overlooked the aspirations and needs of democratic forces in Nepal who expressed shock and surprise over the Indian steps.

Decision of the Government of India on the recent developments in Nepal had provided the democratic forces in the Kingdom an opportunity to criticize New Delhi on the issue. In the palace itself it was a cause for concern as New-Delhi's arms have played a key part in the country's struggle. India has provided arms worth more than US $ 100 million over the past few years to the Royal Nepalese Army that is fiercely loyal to Gyanendra. The RNA led the coup in Nepal, and is fighting the Maoists as well as taking on the pro-democracy protesters. In addition the coup also proved disastrous for the democratic forces in the country. Immediately after the declaration leaders of the democratic political parties were arrested, and armed personnel were stationed at most media houses. The military captured the telecommunications office turning the phone lines off and on at will to keep people from meeting and networking from each other and with the outside world. It was a powerful means of enforcing fear. Upto a dozen armed forces and personnel guarded the houses of prominent civil society personalities. All this amounts to totalitarianism. Thus, King Gyanendra has turned the Kingdom into a chaos whose sole source of strength is the military which he can now deploy without any accountability.[17]

However, it was a fact well-known by the democratic forces in Nepal that India has a vastly influential position vis-à-vis all three of Nepal's forces. No government in Nepal can support itself in the absence of grants and loans to cover up to 60 per cent of the national budget. And approximately 70 per cent of all foreign aid that the military receives comes from India. In the circumstances what best New Delhi can do easily was to persuade the king if it abandons its insistence on bilateralism, and involves the US, Britain and the European Union in search for a solution. Such a multilateral initiative stands a far better chance of persuading the king to restore democracy and concede the Maoist demand for a Constituent Assembly, while simultaneously reassuring him that it will fully support the preservation of the monarchy.

India extended limited support to King Gyanendra despite the fact that Keshab Badal, former Nepalese Minister for Industries and senior leader of the Communist Party of Nepal urged the Indian government not to lend any support to the Nepal Government that could end up with the latter turning even more repressive towards the movement for democracy in Nepal. We seek the sympathy of the Indian Government in our endeavours to replace the monarchy in Nepal with a democratic republic. The Government headed by the king is stockpiling arms and procuring weapons in preparation for the bloodiest civil war in the country.[18] But heart of the matter lies elsewhere. Under a 1965 agreement, Nepal has the right to procure weapons form other countries if New Delhi cannot, or will not, provide them. The king has sent signals that if his request for arms is turned down, he will turn to Britain, the US, Pakistan and China. The US and Britain are as reluctant to get sucked into the Nepali quagmire as India but New Delhi fears that Pakistan and China may not be able to resist the bait. If either country establishes a permanent military presence in Nepal, India's northern ramparts will be decisively breached.

India has to date held its hand, fearing that a strong stand against Gyanendra would drive him into the arms of Pakistan and China, two countries whose influence India wants to minimize in Nepal.[19] In the past, Pakistan had said that it is ready to provide arms and counter insurgency training to help Nepal tackle the Maoists. Beijing had not helped matters by declaring that the royal takeover was Nepal's internal matter but in close touch with Kathmandu through the exchange of bilateral visits on both sides. New Delhi remained watchful following interaction between China and Nepal. At last India's policy, once again found its clear expression in December 2005 when Shyam Sharan, Indian Foreign Secretary, visited Kathmandu as a leader of the four-member delegation. He addressed a press conference on the Indian embassy premises, Kathmandu and said, 'there has been no change in the India's stance on the early restoration of multi-party democracy and constitutional monarchy in Nepal. Restoration of peace and stability and economic recovery in Nepal is not only in the interest of Nepal, but also in the India's interest. Unity among constitutional forces is essential to achieve the goal of peace and stability in the country. India is always ready to support all efforts aimed at bringing a peaceful resolution to the problems confronting Nepal'.

Now it was the turn of Maoists and other democratic forces to take their course of action. Gyanendra's power play worked to the advantage of the Maoists. However, it all began in 1996 when the Maoists presented a 40-point demand list to the Nepali-Congress Government, headed by then Prime Minister Sher Bahadur Deuba. Among others the major demand was to abolish monarchy. At a time when King Birendra Shah had restored democracy, no one really thought it was possible to remove the institution that had ruled Nepal for two and a half centuries. When the Maoists 15-day ultimatum expired they took up arms. They started attacking security forces across the country. In the course of their 10-year insurgency, they were termed 'terrorists' by the government: even the international communities accepted that tag. In 2001, the Nepal Army had taken complete control of the Maoist Militia and Girija Prasad Koirala, the then Prime Minister of Nepal, asked King

Gyanendra Shah to give orders to finish the Maoists, but the latter did not support the idea.

The Maoists of Nepal played the most significant role in mobilising the rural poor and their issues. Neglected rural Nepal and centralised development in Kathmandu were the main factors that helped Maoists win over the people. Corruption and politicization of almost all institutions had vexed people even after the restoration of democracy. When King Gyanendra Shah dissolved the House in 2002, his downfall started. The royal coup in 2005 gave the Maoists a chance to work with the Seven-Party Alliance (SPA) against his direct rule. In the changed, situation the democratic and Maoists forces of Nepal began to come closer to each other to fight against the autocratic rule of King Gyanendra. The first such effort was made in November 2005 when they signed the 12-point agreement which was denounced by the palace and the United States of America. As there seemed no way out the SPA and the Maoists undertook the second understanding on 19 March 2006. On the day of agreement they both released identical statements separately and unequivocally declared that people's movement is the only means of ending the conflict, establish democracy and restore people's sovereignty in Nepal.[20]

Eventually, cn April 24, 2006, the king was forced to relinquish power and reinstate the House of Representa-tives. On April 30, 2006, Girija Prasad Koirala was administered the oath oi the office of Prime Minister of Nepal. The reinstated Parliament unanimously approved a proposal to hold elections for a special Constituent Assembly to draw up a new constitution that would decide the future of monarchy in Nepal.[21] As a further development in November 2006 the Maoists formally ended their decade long war by agreeing to a Comprehensive Peace Accord, signed by two historic figures-Pushpa Kamal Dahal popularly known as Prachanda and Girija Prasad Koirala. It formed a grand alliance between seven political parties and the Maoists.

By the time the political thinking in Nepalese society had also witnessed a clear shift in favour of the Maoists. The transition from April 2006 to March 2007 had not been easy.

The process of sequestering rebel and army weapons and combatants under United Nations supervision took a long time to get off the ground. Despite delay and deliberations over apportioning of ministerial portfolios the alliance had set a sign of the can-do attitude of the new coalition. For a safe side the interim constitution had been amended to allow the interim legislature to abolish the monarchy by a two-thirds majority vote to prevent the king from disrupting the political process.[22] In reality, years of compromise with the monarchy had destroyed the credibility of two political parties-NC and UML and the subterranean balance of forces inside Nepal had already tilted in favour of the Maoists. It was the Maoist demand for an end to the monarchy and the election of a Constituent Assembly which had captured the imagination of the people. In the past two years they succeeded in pushing the envelop further winning popular acceptance for their slogans of an inclusive, federal republic as well as for a more equitable voting system.

As scheduled earlier the election to the members of Constituent Assembly was held on 10 April 2008 and in the results the Maoists gained a clear majority. Emergence of Maoists as the first force of the country was a total failure of New Delhi's diplomatic calculation. It was despite receiving reliable field reports of the widespread support the Maoists were enjoying across the country, South Block eluded itself into believing that the former rebels would be at best a distant third. Bogus surveys commissioned by the US embassy in Kathmandu in which the Maoists were shown as winning only 8 to 10 per cent of the popular votes. Being confident about the weak position of the Maoists no attention was paid to exploring the consequences of a Maoist victory. Even surprisingly M.K. Narayanan, National Security Advisor in the present government had issued a certificate of approval that India was extending a helping hand to the campaigns of the Nepali Congress as well as the Communist Party of Nepal (United Marxist-Leninist), and that proved later on not only improper but unwise too.[23]

At the juncture there is no doubt in the fact that New Delhi had erred in assessing the ground realities in Himalayan Kingdom and blindly believed on reports presented by the US agencies. Maoists crushing success in Nepal made India quick to correct the impression that it has been discomfited by the verdict. Pranab Mukherjee, India's Minister for External Affairs, had described the result as a positive development and senior officials said that they are looking forward to working with the Maoists-led coalition government which will rule Nepal. The official also added, 'India's policy towards Nepal in recent years had two broad aims. The first was the strengthening of democracy and the second the mainstreaming of the Maoists. Nepali people wanted a clean break from the past and this offers India an opportunity to re-examine the bilateral relationship to see how it could be taken forward.[24] India was also in favour of the US withdrawing its designation of the Nepali Maoists as a terrorist organization. Even former American President Jimmy Carter, who has monitoring the election as head of a delegation from his Carter Center, put the seal of approval on the former rebels, saying Washington, that had still kept the Maoists on its list of terrorist organizations, should now start to do business with them. 'It serves no purpose for the US government to continue to boycott the Maoists after they laid down arms and began to participate in the peace process on an equal basis with the other parties.'

Although diplomatically India's bilateral relations with Nepal is not at stake it needs some corrections to be made at the earliest. In this context it is also certain that Kathmandu would not move from the path of democracy as reiterated by Ram Baran Yadav, the first President of the new republic, and Pushpa Kamal Dahal 'Prachanda', the newly elected Prime Minister of the Himalayan Kingdom. After defeating Maoists candidate Ramraja Prasad Singh by 26 votes he said, "It is a victory of democracy; I will work towards strengthening it," In a talk to *The Hindu* he admitted that his challenge ahead was to write a timely democratic constitution and added that we need to adopt a best-suiting model for Federal Democratic Republic of Nepal.[25] Within a month of President's election Pushpa Kamal Dahal 'Prachanda' was elected Nepal's first Prime Minister of the republic in August 2008 heading a Maoist- led coalition which included the Communist Party of Nepal (United Marxist-Leninist) and the Madhesi Janadhikar Forum. Two weeks after his election he said at a programme in Kathmandu 'The international community doubts that the Maoists could go for autocracy but we believe in the norms and values of democracy. He also added further that we believe in the politics of understanding and we will stick to it.'[26] In this context he laid emphasis on winning the people's faith.

The new government and constitution are likely to place Nepal's relations with the outside world and with India on a sounder footing. A stable, peaceful, and prosperous Nepal is decidedly in India's favour and New Delhi must now do all it can to assist the new government during the period of transition. As a gesture of goodwill India expressed its readiness to review the treaty of 1950 and extended India's help in other fields, particularly on water management when Nepalese Prime Minister Prachanda came to India in September 2008.

**Strategy for Security**

Nestled between giant neighours, the main challenge that Nepal is facing is to maintain an equidistance between India and China. Undoubtedly, it is an arduous task which needs distancing away from the preponderant Indian influence. China encourages Nepal to be more independent, but in contrast to what many Indian analysts believe, does not intend to build a military alliance with Nepal. The geostrategic location of Nepal makes it imperative for China to maintain an intimate relationship with Nepal in order to protect its southwestern border.[27] So far as the policy of Nepal is concerned it has been experienced by New Delhi that Nepalese autocrats, in general, had played a China-card effectively in the regional politics for continuing their unjust and undemocratic regimes. Whenever Nepal had democratically elected governments, the Chinese autocrats lost the partners in autocratic governance giving way to the democratic countries such as India, the US, the UK and other European democratic governments to have more influence on the elected governments in Nepal than the Chinese government. Naturally, often the Chinese Autocratic Proletarian Government got sidelined, and found ignored by the elected governments in Nepal. The elected governments in Nepal tended to loosen their control over the Tibetan refugees in Nepal, and let them freely travel and engage in their activities for freedom in Tibet. Therefore, the Chinese autocratic proletarian government always found democracy in Nepal as a threat to their oppressive rule in Tibet.

China and Nepal are close neighbours on the two sides of the Himalayan Mountains and have a long history of more than two thousand years. The earliest defence pact that Nepal had signed with China was the Sino-Nepalese Treaty of 1792 after the Chinese had defeated the forces of the Gorkha Kingdom at Nawakot, some seven Kilometers northwest of modern Kathmandu. Under this treaty, the signatories agreed that they would regard China as a 'father' to them and affirmed their understanding that China would come to the aid of Nepal should it ever be invaded by a foreign power. Again in the mid-nineteenth century when the forces from the Kingdom of Gorkha were on the move northward, the Nepalese-Tibetan Treaty of Thapathali signed in 1856 which stipulated that Tibet pay annual tribute to Nepal and grant certain extraterritorial rights to Nepalese traders.[28] A century later in September 1956 the agreement was replaced by a treaty of amity and commerce with Chinese that ended Nepal's tributary income and extraterritorial privileges.

From 1996 onwards Nepal faced a serious internal problem when the Maoists presented their 40-points demand before the Nepali-Congress government. As we are aware the success of the Chinese revolution had a profound impact on the world, creating a wave of joy amongst the oppressed countries in South Asia on the one hand and sending shivers down the spine of the developed capitalist countries of Europe and especially America on the other. Chinese revolution served as the required fuel to ignite the hidden passions of freedom for many a third world countries.[29] The Himalayan Kingdom was no exception to this where Maoism took birth and reached to political power with the active and open support from the Chinese. The Maoists in Nepal had demanded several basic changes in Nepalese political system including the abolition of monarchy which had continued for centuries and establishment of a federal democratic republic.

Since 1998, the Nepal Army has sent officers and soldiers to study in Chinese military universities and military relations and cooperation between China and Nepal have experienced continuous development. Nearly all the former Army Chiefs and Defence Secretaries of Nepal have visited China. The Defence Minister and the General Chief of Staff of China have also visited Nepal. China has rendered help and assistance to Nepal within its own capacity. The two armies have conducted good cooperation in personnel training as well. Although considerable weightage was given to security issues by both sides, they also strengthened their relations in other spheres. In order to sustain the deep rooted cultural relations at present times, the two countries have reached an agreement on cultural cooperation in 1999. It followed various cultural programmes and activities. In 2001, the two countries signed the Memorandum of Understanding on Tourism Cooperation, including Nepal into the list of the tourism destination for outbound Chinese travelers. Relations between the two also strengthened when Zhu Rongji, the Premier of China, visited Nepal in May 2001.

As earlier increasing Maoists insurgency and influence remained a cause of concern for New Delhi and depite unfavourable political developments in the Himalayan Kingdom India witnessed bilateral contacts at all levels. In general both imports and exports of Nepal have increased over the years. In the year 2000-01, Nepal's global imports were worth 113 billion of which 46 billion were from India and Nepal's global exports were around 57 billion of which around 27 billion worth were to India. Under the liberal trade regime adopted by India as a follow up of the Treaty of Trade has continuously been instrumental in boosting Nepalese exports to India. The figures issued by Nepal Rastra Bank for the Nepalese fiscal years 1998-99, 1999-2000 and 2000-01 showed a surge in Nepalese exports to India amounting to 42.5 per cent, 80.5 per cent and 28.7 per cent respectively. Apart from traditional Nepalese exports to India a number of new commodities were added to the Nepalese export basket subsequent to the Trade Treaty, such as Vanaspati, toothpaste, acrylic and polyester yarn, Ayurvedic medicine, soap, copper wire and other copper products, paper and wax products.

Frequent significant political visits of high dignitaries from both the sides also took place and they discussed bilateral, regional and international issues of mutual interest. K.R. Narayanan, the President of Indian republic, accompanied by Commerce Minister and four members of Parliament paid a state visit to Nepal in 1998 and at his invitation King Birendra and Queen Aishwarya paid a return visit to India in January 1999. In continuation both sides took an opportunity for an exchange of view on bilateral matters when Dr. Ram Sharan Mahat, the Nepalese Foreign Minister visited India in August 1999 and Jaswant Singh, the Indian External Affairs Minister visited Nepal in September 1999. However no major political gain was hoped due to hectic developments in Nepal which posed an unfriendly atmosphere for New Delhi.

From strategic points of view India's political relations with Nepal received a sudden, severe jolt with the Palace Massacre which happened on the night of June 1,2001, and took the precious life of King Birendra, Queen Aishwarya along with 10 other members of the royal family. It followed the coronation of King Gyanendra, the late king's younger brother. The turn of events in Nepal as believed by official circles in India, has not only anti-India mindset but is also believed to have patronised the elements having close links with Pakistan. 'It is really a pity that Gyanendra has been installed as king. It does not bode well for Indo-Nepalese ties'.[30] However, some others including Bimal Prasad, a noted scholar and former Indian Ambassador to Nepal, did not share King Gyanendra's alarmist appraisal who said, 'I did not find any indication of hostility towards India in my interaction with Gyanendra'. He continued the impression even now about the king, 'Indo-Nepal relations will operate on the same wave-length in which they existed. There is every likelihood that the old policy will continue.[31] His assessment was based on two counts. One, that Gyanendra was closely associated with the late monarch and agreed with his policies and two, relations between countries are not determined by the predelictions of one individual but strategic interests. Just because there is a change in monarch, it does not mean there will be a change in policy.

In a further news analysis it was made clear that India's enemies would benefit the most from Nepal's chaos. The two democratic parties, the Marxists and the Nepali Congress refused to let the other rule for even a month in peace. The ruling Koirala Government was hanging by a thread. Hence in the period of the new king the primary beneficiaries would be forces inimical to India. In line the first is a Maoist insurgency that now controls about half the country at that time. In past the Maoist guerillas had penetrated Kathmandu Valley whose slogan is Kathmandu first, New Delhi next. The second beneficiary is Pakistan and the Inter Services Intelligence. The ISI has found Nepal a useful base for two reasons. One, a porous border with India. Two, a growing militant Islamic presence in southern Nepal. India can get Nepal to sign agreement after agreement but Kathmandu is almost beyond the ability to enforce them.[32] A vacuum exists in Nepal and the new regent is expected to see this as an opportunity.

Exactly the same as estimated by the analysts above in Post-Massacre phase Nepal's mutual understanding with China had strengthened further through exchange of visits and fruitful cooperation achieved in various fields. In April 2002 Nepalese Foreign Secretary Achariya visited China and briefed the Chinese side on the latest developments in Nepal. The same year in July Nepalese King Gyanendra paid a State visit to China and met the President, Vice President and Premier of the country. They spoke highly of Sino-Nepalese neighbourly friendship and cooperation and reached broad consensus on further deepening and expanding exchanges and cooperation in various fields. Both sides also signed agreements of mutual interest in course of the visit. In 2004 Nepal and China also signed 'Air Service Agreement' according to which China opened a direet air link with Nepal by route of Chengdu-Lasha-Kathmandu.

The Himalayan Kingdom had leaned more towards the Peoples' Republic of China than to New Delhi in the period of King Gyanendra. In addition as Beijing is a permanent member of the United Nations Security Council, Nepal is of the conviction that only with the meaningful role of China, the acts and decisions of the UN achieves greater support from the world community. The responsible role being played by China to maintain international and regional peace and achieve a harmonious world will always be laudable for Nepal. With the change of time across the globe they both concluded that peace, stability, cooperation and development are the calling of the period and the common aspiration of the mankind. They felt by seizing this opportunity, the two neighbouring countries should build on past achievements and push ahead to bring China-Nepal good-neighbourliness, friendship and cooperation to a new height.

On a number of issues of mutual interest both China and Nepal have supported each other in recent past. For over a decade Nepal has been affected by conflicts and instability. As an immediate neighbour and close friend of Nepal China had shown great concern. It tried its level best to play a constructive role in urging all sides in Nepal to solve problems through dialogues and talks. The Chinese Government and people respect political system and road of development chosen by Nepalese people and sincerely hope that all constitutional forces in Nepal will set store by the fundamental interest of the country and people and seek to appropriately settle the current difficulties and problems through dialogues, based on the maintenance of Nepal's independence, sovereignty and national integrity. On the other Nepal has also recognized Tibet and Taiwan inalienable part of Peoples' Republic of China. In this connection, the Nepal government has unequivocally supported the Anti-secession legislationenacted by the Naitonal People's Congress in 2005. Nepal has also appreciated 'one country two systems' principle as enunciated by China and applied successfully in Hong Kong and Macao in the form of special administrative regions. Exchange of bilateral visits immensely contributed to further nurturing Nepal-China relations and promoting the understanding between the two countries.

In a significant political development King Gyanendra, firing the democratically elected government on 1 February 2005, took over the executive powers imposing emergency rule and vowing to tackle the Maoist uprising. The army had expressed its readiness to take on the Maoists militarily. The king's coup with restrictions on fundamental rights and freedom, media and communications, national and international human rights watchdogs, and political parties and activities, has created desirable conditions for the army to run riot in Nepal. As said by Brigadier General Deepak Gurung, the chief RNA spokesman, 'Now we can solely go after the Maoists in a single minded manner without having to worry about what is going to happen on the streets.'[33] But at the same time the efforts to keep the political leadership on the run and the cadre confused and directionless may prove to be counterproductive. It was widely believed in academia and in a large section of the people in and outside the Kingdom. On the happenings in Nepal India, the US, the UK and the international community as a whole condemned and suspended the military supplies to the Royal Nepal Army. The king could not convince the international community that his army would not use the arms and ammunition against the people fighting for fundamental human rights and democracy in the country.

As monarchy was battling the last war for its survival in Nepal King Gyanendra, in a calculated move, before the take over had shut down the offices of representatives of Dalai Lama and of Tibetan refugees in the country. Obviously, this was done to keep the Chinese Government happy. The Nepal government also issued a statement in which it reiterated its support for Beijing's 'One China' policy that recognises Tibet and Taiwan as integral parts of China. In return, China, as an honest strategic partner, described the developments in Nepal as an internal matter and refrained from taking any stand on King Gyanendra's take over. The occasion reminded the events of the 1960s when King Mahendra played a China card effectively for suppressing the opposition political activities on the borders with India, expressed obligations for Indian efforts, and said Shriman Narayan, the then Indian Ambassador to Nepal, 'On my part, I and my government have now decided to request China to abandon the eastern sector of the East-West Highway and initiate a fresh survey for another road somewhere in the middle regions of Nepal'.[34] Even at that time, he also suppressed the voices of Tibetan refugees in Nepal, and stopped any political activities of them from Nepal against the People's Republic of China in 1960s.

In the year of take over King Gyanendra visited China and perhaps, in response, Nepal received 18 truckloads of arms and ammunition according to media reports in November 2005. Supplying lethal weapons to Nepal, China had not only demonstrated its disregard for suppression of democracy, civil liberties and human rights but also added fuel to the further bloodshed in Nepal. India's daily newspaper, *The Indian Express*, in its observation, wrote, 'the continuing Chinese arms supply to Kathmandu is more than a tactical threat to India's attempt at promoting democracy and stability in Nepal. The time is runing out for the Indian Government to get its Nepal act together and compel King Gyanendra to pay the costs of the China-card he has chosen to play against India. Unable to engineer a split in the coalition between India and the Anglo-American powers, King Gyanendra has put all his eggs in the China basket'.[35] Shyam Sharan, India's Foregin Secretary, on his return from a three-day visit to Nepal in December 2005, also called on China to stop supplying arms and ammunition to Nepal and join international efforts to force King Gyanendra to restore democracy.[36] However, China continued its moral and material support to King Gyanendra's regime and in early 2006 the Chinese Ambassador to Nepal said that his country accorded a high priority to the construction of the proposed Koshi—Lhasa Highway linking Nepal's eastern zones with China's Tibet Autonomous Region.[37] King Gyanendra toyed with a plan to let China and Pakistan open consulates in the sensitive Indo-Nepal border areas and the Indian Government had already communicated its strong displeasure to Kathmandu.

Turn of events moved fastly in Nepal and King Gyanendra's activities had left no option but to form an alliance of the two opposite forces—the Maoists and the Nepali Congress in the larger interest of the nation. The first such efforts was made in November 2005 when they signed the 12-point agreement which paved the way for second understanding between the SPA and the Maoists in March 2006. As a result of their mass movement in April 2006 the King's absolute rule ended that led to the reconvening of Nepalese Parliament, suspended in 2002. The two fighting forces of the country entered into a grand alliance in November 2006 and the Maoists joined the interim government. As scheduled the election to the new Constituent Assembly was held in April 2008 in which the Maoists emerged as the largest faction. In August 2008 Pushpa Kamal Dahal 'Prachanda' the leader of Maoists, became the first Prime Minister of Nepal's federal republic.

However, the basic change in Nepalese political system did not carry any change in its leaning toward the People's Republic of China, although it assured to maintain equidistance as earlier, in relation to big neighbours—India and China. Nepal's Maoist supremo Pushpa Kamal Dahal 'Prachanda' who later became the Prime Minister of Nepal in an interview to the state—run *China Daily* underlined nation's desire to follow the policy of equidistance and explained, 'Equidistance means not siding with one country against another. My exact meaning of equidistance is to have good relations with both the neighbours. But at the same time showing favour to China added, 'The Maoist-led government would take 'strong measures' against 'anti-Chinese activities in Nepal where Tibetan activists had been staging protests against Chinese rule in Tibet.[38] He even said that the Maoists-led government would discuss with India the open border which enables Tibetan demonstrators to come to Kathmandu from Dharamsala, the Dalai Lamas, base in India.

Hardly within a week of taking the oath as the Prime Minister of Nepal Pushpa Kamal Dahal 'Prachanda' went to China in August 2008 and became the first elected premier to visit China first in the history of Nepal. He discussed with Chinese leaders issues of bilateral relations and said that he considers China as a reliable friend and expects more help from it to achieve and promote economic development in Nepal. Hu Jintao, the President of the Chinese republic met with Prachanda on August 24, 2008, and welcoming him to the closing ceremony of Beijing Olympics, expressed gratitude to Nepal for its support to the games. In course of exchange of views Hu said that the two countries have established a good neighourly partnership and enjoyed friendship generation upon generation. He also thanked Nepal for adhering to the 'One China' policy and firmly supporting China on the Tibet issue.[39] The Nepalese premier on his part, assured him that Nepal would never allow any activity detrimental to China's interests in its territory.

Next to Beijing Kathmandu had made Islamabad its strategic partner keeping in view latter's tense relations with New Delhi. It used Pakistan as a less important pressuring tool because Islamabad had till date fought four declared, unsuccessful wars with India. In the early 1980s, Nepal started sending officers for military training to China and Pakistan, and in 1988 it imported anti-aircraft guns from China, contravening the 1950 agreement stipulating that arms were to be imported only from or through India.[40] In succeeding and particularly from the early 1990s the activities of Pakistan's Inter Services Intelligence have increased in India through the tacit support of Nepalese authorities and a section of the people as well. A large number of underworld ganglords and criminals have been arrested in Nepal who were on the 'most wanted' list of Indian police. Normally Pakistan-supported elements who were assigned to do destructive activities on Indian soil come through Nepal and after doing their jobs returned to Nepal as there is a open boundary system between India and Nepal. Several criminals and terrorists have confessed, during interrogations, their links to the officials of Pakistan's embassy in Kathmandu where they get cash, training, travel documents, and explosives. Security agencies of India have long been warning of ISI activity in Nepal, which started operations there during the Punjab crisis.

Despite all this evidence, India took its first diplomatic initiative only in 1997 when the Prime Ministers of the two countries met and an Indo-Nepal joint working group was established. Later Nepal assured that it would not allow its territory for activities inimical to India's interest. It was told by Jaswant Singh, India's Minister for External Affairs, in the Rajya Sabha, in a written reply, that the two countries are continuing cooperation in this regard to prevent misuse of the open border between India and Nepal. 'Centre is engaged in a dialogue with the Nepalese Government following reports about ISI of Pakistan misusing Nepalese territory against India's interest. 'Suitable mechanism such as the joint working group on border management and regular home secretary—level interactions between India and Nepal have been put in place to prevent misuse of the open border between the two countries.[41] Following the reports of increase in infiltration by Pak—trained militants, ISI agents and also large scale illegal trade in select goods, commodities and narcotics New Delhi had decided to upgrade vigilance across its free borders with Nepal. In addition an action plan was also under active consideration under Union Home Ministry to streamline the existing security network with active involvement of four States— Uttar Pradesh, Bihar, West Bengal and Sikkim who shared the 1751 km. along border with Nepal.[42] However, the new security network was to be within the confines of the Indo-Nepal Treaty of 1950. The issue of ISI agents' activities in Nepal was also raised in September 1999 when Jaswant Singh, India's Minister for External Affairs, visited the Himalayan Kingdom and King Birendra came to New Delhi as chief guest of the Republic Day celebration in January 1998.

Despite Indian efforts and Nepalese assurance that it would not allow any anti-Indian ISI activities on its soil, gradually security system at Tribhuvan international airport at Kathmandu became non-existent as reported by a correspondent of *The Hindustan Times*, a daily newspaper, in December 1999. 'Kashmiri militants came to Kathmandu in flights from Islamabad and they are taken care of by ISI officials who are part of the Pakistani embassy in Kathmandu. These militants stay for a few weeks in Kathmandu and then they go to Nepalgnnj where some Muslim families make arrangements for them. Then they easily cross over to India and travel to their destination.'[43] The Indian government, however, had always raised this issue during dialogue with successive Nepalese Prime Ministers who have always denied the existence of such activities. Thus Nepal has never admitted the role of the ISI behind this racket in Kathmandu. With this soft attitude on the part of Nepalese authorities, the ISI has never faced any problem in sending Kashmiri militants to India to create troubles in Jammu and Kashmir.

Nepalese security lapses at Tribhuvan international airport and soft-handling of ISI agents' activities became public on December 24, 1999 when the hijackers of Indian Arilines IC-814 easily boarded Kathmandu airport and then went to

Kandahar (Afghanistan) and put their initial demands through the Taliban. The incident alongwith others that happened earlier had worried New Delhi while India continued to furnish Nepal with incriminating evidence on Pak-backed anti-India operations from its soil. One of the reasons for this, as held by many and intelligence sources, is that in long previous years the ISI has reported to have managed a great deal of influence amongst its resourceful politico-business circles. Apart from this Nepal had also maintained total silence over India's offer on entering into two bilateral treaties - Mutual Legal Treaty in Criminal Matters and Memorandum of Understanding for Combating International Crime and Terrorism. The proposal was put forwarded by New Delhi in August – September 1998 and in early March 1997.[44] On the issue of hijacking Atal Bihari Vajpayee, the Prime Minister of India, wrote to K.P. Bhattarai, his Nepalese counterpart, in the aftermath and drew attention to the major security lapse despite oft-repeated promise of checking anti-Indian activities on its soil. Visibly lapses on the part of Kathmandu had left India unhappy. Earlier on two occasions in 1986 and in 1996 New Delhi had made security-related offers to Nepal but failed to get any answer.

The Joint Working Group (JWG) of India and Nepal met at Kathmandu in February 2000 and discussed the issue as focal point. In the meeting Indian side was represented by a Home Ministry Special Secretary with inputs from a delegation of civil aviation security experts that had just returned from Nepal after studying the security arrangements at Tribhuvan airport. In previous meetings India had also raised the introduction of a passport-visa regime, patrolling of Indo-Nepalese border by Para-military forces and tightening of custom controls as safety measures. The Indian delegation pointed to their Nepalese counterpart the need for effective sharing of intelligence between the two countries and review of the effectiveness and adequacy of the existing arrangements for exchange of information on criminal and terrorist activities.[45] In course of the discussions New Delhi also expressed its readiness to provide help in the form of sharing expertise on counter-terrorism and to impart training to Nepalese police and security forces for tackling left-wing extremist violence. Further Nepal's security nexus with Pakistan-backed ISI gained its base stronger in the Himalayan Kingdom in post-palace Massacre period which took the life of king and queen along with other members of the royal family on June 1, 2001.

In addition continuing political instability in Nepal had paved the way for pro-ISI elements operating in Kathmandu and found a new lealse of life in February 2005 when King Gyanendra declared emergency in the country and took over executive powers of the government. The new incumbent had a plan to let China and Pakistan open consulates in the sensitive Indo-Nepal border areas to which the Government of India has communicated its displeasure to Kathmandu. Pakistan is keen to open shop at Birganj in central Nepal region that also touches borders of Bihar. King Gyanendra is thinking that his threat to draw to China and Pakistan would force New Delhi to soften its policies but indications are that the move could be counterproductive and undermine further the limited support the monarchy enjoyed in New Delhi.[46]

There are also deep strategic signals on the part of Pakistan in which its foreign office warned its government on the news that India, and Nepal were in the process of finalising a secret extradition treaty that might endanger safety of Pakistanis there as the agreement would give full power to New Delhi to get hold of any Pakistani national working or visiting Kathmandu. In this context the foreign office has proposed to the Pakistani Government that as a counter step Pakistan should immediately sign an agreement with Nepal to save its own citizens from being extradited to India from Kathmandu.[47] In the light of foreign office's recommendation the cabinet had approved the signing of an agreement with Nepal in one of the recent meetings which was presided over by Prime Minister Shaukat Aziz. In between the period due to mass movement launched by the Maoists and the democratic forces in April, 2006 King Gyanendra had to left all powers and agree for democratic process in the country. As scheduled the elections to the new Constituent Assembly held in April 2008 and the Maoists emerged as the largest group. Centuries old monarchy in Nepal was abolished that followed the election of President and Prime Minister of the new republic in July and August 2008 respectively. Pushpa-Kamal Dahal

'Prachanda', the new Prime Minister of Nepal has said that his country would follow the policy of equidistance, as earlier, while dealing with two giant neighbours-India and China. In his first address to the nation said that Nepal's relations with other countries would be based on the five principles of coexistence, the Panchsheel.

**Exchange of Visits**

Normally exchange of visits undertaken by several leaders of the country strengthened understanding between them and also provide an opportunity to know each other's view on various bilateral and international issues. The first important visit was paid in post-nuclear explosion phase by K.R. Narayanan, the President of Indian republic, accompanied by Commerce Minister and four Members of Parliament. His State visit to Nepal started in May 28-30, 1998 and in Kathmandu he declared India's determination to continue efforts aimed at global elimination of nuclear weapons which it could now pursue with greater credibility and persuasiveness. Following the five underground nuclear tests earlier this month, he observed India was in a position not to further press its call which earlier had gone unheeded.[48] At the State banquet hosted in his honour by Nepal's king the Indian President narrated the history of Indian call for ban on nuclear testing from 1954 and expressed the belief that today India is in a position to pursue this objective with greater credibility. Describing his visit to Nepal as one of pilgrimages he said that Indo-Nepal bilateral cooperation offered a model for the multipolar pluralist one-world that was emerging as a result of the ongoing worldwide phenomenon of liberalisation, economic reforms and opening up to the world. He also called upon Nepal to ensure that misgivings and apprehensions did not come in the way of realising the larger and nobler objectives of bilateral cooperation.[49]

At another function where the President of India was accorded a civil reception he lauded the progress of democracy in Nepal and expressed confidence that the furture of Nepal's multi-faceted development within a progressive democratic framework was assured and both India and Nepal would enter the coming millenium with confidence in ourselves and goodwill towards all.[50] The visiting President remembered with deep gratitude the support that India received during its freedom struggle from Nepali leaders and the people of Nepal and said further that India, on her part, had often voiced its support to democracy in Nepal through its leaders like Mahatma Gandhi, Jawaharlal Nehru and Jayaprakash Narayan. The highlight of Narayanan's visit was that he was being honoured with D. Litt. by the Tribhuvan University. He was the second President after President S. Radhakrishnan, to receive an honour.

In course of the visit Narayanan touched various aspects of bilateral and multilateral relations. In relation to China he declared that India was keen and indeed determined to go along this process of dialogue, reconciliation and cooperation with China even further than hitherto. Describing the regional organizations like ASEAN, APEC, and SAARC he added that SAARC so far has not become an effective grouping but ASEAN has established itself as a major and most successful regional cooperation organization. APEC is advancing as a vast grouping of immense potentialities.[51] President Narayanan appreciated the initiatives taken by Nepal for sub-regional cooperation under the auspices of South Asian Association for Regional Cooperation, but at the same time ensured Nepal that misgivings and apprehensions would not come in the way of realising the larger and nobler objectives of bilateral cooperation. He was satisfied at the end of his three-day goodwill visit to the Himalayan Kingdom.

At the invitation of the President of India a return visit was paid by King Birendra and Queen Aishwarya of Nepal to India from January 24-29, 1999. They were chief guests at the Indian Republic Day parade and the opportunity provided an occasion for an overview of bilateral relations and exchange of views on matters of mutual interest. During the visit the King called on the President and also had separate meetings with Vice-President, Prime Minister, External Affairs Minister, Home Minister and Commerce Minister. King Birendra's discussions with them covered the entire gamut of bilateral relations, in particular the potentials for long-term bilateral cooperation incore sectors including water resources, trade and transit, tourism etc. The Indian leaders when met with the visiting King recalled his personal contribution to strengthening democracy in his country and promoting Indo-Nepal relations.[52] India also gave credit to the king for the significant upgradation of bilateral relations as symbolised by milestone agreements on water resources cooperation, trade and transit, investment, power trade and civil aviation. These treaties represented the continuity and the sense of direction in Indo-Nepal relations.

King Birendra's visit to New Delhi was followed by the visit of Dr. Ram Sharan Mahat, Nepalese Foreign Minister in August 17-19, 1999 for consultations prior to the forthcoming SAARC Summit in Kathmandu. The visiting Foreign Minister called on the President and Prime Minister, besides meeting with his Indian counterpart. Dr. Mahat handed over his government's invitation to Prime Minister Atal Bihari Vajpayee to attend the SAARC summit and the latter had took the opportunity to stress the importance of SAARC to focus efforts on economic issues upholding the provision of its Charter.[53] Although the visit was primarily in the SAARC context, it did provide opportunity for an exchange of views on bilateral matters as well.

A return visit to Nepal was paid by Jaswant Singh, India's Minister for External Affairs from September 8-11, 1999. Besides inauguration of B.P. Koirala Institute of Health Sciences at Dharan, the visit provided an opportunity to renew the existing areas of cooperation, including the issue of the accentuated menace of Islamic extremists creating disturbances and their access through the open Indo-Nepal border. While India would like Indo-Nepal ties to be strengthened further through cooperation, it would not like third countries to misuse the relationship to the detriment of both countries.[54] Given the subversive agenda that the ISI had been pursuing vis-à-vis India, it was but natural that it should try to avail itself of the easy access facility to push in its agents and mercenary operatives. Over the past few years, a growing number of ISI agents carrying large quantities of lethal weapons and ammunition, including RDX, seized in different parts of the country had been traced to the Nepalese route.[55] The visiting Indian Foreign Minister had not only conveyed the Indian concerns but also discussed specific measures that needed to be taken to prevent misuse of the route by alien agents. Jaswant

Singh was also apprised of the corresponding Nepalese anxieties about the activities of Maoist insurgents who often slipped across the border into India for cover. In the meeting they agreed that better vigilance and intelligence coordination along the border as well as effective checks at the entry points into Nepal would go a long way in addressing these problems.

In Kathmandu on the last day of his visit Jaswant Singh described it as a very productive one and said that India and Nepal had agreed to review the existing extradition treaty between the two countries and to take appropriate steps to combat the menace of terrorism more effectively. In a statement he disclosed that there was a two-fold goal behind his visit, the first being towards effective implementation of important understandings reached, and the second being to identify new areas of cooperation. In both instances, good progress had been made.[56] Both sides also recommended that an India-Nepal Parliamentary Forum be set up to facilitate closer interaction between the Parliamentarian of the two countries and to demarcate the boundaries in a more effective manner. Further in May 2000 Chakra Prasad Bastola, the Foreign Minister of Nepal, visited India and in the same month Lalit Man Singh, India's Foreign Secretary paid a return visit to Nepal. They both met several leàders of the visiting country and had useful discussions on matters of mutual interest.

On 1 June 2001 a mid-night massacre occurred in the Palace of Kathmandu in which King Birendra and Queen Aishwarya along with other members of the royal family were gunned down. It followed an anarchy in Nepal and ultimately Gyanendra, the younger brother of King Birendra was made the new king of Nepal. Political instability and increasing Maoist insurgency remained on the top of national agenda and the king on the other was busy in its clues to survival. During the kingship of Gyanendra the Maoists of Nepal became stronger making a large part of territory and population under their control. Hence in comparison to India Nepal continued to be active politically with the Peoples Republic of China. Although several important political visits were undertaken from both the sides, despite discussions and agreements no effective steps were taken to check the ISI agents activities on Indo-Nepal border.

Even democratic forces of Nepal who held a decade-old sympathy for India, have now began to support China on several counts more to weaken India politically in Nepal than to maintain a policy of equidistance between the two giant neighbours. Having faced groupings of democratic forces and a torn kingdom due to Maoists insurgency and blockades, King Gyanendra, using his constitutional powers, declared emergency and taken over all the executive powers of the government in February 2005. King's action was condemned by several countries of the world-western democratic and India alike in particular which put a halt on exchange of visits between the two for months to come.

At a time when Nepal was passing from its crucial phase Shyam Sharan, Indian Foreign Secretary and former Indian Ambassador to Nepal went to Kathmandu on a three-day visit as a leader of the four-member delegation on 11 December 2005. The visit of Indian Foreign Secretary to Nepal was in the background of the meeting between King Gyanendra and Prime Minister Manmohan Singh in Dhaka in which both the King and the Prime Minster agreed to be in touch at different levels. At Kathmandu the Indian Foreign Secretary apart from other leaders also met King Gyanendra and the latter had conveyed to him that he remained committed to multiparty democracy and constitutional monarchy and that there should not be any doubt in his commitment. On December 13, 2005, before leaving for New Delhi, in an address to a press conference, Sharan reiterated India's policy towards Nepal and stressed that there has been no change and his country wanted the earliest restoration of multi-party democracy and constitutional monarchy in the Himalayan Kingdom. In his 10-minute long press conference concerning the military assistance to Nepal he said, 'At the moment we do not have Indian arms coming to Nepal but other aspects of our cooperation to Nepal including the Royal Nepalese Army is continuing and quoted the training for RNA. After returning from Nepal he made it clear, 'We would trust that India and China are not seen as somehow competing with each other for any kind of influence in Nepal and added that India believes both New Delhi and Beijing share a common objective of seeing the return of peace and stability to Nepal.[57]

In later developments of immense significance in post-emergency phase of Nepal the Maoists and the democratic forces had come together to fight the misrule of King Gyanendra. They succeeded in April 2006 and the king had to left executive powers and the Parliament suspended in 2002 was restored that paved the way for an interim government to be constituted till the election to the Constituent Assembly. As scheduled elections to the Constituent Assembly was held in April 2008 and the Maoists emerged as the single largest Party. In August 2008 a Maoist - led coalition government was formed under the premiership of Maoist leader Pushpa Kamal Dahal 'Prachanda'.

However, the most significant visit undertaken by Nepal was the visit of Pushpa Kamal Dahal 'Prachanda', the new Prime Minister of Nepal, to India 14-17 September 2008. Before his four-day official visit to New Delhi, 'Prachanda' took his first visit to Beijing in August 2008, about a week later of his assumption of office and discussed with Chinese leaders bilateral and multilateral issues. According to official sources India had decided, even before the visit, to respond positively to any proposal for revising the 1950 Indo-Nepal Treaty. India was also looking forward to the visit of Prachanda as it would provide an opportunity for New Delhi to establish a political equation with the new Maoist - led dispensation in the Himalayan republic. The sources also added as regard to India's agenda with Nepal and reiterated that it did not depend on which party or government was in power in Nepal. As earlier, this time too, India's concerns revolved around questions of security and border management - including the potential misuse of Nepali territory by elements inimical to Indian interests -as well as the imperative of promoting economic cooperation, especially in the hydroelectric sector.[58] As to the devastating flood and maintenance of barrages and embankments along the Kosi, the sources hoped to figure during Prachanda's visit to India.

On the other the Nepalese Prime Minister who was to visit India with Upendra Yadav, his Foreign Minister, before coming, in an interview to *The Rising Nepal* disclosed; We have already prepared a draft which I am carrying to India. He did not stick to the point that India should accept his proposed draft but was of the view that it should be done in such a way that all matters be included in the treaty are worked out following the formation of a task force of the officials of the two countries.[59] But he also said that during the visit primary focus would be 'to remove the crisis of confidence between Nepal and India at a political level.

The present leadership in Nepal is self-confident, pragmatic and resilient. They are intelligent enough to understand and acknowledge that in the interest of their own political consolidation and delivery of promised development to the Nepali people, India's goodwill and help is indispensable. They sought India's recognition and respect even during the insurgency years, particularly since 2002 and loudly acknowledged India's support in the Jan Andolan II. It was India's confused and contradictory responses during the two post - Jan Andolan-II transition phases in Nepal from Constitutional Monarchy to the Republic and from Constituent Assembly elections to the formation of an elected government, that alienated some of them.[60] According to the policy document released in Kathmandu the primary concerns on which Nepal needed India's creative responses were counted as; political stability of the coalition regime, culmination of the peace process through security sector reforms, timely conclusion of the constitution drafting and implementation of the vision of 'economic revolution' in a decade.[61] The first visit of Prachanda would mark the beginning of a new relations between the two countries.

In course of the visit Prachanda met, apart from his Indian counterpart Manmohan Singh, with Pranab Mukherjee India's External Affairs Minister. He was called on President Pratibha Patil and interacted with leader of the Opposition L.K. Advani. Prachanda on 15 September 2008 described his country's relationship with India as unassailable and said that it can not be compared with any other country. With history having created a new atmosphere he would like to start afresh on issues of discord such as water resources. 'Nepal is in a very delicate and sensitive transition period. I have full confidence that we can create very conducive conditions in a very short span of time'.[62] On the same day at a luncheon organised by India's three leading chambers of commerce and industry he added further, 'Due to our specific history, geography, cultural ties and tradition of economic interdependence, our relationship with India is crucial. Although we wish to develop ties with China, there is no question of comparison.' He also took the opportunity to invite Indian investors to Nepal and assured them of Nepal government's commitment to adopt every possible measure to provide them the necessary securities including repatriation of capital and profit earned by them in the country. We will do all we can to ensure industrial security in Nepal and also a fair collaborative relationship between labour and industry as well.'[63]

During the visit of Nepalese Prime Minister India expressed its readiness to revise the treaty of 1950 in the new circumstances and as an immediate package to help Kathmandu, New Delhi would release Rs. 20 crore for Nepalese victims of the Kosi barrage breach and continue with supplies of petroleum products, wheat, rice and sugar. On management of river waters, Shiv Shankar Menon, India's Foreign Secretary, said that his country wanted to rationalise the existing mechanism and hasten the progress of hydel projects. The Nepalese Prime Minster had also expressed his desire to expedite work on the outstanding water projects and in their talks on 16 September 2008 India and Nepal agreed to set up a three-tier joint water management mechanism. They agreed that there will be a ministerial-level Joint Rivers Commission, under which there will be a secretary level joint committee and then project-level technical committees for each project. The agreement was hailed as a new era of mutual cooperation and trust in water management. At a lunch hosted by Janata Dal (United) President Sharad Yadav, Bihar Chief Minister Nitish Kumar also met Prachanda and found him very positive about completing water projects that would, to a large extent, tame the Kosi and help the State rid of perennial flooding.[64] In the meeting Nepal had sought India's cooperation in construction of 190 meter-high Naumure hydro-power dam on the Rapti river that would generate 240 MW. The estimated cost of the project is Rs. 2500 crore.

At the end of the visit a joint statement was issued which covered wide range of subjects discussed by the leaders of the countries during the four-day official visit. As mentioned in the statement India and Nepal would undertake mega projects, including for infrastructural development. Kathmandu will provide a conducive environment for Indian business which has complained of sccurity issues and labour problems. On its part New Delhi will seek to reverse the erosion of gains to Nepal under the 1991 trade treaty. It will undertake a comprehensive review of the existing trade and transit arrangements with a view to promoting industrialisation in Nepal.[65] On water management the joint statement promised a wide array of measures. Both sides decided to launch relief and rehabilitation measures for the victims, and to reconstruct infrastructure damaged by the breach in the Kosi. Both sides also agreed to enhance cooperation in handling cross- border crime and security concerns with the Home Secretaries meeting soon to implement the decision according to the statement.

With the joint statement and issues discussed between the Indian and Nepalese leaders a new chapter has been opened in their relationship. The statement had fully covered the wishes and needs of new Nepal in bilateral sphere. On India's part, traditional attitude towards Kathmandu should be left behind because peace and political stability in Nepal are in India's genuine interests. The successful visit, to a large extent, has been able to remove suspicions and misunderstandings towards each other.

## Politics

As a true follower of tradition and practice, Nepal continued its policy of equidistance in its relations with two big neighbours India and China. In this phase of post-cold war, a disintegrated eastwhile super power Soviet Union had made the United States of America a single super power of the world who wanted to design, regulate world politics in its own way, the Himalayan Kingdom had nurtured its relations with Pakistan with a view to put pressure on New Delhi off and on to have a favour for Nepal. Once again in May 1998 the region South Asia became a tense area due to detonation of a series of nuclear devices by India and Pakistan. The incident had triggered the relations between them and Girija Prasad Koirala, the then Prime Minister of Nepal, while addressing a press conference after returning home from the 10th summit of the South Asian Association for Regional Cooperation, offered Kathmandu as a venue for Indo-Pakistan talks to ease tension in the South Asian region.[66] Earlier in May 1998 in the light of a decision taken at the Environment Ministers of SAARC member nations at Male in October 1997, a seminar was organised by the United States Information Service '(USIS) in which non-Government experts from India, Pakistan and Nepal participated and said that new initiatives and partnerships were needed for environmental management.[67] Presenting the paper Dr. Biplap Bhusan, director of the Calcutta based school of fundamental research held the view that these three developing countries of the Indian sub-continent in South Asia are uniquely placed in the global context are bestowed with immense natural resources, vast fertile plain, land, thick forests and extended shoreline. Hence these neighbours have to go hand in hand and tackle the problems jointly.

Nepalese policy to placate China-card in its dealings with India has been an oldest one. Especially the monarchy of the Kingdom in order to pressurise New Delhi and its policymakers but more to protect their position have sought to manipulate India by threatening it with the PRC. Sometimes there is a hint of arms supplies from Beijing and at other times a possibility of allowing them to open a consulate on the Indo-Nepal border. But in fact there is no China-card that Kathmandu can play. Western diplomats are impatient with any such suggestion and Indian diplomats certainly do not believe in its existence. As explained by an European diplomat based in Kathmandu, 'There is no China card. But the perception of the China-card is more important than the card. It is a classical case of manipulation by the palace. If people believe that there is a China card, the King's purpose is served. The China-card seems all about trying to force India to help legitimize the king and his actions. The democratic political-parties are also dismissive of Nepalese China-card and Girija Prasad Koirala, prominent leader and several times Prime Minister of Nepal, held the view that the Indian diplomats were in constant dialogue with the Chinese and there was a lot of understanding between them.

However, this China-card has also a lease of life. As long as the Chinese occupation of Tibet will be intact, the Nepalese autocrats could play the China-card. Therefore, not only the Nepalese autocrats but also the Chinese occupation of Tibet is a threat to democracy in Nepal. The Chinese Proletarian Government would do its best to block the flourishing of democracy in Nepal, as democrats would be in favour of Tibetans fighting for the freedom from the foreign occupation of their homeland. Thus, the root cause of unstable democracy in Nepal is the loss of Tibet to the Chinese Proletarian Government making it possible for the Nepalese autocrats to play the China-card whenever the need arises.

The issue of Tibet may not be only but one of the main factors that binds the Chinese with the Himalayan Kingdom on permanent basis. The Chinese Government has continuously pursued a policy of friendship towards Nepal attach great importance to developing the comprehensive and friendly relations with Nepal. Under a policy adopted much earlier China would never change its friendly policy towards Nepal irrespective of changes both internationally and in our two countries. It is committed to pursuing cooperation with Nepal in all areas. As developing countries China and Nepal are both faced with the arduous tasks of economic and national development. Strengthening cooperation of mutual benefit and promoting common development the Peoples' Republic of China has expanded with Nepal bilateral exchanges and cooperation in politics, economy, trade, culture and tourism.

From mid-1990s, the Chinese Government has been pledging grant assistance to the Nepalese government under the Economic and Technical Cooperation programme in order to implement mutually acceptable development projects. Apart from an agreement on cultural cooperation in 1999 in the year 2001 an agreement on the construction of Syaprubesi- Kerung Road have broadened the possibilities of bilateral trade. The Government of the Peoples Republic of China has since 2001 designated Nepal as one of the tourist destination, which has rendered a great potential for Nepal to attract many tourists from China. As a mark of their enhanced understanding China had organised a cultural fair in Kathmandu in 2003 and also the Chinese Embassy in Kathmandu organised China Festival in Kathmandu in 2005, on the occasion of the 50th anniversary of the establishment of diplomatic relations. In nutshell, the adoption of liberal economic policy in Nepal, China's move towards freer economic system and their membership with the WTO have together brought two countries more closer in economic agendas.

In post-nuclear explosion period and even earlier Nepal tried to involve though unsuccessfully, China in its border dispute with India. It was Nepal's dispute over Kalapani— a strategically important tri-junction that has assumed frightening dimensions and is likely to snowball into a major controversy. It surfaced first during the Sino-Nepal Border Agreement (1961), Sino-Nepal Border Protocol (1963) and in the subsequent 1979's Border Protocol. It involves about 75 sq. km. of area in Kalapani, where China, India, and Nepal meet. Indian forces occupied the area in 1962 after India and China fought their war.[68] Three villages are located in the disputed zone: Kuti, Gunji and Knabe. India and Nepal disagree about how to interpret the Sugauli treaty between the British East India Company and Nepal, which delimited the boundary along the Maha Kali River, known as Sarda River in India. Significantly as against other neighbouring countries, India's borders with Nepal have for long been clearly demarcated since the earlier phase of British rule. India and Nepal differ as to which stream constitutes the source of the river. As per Nepalese claim, quoting the Sugauli treaty this area lies at the junction between the Tibet region of China, India and Nepal belongs to the Kathmandu regime and that India is illegally occupying it. Nepal has reportedly tabled an 1856 map from the British India office to support its position.

But India has contradicted this position saying that the river Kali begins only from the meeting point of the Lipu Gad with the stream from Kalapani springs. In the survey of India maps, the border leaves the mid stream of the Kali river below Kalapani turning Eastward away from the river, to follow the high watershed. It is also important to mention here that the first regular surveys of the upper reaches of the Kali river were conducted during the time of British India in 1870s. Such a map of 1879 vintage shows the whole Kalapani area as part of

India.[69] Even a fresh set of surveys conducted by the Nepalese surveyors in the 1920s, confirmed the 1879 border alignment.[70] Apart from this, official sources claim that administrative and revenue records dating back to 1830s, available with the UP state government, show that Kalapani area has traditionally been administered as part of Pithoragarh district.

The dispute over Kalapani intensified in 1997 as the Nepali Parliament considered a treaty on hydro-electric development of the river. The two countries have held several meetings about the dispute and discussed jointly surveying to resolve the issue.[71] It was officially taken up by Nepal during former Prime Minister I.K. Gujral's visit to Kathmandu in June 1997 who had told to send the papers relating to its claim to the government of India for examination. Kathmandu raised the matter when its Prime Minister Girija Prasad Koirala met his Indian counterpart Atal Bihari Vajpayee on the eve of 10th summit of SAARC countries held at Colombo in August 1998. This issue between India and Nepal is not likely to set aside soon because it is the result of Nepalese understanding with China on border issues. In this context Nepal has also suggested that sensitive western extremely along the junction be discussed trilaterally between China, Nepal and India, and has added yet another dimension to the dispute. It was feared that the continuing border dispute may endanger the safe movements of traders and pilgrims along the strategically - located Lipu Lekh Pass - the all weather and reliable entry point into Tibet from Almora.

Nepal's diplomatic relations with the People's Republic of China continued further and a Nepalese non-governmental friendship organization called China Study Center (CSC) founded in the year 2000 set up its Eastern Region Chapter in Biratnagar, about 400 km. from Kathmandu. It is of great important because this city is known in Nepal for its status of industry, trade center and the second largest town of the country. Inaugurating the function Sun Heping, the Chinese Ambassador to Nepal, said that there are more opportunities for China-Nepal trade cooperation and will surely bring the entrepreneurs in eastern part of Nepal closer to China.

Unfortunately as a result of the Palace Massacre in Kathmandu in June 2001 King Birendra and Queen Aishwarya was gunned down and his younger brother Gyanendra took over the charge of Administration in Nepal. Pursuing the policy already continuing for decades in April 2002 Achariya, Nepalese Foreign Secretary, visited China and briefed the Chinese side on the latest developments in Nepal. In July the same year the new king of Nepal paid a state visit to China and met Jiang Zemin, the President, chairman Li peng, Premier Zhu Rongji and Vice-President Hu jintao. Leader of the two countries spoke highly of Sino-Nepalese neighbourly friendship and cooperation and reached broad consensus on further deepening and expanding exchanges and cooperation in various areas. Exchange and interaction between them at various levels also continued further.

In March 2003 they exchanged congratulatory messages that strengthened Nepal's understanding with China. King Gyanendra continued to work under the influence of China and needed the country most because perhaps on account of the Maoists insurgency whose primary demand included the abolition of monarchy in Nepal and establishment of a democratic republic. As the Maoists insurgency and influence increased the king began to depend more and more on Chinese sympathy. At the instance of China in January 2005 the Nepali government closed the office of the Representatives of His Holiness the Dalai Lama. About the sametime Human Rights Watch urged China, India, and Nepal to uphold their obligations to respect the freedoms of expression and assembly, and due process guaranteed under domestic law and by the International Covenant on Civil and Political Rights (ICCPR).

In an unprecedented political event on 1 February 2005, King Gyanendra imposed emergency in Nepal and took over the executive powers of the government. It became a matter of world-wide condemnation particularly from India and Western countries and they, all urged the king to restore democracy at the earliest. Even on the occasion the People's Republic of China had termed the event as an internal matter of Nepal and assured the king to help otherwise. This sudden development had worsened the political situation in Nepal and as a result the

Maoists and the democratic had come together to fight jointly the autocratic rule of King Gyanendra. Consequently in April 2006 due to large scale mass movement the king agreed to left his executive powers and restore the Parliament suspended in 2002. However, inspite of political changes in Nepal its policy towards China did not make any alteration and K.P. Sharma Oli, the visiting Nepali Deputy Prime Minister of Nepal, hailed China's plan to extend Tibetan railway to Nepalese border and said that it would greatly facilitate bilateral trade, tourism and people-to-people contacts. In the year 2007 Nepal took the unexpected step of deregistering the Bhota Welfare Office, a local organization assisting Tibetan living the Himalayan Kingdom. Initially, King Gyanendra hoped for sustaining his military option with the military and moral support from the international community. For this purpose he also began mobilising China, Russia and Pakistan.

The Tibetans all over the world and particularly in Tibet itself, on their 50th anniversary of revolt, staged demonstrations for their freedom from Chinese domination in March-April 2008. During the demonstration at New- Delhi and elsewhere the Government of India remained harder towards the Tibetans and did not say anything openly against the Chinese. Perhaps it was not in a position to take Chinese displeasure on the issue and on March 10, 2008, the Indian police detained 100 exiled Tibetans who attempted to March to Tibet from Dharamasala, the site of the Tibetan government-in-exile, in Kangra District in India. On the same afternoon, Indian police issued a restraining order barring the protesters from leaving the district. Three days later, Indian police forced the marchers to stop, loaded them into police buses to a destination of police station. New Delhi also kept silence over the deployment of forces on the Nepalese side of the border with Tibet and the huge diplomatic snub by China as it summoned India's ambassador Nirupama Rao, at 2.00 am to give her a list of demonstrations that Tibetans planned to organize in India. It also included Chinese protest against Tibetan activists breaking into the Chinese Embassy in Delhi.

Unlike India, Nepal came openly in support of the Chinese and their 'One China Policy'. On March 10, 2008, Nepal's metropolitan and armed police force violently suppressed demonstrations in Kathmandu with more than150 Tibetans arbitrarily detained for several hours in Gau Shala, Kamal Pokhari and Boudha police station. The Nepalese regime and its Prime Minister Girija Prasad Koirala during his meeting with Zheng Xianglin, the Chinese Ambassador to Nepal reiterated his country's adherence to one China Policy and said that the Government of Nepal would never allow anyone or any force to engage in anti-China separatist activities on the soil of Nepal.[72]

However, on the issue of Tibet many western countries and a section of Indian and Nepali people continued to support Tibetan cause. They held China responsible for their atrocities for the last 50 years and said the Chinese authorities to initiate dialogue with the Tibetans and their leader. They urged China, India and Nepal to free Tibetan protesters who are entitled to freedom of movement, assembly, and association. On March 14, 2008, Sophie Richardson, Asia advocacy director at Human Rights, Watch, Washington, said, 'Peaceful demonstrations are protected under international laws and they should be permitted, not violently dispersed. Instead of arresting peaceful protesters, why don't these governments meet with them and attempt to address their grievances. Over the past half century, the Chinese government has arrested, detained, and tortured countless Tibetans including monks, nuns and children protesting Chinese rule intended to quash alleged separatism. We are witnessing the most visible wave of peaceful dissent against Chinese rule in the Tibetan capital for the last two decades.' He also expressed surprise over New Delhi and Kathmandu's attitude and added what is unusual is the harsh crackdown on similar protests in democratic India and Nepal, which raises concerns about whether China is pressuring those countries to silence Tibetans.

The year 2008 also witnessed a basic change in Nepalese political system - abolition of monarchy and establishment of federal republic. In the election of Constituent Assembly the Maoists emerged as the largest faction in Nepalese politic who had even before coming to power had been demanding of the revision Indo-Nepal Treaty of 1950. Pushpa Kamal Dahal 'Prachanda' the

Maoist leader who later in August 2008 became the first Prime Minister of the Nepalese republic, in an interview to *The Hindu*, had held the view that the 1950 treaty exists but based on the situation in the first decade of the 21st century, we feel it will be better for Nepal and India to have a new treaty. Our people have the feeling that somewhere along the line, the kind of benefit Nepal could get is not there, so the Nepali people's aspiration has been to change this. He also said that we would like to review all the other treaties to see what revision or further enhancements are necessary. What we want is new unity on a new basis with India. Far from wanting to damage our relations, we want to make them even better.[73] After taking over as the Prime Minster of Nepal he preferred to visit China first and reiterated to pursue Nepal's policy of equidistance between India and China.

**Analysis of the Attitude**

The Government of Nepal was initially happy with the coming of a BJP- led government under the premiership of Atal Bihari Vajpayee in March 1998. As earlier the new Government of India had reiterated its intention to follow a policy of friendship and cooperation with neighbours. In earlier phase too the small neighbours of India had been benefited form the Gujral Doctrine and pinned a hope in the current regime. For a short while the Himalayan Kingdom felt uneasy when the new government exploded its nuclear device in May 1998 and the suit was also followed by Pakistan in the same month. Economic help and cooperation, made on the part of India continued further in this phase and trade turn over increased in comparison to the previous years. However, in political sphere the issue of Pakistan - based ISI agents' activities on Indian soil remained a tension area on the New Delhi's side. Nepal had reached an understanding with Islamabad to put India under pressure and as an alternative to the Peoples' Republic of China as Sino-Indian relations were mending day by day and in view of United State's improved relations with the Beijing and New Delhi, China became less interested in Indo-Nepal affairs.

But in relation to India Nepalese political relations with the Chinese improved rapidly and it became a cause of concern for New Delhi. A change of guard took place in India in the year 2004 and the Congress Party with the support of leftists formed the government under the premiership of Dr. Manmohan Singh. The new government continued India's earlier policy with Nepal but latter's unwillingness to check the ISI activities on its soil and its growing connections with the Beijing remained a matter of grave concern. The Congress government of India continued to be anxious on the growing popularity of the Maoists in Nepal and in future alertness is required on the part of India because the system of century—old monarchy in Nepal had been abolished. It had now become a federal republic with Maoists a vital, permanent for future Nepal. As the basic political system of Nepal has taken a 'U' turn, New Delhi needs to realise the ground realities in Nepal and make policy adjustment on its part to have a fruitful relations with Kathmandu in future.

In comparison to India the Himalayan Kingdom witnessed several basic changes in its political system and in its relations with other countries as well. As earlier Nepal depended more on India for its economic development but did not miss any occasion to play its old China-card to pressurise New Delhi. Internally from the mid-Nineties the influence of Maoists increased rapidly and controlling of Maoists' violence proved a challenging task for the Nepalese regimes. In transition the incident of Palace Massacre occurred in June 2001 had also cast a dark shadow on Indo-Nepal relations. The democratic forces of Nepal also remained divided and no consensus emerged among them on political matters that led to the mass dissatisfaction and a general wave in favour of the Maoists became dominant. From the beginning the Maoists had demanded the abolition of monarchy and establishment of a federal republic in the country.

As a result of the Palace Massacre Gyanendra became the new King of Nepal in June 2001 and faced a difficult time on account of political instability and Maoists insurgency in the larger parts of the country. Coronation of the new king also received mixed reactions in India as, from earlier, he was famous for his anti-Indian attitudes. In a significant development on 1 February 2005 King Gyanendra declared emergency in the country and took over the executive powers of the government. King's arbitrary misrule provided an opportunity to shake hands between the Maoist and democratic forces of the country. A mass movement was started jointly in April 2006 which compelled the king to bow down and relinquish the executive powers taken over earlier. In the election of the new Constituent Assembly the Maoists forces found a lion's share and a Maoists-led coalition formed the government. The new Prime Minister Prachanda had demanded revision of the Indo-Nepal treaty of 1950 in the new context. Nepal's political relations with India remained tense as earlier on the issue of ISI activities and other security matters. Beijing's growing influence in Nepal is also a grave concern for New Delhi. Installation of a Maoist government in Kathmandu would certainly serve Chinese purpose more in comparison to India and the latter would left with no option but to move consciously in its relations with Nepal.

## Notes and References

1. Raj Kumar Kothari, "Democratic Transition in Nepal: Banes and Boons for India," Subhash C. Kashyap, ed., *South Asia Politics*, Vol. 7, No. 2, June 2008, New Delhi. pp. 24.
2. Kalyan Chaudhuri, "A Realignment in Nepal and Changing Political Realities," *Frontline*, April 4, 1997, pp. 51-52.
3. Uddipan Mukherjee, "Maoism and Its Future in India," Subhash C. Kashyap, ed., *South Asia Politics*, Vol. 7, No. 3, July 2008, New Delhi, pp. 26-27.
4. Rajkumar Singh, "Democratic Experiments in Nepal," Babuddin Khan, ed., *Third Concept*, Vol. 21, No. 251, January, 2008, pp. 16-17.
5. *The Hindustan Times,* 4 August 1998.
6. *The Times of India*, 4 August 1999.
7. *Ibid.*
8. *Ibid.,* 5 March 1999.
9. *Ibid.,* 4 March 1999.
10. *Ibid.,* 7 January 2000.
11. *Ibid.,* 4 June 2001.
12. Manoj Joshi, "A Tale of Two Countries," *Ibid.,* 5 February 2005.
13. Rajkumar Singh, *op. cit.,* p. 17.
14. *The Hindu*, 2 February 2005.
15. *The Hindustan Times*, (editorial), 2 February 2005.

16. Prem Shankar Jha, "Royal Plural" *Ibid.*, 11 February 2005.
17. Manjushree Thapa, "Exile and Kingdom," *Ibid.*, 7 February 2005.
18. *The Financial Times*, 14 December 2005.
19. *Ibid.*
20. Siddarth Varadarajan, "The Countdown in Kathmandu has Begun," *The Hindu*, 30 March 2006.
21. *Ibid.*, 1 May 2006.
22. *Ibid.*, (editorial), 3 April 2007.
23. Siddarth Varadarajan, "Triumph of the New Mainstream in Nepal," *Ibid.*, 16 April, 2008.
24. *Ibid.*
25. *Ibid.*, 22 July 2008.
26. *Ibid.*, 1 September 2008.
27. Mahinda Werake, 'China and South Asia in the Eighties,' Shelton U Kodikara, ed., *External Compulsions of South Asian Politics*, New Delhi; 1993, p. 90.
28. For detail visit http://www.photius.com/countries/nepal/national_security.
29. Uddipan Mukherjee, *op. cit.*, 26.
30. *The Hindustan Times*, 4 June 2001.
31. *Ibid.*
32. *Ibid.*
33. S.D. Muni. "Thy Hand, Great Monarch," *Ibid.*, February 2005.
34. Shriman Narayan, *India and Nepal: An Exercise in Open Diplomacy*, New Delhi, 1971, p. 124.
35. *The Indian Express*, 28 November 2005.
36. *The Financial Times*, 14 December 2005.
37. *Xinhua*, 3 January 2006.
38. *The Hindu*, 14 June 2008.
39. *Ibid.*, 25 August 2008.
40. Verghese Koithara, *Society State and Security, The Indian Experience*, New Delhi, 1999, p. 72.
41. *The Hindustan Times*, 5 March 1999.

42. *Ibid.*, 6 August 1999.
43. *Ibid.*, 27 December 1999.
44. *Ibid.*, 6 January 2000.
45. *Ibid.*, 6 February 2000.
46. *The Indian Express*, 10 January 2006.
47. *Pakistan Link News*, 28 December 2005.
48. *The Hindustan Times*, 29 May 1998.
49. *Ibid.*
50. *Ibid.*, 30 May 1998.
51. *Ibid.*, 31 May 1998.
52. *Ibid.*, 23 January 1999.
53. *Ibid.*, 20 August 1999.
54. *Ibid.*, 8 September 1999.
55. *Ibid.*, (editorial), 11 September 1999.
56. *Ibid.*, 13 September 1999.
57. *Daily Times*, 15 December 2008.
58. *The Hindu*, 14 September 2008.
59. As quoted in *Ibid.*
60. S.D. Muni, "Dealing With a New Nepal," *Ibid.*, 15 September 2008.
61. *Ibid.*
62. *Ibid.*, 16 September 2008.
63. *Ibid.*
64. *Ibid.*, 17 September 2008.
65. *Ibid.*, 18 September 2008.
66. *The Hindustan Times*, 4 August 1998.
67. *Ibid.*, 27 May 1998.
68. *Kyodo* (Tokyo), 1 September 1997.
69. Rajkumar Singh, India-South Asia Minus Congress Regimes, Patna, 2000, pp. 125-26.
70. *Ibid.*
71. *The Kathmandu Post*, 16 July, 1997 and Xinhua, 11 April 1997.
72. *Xinhua*, 7 April 2008.
73. *The Hindu*, 28 April 2008.

# 13

# A REPORTCARD OF INDIA AND CHINA IN NEPAL

## CASE OF CHINA

### Political

The people's Republic of China and Nepal are close neighbours and enjoy over a thousand years of friendly contacts. It is well known that Nepal and China have very long and constantly sustained relationships. These have been marked by friendliness, mutual support, understanding and appreciation of each other's aspirations and sensitivities. In recent past they both have been unequivocally abiding by the ideals of Panchsheel and the Five Principles of Peaceful Co-existence. Such friendship is a great asset of the peoples of the two countries. Regular exchange of high level visits has played an important role in further consolidating their mutual beneficial relations. Since the establishment of Sino-Nepalese diplomatic relations on August 1, 1955 traditional friendship and friendly cooperation between the Chinese and Nepalese people have witnessed continuous development. Frequent have been the contacts between the leaders of the two countries. Nepalese King and Prime Ministers visited China many a time and the same response the former had taken on Chinese part. The leaders of both past and present, have brought about the flowering of China-Nepal friendship with their wisdom,vision and unremitting efforts. The untiring efforts of leaders made over half a century, exchanges and cooperation between China and Nepal in political, diplomatic, economic and trade, cultural, educational and other fields have borne rich fruit.

The foreign policy of Nepal took a dramatic turn politically after the death of King Tribhuvan and succession of his son,

King Mahendra. The new king did not feel the same commitment to and sympathy for India as his father did and palace politics soon came to be dominated by elements and forces not-too-friendly to New Delhi. Mahendra initiated the policy of Nepalese quest for diversification of foreign relations. The main emphasis in the new innovations introduced in 1956 was an effort to diversify, to the extent possible, Nepal's diplomatic and economic relations in order to modify the 'special relationship' with India. In the new framework China was perceived as the principal instrument for the attainment of diversification by the king. Tanka Prasad Acharya, the new Prime Minster of Nepal, now openly spoke that Nepal's foreign policy was based on the principle of 'equal friendship' with India and China.

Equal relationship with India and China is one of the basic tenets of Nepalese foreign policy since the days of King Prithvi Narayan Shah who founded and unified the Kingdom. He described the Kingdom of the Kathmandu Valley as 'a fort built by God himself and a root between two stones'. As the first king was the friend, philosopher and guide of modern Nepal he suggested to maintain friendly relations with the Emperor of China. Great friendship should also be maintained with the Emperor beyond the southern seas, but he is very clever. For future he advised the country not to engage in offensive attack. Fighting should be conducted on a defensive basis......If it is found difficult to resist in the fight, then even means of persuasion, tact and deceit should be employed. King Prithvi Narayan Shah, during his term of office followed this policy in dealings with the British in India. The most formidable problem in the formulation and implementation of foreign policy had been the preservation of its independence in the face of the two concurrent but separate threats posed by the newly emerging dominant power in northern India, the British East India Company, and the slowly but steadily expanding Chinese presence in Tibet. Although Nepal's policy of balancing China against British India could not succeed to the extent desired by Kathmandu, it however, persisted in its game of balancing the one against the other with a view to preserve at least its internal independence.

King Mahendra not only diversified the external relations of Nepal but, in the new international perspectives, added three strong urges in its foreign policy formulation and execution. George Liska, in his book *Alliance and the Third World,* has counted these urges as security, stability and status. The urge for 'security' has found expression in the objectives of (a) preservation of autonomy and independence in taking and implementing foreign policy decisions; and (b) preservation of territorial integrity. The first objective has a politico-diplomatic connotation and its task may be described as one of counteracting undesirable external pressures and influences. The second objective has a politico - military - strategic connotation and its task is defence against external aggression for the preservation of territorial integrity. The urge for stability has also two dimensions, namely (a) stability of the domestic power structure in which every ruling group has the highest stakes, and (b) stability through economic development. These dimensions have been accordingly expressed as objectives of foreign policy. The urge for 'status' is psychological in nature and it has been one of the forceful drives behind Nepal's foreign policy behaviour.

A clear shift in Nepalese foreign policy and relations witnessed after the dismissal of the first elected government by King Mahendra on 15 December 1960. In the years following the royal coup the monarchical regime of Nepal looked for legitimacy at home, faced the Nepali Congress rebels harboured and sympathized in India, resisted India's pressure and persuasion to look for reconciliation with the rebels and as a result it looked to China against India. King's policy changed abruptly towards the end of 1961 when it became apparent that New Delhi was unwilling to provide the kind of guarantee that his royal regime considered vital to its survival. At the juncture his visit to China in October 1961 had paved the way for strong Nepal - China relations and the two had signed boundary treaty and an economic aid agreement providing for the construction of a road connecting Kathmandu with Tibet. Further India's defeat at the hands of Chinese in October 1962 also helped and encouraged Nepal to have a strong strategic ties with the Beijing. Apart from Nepalese designs China had also limited objectives in Nepal primarily directed at complicating India's relationship with neighbouring states in order to limit New Delhi's ability to take effective action outside the South Asian region. The Chinese presence in Nepal expanded considerably after 1962 but not to the point where it might have been reasonably viewed as dominant by New Delhi or threatening by Kathmandu.

In history as a general rule Nepalese autocrats had played China - card effectively in the regional politics for continuing their unjust and undemocratic regime. Whenever Nepal had democratically elected governments, the Chinese autocrats lost the partners in autocratic governance giving way to the democratic countries to have more influence on democratic governments in Nepal than the Chinese government. The elected governments in Nepal tended to loosen their control over the Tibetan refugees in Nepal, and let them freely travel and engage in their activities for freedom in Tibet. Hence, the Chinese autocratic proletarian government always found democracy in Nepal as a threat to their oppressive rule in Tibet. Thus the first victims of Nepalese China card were the Tibetans fighting for freedom from the autocratic rule of the Chinese proletarian leaders, and another victim, of course, was the democracy in Nepal. This was true in 1960 when King Mahendra played the China-card to kill the infant democracy and in recent past in 2005 when King Gyanendra used the China-card to throttle the flourishing democracy. In 1960s the then king of Nepal had suppressed the voices of Tibetan refugees in Nepal, and stopped any political activities of them from Nepal against the People's Republic of China. Later on the king had also eliminated the Khampa rebels fighting against the Chinese rule in Tibet from the northern border of Nepal in 1970s.

Likewise before taking over the executive powers King Gyanendra shut down the offices of Dalai Lama and of Tibetan Refugees in Nepal. Obviously, this was done to keep the Chinese government happy. The king was sure that India and the western democratic countries would not support his actions of upsurging the power from the elected government and so he wanted to keep at least one neighbour happy and in his favour. China too, perhaps in response, described the developments in

Nepal as its internal matter and refrained form taking any stand on the take over. It had taken a friendly attitude towards the king in Nepal. As reported by media the Nepali monarch desperately sought arms from China and the Chinese army escorted eighteen trucks carrying arms and ammunition to Nepal's borders where plain-clothes Nepalese troops took over in November 2005. By supplying lethal weapons to Nepal China had not only demonstrated its disregard for democracy, civil liberties and human rights but also added fuel to the further bloodshed in Nepal. It is perhaps due to the fact that the communists believe in subjection of individuals to the dictatorship of the proletariats.

Once again in March 2008 the problem of Tibet became a hot issue when the Tibetans wherever they reside, attempted to observe 'Tibetan National Uprising Day', the anniversary of the Tibetan rebellion against Beijing's rule in Tibet in 1959. They organised peaceful protests calling for an end to religious restrictions and release of imprisoned monks. Perhaps at Chinese instance on March 10, 2008, Nepal's metropolitan and armed police force violently suppressed demonstrators in Kathmandu with more than 150 Tibetans arbitrarily detained for several hours at different police stations of the Kingdom. In fact many Tibetans who arrived in Nepal before 31 December 1989 are officially regarded as refugees. But the Nepalese government has refused to register as refugees Tibetan asylum seekers arriving after that time. As a result, new arrivals are at risk of summary repatriation and encounter great difficulty integrating into Nepali society and accessing education, health care, and employment. It is also impossible for them to leave the country unless granted an exit permit. King Gyanendra too during his term of office had taken several steps inimical to Tibetan interests just to please the Chinese dispensation. In addition, for long Nepal has been consistently pursing the 'One China' policy and considered Tibet and Taiwan as the integral parts of the Chinese territory. It is said that to look back the friendly history of China-Nepal relations there are three factors which have enabled their friendship to maintain its strong momentum of growth over the years. The first is trust. The two countries never threat each other, harm each other or doubt each other, but always respect each other, believe each other and help each other. The Chinese government and people firmly pursue the principle of non-interference in the internal affairs of Nepal. The second is equality. The Chinese government and people firmly pursue the principle that a country is equal with others no matter how big or small it is. In the last 50 years, abiding by the Five Principle of Peaceful Co-existence, through equal dialogue, communication and coordination, China and Nepal have made excellent cooperation and achieved great accomplishments in bilateral political relations, regional affairs and international forums. The third is sincerity. China treats Nepal as its closest neighbour and best friend. Over the last 50years, with China's financial and technical assistance, more than 30 projects have been completed in Nepal. China has also appreciated the strong support that Kathmandu extended over the years on the question of Taiwan and Tibet and other major issues related to China's sovereign rights and interests. In recent years, the relations between China and Nepal have developed more rapidly.

**Economic**

As a friendly neighbour of China, Nepal is one of the first group of countries China has provided with aid. Since 1956, China has rendered the Nepalese government 64 sums of aid, all free, with the total amount close to RMB 1.4 billion. With the help of this financial assistance the Nepalese has mainly built highways, brick-kilns, paper mills, hospitals, schools, hydro-power stations, textile plants, tanneries, irrigation projects, sugar refineries and International Conference House. China and Nepal are both faced with the arduous tasks of economic and national development. Strengthening cooperation of mutual benefit and promoting common development are shared aspirations that serve mutual interests. China is ready to increase friendly exchanges with the Nepalese government, political parties and people of all walks of life, and expand bilateral exchanges and cooperation in politics, economy, trade, culture and tourism. China will continue to support economic and social development in Nepal to the best of its capacity.

Initially China endeavoured to cement its friendly ties with Nepal further by giving economic aid and perhaps the first agreement on economic matters they signed was on the maintenance of Friendship and Trade and Transport between Tibet Autonomous Region on September 20, 1956. It followed in October 1956 Peking's promise to give Kathmandu assistance worth Rs. 60 crores in cash and material without any condition attached to the use of the aid. It was said that Nepal would be free to use the money and materials as it wished and the Government of the People's Republic of China would not interfere. Further economic agreement was signed between the two in March 1960 when Nepalese Prime Minister B.P. Koirala visited Peking which stipulated that China would give Nepal a free grant of aid to a total value of Rs. 100 million in Indian currency within a period of three years and without any political condition attached.

The Chinese aid programme caught the imagination of the Nepalese more by its methods of operation than by its size. It was different from the Indian or the American aid programme which were executed under the strict supervision of the technicians of the donor country. In contrast, the Chinese aid programme did not insist on examining the soundness of specific projects on which the amount was to be spent. To the Nepalese people the outright grant of foreign aid with no restriction on its utilisation by China amounted to a recognition of their capacity to administer their own economic development without outside foreign supervision. China's economic aid to Nepal demonstrated that China was keen to get a strong foot-hold in Nepal's political life.

Behind the Chinese aid programme in Nepal, the main purpose was political and strategic. Despite the differences, between the two on the question of Mount Everest and the Border incident, they came closer to each other due to their own reasons. In post - royal coup period King Mahendra needed Chinese help for himself and his regime. With a view to broaden the base of Nepal's relations with China King Mahendra visited China in 1961 during which he obtained Peking's assurance that China would be more than careful to respect Nepal's national sentiments. The agreements signed in course of the visit proved a major breakthrough in Sino-Nepal relations. It was a great victory for the Chinese diplomacy in Nepal. Obviously this was more than good neighourliness or even the desire to expand Chinese influence in the region.

Formerly China viewed Nepal as an area of Indian influence and did not come in the way of Nepalese relations with the British India. Rana regimes in Nepal maintained a very good and close relations with the British India but later on after the withdrawal of the British, it was not liked by the Chinese. As the imperial designs of the Chinese increased it posed a security problem for India at the close of the forties. Among India's small neighbours, Nepal was of some significance to Peking because of its monarch's desire for external support to counter military and economic pressures from New Delhi that threatened its independence. Chinese diplomacy exploited this need with some success and there were incidental benefits. From the regional point of view China's increased power and influence in the Himalayan was not a good sign for India. The elimination of Tibet as a buffer state, change of Tibet into a Chinese military base, combined with increasing Chinese pressure for direct contacts with Nepal had vastly upset the balance.

From the beginning, Chinese economic assistance to Nepal was worth in name. The main Chinese objective in the region was political and strategic. Keeping in view its strategic position it continued to provide economic assistance in order to complicate India's relationship with the Himalayan Kingdom and limit New Delhi's ability to take effective action outside the South Asian region. With a view to achieve this objective China tried its best to hurt India's relations with Nepal, isolate India, eliminate Indian influence and draw Nepal into its own sphere of influence. However, the Chinese objectives in Nepal changed with the passing of time. In the early fifties it started its relations with Nepal very polite way but later began to challenge India in each and every field. From mid-sixties it started to make its role in the Himalayan Kingdom more assertive or forceful.

China continued to help Nepal further its economic development. Trade and aid were the two important instruments but nevertheless remained rather limited in comparison to India. China had helped Nepal in the establishment of a shoe factory, some brick and tile factories and ware houses. But the aid had gone principally into road building and power generation. The major project China took was the construction of the 67-mile Kathmandu- Kodari Highway and committed itself to build some 200 mile roads. In the field of power-potential, Peking, agreed to assist in the construction of a 10,000 kw hydro-electric station. In 1967 the two countries concluded an agreement proposing aid for constructing a hydro-electric station on the Sunkosi river, 20 mile south from the Nepal- Tibet border. Further China agreed in December 1970 to provide financial and technical assistance in setting up power transmission line from Sunkosi hydel project to Barhibise and Chatura in east Nepal.

Nepal's trade with China is largely conducted through Tibet and Hong Kong. Six points along the Nepal-China border have been opened for overland route trade. Nepal and China have established Inter-governmental Economic and Trade Committee (IGETC) in October 1982. Its meetings have become the main forum for discussions on Nepal-China bilateral economic and technical cooperation. The IGETC meetings focus on economic and technical assistance, bilateral trade and tourism. The adoption of liberal economic policy in Nepal, China's move towards freer economic system, and their membership with the WTO have together brought two countries even more closer in economic agendas. However the current trade statistics show that there exists a huge trade deficit. In 2005-06 Nepal imported Rs. 6,63,55,06,000 worth of goods from China which stood as second biggest import source. In the same period, Nepal exported Rs. 10,81,68,000 worth of goods to China, which stood as 21$^{st}$ export destination. It is a matter of concern for Nepal that an ever increasing trade deficit continues to dominate the economy.

Nepal has been receiving financial and technical assistance from China as a reliable development partner, despite its own status as developing country. Chinese aid is focussed mainly in infrastructure such as roads, bridges, hospital, hydro-power project, sports facilities and industrial set ups. It is geared towards the long-term goals of promoting Nepal's trade capability with China, particularly with Tibet via overland route. The China Study Center (CSC), which was founded in 2000 has recently set up its Eastern Region Chapter (ERC) in Biratnagar to boost opportunities for Nepal-China trade cooperation.

In 2001 the Government of the People's Republic of China has designated Nepal as one of the tourist destinations and they have signed the Memorandum of Understanding on Tourism Cooperation. It has rendered a great potential for Nepal to attract many tourists from China. Chinese Yuan has been made convertible for tourists and businessmen in Nepal,while visa fee for Chinese tourists has been waived. Later on, the two countries signed Air Service Agreement according to which, Air China opened a direct air link between China and Nepal in 2004, by route of Chengdu-Lasha-Kathmandu. In addition, the China Southern Airline has also started operating air service between Guangzhou and Kathmandu since February 2007. Likewise, the Nepal Airline is operating air service between Kathmandu and Shanghai, Kathmandu and Hongkong. In addition to direct air links, bus service between Kathmandu and Lhasa has been in operation since 2005. In 2007 about 14,500 Chinese travelled to Nepal via air route. In order to sustain the deep rooted cultural relations the two countries have reached an agreement on cultural cooperation in 1999 and as a follow up various activities have taken place in each others territories.

In sphere of investment the Chinese status in Nepal is growing and has potential to further growth. Chinese investors are found interested in making investment in hotels and restaurants, electronics, telecommunications services, readymade garments medical services, hydropower, civil construction, etc. Recently the Chinese government has encouraged its viable enterprises to invest in friendly countries. There are ample possibility of developing bilateral cooperation through large scale induction of Chinese technology and capital in the form of joint ventures. China has also increased its activities in various aspects of the Nepalese life. To develop overall economic activities the Chinese people's Association for Friendship with Foreign Countries (CPAFFC) and Nepal-China Executive Council (NCEC) have signed a Memorandum of Understanding on December 25, 2005 according to which both the organizations shall cooperate on the promotion and expansion of cooperation in the field of trade, tourism and cultural exchanges, and shall act as facilitators to promote and strengthen investment and entrepreneurial relationship between the two countries.

In 1996 the two countries had also established the Nepal-China Non-governmental Cooperation Forum. The Forum is being led by FNCCI from the Nepalese side and All China Federation of Industry and Commerce (ACFIC) from the Chinese side. In the same year the Consultation Mechanism was arranged for foreign secretaries meeting between the two countries under which foreign secretaries visit each other's capitals to hold meetings regularly. It has proved to be an effective tools of interaction with each other. The seventh round of the Mechanism was held in Kathmandu in 2008.

In the filed of education China has been providing 100 scholarships annually to Nepalese students to study in China. Many Nepalese have found China as an attractive destination for higher studies, particularly in medical sciences. This has helped Nepal to meet the ever-increasing demand for technical manpower in the country. It has also contributed to promoting understanding and appreciation of each others' culture and tradition.

**Defence**

Located in the centre of the Himalayas between the Tibetan regions of China and India, Nepal is a land-locked country, cut off from the rest of the world by high mountains. Among these distinct states Nepal happens to be the largest on the southern slopes of the great mountain divide which has always been regarded vital from the viewpoint of Indian security. By virtue of its strategic position it has always been felt that Nepal could influence the course of events in central Asia. This feeling in the Nepalese mind is part of its ancient heritage and rooted in the awareness that one of the main land routes between India and China lay in Nepalese territory. Though the opportunities to exploit the geographical influence was rare, Nepal however, was aware of its immense potential. For China, Nepal had all along been a distant neighbour and the former could come into contact with it only through Tibet. In the early fifties Peking's security interests in Nepal could no longer be regarded peripheral as the United States of America was setting up bases, wherever possible, encircling China.

Nepal's security relations with China dated at least as far back as the eighteenth century. In the nineteenth century, Nepal gained the upper hand over Tibet, then a semi-autonomous vassal state of China. The earliest defence pact with China was the Sino-Nepalese Treaty of 1792, signed after the Chinese had defeated the forces of the Gorkha Kingdom. Although it mentioned in the treaty that China would be regarded as a "father" for the Nepalese and the former would come to the aid of Nepal should it ever be invaded by a foreign power, no such assistance occurred during the Anglo-Nepalese war of 1814-16. The Nepalese-Tibetan Treaty of Thapathali was signed in 1856 and stipulated that Tibet would pay annual tribute to Nepal and grant certain extraterritorial rights to Nepalese traders. And lastly a century later in September 1956, the treaty of 1856 was replaced by an agreement of amity and commerce with China's new communist regime, ending Nepal's tributory income and extraterritorial privileges. China, on several occasions had offered to sign non-aggression or mutual defence pacts with Nepal the latter had always turned down the offers in deference to Indian sensitivities.

After the establishment of communist rule in 1949 throughout the 1950s, Nepal's anticommunist rulers spured on by Indian advisers, regarded China as a potential threat and enacted various military reforms and laws to combat Chinese propaganda and subversion. Nepal's defence relations with China was also badly affected by a security pact the former had signed with India in July 1950. Of the two treaties signed at a time between India and Nepal the Treaty of Peace and Friendship, stipulated in Article '5' of the treaty, 'The Government of Nepal shall be free to import from or through the territory of India, arms, ammunition, or warlike material and equipment necessary for the security of Nepal. The procedure for giving effect to this arrangement shall be worked out by the two Governments acting in consultation. In a further move the exchange of letters took place between India and Nepal in which the Nepalese ambassador had confirmed that these letters constituted an agreement between the two countries. In the exchanged letters the understanding was that India would supply the entire requirement of the Nepalese army to the best of its ability, with Britain and the USA being allowed to step in only when Indian was unable to do so. Moreover, the agreement further provided that even when Britain and US arms were permitted, they would have to be routed to the land-locked Kingdom, only through Indian territory. The provisions had tied the hands of both China and Nepal as well on security matters.

Thus despite political and economic interactions between China and Nepal security-related concerns remained scarce between the two for a long time. Even understandings between them on defence matters faded due to non-application in the circumstances. It was only in the year 1988 that Nepal dared to purchase certain arms and ammunition from the Chinese that too proved fatal for the Kingdom and resulted in the delay of renewal of trade and transit treaty with India creating a lot of hardships for the common people of the country. Perhaps being fearful from the development in India-Sri Lanka relations and sending of Indian Peace-keeping Forces there to protect the national unity and integrity of the country, Nepal became apprehensive of Indian motives and felt insured. In March 1988 King Birendra directed the Nepali negotiators to finalise a deal with the Chinese and Nepal received the equipments in June-July, the same year. The delivered military supplies included anti-aircraft guns, medium range missiles, A.K. 47 rifles, huge quantities of ammunition and uniforms, etc. Purchase of arms from China without taking India into confidence was against the Indo-Nepal Friendship Treaty of 1950 and negation of the 1965 agreement on import of arms between the two countries. Nepal violated both and the deal seems to be a step forward in Kingdom's search for strategic diversification and distancing from India. It had generally preferred to keep relations with China low-key to avoid offending India. The 1988 decision was a glaring exception to this rule.

Clarifications on Nepalese part came in which Marich Man Singh Shreshtha, the Prime Minster of Nepal, denied the charge of using China as a counter balancing force against India and favouring the deal said that our defence arrangements are related only to our internal security and at the same time rejected the question of any threat to neighbours. In the mid-1980s, small antimonarchist and communist groups conducted a series of bombings in the Kathmandu Valley to dramatize their opposition to Birendra's rule. In June 1984, clandestine Maoist bands such as the Samyuktha Mukti Bahini, the Democratic Front, and the United Liberation Torch Bearers mounted a campaign of bombings and assassinations intended to spark a revolution. To deal with the situation the Rashtriya Panchayat passed a stringent anti-terrorist ordinance to put down the threat. The following year another sensational crime was perpetrated by the Jan Morcha (People's Front), a Tarai-based anti-monarchist group. The strong communist showing in succeeding years was also a disturbing development from the perspective of King Birendra and the army alike.

However, Nepalese explanations failed to satisfy Indian sentiments and policy makers and in the closing years of the eighties, the Kingdom had to face two developments in her international relations. Firstly, Nepal could not count on China's armed support in any confrontation with India brought about by Nepal's own actions. Secondly, in March 1989, the trade and transit treaties with India lapsed and the world, including China, simply watched when India refused to allow Nepal any more benefits than what international practice and usage allowed. Even a change of government in Delhi made little difference. At the time economy of the country was in disarray and the prices of essential goods like petrol, kerosene, sugar and salt made life expensive and troublesome for the common people.

Strong understanding on defence matters increased between China and Nepal despite New Delhi's complains and anxieties. From 1990 onwards even the Army officers of RNA, most of whom rejected the anti-monarchist platform of the communists, invariably regarded the communists as a potential security menace and a threat to the throne. There was no evidence in late 1991 that some twenty Nepalese communist factions then in existence commanded any appreciable support within the army rank-and-file. Gradually the relations between the armies of China and Nepal became an important component of their overall relations. In the past years, the military relations and cooperation between them have experienced continuous development. Nearly all the former Army Chiefs and Defence Secretaries of Nepal have visited China. The Defence Minister and the General Chief of Staff of China have also visited Nepal. China has rendered help and assistance to Nepal within its own capacity. The two armies have conducted good cooperation in personnel training as well. Since 1998, the Nepal Amry has sent officers and soldiers to study in Chinese military universities. In the academic year 2006-07, in particular 21 officers and soldiers of the Nepal Army went to China for training. China has also sent military officers to participate in the adventure trainings organised by the Nepal Army since 2002. On several occasions the Chinese government had expressed its pledge to continue a policy of friendship towards Nepal and made it clear that it attached great importance to developing the comprehensive and friendly relations with Nepal.

On 1 February 2005, King Gyanendra took over the executive powers and put a ban on all political and democratic activities. Barring China, who termed it as the internal affairs of Nepal, India, the US, the UK and the international community as a whole had condemned the development and suspended the military supplies to the Royal Nepalese Army. They did not believe at King's word that their army would not use the arms and ammunitions against the people fighting for democratic rights. At the juncture while the Government of India sided with the democratific forces and mounted pressure on King Gyanendra to compromise with them the Chinese authorities proved opposite number. The Nepalese monarch when sought arms from China the latter had sent 18 truckloads of arms and ammunition. The Chinese army escorted trucks carrying arms and ammunition to Nepal's border where the plain-clothes Nepalese troops took over in November 2005. By supplying lethal weapons to Nepal, China had displayed its disregard for civil liberties and human rights in the country.

China's supply of arms and ammunition to Nepal at a time when it was passing through the most difficult situation in nation's history was criticized by democratic forces of the world including India. Some newspapers viewed it more than a tactical threat to India's attempt at promoting democracy and stability in Nepal and expressed the opinion that India should compel the King Gyanendra to pay the costs of the China-card he has chosen to play against India. But in Nepalese circle there are two divided opinions on the issue. While a section of the people blamed India for its refusal to supply arms and equipments to the King which he needed perhaps to combat the Maoist terrorists, and it forced the Kingdom to look toward China, others criticized foreign powers and campaigners who are making the Chinese military assistance to Nepal a case of intervention in Nepal's internal affairs. Such forces are also effortful to prove that Nepal has tilted toward China and there is increasing Chinese influences in Nepal. Academic circle of Nepal still held the view that still country's foreign policy remains unchanged and the Kingdom of Nepal believes in the policy of neutrality and non-alignment.

## CASE OF INDIA

### One Culturally and Emotionally

Although landlocked Nepal is surrounded by both India and China, the Himalayan Kingdom's ties with New Delhi is direct and deep in spheres of history, geography, religion social relationship, mutual faith, values, customs and conventions, politics, economy and defence etc. As mentioned in several religious books the pre-Vedic Shiva who lived in the eternal city of Banaras was wedded to Parbati, the daughter of the Himalayas. Shiva and Parbati stayed at Banaras during day-time but left for Mansarowar every evening and returned to Banaras at day break next morning. This established the necessary harmony between the Vedic and the indigenous traditions or between the 'Nigams and the Agamas as the Hindu priests put it. Shiva also became the Pashupati Nath-Lord of all animals-of the Kirati rulers of the Kathmandu valley. These were the binding social links between the people of Nepal and early India. Coming to facts established by archaeological findings we come to the time of Gautam Buddha, who was born at Lumbini the Nepal Terai and spent a good deal of his wandering life near that area. It followed the period of Ashok who built the stupas at Patan, and whose daughter Charumati dedicated her life to the spread of the Dharma relating to the Buddhist faith amongst the people of Nepal. All these expanded interactions between the rulers and people of India and Nepal. Even the Shah dynasty of Gorkha and later of Nepal claims descent from the Rajput ruling family of Chittor and along with the Shah family came several collateral chiefs including Ranas, Kunwars and others.

Between India and Nepal Hinduism has been, and continues to be the strongest common bond. Nepal is a Hindu Kingdom, and the King is looked upon as the protector and is defined as the early manifestation of the Hindu god Vishnu. This central place of Hinduism in Nepal's political set up has been accepted by all segments of the population. Even before the advent of the Gorkha rule in the $18^{th}$ century, Buddhism was a flourishing religion in the region. The Gorkha rulers projected Nepal's distinct identity as Hindu state. The Hinduisation of the Kingdom was completed by the Rana rulers who brought the various ethnic groups into the Hindu social hierarchy through the civil code of 1854. The codification and standardisation of religious and social practices led to the assimilation of many ethnic groups into the dominant Nepali culture. A vast majority of today practice a syncretic blend of Hinduism, Buddhism and/or animist traditions. They worship the same gods/goddesses and celebrate some festivals commonly. Thus, the basic value system of Nepal-their metaphysics systems of thought and aesthetics-owes overwhelmingly to Hinduism and India. Hinduism has been the religion of the ruling class in Nepal and it is not surprising that Hindu social and ritual practices carry the highest prestige and value even among communities of Mongoloid origin.

The social systems of India and Nepal bear striking similarities. Some of the Hindu Kings of Nepal, notably, Jayasthiti Malla of Kathmandu (138-1395), Rama Shah of Gorkha (1606-1633), and Jang Bahadur Rana (1846-1877) made significant contributions in this direction. They made attempts to impose Brahmanical social system and codes on the Nepali society. They tried to structure the Nepali society within a basically orthodox Hindu framework. The Indian caste structure is accepted almost throughout Nepal.

Indians and Nepalese have been intermarrying in families of equivalent caste status. As such, in the Terai in particular, a large number of families have kinship and marriage ties across the border. The ruling Nepalese families especially have preferred to marry in India. Such marriages have been a significant vehicle of continued Indian cultural influence. Nepali, the national language of Nepal, is a derivative of

Sanskrit and is closely related to Hindi. They both are written in the Devnagri script. Several of the dialects of Hindi, such as, Maithili and Bhojpuri, are widely spoken in Terai and are often the medium of education. Indian radio and films have become part of Nepalese life and imperceptibly influence Nepali life. Kathmandu itself imports its culture and standards from India and thus the influence of Indian thought and civilisation gradually percolates to the remotest corners of Nepal. Thus cultural influences from India have been extremely important in determining the character of the contemporary Nepali society. In the fields of religion, art, literature, music, and education and practically in everything of consequence, the impact of India is bound to be both- deep and durable.

The impact and influences of Indian political ideas and events extended to Nepal due to close proximity between them. The nineteenth century Indian renaissance, resulting from India's exposure to modern ideas, had their impact on Nepal as well. The end of the Sati Pratha in India led to its end in Nepal. Subsequently, the Arya Samaj movement of Dayanand Saraswati (1824-1833) attracted a few Nepalese at the close of the century. The Indian national movement continued to inspire the Nepalese in India with nationalistic feelings. The Civil Disobedience movement launched by Mahatma Gandhi in 1920 also started influencing the course of events in Nepal from the very early twenties. Since the Rana regime had the protective patronage of the British raj in India, the Nepalese influenced by Gandhi realised that the end of the British rule in India was necessary for the overthrow of Nepal's Rana regime. With that kind of realisation many of them started taking part in the Indian National Congress and Satyagrah movements of the 1920s and 1930s and received instructions and practical training in the new ideology and methods of mass movements initiated by Gandhi. Thus, India became the base of the Nepalese expatriates from where they carried on propaganda against the Rana regime and tried to arouse the political consciousness of their people.

In past all anti-Rana agitations derived their inspiration form India and a very positive role was played by the India-centered Nepali newspapers and magazines. In 1921, Thakur

Chandan Singh established the Gorkha League and published form Dehradun in India two weekly papers, namely the *Gorkha Sansar* and the *Tarun Gorkha,* with a purpose to effect social reforms in Nepal, arouse political consciousness among the Nepalese people and to carry anti-Rana agitation in India. At about the same time another weekly, *Gorkhali,* was started from Banaras with the similar objective of arousing public consciousness against the Rana-rule. The Banaras group in particular, functioned openly and conducted its programmes through newspapers, magazines, public meeting and public organizations. Both the groups who were working for the purpose received inspiration from Indian nationalist movement. A group of Nepalese youth, believing in violent revolutionary underground activities, organised in 1931 a secrct society called Prachanda Gorkha, for overthrowing the Rana autocracy and establishing in its place a democratic regime as its objective. The Praja Parishad, a secret society, organised in 1935 with the same objective was the other significant anti-Rana organization of the thirties. This organization, too, was inspired by the Civil Disobedience Movement and the activities of underground terrorist groups in India in the early thirties.

A number of Nepalese youth actively participated in the Quit India movement in 1942. Prominent among those who were arrested by the British government in India were B.P. Koirala, K.P. Upadhyaya and D.R. Regmi. A wave of enthusiasm spread throughout Nepal when, in September 1946, the Interim government was formed in India as a prelude to its full independence. Common participation in the Indian freedom movement had established intimate relationship, even camraderie in certain cases, between the Nepalese leaders and the Indian leaders, particularly the socialists with whom the Nepalese leaders found themselves especially closer. This contributed significantly in subsequent years to the shaping of independent India's attitude towards the various factions of Nepalese politics.

The Britishers in India too had a commercial and diplomatic relations with Nepal although they received initial setbacks because the rulers of Nepal were suspicious of them. The British themselves and through the East India Company failed to penetrate Nepal but it did not deter the British and they continued the efforts. But ultimately when Kathmandu involved in a war with China, it signed a commercial treaty with East India Company on 1st March 1792 in the hope of securing British assistance in the war. Even till then the Nepal Darbar was strongly averse to the British and had signed the commercial treaty of 1792 in compelling circumstances and, as soon as these were over, the treaty was considered to have outlived its necessity. Nepal continued to be cold to British India's repeated overtures and the Kirkpatrick (1793) and the Abdul Quadir (1795-96) missions sent to Nepal to improve Anglo-Nepalese relations, particularly commercial relations failed to achieve any tangible results.

The British had their first success in 1801 when, taking advantage of the dissensions in Nepal Darbar and siding with the ruling faction, they obtained a treaty of commerce and alliance with Nepal. The treaty provided for the stationing of a British Resident in Kathmandu and despite bitter opposition by the Nepal Darbar this first entry of British influence in Nepal lasted in one form or another until the departure of the British from India in 1947. Further in the phase when the Shah rulers of Nepal adopted a policy of territorial expansion, it brought Nepal into conflict with British India. It culminated in the Anglo-Nepalese war of 1814-16. The Nepalese lost the war and the Treaty of Sugauli was signed on 2 September 1815 and ratified by Nepal in March 1816. The anti-British policy of Nepal continued until the establishment of the Rana rule in 1846, when a radical change took place in Nepalese policy towards the British.

By the time Nepal changed its policies in favour of the British, China was both unable and unwilling to come to the rescue of Nepal against the British expansion due to its defeat in the opium war. Jang Bahadur Rana, the first Rana Prime Minister, initiated a policy of friendship and cooperation with the British as this appeared to him to be the only way to save Nepal's independence from the British imperialism. He signed a treaty of extradition with the British India in 1855 and finally, succeeded in convincing the British of his friendly intentions by dispatching Nepali forces to crush the rebellion in India in course of India's first struggle for freedom in 1857-58. Now onwards, the foreign policy of Nepal went under the British control and it slipped to a 'quasi-subordination in relation to British India. In subsequent years the Nepalese rulers followed the policy of cooperation with the British. In later years and particularly during the regime of Chandra Shamsher (1901-1929) the Nepali goals became servile to the British and it turned into a virtual appendage of the British India empire. In 1923 Britain and Nepal signed a new treaty by which Britain formally recognised the independence of Nepal. Earlier after witnessing the performances of the Gorkha soldiers in the Anglo-Nepal War of 1814-15, Sir David Ochterlony conceived the idea of recruiting the Gorkhas in the British Indian Army. Having seen the bravery of the Gorkhas their enlistment started almost immediately after the war as the British realised that it was not as easy task to subdue them and their alignment with an enemy power or the native power could be fatal to the British regime in India. In independent India the arrangement continued under the Tripartite Agreement signed between the Government of UK, Nepal and India on November 9, 1947. By this India had anticipated that the enlistment of Gorkhas in the Indian Army, employment would be generated amongst the Nepalese and the soldiers, through their salary or pension would in turn generate goodwill amongst their families and also help their country earn foreign exchange.

Thus, in the background of multi-layered proximities with Nepal, India, after its independence in 1947, started relations with the Kingdom of Nepal on an equal footing. As the British had left India with a peaceful Himalayan frontier New Delhi allowed the old British pattern of India-Nepal relationship to continue for the time being, but the British withdrawal from the Indian subcontinent constituted a setback to the then Rana regime as it lost sympathy of the regime that replaced the throne of New Delhi. However, Jawaharlal Nehru, the first Prime Minister and chief architect of India's foreign policy, due to his liberalism treated Nepal even in British days as a fully independent country and clearly envisaged close cooperation between India and Nepal. Even before independence, Nehru as the vice-President of the Interim government remarked on 27

September 1946 at a Press Conference on Indian foreign policy, 'Nepal is an independent country so far as we are concerned. If, in future, Nepal chooses to have some kind of close union with India, we shall welcome it'. Recognising Nepal's international stature, the Indian leaders, when organised an Asian Relations Conference in Delhi in March-April 1947 they also invited Nepal to participate in the conference. In 1949 the Government of India promised full support to Kathmandu in seeking admission into the United Nations.

Though immediately after independence, India was confronted with serious domestic problems, under the conditions, prevailing at that time, India adopted a policy towards Nepal which was guided by four main considerations. They were first, to keep Nepal away from cold war tensions; second, to promote the process of democratization in Nepal; third, to assist Nepal in achieving its political stability and economic prosperity as an instrument of effective guarantee against any foreign encroachment; and fourth, to ensure Nepal's security against the communist menace that might eventually developed from the Chinese side. In nutshell, the above points may also be summarized as-Political, economic and defence.

**Political**

Following independence India as a part of its general policy, was engaged in planting the institutions of demoracy in its own land and desired that these be planted and may take firm roots and flourish in all the newly emerging states of Asia and Africa. It looked for democratisation of Nepal for the political health of that country as much as for the sake of its own security. In fact, the movement for democracy in Nepal had its origin on Indian soil and, to a large extent, the Indian nationalist movement served as a model and an inspiration to the Nepalese. The independent India for a number of reasons, initially only sympathised with the nascent democratic forces in Nepal and later extended its help and support to them. The new Indian rulers themselves viewed the emerging democratic forces in Nepal as their natural allies. The nationalist leaders of India and Nepal had fought shoulder to shoulder in the freedom movement of India. Besides, the objectives of the Nepali

Congress were in conformity with the policy of the Indian National Congress to help the democratic and progressive forces in Afro-Asian countries. The Socialist Party of India, being out of government and free from the charge of interference, actively associated itself with the Nepalese struggle.

At the time of India's independence the rule of corrupt Ranacracy was continuing in Nepal. It was established in 1846 by Jang Bahadur Kunwar, better known as Jang Bahadur Rana. According to a decree of 1856 Jang Bahadur and his successors were granted absolute authority in civil and military administration justice and foreign relations including the right to ignore the commands of the King if these were found to be inappropriate or contrary to national interest. From there onwards monarchy was retained in form, but the powers of the King were usurped by the Rana Prime Minister. In the new system the people had no say in the governance and the politics of the Kingdom were nothing more than the rivalry and interplay among the personalities of the Rana family for power and position. But the Rana system was sustained owing to the weakness of the kings and the support of the British authority in India which found in the Ranas a reliable protege in promoting their interests in India and the Himalayan Kingdom. The British withdrawal from India weakened the Rana regime which draw support from them in times of crisis. On the other the Rana regime of Nepal was hostile to and incompatible with the modern concepts of power, authority and legitimacy which, in a nutshell, required the broadening of regime's base in the changing circumstances. Thus a ground was ready for the basic change in Nepal's political system. The new Indian government also disliked the Rana rulers for their British connection and the negative role played by them during the national movement.

At first India, despite its sympathy and support for the democratic forces in Nepal moved consciously in case of the kingdom and avoided for about two years doing anything that might invite the charge of interference in the external affairs of a small neighbour. It refused to extend any substantial support to democratic forces and confined its role to offering friendly advice to the Ranas to keep the pace with the democratic forces and wanted to make at least some advance in the ways of democracy. In February 1950 Nehru himself exercised his persuasive talents on the Nepali Prime Minister Mohan Shamsher when he was in New Delhi but failed to convince him on the issue and necessity of reforms. The second line of India's approach which at times, went side by side with the first was to exercise pressure on Nepal for the liberalisation of its regime. But finally, when the first two failed to produce satisfactory results, India began to favour the democratic and progressive forces of Nepal.

By the time it became clear that what India wanted in Nepal was at least a semi-democratic regime. Although because of its tyrannical and feudal character the Rana regime was an anthema to the new fervently democratic, modernist and anti-feudal rulers of India the latter was moving slowly in case of Nepal. The leader and the public opinion in India was strongly in favour of the democratic forces and against the Rana regime. Apart from Socialists, Maulana Abul Kalam Azad condemned the continuation of Rana regime in Nepal and said that it is amazing that in the middle of the twentieth century naked autocracy should reign in any part of the world. It is unthinkable and intolerable. There is not one Indian who does not sympathise with the cause of the Nepalese people. Maulana Azad's statement rightly explained the general feeling of Indian people.

Gradually the internal position of Nepal on political front deteriorated mainly due to power struggle among the contending factions. The liberal section of the ruling Ranas led by the then Prime Minister Padma Shamsher tried to contain the Nepalese movement by granting a constitution but having failed to satisfy the opposion the Prime Minister had to resign. In this confrontation, the leaders of the democratic movement in Nepal got support from the monarch, who was being kept in virtual captivity by the Ranas and who were deprived of their share of ruling positions. Ultimately the situation was dealt under the guidance of Indian Prime Minister Jawaharlal Nehru in which the three segments of Nepali Politics at that time—the Ranas, the popular leaders and the Monarch worked out a settlement. As per terms of the Delhi Settlement the position of

King Tribhuvan was restored and as monarch he became free from the control of the Ranas. In February 1951, a coalition cabinet headed by Mohan Shamsher was formed with five Ranas and five Nepali Congress Party members. It was an interim arrangement till the installation of a democratically elected government. It was also agreed to have a constituent assmebly for framing of the constitution and holding the general election within a period of two years. The understanding amongst the King, the Rana rulers and the Nepali Congress leaders evolved through the efforts and influence of the Government of India. The new arrangement of Nepal was a transition from authoritarian to democracy. Under pressure from New- Delhi both the custodians of the status quo and the advocates of change had given up their extreme positions, and adopted a political system that involved both. It was hoped at the moment that the arrangement would ensure stability and would also progressively lead Nepal on the path of democracy.

Since the Indian government had helped Nepal's new ruling elite to come into power and assured them to support for the establishment of a democratic system, the Nepalese government found in India a friend to be trusted, a philosopher to be consulted and a guide to be relied upon. In the changed circumstances it was suite natural for the Nepalese ruling elite to remain in close contact with New- Delhi particularly on issues that might hamper the birth and growth of genuine democracy in the Himalayan Kingdom. The new dispensation urgently confronted with three perplexing, questions-the problem of law and order, of forming the new ministry time and again and the task of administrative and economic reforms in the country. On almost all issues the Government of Nepal requested its Indian counterpart for substantial help which the latter was bound to do morally and it was not possible for the ruling elites of India to ignore or overlook the problems, which were basics of democracy in Nepal.

For the new set up of Nepal the civil service machinery inherited from the Ranas was outdated and on the urgent request of the Government of Nepal, New Delhi lent the services of three experienced civil servants to Kathmandu to help reorganise the administration. Of them two were to function as advisers on administrative reorganisation and the third was to function as a private secretary to King Tribhuvan. The sent officers prepared the administrative rules and instructions for office procedures on the pattern of the Indian secretariat manual. They also assisted in the preparation of the Interim Government Act of 1951 which provided the basis for the new political order. Not only that whenever Nepal needed an experienced man to take charge at the highest level of a department, it sought India's assistance. The first Attorney-General of Nepal and several officers of Nepal, holding key posts were an Indian.

However, despite all help and assistance by the Government of India and sympathy of the Indian public at large the experiments in Nepal failed one after another. The coalition government of incompatible elements could not last more than a few months and the entire bloc of Nepali Congress ministers resigned over police brutality in November 1951. It followed the formation of a new ministry excluding the conservative Rana power bloc by King Tribhuvan. But even now the political leaders due to their inadequate socialisation in democratic norms and practices and greed for power could not bring political and the same situation for some years to come. There was a succession of short-lived governments ruling under terms of the interim constitution or under the direct command of the King. The death of King Tribhuvan in 1955 and succession of his son Mahendra Bir Bikram Shah as the new King of the Kingdom made several shifts in country's national and international policies. King Mahendra was publicly opposed to democracy in principle carried on as before, experimenting with types of councils or ministers that would do his will behind a democratic façade. As he was under intense pressure he hold country's ever first national election in February 1959, but a week before the election he gave the country a new Royal Democratic Constitution in 1959 which envisaged a Parliamentary system under a constitutional monarchy, it however, conferred unlimited and overriding authority on the King in every sphere.

The first general election of Nepal held in February 1959 brought victory for the Nepali Congress and its leader B. P. Koirala became the Prime Minister of Nepal. Results of the election and popularity of the new government which initiated and proposed several reforms of public interest threatened the traditional power base of the army, the former aristocracy and the conservative landowning groups. Even King Mahendra became fearful of his position and apprehended that a popular Prime Minister backed by a popularly elected parliament might impose severe restrictions on his personal power and reduce him to a constitutional figurehead. Political relations between India and Nepal touched a new height when Jawaharlal Nehru visited Kathmandu in June 1959 and a return visit was paid by B.P. Koirala in January 1960. New Delhi began to appreciate Nepal's independent line in foreign policy and had the psychic satisfaction that Koirala would not at least allow the Chinese to act to the detriment of India's interests in the Kingdom. The two countries signed the new Treaty of Trade and Transit in 1960 whereby Nepal secured the desired facilities for its trade with third countries through Indian ports and territories. Nepal too cooperated with India by signing the agreement on the Gandak Project and agreed to give the necessary facilities within its territory for execution.

Nepal's democratic baby was too good to last long. King's apprehension and fear of his personal position took the life of democracy in Nepal. On 15 December 1960 the King invoked the emergency powers to dismiss the cabinet and arrest its leaders on the charge that they had failed to provide national leadership or maintain law and order. King's action was disliked by the Government of India and criticized sharply by all shades of public in general. In the Indian Lok Sabha, Prime Minister Nehru while replying to a adjournment motion said on the issue that it is not for me to criticize the action taken by them but obviously it is a matter of regret for all of us that a democratic experiment or practice that was going on her suffered a setback. He also viewed King's action as a complete reversal of the democratic process. The wide criticism by the Indian government and the public alike was not liked by the king and his sycophants who latter misguided King on country's relations with India and charged the latter of interference in the internal affairs of a sovereign country.

However, King's dislikings did not deter India in extending moral support to the thousands of Nepalese political workers, particularly belonging to Nepali Congress who escaped to India from where they were preparing to start a wide spread movement against the ruling elites of Kathmandu.

In post-dismissal phase a new so called Panchayat system was introduced in 1962 under which the King held a very strong position and was advised by a Council of Ministers and by his own palace secretariat. Political parties were banned. In their place a monolithic three-tier system of village/town, district and national assemblies (Panchayats) was installed. This partyless Panchayat system was dominated by traditional elites mainly drawn from the three major upper castes. Although the new system was termed as partyless democracy, free from the ills of the party politics it failed miserably in bringing genuine decentralization and helped in greater concentration of power in the palace. The panchayat constitution underlined that sovereignty was located in the hands of the King by constitutional laws, customs and usages of the land. The King was to be the executive legislative, and judicial power. Of the two opinions arguing in favour of a multi-party Parliamentary system with a limited monarchy or Panchayati democracy with a king at the helm of affairs initially Indian leadership openly supported the movement for the restoration of Parliamentary Democracy in Nepal for two reasons; one, that the Nepali leaders associated with the movement had close affinity with the Indian leadership and two, that India has a Parliamentary system, so its preference for the same in Nepal was but natural. Later when situation became unfavourable because of a changing power equation in the sub continent, India desisted from this ideological bent and declared that all sovereign countries were free to emulate a convenient model for their governance.

After the death of King Mahendra in 1972 King Birendra inherited the system with absolute authority to rule the country. In comparison to his father King Mahendra King Birendra was more liberal and sympathetic towards the democratic aspirations. With a view to lessen the pressure for change he announced various steps and membership of the National Panchayat was raised form 90 to 112 and the King's power to nominate 15 per cent of its members was raised to 20. An extra-constitutional body named Back to the Village National Campaign, under the direct control of the King was elevated with enormous powers to control the political process at the level of village Panchayat. However, these cosmetic changes did not affect the fundamentals of Panchayat system and the left as well as Nepali Congress became active at the close of the seventies. By the time failure of the system also became visible which led to the announcement of a referendum to decide whether to exist with the existing system with suitable reforms or go for a multiparty system. The referendum held in December 1980 went in favour of the Panchayat system with a narrow margin of 54 per cent. But the results of the referendum made it amply clear that a large number of people were against the existing system which compelled the King to broaden its base. Several amendments were made in the Panchayat constitution keeping in view the facts and the political system was moulded on Parliamentary lines. As the democratic forces of the country were struggling for decades they wanted nothing less than a multiparty democratic system and as a result the Nepali Congress and other political parties boycotted the 1981 and 1986 elections. The inching of Nepal towards genuine democracy was welcomed by Indian establishment and its people at large.

The closing years of the eighties witnessed change in political relations at global level which affected the political events of the Himalayan Kingdom. In 1989-90, several east European dictatorships had submitted to democratic revolutions. In Nepal, transistor radio sets were the cheapest as compared to other South Asion countries and were of superior quality. Many countries broadcast in the Nepali language and as every household in Nepal has a radio set, every Nepalese citizen knew what was happening in eastern Europe, China, India, South Africa etc., as the broadcast in Nepali kept him abreast of all political developments and thinking in these countries.

In India too, the success of V.P. Singh in building an anti-Congress front in the country in 1989, showed that centrist and leftist parties could join hands political for a clearcut objective. In Nepal efforts had been made from time to time to get the

Nepali Congress and the Leftist parties, consisting of different Communist groups to work together, but they had always failed. In 1989, a common objective, however attracted both the parties. It was to have a multi-party political system in Nepal in place of the partyless panchayat system which did not recognise officially any of the several political parties registered under legal cover names or otherwise. In the same year the main leftist parties formed a Unit Left Front and decided to cooperate with the Nepali Congress in asking for a multi-party political system in which the King was bound to appoint the leader of the majority party as his Prime Minister. This meant the new political grouping was intended to organise a political struggle for democracy. Ganesh Man Singh who became the supreme leader of the Nepali Congress after the death of B.P. Koirala in 1982, earlier did not favour taking part in political activities of the ruling elite but thought later that Mikhail Gorbachov's glasnost and Perestroika had brought liberalisation all over the world and that these winds of change were bound to affect Nepal also. He actively supported the plan for a joint mass movement by the left parties and the Nepali Congress. Now the movement for democracy had become a historical compulsion.

The final blow to the Panchayati system came in the form of a pro-democracy movement launched by the Nepali Congress and the Communist parties jointly on 18 February 1990. The two groups agreed to work for certain common goals, namely, the restoration of a full-fledged democracy, amending the constitution ushering in genuine parliamentary democracy and to that end holding several election, hopefully within a year. In other words the main aim of the movement was to change the existing constitution. As a forward movement they organised Satyagraha demanding the government to lift the ban on political parties and restore fundamental rights. With the political parties acting in concert, the pro-democracy movement gathered momentum commanding the loyalty and imagination of the over whelming majority of the urban population. Meanwhile a decline in agricultural production and decision of the Indian government to close all entry points except the two in March 1989 added to the woes of the Pańchayat system. In course of the movement much blood had been shed with promises of much more, and ultimately King Birendra decided to capitulate. On April 8, a royal declaration announced the dropping of the word partyless from the preamble to the constitution and the ban on political parties was lifted. In response to King's gesture the leaders of the opposition decided to withdraw the move and it paved the way for swearing-in of a new ministry by the King on 9 April 1990 with Krishna Prasad Bhattarai, the Nepali Congress leader as the Prime Minister of Nepal. On April 30, the new Prime Minister wrote a letter to his Indian counterpart and expressed gratefulness for his friendly sentiments and assured him of his whole-hearted resolve for Nepal-India relationships.

Under the first promulgated democratic constitution of Nepal general elections held in May 1991 in which Nepali Congress and the United Marxist Leninist Communist Party of Nepal shared most of the votes. Girija Prasad Koirala, leader of the Nepali Congress became the Prime Minister but factionalism soon engulfed the ruling party and a mid-term elections held in November 1994. In this election the Communists (UML) emerged as the single largest party with 89 seats, it however, managed to form a minority government with the support of small parties. Splits became popular in this period among the major parties and four coalition governments were formed before the next general elections in 1999 which gave a clear majority to the Nepali Congress with 113 seats and K.P. Bhattarai was made the Prime Minister. Factionalism prevailed in the Party and Bhattarai was replaced by G.P. Koirala in early 2000 but he too could not last long and in his place Sher Bahadur Deuba became the Prime Minister in July 2001.

Earlier June 1, 2001, brought a black night for the People of Nepal when in a palace massacre King Birendra, Queen Aishwarya along with other family members was gunned down by the eldest son. India expressed shock at the tragic and untimely demise of King Birendra, Queen Aishwarya and other members of the royal family. It declared a three-day state mourning across the country during which the national flag will be flown at half mast and there will be no official entertainment. The emergency cabinet meeting convened by the Prime Minister Atal Bihari Vajpayee also passed a resolution which termed the demise as a very great tragedy and an irreparable loss to Nepal and its people. It said, 'As a neighbour and close friend, in this hour of Nepal's grief, we share the feelings of immense sorrow. We pray that the mourning nation and its citizens are bestowed the strength and courage to bear this irreparable loss. India stands by them in this hour of national grief.'

Prince Gyanendra succeeded as the next King of the Himalayan Kingdom after the sudden demise of King Birendra. By that time the Maoist insurgency had become one of the main problems of the nation as it controlled most part of the territory in rural and sub-urban areas. It affected for most of the period in coming days the functioning of the democratic politics of Nepal. In May 2002 although Deuba government recommended the dissolution of the Parliament but found difficult to hold election because of the Maoist insurgency. Taking advantage of the situation the new King Gyanendra invoked Article 127 of the Constitution to dismiss the Prime Minister and his Cabinet in October 2002 and nominated Lokendra Bahadur Chand to head a nine member interim government in which major political parties refuse to participate. Since then a tripartite power struggle dominated Nepali politics-the King, the mainstream political parties and the Maoists. In this context the role of the Royal Nepal Army increased which sought to resume its role in the national politics that it enjoyed before the 1990. While the mainstream political parties were demanding a return to constitutional government through restoration of the dissolved parliament or the creation of an all-party interim government, the Maoists remained adamant for Creation of a Constituent Assembly and draft a drastically revised constitution.

The Himalayan Kingdom entered into deep turmoil and factionalism during the reign of King Gyanendra. Expectations that the new King would stabilise the country following the 2001 palace massacre have been belied. Instead of becoming a force for stability and moderation, the monarchy displayed the very wayward ways that brought Nepal to a sorry pass. Neighbours like India and well-wishers like the US or China could do little to help the Nepalis when they seem determined not to help themselves. They all felt the need to convince the king that only through unity and dialogue Nepal would be able to step back from the brink. At the juncture New Delhi sided with the King due to its dislike for corrupt and power hungry political leaders as well as its near hatred for the Maoists who are seen as supporters of the Naxalite and insurgent groups in India.

In fact India has a vastly influential position vis-à-vis all three of Nepal's political forces. No government in Nepal can support itself in the absence of grants and loans to cover up to 60 per cent the national budget. It is also to mention that approximately 70 per cent of all foreign aid that the military receives comes from India. It is the place where Nepal's political parties were founded. Before going to Nepal in 1947 to head the democratic struggle there, B.P. Koirala spent three years in jail for his involvement in India's push for independence.

Before any concrete initiative on the part of India the political situation in Nepal worsened further and King Gyanendra took the decision to declare an emergency, sack his government and assume direct control. As a result the leaders of the political parties were arrested and armed personnel were stationed at most media houses. The events that took place in Nepal had confronted India with the most acute foreign policy dilemma that it has ever faced; to back the King in what is bound to become an all-out conflict with the Maoists, or to back away from him and let Nepal slip out of India's sphere of influence. Initially when India decided to continue military aid to Kathmandu it was criticized for overlooking the democratic forces in Nepal embodied by the political parties and by civil society institutions. But it should be noted here that India had temporised by agreeing to send the arms that were already in the pipeline and deferred a decision on agreements that had not as yet been signed.

Apart from this New Delhi had also condemned the take over in Nepal and asked King Gyanendra to start immediate dialogue with political parties to end the instability. After a high-level meeting chaired by Prime Minister Man Mohan Singh, India's ambassador to Nepal met with the King in Kathmandu and conveyed to him India's concern at the situation and the immediate need for holding dialogue with the democratic forces of the country. The United States of America had described the monarchy as having failed to restore democracy in the Himalayan Kingdom and along with India and Britain suspended military aid in Nepal in protest against the coup. India subsequently partially lifted the arms embargo but only for non-lethal supplies. This was also because New Delhi believed that a democratically elected government is the best bet to solve the problems with the Maoist rebels, who nursed a deep hatred against the monarchy.

Months after the take over by King Gyanendra New Delhi played a very positive role in June 2005 in forging an understanding between the Parliamentary parties and the Maoists who were fighting against the King separately. It was a 12-point understanding reached between them that changed the entrie nature of their fighting and the King later had to bow down before a mass movement launched jointly by the potential forces of the country. As a result of the 19-day andolan the King agreed in the last week of April 2006 to relinquish his arbitrary power and reinstate the Parliament suspended in 2002. It also paved the way for election of a Constituent Assembly which was held in April 2008 and the public in general, gave weitage to the Maoist pleadings. Importance of the understanding reached between the SPA and the Maoists at New Delhi was accepted by Pushpa Kamal Dahal Prachanda who was of the opinion that the agreement would not have been possible if the Indian government's support had not been forthcoming. It was from there that a new relationship between India and Nepal begins.

In April 2008 the Government of India became the first foreign government to hail the holding of the twice deferred polls and Navtej Sarna, the spokesman at India's external affairs ministry, in a statement called the successful constituent assembly election in Nepal a welcome and historic step towards realising the aspirations of the people of Nepal for a democratic future. This happy outcome is a product of the determination of the people of Nepal with significant contribution by the political parties and the Election Commission of Nepal. Again India reiterated its commitment to stand by the people of Nepal in the major tasks of demoratization and development that lie ahead while building a stable, prosperous and peaceful Nepal.

New Delhi's genuine effort for the democracy of Nepal has also been accepted by Pushpa Kamal Dahal 'Prachanda' who became the first Prime Minister of the Nepalese republic disclosed in an interview to the correspondent of *The Hindu* that India has consistently been in favour of elections. He expressed happiness about the growing political understanding between India and Nepal because of cultural, historical and geographical relations. He also added that India is a fast growing economy and without its cooperation it is not possible to bring stability and prosperity in Nepal. Thus, India in line with its democratic commitments helped Nepal in achieving its goal gradually-from absolutely to constitutional monarchy and ultimately to a fedral republic in the year 2008.

## Economic

### General Assistance

The Political and economic development of modern Nepal began with the end of the rule of Rana family and establishment of constitutional monarchy in 1951. The new democratic government virtually had no modern means of development. All that was inherited from the despotic regime was a weak transport and communication system, a few educational institutions and an antiquated bureaucracy. As educational opportunities were limited to a few colleges in townships and some traditional schools, only two percent of population was literate. The economy, which was self-sufficient at the bare subsistence level, was already facing the problem of population growth. Like all newly independent developing countries initially, Nepalese leadership also assured the people that it would fulfil their aspirations of economic development. But in feudal social structures the resources of production are generally cornered by the elite in the society. Obviously, in Nepalese domestic life also two forces are competing with each other with divergent economic interests. On the one hand if, the majority is trying to find out opportunities for their livelihood, the minority including the royal family, insists on trade diversification, foreign assistance and more transit facilities, all of which would enable it to earn for itself. As such, being the closest next door neighbour and a littoral country, it is India which has been bullied by the Nepalese elite every now and then for extracting increased economic facilities on favourable terms.

India-Nepal economic cooperation was built upon the pillars of the 1950 Treaty of Peace and Friendship between India and Nepal, which in turn, derived its inspiration and strength from the centuries-old cultural, religious, historical and political ties between the two countries and above all from the geographical factors. For ages, Nepal's access to the world has been through India which holds good even today to a very large extent. Nepal enjoyed the facility of multiple entry points under the Treaty of Peace and Friendship of 1950 and also two treaties on trade and transit. To avoid any confusion further on either side Articles two and five of the treaty provided that they will inform each other of any serious friction or misunderstanding with any neighbouring state likely to cause any breach in the friendly relations subsisting between the two and whenever war-like material is to be imported by the Nepalese Government the arrangement for the same will be worked out with the consultation of India. Under these treaty provisions the relationship between the two remained quite intense and India wholeheartedly Nepal in the pursuit of its economic, political and administrative development.

India's economic relations with Nepal was founded on New Delhi's contention that an economically developed, militarily strong and politically stable Nepal will only be able to sustain itself but may be in a position to ward off all security hazards from the north. But in the light of treaty provisions the Nepalese elite criticized this relationship in the terms that Nepal had virtually been made a satellite of India, they also condemned India for imposing a Parliamentary system of government on Nepal insisting that Indian aid is used in the areas of strategic importance and not for developmental purposes, obstructing the ways of free trade extending shelter to anti-Nepalese elements in India and playing a hegemonistic role in the subcontinent. Venturing a guess about possible reasons we could think of many. First, in the political thinking of a small and weak nation fears from a big and strong neighbour are everlasting. When such fears exist, economic cooperation may not be favoured by the small neighbours. Second, lack of understanding and friendship between the governments of the two countries might have made economic cooperation a casualty. Third, Nepal might have nourished a desire for all these years to have trade relations with other countries as well so that it did not come to solely and totally depend upon one country.

Even today no one can deny that India-Nepal trade and economic cooperation is a living example of the extent to which economic cooperation in the South Asian region could succeed and yet, keep the weaker economy independent and free from exploitation by stronger economy. The treaty of 1950 has lasted for almost sixty years, yet, it has not resulted in any kind of domination of Nepal-political or economic, by India. Political and economic analysts have never alleged that India-Nepal trade and economic cooperation resulted in economic exploitation of Nepal. Rather, Nepal enjoyed privileges not only in the field of trade and transit but also in the field of education, hospital services, recruitment of Nepalese in the India armed forces, etc., as well. In addition India-Nepal trade and economic cooperation had comprised of preferential trading arrangements, plentiful transit facilities to Nepal and also the Indian Rupee as the medium of their mutual trade. Besides, the India is the most advantageous source of Nepal's moderate exports. In a sense, India, all along these years, has been the single important trading partner in Nepal's foreign trade.

India, from the beginning has been deeply involved in Nepal's economic development. Indian financial and technical assistance to Nepal began in the early 1950s with the main objectives: first, to assure Nepal's political stability through economic growth; second, to emphasise India's special relationship with Nepal by strengthening the economic ties between the two countries; third, to gain the goodwill by winning the support of the people and the Government of Nepal; and finally, to advance India's strategic interests by accomplishing at least a partial fortification through an aid programme. Thus India's attitude towards Nepal may turn the idea of South Asian Regional Cooperation into reality. The prominent areas where such cooperation between India and Nepal had been identified were exploitation of water resources, trade diversification, joint ventures, industrial, scientific and technological development. The initial focus of India's assistance, in deference to His Majestic Government of Nepal's priorities, was on infrastructural projects, involving the construction of roads, bridges, hospitals and airports. While infrastructure continued to remain the priority focus, projects also began to include health, industrial estates and other sectors including quick disbursing items such as 'solid waste handling equipment for Kathmandu and Lalitpur Municipalities' and railway locomotives and coaches. The following table will provide an idea, about India's role in first three decades in this respect

**TABLE-I**

**India's Share in Major Areas of Development**

(In Crores (IC))

| *Areas of Assistance* | *Quantum of Help* | *Percentage* |
|---|---|---|
| Irrigation, Power and Water resources | 44.27 | 27.2 |
| Industries | 1.84 | 2.5 |
| Technical and Scientific research | 7.84 | 4.5 |
| Socio-Cultural activities | 2.8 | 1.2 |

On an average about 35.4 per cent of India's aid had been diverted to the Nepalese priority sector. It is also to be noted that dozens of joint ventures with Indian entrepreneurs remained operative in Nepal, providing a boost to the hotel, blanket, electric, automobile textile, transport and food industries, etc. With a view to promote the economy of Nepal, a separate body was set up to execute projects with Indian assistance in the country.

India had always evinced interest in Nepal's economic development. King Mahendra after his accession to the throne in 1955, devoted his attention to the subject and in October announced that a National Planning Commission would be formed to formulate a five year plan to raise the standards of living of the Nepalese people. When Nepal prepared a plan of national development, New Delhi welcomed it and was willing to assist Nepal in its implementation. For the first two Five Year Plans of Nepal, India was the only country involved with Nepal's development. India had agreed to helped Nepal in planned development to the best of its capabilities as indicated in the table given below.

**TABLE-II**

**Share of India's Assistance in Nepal's Planned Development**

(in Million Rs.)

| *Plan* | *Total Outlay* | *Foreign Assistance* | *Percen-tage* | *Indian Assistance* | *Percen-tage* |
|---|---|---|---|---|---|
| First Plan | 214.4 | 382.9 | 100 | 82.1 | 21.44 |
| Second Plan | 596.7 | 476.0 | 76 | 110.0 | 23.11 |
| Third Plan | 1779.0 | 967.8 | 54 | 550.0 | 54.8 |
| Fourth Plan | 3315.5 | 1508.9 | 46 | 563.7 | 37.36 |
| Fifth Plan | 8870.6 | 4240.8 | 48 | 643.6 | 15.18 |
| Sixth Plan | 21750.0 | 13920.0 | 60 | 530.6 | 26.23 |

Thus, it is clear that for decades Nepal could hardly accumulate fifty percent or less resources for its ambitious plans domestically. The rest were arranged from external sources in which India's share remained twenty five percent on an average. As part of its policy the Government of India continued to assist Nepal in its economic development and Indian assistance to Nepal has increased over the years. Since 1997 annual Government of India's disbursement has been around Rs. 70 crores. Apart from this the Government of India also provide subsidy for the supply of commodities like sugar, rice, cement, fertilisers, petrochemicals, etc, and refund of excise duty levied on items exported form India, Rs. 50 crores stand-by credit facility etc. A high level task force at the level of Principal Secretary to Prime Minister and Chief Secretary to the Government of Nepal oversees progress in Indian assisted projects to Nepal.

### Trade

Nepal's geographical location and historical ties have linked the Nepalese economy irrevocably with India. Hence New Delhi is the main trading partner of Nepal. Nepal exports nearly 48 percent of its goods to India followed by United States and Germany with 26 percent and 11 percent of the total exports of

Nepal respectively. Similarly, Nepal imports 39 percent of its goods from India followed by Singapore with 10 percent and China with 9 percent of the total imports. In the 1950s over 90% of the foreign trade was carried on with India. The share of India's trade is actually higher than the official statistics would imply. It is estimated that most of the trade between the two is unrecorded as it is done through informal channels using barter-like payment arrangements by and between the closely knit mercantile classes of West Bengal, Uttar Pradesh, Bihar and Uttaranchal. Over the years the total number of trade between India and Nepal has reduced substantially, but despite several attempts to diversify foreign trade and make it less dependent on India, New-Delhi remains the main trading partner of Nepal. It is also to note here that Nepal's trade with other countries other than India involves the transit of goods to and from foreign countries through Indian territory. Therefore, the smooth transit of goods over India depends on the friendly relations between the two countries.

In 1950, under the Treaty of Trade and Commerce between India and Nepal, India agreed to provide transit facilities to Nepal. Subsequently, custom duties on goods transited through India was waived, 21 border transit points provided and a warehouse in Calcutta port was made available to Nepal for storing goods in transit. The Indo-Nepal Treaty of Trade and Commerce was revised further in September 1960 to gain the goodwill of Nepal and aimed at encouraging the collaboration between the two countries in economic development and at facitating trade with third countries. Article two of the Trade Treaty of 1960 stated, 'goods originating in either country and intended for consumption in the territory of the other shall be exempt from custom duties and other equivalent charges as well as from quantitative restrictions,' and as such raw materials finished goods having eighty per cent or more indigenous Nepalese content would have an unchecked flow in the Indian market. Though the negative economic policies of Nepal, like gift parcel and Bonus Voucher Schemes, the Indian economy received a setback, yet because of its policy of strengthening the economic infrastructure of Nepal in an effort to provide political stability, India willingly accepted this and continued with the facilities even thereafter.

The Trade and Transit Treaty of 1960 expired on 31 October 1970 and after a gap of more than a year a new Treaty of Trade and Transit was signed on August 13, 1971. The agreement provided ***i.*** that the two countries would give most favoured nation treatment to each other's products; ***ii.*** that Nepalese manufactures made from Nepalese or Indian materials would have access to the entire Indian market without any quantitative restrictions and would be free to impose import duties on Indian products on a most favoured nation basis; ***iii.*** that each country would prohibit the export of other country's products and products mainly made from the other country's raw materials; ***iv.*** that goods may be transported between Calcutta and Nepal both by rail and road. This clearly indicates how India, maintaining a special relationship with Nepal nursed the trade and economy even at its own peril.

India in its policy to accommodate the needs and aspirations of its neighbours, accepted Nepal's demand for separate treaties for trade and transit. On 17 March 1978, the two treaties signed in New Delhi, which replaced the Indo-Nepal Treaty of Trade and Transit of 1971, which had expired in August 1976. Valid for a period of five years from the date of signing, the Treaty of Trade provided that India would assist in the industrialisation of Nepal by enlarging the scope of preferences for Nepalese manufactured products in the Indian market, that the two countries would give preferential treatment to each others' primary products on a reciprocal basis, and that necessary arrangements would be made to maintain supplies of essential commodities needed by each other. In the Treaty of Transit India had conceded a long standing Nepalese demand for an alternative transit route for goods originating from and destined to Nepal. It also threw upon the use of overland routes for the export of Nepalese goods to Bangladesh as also for Nepal's trade with third countries through Bangladesh. An agreement between the two countries was also signed to ensure that the economic interests of either country were not adversely affected through unauthorised trade between the two countries. The said treaties were signed by the then Janata Government under its policy of 'beneficial bilateralism.' It was renewed in March 1983 which subsequently expired in March 1988 and India modified these significantly in 1991 with the coming of a democratic government in Nepal to provide unilateral concessions.

The renewal of the Treaty of Trade (1991) in December 1996 with the provision for automatic renewal of the Treaty every five year provided, on a non-reciprocal basis, duty free access, without quantitative restrictions, to the Indian market for all Nepalese manufactured articles barring a short negative list. The protocol to the India-Nepal Treaty of Trade was renewed with some modifications in February 2002 which included 12 Articles. The treaty in its revised form is proving to be an effective instrument in providing a strong impetus to industrial growth and economic development in Nepal and in expanding bilateral trade ties with India. In general, both imports and exports of Nepal have increased over the years. The Nepalese exports to India have been growing at a rate which far exceeds the growth of Nepal's overall exports. India's share in Nepal's exports, imports and total volume of trade in past few decades is given below.

Thus, the entire gamut of trade relations between India and Nepal right from 1950, clearly indicates that Indo-Nepalese trade has always been regulated by special provisions. Whether the objective was to create a common market or to provide the treatment of most favoured country, India had a privileged place in Nepal in comparison with others just as Nepal enjoyed a special place in India as per different treaty provisions. As such Indo-Nepalese trade witnessed an upswing on regular basis.

**Surface Transport**

In the early 1950s on a request from His Majesty's Government of Nepal, the Government of India agreed to the construction of the Tribhuvan Airport at Kathmandu and the Tribhuvan Rajpath connecting Kathmandu to Birganj in the south of Nepal bordering Raxaul in India. About 78.5% of the Mahendra Raj Marg, a highway that runs the entire length of Nepal from the east to the west along the southern terai, has been constructed by India. In addition, roads from Kathmandu to Dakshinkali, Trishuli, Balaju, Godavari and Raxaul via Hetauda, Sunauli to Pokhara, Rajbiraj to Kosi Barrage and Janakpur town road are contributions of Indian assistance. India has also constructed a number of bridges on these roads and

**TABLE-III**

**India's Share in Nepalese Foreign Trade**

| *Periods* | *1970-71* | *1980-81* | *1990-91* | *1991-92* | *1993-94* | *1994-95* |
|---|---|---|---|---|---|---|
| Nepal's export | 98.7% | 61.7% | 21.0% | 10.6% | 12.5% | 17.0% |
| Nepal's import | 88.2% | 49.2% | 31.5% | 35.2% | 33.0% | 31.7% |
| Total volume of trade | 92.0% | 52.5% | 29.0% | 27.8% | 27.4% | 28.3% |
| *Periods* | *1995-96* | *1996-97* | *1997-98* | *1998-99* | *1999-2000* | *2000-01* |
| Nepal's export | 18.5% | 23.1% | 31.9% | 35.5% | 42.8% | 46.7% |
| Nepal's import | 32.7% | 26.6% | 30.7% | 34.9% | 34.8% | 39.0% |
| Total volume of Trade | 29.7% | 28.9% | 31.0% | 35.0% | 37.2% | 41.8% |

The last column of the second block reads *2001-02*: Nepal's export 60.7%, Nepal's import 42.5%, Total volume of Trade 48.1%.

separately two bridges on the river Bagmati at Kathmandu and one on the river Mohana.

A bilateral agreement for the construction of 22 bridges on the Kohalpur-Mahakali sector of the East West Highway in Nepal was signed in February 1996 when Nepalese Prime Minister Sher Bahadur Deuba visited India. The 22 bridges have been constructed between 51 kms to 127 kms stretch on the Kohalpur-Mahakali sector at a total cost of Nepalese Rupees 1088 million. These have been completed and opened for traffic but some of them situated in the most difficult terrain. These difficulties were compounded due to the presence of artesian wells that caused piers and foundations to tilt and sink, and the occurrence of flash floods. Other contractors and countries had given up this work earlier due to these obstacles.

**Health**

India has been traditionally associated with the development of some hospitals in Kathmandu. These include Bir Hospital, Paropakar Maternity Hospital and the Police Hospital. In addition, The B.P. Koirala Institute of Health Sciences has been established recently. The Bir Hospital of Nepal was set up by India in the 1970s and an expansion project for the hospital was finalised when the prime Minister of India went to Nepal in June 1997. He during the visit, laid the foundation stone of the 200- Bed Emergency and Trauma Centre. A high- level Experts Group, led by the Director of the All India Institute of Medical Sciences, has been set up to advise the Government of India on project parameters. A team of architects from Central Design Bureau, of the Ministry of Health visited Kathmandu in Februray and September 1998 to prepare the project design and parameters. A four-member experts group led by Dr. P.K. Dave visited Kathmandu from 31st May to 4th June 2000 for holding discussions with Bir Hospital Authorities and the Nepalese government to firm up the project parameters. Apart from this over the last 24 years the Government of India have assisted in the control of iodine deficiency in hill areas of Nepal through the supply of iodised salt to Nepal. Our commitment on the programme ended in March 1998 and has been very successful in meeting its objective of making the iodised salt available in the remote areas of Nepal and controlling the incidence of goitre.

The Paropakar Maternity Hospital was established in 1959 by the Government of India and since then it has continued its assistance to the hospital. Recently an assistance was extended to the Paropakar Maternity Hospital in Kathmandu for procuring sophisticated medical equipment to facilitate the setting up of Maternity and Neo-natal Intensive Care Unit at the Hospital. The supplies have since been completed and the ICUs were formally inaugurated and handed over to the Hospital authorities on September 10, 1999, during the visit of India's External Affairs Minister to Nepal. As part of our continuing cooperation and assistance the providing facility included the gifting of a Mobile Medical Clinic-cum-Ambulance, three workshops for the physicians and nurses in maternal and child care and learning aids and resource material consisting of books, computer, VCR and TV.

Likewise the B.P. Koirala Institute for Health Sciences (BPKIHS), Dharan, is one of the outstanding symbols of Nepal-India friendship. It was inaugurated and dedicated to the nation in September 1999 by the Prime Minister of Nepal in the presence of the External Affairs Minister of India. During the inauguration, an announcement was made by India's minister to extend the facility support to the institution for an additional 5 years till 2009 on the basis of the request received from the Nepalese government. This institute is now making a very significant contribution in the health care sector for the entire Eastern Region of Nepal. A large number of patients from India are also benefiting from the facilities which have been created. It is the most prestigious project undertaken in Nepal.

**Education**

India has contributed towards the development of various institutes and organizations in Nepal including the Tribhuvan University, Engineering School and National Archives. A Museum, Library-cum-Documentation Centre was constructed by India at the Institute of Forestry, Hetauda. The Government of India had also contributed towards the development of the Lumbini Museum. Quite a good number of books were also presented by the Government of India for the Lumbini Library. India has been regularly deputing experts to various departments of University and Hospitals. The Indian government provides financial assistance every year for purchase and presentation of books to various educational institutions in Nepal including Tribhuvan University, Kathmandu University, colleges and various libraries.

As per the documents of the embassy of India, Kathmandu, there are several schemes that regulate the education in the Himalayan Kingdom. All the courses offered by any University or Institution in India is open to Nepalese scholars under the foreign students category. While for some general courses like BA, BSc, etc., the students can approach the University directly, for some other professional like MBBS, BE, etc., the scholar has to approach the Embassy of India and complete required formalities. Government of India, through its various schemes, offers a large number of scholarships to meritorious Nepalese students.

For general courses such as Bachelor's and Masters degree in arts, pure science, commerce, education and law Nepalese students can approach Foreign Students Advisor of any Indian University for admission provided 12 years of schooling have been completed successfully. No clearance from the Government of India is required and Nepalese students even do not require visa. For MCA, MBA, Hotel Management and other professional courses; M. Phil, Ph. D. in any subject Nepalese students can approach the concerned University/Institution directly subject to obtaining No Objection Certificate from the Government of India. For obtaining NOC, the students may apply in the format available at the Education Wing of the Indian Embassy. While in case of MBBS, BDS, BE, B Pharma, Agriculture and Veterinary Science courses, Diploma in Engineering they should send their applications to Education Wing of the Embassy of India as per notification issued in local newspapers form time to time. Eligibility is 60% marks in aggregate in plus two and 60% in PCM or PCB, depending on the course opted.

Apart from this the Government of India also provides Nepalese students admission to post graduate courses in medicine at All India Institute of Medical Sciences, New- Delhi, and the post-graduate Institute of Medical Education and Research, Chandigarh, through a written competitive examination twice a year. A No Objection Certificate from the Government of India is necessary to enable the candidates to appear in the competitive examination, for which Nepalese nationals may consult Embassy of India for necessary guidance and advice. Admission to Post Graduate courses in Engineering and Technology is available only after Nepalese nationals have passed 'Graduate Aptitude Test in Engineering' (GATE), conducted annually by Indian Institute of Technology at different centres in India. A No Objection Certificate from the Government of India is necessary to enable the candidates to appear in the competitive examination, for which Nepalese nationals may consult Embassy of India for necessary guidance and advice.

In the sphere of education establishment of B.P. Koirala India-Nepal Foundation in December 1991 is a new landmark decision to promote the educational avenues between the two countries. It was instituted through a Memorandum of Understanding between His Majesty's Government of Nepal and the Government of the Republic of India. Its establishment in the country was a symbol of Nepali renaissance. The ideas and vision of B.P. Koirala had made him a unique mixture of liberalism, humanism and social justice. He was a crusader against all forms of injustices perpetrated in various forms and through various agencies-state and non-state. He occupies a unique place in politics, literature and intellectual thinking process making him a statesman. Hence to foster educational, cultural, scientific and technical co-operation between India and Nepal to promote mutual understanding and cooperation through the process of wide sharing of knowledge and professional talents in both academic pursuits and technical specialization. The thrust areas of activities identified for promoting understanding and cooperation are: education and culture, agricultural research, science and technology, health, technical training and development studies etc.

The B.P. Koirala foundation extends financial support to higher studies, research and other educational activities and in-service training, visits and exchanges of scholars, writers, politicians, mediaperson, administrators, businessmen and other professionals in various fields. It is financed through revenues generated from a Trust Fund which has been set up principally through grants made available by His Majesty's Government of Nepal and the Governments of India. It also accepts unconditional grants from other agencies, both public and private. The institution is managed by a ten-member Board of Directors headed by the two Co-Chairpersons. The Ambassador of India to Nepal and the Royal Nepalese Ambassador to India are the co-chairpersons of the Board. Other members of the Board are nominated by the two Governments from amongst the distinguished persons in their respective while fields, the Joint Secretaries incharge of their respective foreign officers of India and Nepal desks and the two officials of respective Embassies are designated to act jointly as Secretaries of the Foundation. The Board manages, supervises and controls the affairs of the Foundation. It meets twice a year to consider various proposals and projects received by the Foundation, and sanctions funds. Towards meeting the stated objectives, individuals, institutions or groups can approach the Foundation for consideration of their proposals through prescribed format made available in Foundation offices in Delhi and Kathmandu.

**Welfares of Gurkha Indian Army**

India has always been proud to have Nepalese as soldiers in her Defence Forces and has made every effort to ensure that they are looked after and cared for in their twilight years. From the first quarter of the 19$^{th}$ century, Gurkhas from Nepal had served under the British, first in the armies of the East India Company, and then the British Indian Army. At that time the terms and conditions of service for the Gurkhas were solely a matter for the British Indian authorities, without reference to the British Government in London. In 1947 when India became independent the two governments decided to split the Gurkha regiments between the British and Indian armies-six Gurkha units became part of the new Indian Army, while four were transferred to the British Army. It was agreed as a part of the arrangement that Gurkhas in British and Indian service should enjoy broadly the same conditions of service, to ensure that there was no unfair advantage to serving in one or other, thus maintaining economic stability and social harmony in the Gurkha recruiting areas. In this regard a Tripartite Agreement was signed which applied to the 3,500 Gurkhas serving in the British Army, and close to 100, 000 Gurkhas in the Indian Army. The Agreement provided the unique terms and conditions of service of the Gurkha soldier which in a number of key areas differ markedly from those of his British or Commonwealth counterpart. To remove the anomalies in May 2007 a number of proposals were adopted regarding nationality and status, recruitment and selection and pay, pension and allowance.

The Government of India has made every effort to ensure that the ex-servicemen, their families and dependents are looked after in the best possible manner. To ensure this New Delhi has established 'The India Ex-Servicemen Welfare Organisation in Nepal (IEWON) functioning within the Embassy of India under the chairmanship of none other than Ambassador of India to Nepal. The welfare schemes are also undertaken in the remotest areas of Nepal where our brave ex-servicemen settle down to lead a quiet and contended life. For this the Government of India has formed District Soldier Boards (DSBs) that function in various locations wherever the soldiers have chosen to reside. For disbursement of pension apart from Kathmandu two pension paying offices are functioning at Pokhara and Dharan.

Under medical facility scheme each ex-servicemen is provided with a medicine pack once a year containing essential basic medicines with direction for usage. A sum of rupees 70 lacs is expended on this account annually. For the next stage of their treatment there are two Medical Inspection Rooms at Pokhara and Dharan, each manned by a male and a lady doctor. These facilities are fully equipped with X-Ray Lab and ECG, such alike. Presently the Indian Embassy doctor visits the Medical Inspection Room at Kathmandu and provides free treatment to the ex-servicemen. For cases where specialist treatment is required, 13 Indian Army Medical Welfare Teams visit Pokhara, Dharan and various DSBs each year. A sum of Rs. 90 lacs is expended on making these specialist teams available for our ex-servicemen in Nepal. In addition the Nepali ex-servicemen can visit Army Hospital in India for free treatment. The Government of India has also introduced a scheme for eligible ex-servicemen wherein, by joining the extended Medical Benefit, they are given financial assistance up to 1.6 lakh. This assistance covers illness such as Heat Diseases, Cancer, Renal, Transplant/Dialysis and Limb Replacement which includes the pensioner and his spouse. Attached to health is the Drinking Water Projects under which HDP pipes, CGI sheets and cement are made available for construction in villages where the ex-servicemen population is large. The villagers through voluntary service also subsequently execute the project on ground. So far 877 water projects have been implemented in various remote areas of Nepal.

The ex-servicemen of Nepal receive Indian assistance in the filed of education in the form of educational scholarships, scholarship to wards of those killed in action, financial assistance to schools and vocational training schools. To assist the ex-servicemen in educating their children scholarships are provided at the rate of 400.00 for children up to class 4$^{th}$, Rs. 750.00 for children up to class 8$^{th}$, and Rs. 1200.00 for children beyond class 8$^{th}$ and upto graduate level studies. Each year a sum of Rs. 8 lac is disbursed on this account. For those wards who undertake professional studies such as MBBS, BE, MBA, CA, LL.M, MSc, MEd. MA both in India and Nepal, especial scholarships in addition to complete tuition fees, cost of books etc is provided. Another operative scholarship scheme is given to wards of those ex-servicemen who died in 1962, 1965, 1971 operations–OP PAWAN, OPVIJAY and OP MEGHDOOT. This scholarship package includes complete tuition fees, boarding and lodging charges, school bus charges, books and stationary charges, cost of uniform and clothing etc is re-imbursed on an annual basis by Army Headquarter.

Apart from this the Government of India provides financial assistance to schools where the majority of children are wards of ex-servicemen. Assistance is provided for expansion and repair of existing school building, purchase of furniture, books, sports equipments etc. A sum of Rs. 8 lac is expended annually on this account. The Indian government has also expanded its efforts to vocational training schools for wards of ex-servicemen in order to enhance their opportunities for employment business etc. The courses conducted include stitching, knitting, typing (English and Nepali), English language and computer training. The most popular of these is the course training on computers which is run at Kathmandu, Pokhara and Dharan. Recently computer training at DSB Butwal and DSB Gulmi has been introduced with stitching and knitting classes. Now we also provide ex-servicemen of Nepali origin the CSD facilities through Cooperative Stores functioning at Kathmandu, Pokhara and Dharan. Under the Naitonal Defence Fund Package the Government of India has announced financial help for soldiers killed in action and disabled during various operations since 1947. It also provides from April 2000 a funeral grant of 3,200,00 NC of an ex-servicemen in the event of his death.

Pension of ex-servicemen has been an important issue and before 1947 they and their families were drawing pension from border treasuries in India. After independence the responsibility of pension payments was taken over by the Indian Embassy. The first Military Attache posted in 1949 took over the responsibilities thereafter. Initially, temporary pension camps were established at Pokhara in 1955 and Dhankuta in 1959. These were converted into permanent pension paying offices in 1960. Presently the Embassy conducts 32 Seasonal Pension Paying Camps annually, in the interiors of Nepal for the convenience of ex-servicemen. The Military Pension Branch of the Embassy of India is responsible for payment of pension and other dues to the Nepalese ex-servicemen and their families residing in Nepal. The branch alongwith its offices at Pokhara and Dharan are today catering for more than one lac eight thousand defence and civil pensioners who have opted to draw their pension in Nepal. It also ensures that all requirements of the pensions in terms of Medical, Educational Scholarships, Army Group Insurance claims etc. are all dealt under the concept of single window service thereby obviating the need for the pensioners to report at different places. In the year 1999-2000 Rs. 370.6 crores were disbursed as pension payments. Thus the Government of India covers a large and expanded life of the Nepalese Government and people as well.

**Defence**

Since the British times Nepal has been considered an integral part of the security system of India. For the British it was the classic 'buffer state' separating India from the vast expanse of China beyond the Himalayas, a role played to a lesser extent by the less independent entities of Bhutan and Sikkim. With the exit of the British from the subcontinent, India did try to build a security community of the Himalayan neighbours when she formulated the Southern Himalayan policy network and brought Nepal, Bhutan and Sikkim under its security umbrella. As regards Nepal, Nehru himself laid down the crucial parameters of Indo-Nepal relations and before the signing the 1950 Treaty of Peace and Friendship, he declared in the Lok Sabha: 'We can not tolerate any foreign country in any part of the Indian subcontinent. Any possible invasion on Nepal would inevitably involve the safety of India. A later variant of the same outlook was expressed by Atal Bihari Vajpayee, the Minister for External Affairs in Janata Government in 1977 when he declared that God and geography have linked our two nations and decreed that we live in friendship.

However, around 1960 and especially after 1962 when India's relations with China was tense on account of border dispute Nepal was more favourably placed to profit from the adversary relationship between India and China. The new pro-China policy was initiated by King Mahendra in 1955 and there onwards China became an important variable in Nepalese foreign policy. For decades despite public statements and accusations against the treaty of 1950 no formal representations have been made to New Delhi for its revision. Indeed, the greater influence which India has wielded in Nepal in numerous ways has not diminished significantly in consequence of its new relationship with China. The Indo-Nepal border remains open; Indian currency is still legal tender in Nepal; Chinese influence and road building has been restricted to the northern parts of Nepal; and India remains Nepal's main trading partner, and Nepal's outlets remain located mainly through India.

Emergence of China as a communist country in 1949 and its occupation of Tibet by force was a motivating factor for signing the Indo-Nepal Treaty of Peace and Friendship in 1950. The geo-strategic linkage of China with the South Asian region, ideological difference with India and aspiration to be a counterweight to its dominance in the region disturbed India. To make its exposed frontiers more secure, India tried to consolidate its security interests in the north. Even later the roads constructed from Kathmandu to Tibet such as the Kathmandu-Kodari road, in the 1960s, connect Nepal with Tibet through the Kuti Pass. Towards the south the entire border is open. And it is through these passes in the north and the open border in the south that any enemy can have excess to India's populous states of Uttar Pradesh, Bihar, West Bengal. Under such geo-strategic compulsion, Nepal's importance in India's security concerns is enhanced due to its relations with China. Thus, Nepal came to play a much larger role in India's security calculations.

In fact, geography has played a very significant role in shaping Nepal's foreign policy considerations. The 1750—km-long open border between Nepal and India has led to the crossing of the border by hundreds of people every day influencing each other's history, culture and tradition. The situation available has forced Nepal to look southwards where the main population centres of the Indian plains are easily accessible to Nepal due to the open borders. In addition Nepal was also apprehensive of China's southward expansion. The Ranas, in order to resist the democratic opposition, tried to win India's support by agreeing to sign the Treaty of Peace and Friendship. From the beginning New Delhi had insisted that stable, independent neighbours were vital to India's security, but many Nepalese regarded India as regional bully and to assuage Nepalese fears of Indian domination, the treaty also stipulated that Indian forces could be introduced into the country only at the invitation of the Nepalese government.

The Government of India and the Government of Nepal recognising the ancient ties which have happily existed between the two countries for centuries and desiring still further to strengthen and develop these ties and to perpetuate peace between the two they resolved to enter into a Treaty of Peace and Friendship on 31 July 1950. Through the treaty, India and Nepal tried to make their security concerns complementary in nature. The treaty was not a military alliance but an agreement which identified the concerns and threat perceptions of the two governments and attempted to thwart these together. It contained 10 Articles in total and the main thrust of the agreement was on the reorganisation and modernisation of the Nepalese Army. With the purpose of strengthening the security of Nepal, the Government of India undertook 'to supply arms, ammunition and equipment for the entire Nepalese Army on the basis of a total strength of about 17,000 men comprising four recognised brigades-Clause 3 (a) and to replace the existing stock of Nepalese weapons Clause 3 (b).

India also agreed to provide training facilities required for the Nepalese armed forces personnel in the training establishments in India, as necessary, and also by sending training personnel to Nepal at the request of His Majesty's Government – 3 (c). However, the military assistance to Nepal was to be provided on a grant basis and not to be diverted to any third party. Thus, the agreement ruled out any possibility of arms being diverted to any subversive agency. As a part of security understanding soon after the Chinese annexation of Tibet, checkposts were set up on the Indo-Nepal border which were jointly monitored by the Indian technicians and Nepalese Army personnel. The Indian wireless operators kept an eye on the military activities along the Tibetan side of the border and passed on coded intelligence messages to the Government of India and Nepal through the Indian Embassy at Kathmandu.

On the request of the Government of Nepal, India also sent its troops when the Raksha Dal led by K.I. Singh had revolted against the compromise formula which brought the monarchy back to power, and the Ranas and Congress had to jointly form an interim government.

In response to the Nepalese request to modernise Nepal's Army, India in 1952 sent a military mission to Nepal which consisted of a Major General and 20 other Army personnel. The strength of the mission was later extended to 197. The Indian Military Mission arrived in Kathmandu to reorganise Nepal's armed forces and bring the Kingdom's defences more in line with India's security requirements. In implementing changes, Nepal drastically reduced the size of its postwar army and revamped its training and organization along Indian lines. The strength of Royal Nepal Army was reduced from 25,000 men to 6,000 well-trained and well-equipped men. A few Nepalese Army personnel were sent to Indian military establishments for training. On Nepal's request, the Indian Military Mission was withdrawn on July 16,1958, and was reorganised as the Indian Military Training and Advisory Group (IMTAG) which advised the Nepalese Army on training and reorganisation and assisted it in filling the vacancies for courses of instruction offered by India and helped in arranging attachments for Nepalese personnel in unit installations and establishments of the Indian Army. Again in 1963, soon after the Sino-India war, the IMTAG was recorganised as the Indian Military Liaison Group (IMLG). The group consisting of 23 officials was withdrawn in 1970 on the recommendation of the then Prime Minister of Nepal, K.N. Bista. The Indian Military personnel from the checkposts were also called back but it did not mean an end to the military relationship with Nepal. The tripartite agreement on Gorkha recruitment is still in existence under which the Nepalese military personnel avail the training facility in Indian military establishments.

In the closing years of the eighties Indo-Nepal defence relations received a jolt for a brief period when in June 1988 King Birendra concluded a secret arms purchase deal with China. India protested the agreement vigorously because it was the violation of 1950 treaty and exchange of letters on import of arms which took place in 1965. The concluded agreement of 1965 gives India a virtual monopoly of the Kingdom's defence needs and altogether excludes any Chinese role in equipping the Nepalese armed forces. Although the appearance of a limited number of vintage air defence weapons hardly threatens the Indian Air Force, New Delhi interpreted the sale as a dangerous precedent that could not go unchallenged. Purchase of arms from China had hardened India's attitude when trade and transit agreement signed between the two earlier, came up for renewal. New Delhi refused to extend the agreement and asked Nepal to meet India's defence and commercial concerns. As both sides refused to back down the agreement was allowed to lapse leading to the closing of thirteen out of fifteen border checkposts that regulated most of Nepal's trade with the outside world.

The deadlock on the treaty of trade and transit with Nepal continued for about fifteen months and finally both sides reaffirmed the 1950 treaty, and Kathmandu agreed not to purchase defence items abroad without consulting India. In addition, it made two things clear. Firstly, Nepal could not count on China's armed support in any confrontation with India brought about by Nepal's own actions. King Birendra's other friends were too far away to be of much help because of geographical separation from the land-locked Kingdom of Nepal. Secondly, when the trade and transit treaty with India lapsed, the world simply watched when India refused to allow Nepal any more benefits than what international practice and usage allowed.

The early years of the nineties witnessed a lot of changes in global geo-political perspectives—the disintegration of the Soviet Union, end of cold war and opening of doors to foreign investors by India and China. All these shifted the focus of international actors from geo-politics to geo-economies in which no particular nation asserts supremacy. By the time other security related issues were erupted between India and Nepal which paved the way for further misunderstandings. The ISI made its formal debut in Nepal in 1989 as part of its third proxy war in Jammu and Kashmir. Nepal's China-card was also gradually weakening due to latter's growing understanding with India on border issue along with other economic problems facing the two giant neighbours of Asia. And so Nepal chose to play the Pakistan-card instead. However, despite these in the Joint Communique issued at the end of the visit of Nepalese Prime Minister K.P. Bhattarai to New Delhi, on 10 June 1990 both agreed to respect each others security concerns and pledged not to allow any activities on their soil directed against the other.

Once again it was also agreed to have prior consultations with a view to reaching mutual agreement on such defence-related matters which in the view of either country could pose a threat to its security.

In later years too a number of security related issues were discussed between India and Nepal including the ISI activities in the Terai region of Nepal from where anti-India movements are carried out. The Terai region has a concentration of Nepalese Muslims who are vulnerable to ISI and Muslim organisations which can manipulate them. Many Kashmiris came to Nepal as traders and have settled mainly in Kathmandu and Pokhara. The arms and ammunition are sent from Nepal to India by concealing them in vehicles crossing the border. Terrorism is interconnected with acquisition of arms and ammunition and the training for their use for which money is generated through drug-trafficking. India and Nepal have recognised terrorism and drug-trafficking as a new threat to their security and have discussed it at various level. India also criticized Nepal in December 2005 when its King Gyanendra purchased arms and ammunition from China violating its past defence treaties with India, but it however, did not deter New Delhi to assist Nepal in defence matters as disclosed by India's Foreign Secretary that our cooperation with Nepal including on training for RNA is still continuing. The Indo-Nepal security relations can be strengthened with developed confidence-building measures. Cooperation in trade and economics, joint ventures and technical collaboration would enhance closer understanding at both the people and government levels.

Even today when the Kingdom of Nepal has become a republic and a communist-led interim government has been installed to look after the people of the nation it would be useful in the interest of the country to come to terms with New Delhi. It must be clear to the Nepalese leadership and the people as well that the independence, stability and development is ensured if both the countries move together in a cooperative way. The bilateral relations are like two-way traffic-what one expects from the other one is to reciprocate in the same manner as one Nepalese leader has rightly expressed that Nepal's relations with India are more vital than its ties with hundred other countries and that the facts of life and geography cannot be changed.

# SELECT BIBLIOGRAPHY

## PRIMARY SOURCES

### A. Documents


Agreements between the United States of America and the Kingdom of Nepal, respecting friendship and commerce, effected by exchange of notes signed at Kathmandu, 25 April, 1947.

Agreement between His Majesty's Government of Nepal and the Government of India on the Gandak Irrigation and Power Project (Kathmandu, 4 December 1959).

American Assistance to Nepal (1952-1967) (Resources Division, Ministry of Economic Planning, His Majesty's Government of Nepal, Kathmandu).

Annual Report (1967-68, 1968-69, 1969-71) His Majesty's Government, Ministry of Foreign Affairs, Kathmandu.

Asian Relations Organisation, Report of the Proceedings and Documents of the First Asian Relations Conference, New Delhi, March-April 1947, New Delhi 1948.

All India Congress Committee, The Background of India's Foreign Policy (New Delhi, 1952).

Annual Report (Kathmandu, Ministry of Foreign Affairs).

Agreement between the Government of USSR and HMG of Nepal on rendering Economic Technical Assistance by Soviet Union to the Sovereign Kingdom of Nepal, 6 January 1962.

Agreement between His Majesty's Government of Nepal and the Government of USSR on free of charge construction in Nepal of a section of East-West highway, 8 April 1964.

Bahadur K.C. Prakash, Hostile, Expeditions and International Law (Kathmandu: Department of Publicity, 1962).

Bhasin, A.S., (ed.), Documents on Nepal's Relations with India and China 1949-66 (Bombay: Academic Book, 1970).

(ed.), Nepal's Relations with India and China, Documents 1947-1992, Vol. I (Siba Exim, Delhi, 1994).

Constituent Assembly of India (Legislative) Debates-7 (1) 1948; 3 and 4 (1) 1949.

Co-operation for Progress in Nepal (Ministry of External Affairs, Government of India, New Delhi, 1966).

Co-operation for Progress (Indian Embassy in Nepal, Kathmandu, 1961).

Department of State Bulletin, Washington D.C. Vol. 41 (July-December 1959, p. 270, January 1959 March 1960, 1967, Vol. 57, pp. 706-709.

Foreign Policy of India: Text of Documents 1947-1958 (New Delhi, Lok Sabha Secretariat, October 1958).

Foreign Policy of India-Text of Documents 1947-1959 (Second Edition, Lok Sabha Secretariat, New Delhi, 1959).

Foreign Affairs Record (Ministry of External Affairs, External Publicity Division, Government of India, New Delhi, 1977-1980).

Giri Tulsi, Some Speeches of Dr. Tulsi Giri, Kathmandu, Department of Publicity, 1964).

Government of India, Indo-Nepal Economic Co-operation, Kathmandu.

Hamro Par Rastra Sampark (Our External Relations), (Department of Publicity, His Majesty's Government of Nepal, Kathmandu, 1954).

Indo-Nepal Economic Co-operation: 1951-1966 (Indian Aid Mission, Kathmandu, 1967).

Indira Gandhi, Statements on Foreign Policy, January-April 1983 (External Publicity Division, Ministry of External Affairs, New Delhi, 1983).

Khanal Yadunath, Background of Nepal's Foreign Policy, Kathmandu, Department of Publicity and Broadcasting, p. 7.

Nepal-India Relations, Kathmandu, Department of Publicity and Broadcasting, 1963, pp. 22.

Nehru, Jawaharlal, India's Foreign Policy: Selected Speeches, September 1949-April 1961 (New Delhi, Publication Division—Ministry of Information and Broadcasting, 1961).

. . . Speeches (1949-53) (New Delhi, The Publication Division, Ministry of Information and Broadcasting, Government of India, 1951).

Nepal China Boundary Protocol, Kathmandu, Department of Publicity and Broadcasting, 1963.

Nepal Gazette, His Majesty's Government, Department of Publicity and Broadcasting, Kathmandu.

Nepal-India Friendship: Speeches by H.M. King Mahendra in Course of Royal visit to India (18-22 April 1962) (Department of Publicity and Broadcasting, Ministry of National Guidance, HMG, Nepal, Kathmandu,1962).

New Developments in Friendly Relations between China and Nepal (Includes text of treaties with Nepal) (Chinese People's Institute of Foreign Affairs, Foreign Language Press, Peking, 1960).

Nepal Treaty Series (1972-74), His Majesty's Government of Nepal, Ministry of Law and Justice, Babar Mahal, Kathmandu.

. . . On Cultural and Scientific exchanges between HMG and the Government of USSR for the year 1973 and 1974, pp. 63-68.

Nepal Treaty Series (1975-1976), HMG, Ministry of Law and Justice, Babar Mahal, Kathmandu.

. . . Grant Agreement dated 5 June 1975 between HMG of Nepal and the United States of America, Acting through the Agency for International Development, pp. 17-27.

. . . Grant Agreement between HMG and USA/Aid Mission on dated 13 January 1976, pp. 225-35.

Programme on Cultural and Scientific Exchanges between HMG and USSR for year 1975-1976, pp.113-16.

Nepal Treaty Series, Programme on Cultural and Scientific exchange between HMG of Nepal and Government of USSR for year 1977 and 1978, pp. 71-75.

... Project Grant Agreement between HMG Nepal and the USA/Aid dated 21 August 1978, pp. 473-79 and 495-500.

... (1979) and 1980, MHG, Ministry of Law and Justice, Babar Mahal, Kathmandu.

Notes, Memoranda and Letters Exchanged and Agreements signed between the Government of India and China: White Paper: 1954-1959 (New Delhi, 1959).

Policy and Main Objectives of His Majesty's Government (Kathmandu, Department of Publicity and Broadcasting Ministry of National Guidance, HMG, Nepal).

Proclamations, Speeches and Messages of His Majesty King Mahendra, Vols. I to IV (Kathmandu, Ministry of Information and Broadcasting, 1967).

.... Speeches and Messages of King Birendra 1972-1981, His Majesty Government, Ministry of Communications, Department of Information, 1982.

Progress of Nepal-India Cooperation Programme (Kathmandu: Indian Co-operation Mission, 1968).

President Nixon's Report to Congress, February 1972.

Report, Ministry of External Affairs, Government of India, Prime Minister's Statements and Foreign Minister's Statements, New Delhi, 1977-1979).

Report on Human Rights Practices in Countries Receiving USAID (Report submitted to the Committee on Foreign Relations of the US Senate and Committee on Foreign Affairs of the US House of Representatives by the Department of State, 8 February, 1979, pp. 599-605.

Soviet Information Bureau, Naxal Kathmandu, Barho Soviet-Nepal Maitry (Growing Soviet Nepal Friendship, 1982).

"Speech at Dinner in Honour of Nepalese Foreign Minister by Y.B. Chavan, External Affairs Minister of India". Foreign Affairs Record, Vol. XXI, No. 8, August 1975.

Text of Joint Communique, Lok Sabha Secretariat, Foreign Policy of India: Text of Documents 1947-1964 (New Delhi, 1966).

Tuladhar, Tirtha, R., Nepal-China: A Story of Friendship (Kathmandu: Department of Publicity and Broadcasting).

United States Department of State Point Four, A co-operation Programme for Aid in the development of economically underdeveloped area (1950).

United States, Background USA, 8 December, 1983.

United States, Official Text, Exchange of Remarks by President Reagan and HIS Majesty' King Birendra at White House Arrival Ceremony, 8 December 1983.

... Official Text, Remarks of President Reagan and King Birendra of Nepal at State Dinner, 14 December, 1983.

... A quarter Century of US Assistance to the Kingdom of Nepal, Kathmandu, 1976.

. . . Thirty Years of US Assistance to the Kingdom of Nepal, 1981.

... Six Years of Nepal-America Co-operation 1952-1958, Kathmandu, 1958.

United States Foreign Policy for the 1970: Emerging Structure of Peace: A Report to the Congress by Richard M. Nixon, President of the United States, 9 February 1972 (Washington, D.C. 1972).

**B. Books**

*Acheson, Dean,* President at the Creation: My Years in the State Department (New York, 1969).

*Agarwal, Hem Narayan,* The Administrative System of Nepal, From Tradition to Modernity, (Vikas Publishing House, Delhi, 1976).

*Aitchison, C.U.A.,* Collection of Treaties, Engagements and Sunnuds Relating to India.

*Bahadur, Poorna,* Nepal Behind the Screen, Kathmandu : Nepal Youth League Central Committee, 1957.

*Berreman, Gerald,* Hindu of the Himalayas. (Berkeley: University of California Press, 1963).

*Bista-Dor Bahadur,* The People of Nepal (Department of Publicity, HMG, Kathmandu, *1967).*

*Bowels, Chester,* Ambassador's Report (Newyork, 1954).

*Bhattacharjee, G.P.,* India and the Politics of Modern Nepal (Calcutta, 1970).

*Chavan, Yeshwant Rao B.,* India's Foreign Policy (Somaiya Publishers, Bombay, 1979).

*Gange, John,* American Foreign Relations (Ronald Press Company, Newyork, 1959).

*Gaige, Frederick H.,* Regionalism and National Unity in Nepal (Berkeley, 1975).

*Gupta, Anirudha,* Politics in Nepal: A Study of Post-Rana Political Developments and Party Politics (Bombay, 1964).

*Gyawali, S.P.,* Friendship on Trial (Department of Publicity, HMG.

*India 1983,* Compiled by Research and Reference Division (Publication Division, Ministry of Information and Broadcasting, Government of India, New Delhi, 1983).

*J. Bandyopadhyaya,* The Making of India's Foreign Policy (Bombay, 1980).

*Jain, R.K.,* China South Asian Relations 1947-1980 (Radiant Publishers, New Delhi, 1981).

*Kaul, T.N.,* Foreign Relations (Publication Division, New Delhi, 1972).

*Karan, P.P. and W.M. Jenkins,* The Himalayan Kingdom: Bhutan, Sikkim and Nepal (Princeton, 1963).

*Kumar Satish,* Rana Policy in Nepal 1846-1951 (Bombay, 1967).

*Liska, George,* Alliance and the Third World (USA, 1968).

*Mihaly. E.B.,* Foreign Aid and Politics in Nepal: A Case Study (Oxford University Press, London, 1965).

*Muni. S.D.,* Foreign Policy of Nepal (New Delhi, 1973).

*Narayan, Sriman.,* India and Nepal: An Exercise in Open Diplomacy (Bombay, 1970).

*Nath, Tribhuvan,* The Nepalese Dilemma 1960-74 (New Delhi, 1975).

*Ramakant,* Nepal China and India (New Delhi, 1976).

*Rose, Leo. E. and Margret W. Fisher.,* The Politics in Nepal (Ithaca, 1970).

... Nepal Strategy for Survival (Berkeley, 1971).

Shaha, Rishikesh., Nepal and the World (Kathmandu, 1955).

. . . Nepali Politics: Retrospect and Prospect (Delhi 1975).

. . . Politics in Nepal 1980-1991 (Manohar Publishers, New Delhi, 1992).

*Vajpayee, Atal Bihari,* New Dimensions of India's Foreign Policy (Vision Book, New Delhi, 1979).

*Verma, S.P.,* Struggle for the Himalayas: A Study in Sino-Indian Relations (New Delhi, 1971).

*Wright, Daniel,* History of Nepal (Calcutta, 1958).

*Yami, Dharma Ratna.,* The Study of the Critical Situation in Nepal (Kathmandu, 1958).

**C. Articles**

*Ali, S.M.,* "Nepal at the Cross-roads", Far Eastern Economic Review, 22 April 1965,. pp. 159-61.

*An Indian Official,* "India as a World Power", Foreign Affairs, 4 (July 1949), pp. 540-50.

*Anderton, Piers,* "India's Front Lines in the Himalayas", Reporter, (3-16 January 1964) pp. 38-40.

*Appadorai, A.,* "Where India Faces China," Foreign Affairs, 4 (July 1959) pp. 617.

. . . *and Baral,* L.S., "The New Constitution of Nepal", International Studies, 1959-60, pp. 217-47.

*Ayoob, M.,* "India and Nepal : Politics of Aid and Trade", The Institute of Defence Studies and Analysis, 3 (October 1970), pp.127-56.

*Bajpai, Girija Shankar,* "Nepal and the Indo-Nepalese Relations", Indian Year Book of International Relations, Madras, University of Madras, Vol. 3, 1954.

*Baral, L.S.,* "Nepal's Apprenticeship in Democracy 1951-69", India Quarterly, Vol. XXVI, No. 3, July-September 1971, pp.185-200.

*Bhambhari, C.P.,* "The Chinese Aggression and India's Foreign Policy," Political Science Review, Vol. 2, No. 2, October 1963, pp. 42-54.

*Bhatta, Dibya Deo.,* "Soviet Nepalese Relations", Eastern World Vol. 18, No.7, July 1964, pp.11-12.

. . . "Soviet and Chinese Involvement in Southern Asia", Canadian Slavonic Papers, Vol. 12, No. 2, Summer 1970, pp.175-94.

*Bista, K.N.,* "Nepal and India Stand for Co-operation with All Nations," The Rising Nepal, 20 April 1972.

*Brown, M.,* "Diplomatic Development of Nepal," Asian Survey, 11 (July), 1971.

*Bull, Hedley.,* "The Conduct of American Foreign Policy: A view from abroad consisting under Pressure", Foreign Affairs, Vol. 57, 1978, pp. 459.

*Chauhan, R.S.,* "Consolidation and Confrontation: A Study of Nepal Politics 1970", South Asian Studies, Vol. VI, No. 1, January 1970.

*"China in Nepal",* Thought, Vol. XIV, No. 41, October 1962.

*Crocker, H.E.,* "The Situation in Nepal", Contemporary Review, Vol. 186, September 1955, pp. 189-91.

*Desh Pande, G.P.,* "China and the Himalayan States", China Report, Vol. III, No. 1, December 1966.

... "Development in Nepal", India Quarterly, Vol. XXIX, No. 3, July-September 1973.

*Dieter, Bram,* "Changes in South Asia Intra-regional and External Relationship", The World Today, Vol. 34 (London, October 1978), p. 393.

*Dutta,* Som., "The Defence of India's Northern Border", India Quarterly, Vol. 1, No. 22, January-March 1966.

*Gaige, Frederick H.,* "Nepal: Compromise and Liberalisation", Asian Survey, Vol. IX, No. 2 (February, 1967), pp.94-98.

... "Nepal : The Search for a National Consensus", Asian Survey, Vol. X, No. 2 (February 1970), pp. 100-106.

. . . "Nepal: More Problems with India", Asian Survey Vol. XI, No.2 (February, 1971), pp.172-76.

*Ghosh, K.K.,* "Nepal and Its Neighbours", Pakistan Horizon, Vol. XVII No. 4, 1968.

*Hers, Peter.,* "Nepal between India and China", Swiss Review of World Affairs, Vol. 17, No. 6, (September, 1967).

*Khanal, Y.N.,* "Nepal 1972 : A Search for a New Base-Camp", Asian Survey, Vol. XIII, No. 2, (February 1973), pp. 211-16.

*Kumar, Vinod,* "Great Powers and Nepal", S.D.Muni, ed.; Nepal: An Assertive Monarchy (Chetana Publishers, New Delhi 1977), pp.143-59.

*Manandher, R.P.,* "Some New Light on Early Nepal-China Relations", Bulletin Indian Institute of Advanced Study, Vol. III No. 4, July 1970.

*Mukherjee, Dillip,* "Sign of Times", Far Eastern Economic Review, July-September 1969, pp. 126-28.

*Muni, S.D.,* "India's Mutual Security Arrangements with Nepal", IDAS, VoI. IV, No. 1, July 1971.

... "Sino-Nepalese Relations 1955-67", United Asia, Vol. XXI, No. 3, May-June 1969.

*Narayan Sriman,* "India Nepal", United Asia, Vol. XIX, No.4, July 1967.

. . . "Nepal : Present Political Situation in Nepal", Young India, Vol.V, No. 6, January 1975.

*Pannikar, K.M.,* "The Himalayas in India's Defence", India Quarterly, Vol. III, No. 2, 1947.

*Ramakant,* "Nepal's Foreign Policy and China", India Quarterly Vol. XXVI, No. 3, July-September, 1971.

*Ray, Heman,* "Communist China's Strategy in the Himalayas, Nepal, A Case Study," Orbis, Vol. 2, No. 3 1967.

*Shaha, Rishikesh,* "Nepal-China Relations", The Nepal Guardian, No 2, June 1964, pp. 37-47.

. . . "Nepal Tibet and China" Annual Journal of the Council of World Affairs (12 June, 1970), pp.13-82.

*"Y.B. Chavan's Nepal Visit:* Accent on Mutual Co-operation", Socialist India, Vol. XII, No.10, February 1976.

## SECONDARY SOURCES

### A. Books

*Agrawal, Govind R. and Jai P. Rana,* Nepal and Non-alignment (Centre for Economic Development and Administration, Tribhuvan University, Kirtipur, Kathmandu, 1982).

*Aggarwala, Adish C.,* Rajiv Gandhi: An Assessment (Amish Publications, New Delhi, 1993).

*Ahluwalia, B.K. and Shashi Ahluwalia,* Rajiv Gandhi—A Profile in Courage (Intellectual Publishing House, New Delhi, 1985).

*Appadorai, A.,* The Domestic Roots of India's Foreign Policy (Oxford University Press, Delhi, 1981).

*Arthur, S. Banks,* ed., Political Handbook of the World (Newyork, 1978).

*Bahadur, Keshar,* Nepal After Revolution of 1950 (Kathmandu, 1976).

*Bhargava G.S., ed.,* Perestroika in India: V.P. Singh's Prime Ministership (New Delhi, 1990).

*Bailey, T.A.,* A Diplomatic History of the American People (Appleton Century Crofts, Newyork, 1969).

*Baral, Lok Raj.,* Oppositional Politics in Nepal (New Delhi, 1977).

. . . Nepal's Politics of Referendum: A Study of Groups, Personalities and Trends (Vikas Publishing House, New Delhi, 1983).

*Chakravarti, G.P.,* India's China Policy (Indian University Press, Bloomington, 1962).

*Chatterjee, Bhola,* A Study of Recent Nepalese Politics (World Press, Calcutta, 1967).

*Chaturvedi, S.K.,* Indo-Nepal Relations: Tension Areas, Foreign Affairs Report (Indian Council of World Affairs, Delhi, 1989).

*Chaudhuri, Sailen,* Maoist Betrayal : India a Case Study (Sterling Publishers, New Delhi, 1980).

*Dallin, David J.,* The New Soviet Empire (New Haven, Yale University Press, 1951).

*Dutt, V.P.,* China's Foreign Policy 1958-1963 (Asia Publishing House, New Delhi, 1964).

. . . India's Foreign Policy (Vikas Publishing House, New Delhi, 1987).

*Fisher, M.W., Leo E. Rose and R.A. Huttenback,* Himalayan Battle Ground: Sino-Indian Rivalry in Ladakh (Newyork Preager, 1965).

*Frankel, Joseph.,* The Making of Foreign Policy: An Analysis of Decision Making (Oxford University Press, London 1963).

*Gaige, Frederick H.,* Regionalism and National Unity in Nepal (Vikas Publishing House, New Delhi, 1975).

*Gangal, S.C.,* India's Foreign Policy-A Documentary Study of India's Foreign Policy since the Installation of the Janata Government on 24 March 1977 (Young Asia Publishers New Delhi, 1980).

*Gupta, Anirudha,* Politics in Nepal: A Case Study of Post-Rana Political Development and Party Politics (Asia Publishing House, Bombay, 1964).

*Jain, Girilal,* India Meets China in Nepal (Asia Publishing House, Bombay, 1959).

*Jha, S.K.,* Uneasy Partners: India and Nepal in the Post-Colonial Era (Manas, New Delhi, 1975).

*Kaul, T.N.,* Diplomacy in Peace and War: Recollections and Reflections (Vikas Publishing House, New Delhi, 1979).

*Kumar, D. P.,* Nepal : Year of Decision (Vikas Publishing House, New Delhi, 1980).

*Kumar, Satish,* Rana Polity in Nepal 1846-1951 (Asia Publishing House, Bombay, 1967).

*Lohia, Ram Manohar,* A Himalayan Policy for India in the Third Camp in World Affairs (Bombay, 1951).

. . . India China and Northern Frontiers (New Hind Prakashan, Hyderabad, 1963).

*Mallik, D. N.,* The Development of Non-alignment in India's Foreign Policy (Chaitanya Publishing House, Allahabad 1967).

. . . Post-War International Politics : A Quadripartite Survey (Veena Mandir Publishers, Muzaffarpur, 1973).

*Mihaly, E. B.,* Foreign Aid and Politics in Nepal (Oxford University Press, London, 1965).

*Muni, S. D.,* Foreign Policy of Nepal (Delhi, 1973).

*Noorani, A. G.,* Aspects of India's Foreign Policy (Jaicom, Bombay, 1970).

*Panda, Kamala Kanta and Mishra Pramod,* The New Perspectives in India's Foreign Policy : The Janata Phase (Sandeep Prakashan, Delhi, 1980).

*Prasad, Bimal,* Our Foreign Policy Legacy (Perhes Publishing, New Delhi, 1960).

*Rowland, John.,* A History of Sino-Indian Relations (Princeton, 1967).

*Saini, M. K., ed.,* Aspects on the Non-alignment (Kalamkar Prakashan, New Delhi, 1980).

*Sen, Chanakya.,* Tibet Disappears (Asia Publishing House, New Delhi, 1960).

*Sharma, J. P.,* Nepal's Foreign Policy, 1947-1962 (University of California, Unpublished thesis, 1968).

*Singh, J. B.,* India, Nepali Congress and King Mahendra (Mimeograph) (Lucknow, 1964).

*Zaidi, A. M. and Zaidi, S. G.*, eds., The Encyclopaedia of Indian National Congress (S. Chand and Company, New Delhi, 1981).

**B. Articles**

*Acharya, T. P.*, "Nepal's Fight for Freedom", India Today, (1 June 1952), pp. 19-27.

*Alexandrowich, C. H.*, "India's Himalayan Dependencies", The Year Book of World Affairs (London), 10 (1956), pp.128-43.

*Bahadur, Poorna.*, "The Strategic Importance of Nepal", Nepal Today 6 (28 April 1953), pp. 5-7.

*Bhargava, G. S.*, "Nepal between two Giants, "Eastern World", 14 (September 1960), pp.18-19.

*Brahmanand*, "Indo-Nepalese Trade Treaties", Eastern Economist 56 (1971), pp. 508-11.

*Dar, A. N.*, "Mr. Bhattarai Plays it Right", The National Herald, 16 June 1990.

*Ghori, Karamatullah Khan*, "Nepal and its Neighbours", Pakistan Horizon, Vol. 7, No. 4, 1964, pp. 368-84.

*Kapur, Ashok.*, "Emerging Problem in India's Foreign Relations in Seventies", Foreign Affairs Report (New Delhi) Vol. III, No. 3, March 1971, pp.148-56.

*Kumar, D. R.*, "Nepal's Road to China", Far Eastern Economic Review, Vol. 53, No. 8, 20 February 1964, pp. 619-21.

*Kumar, Satish*, "Nepal and China", Indian Journal of Political Science, Vol. 24, January March. 1963, pp. 79-93.

*Kurve, Mavin.*, Nepal's peace Zone Move : Attempt to Change 1950 Treaty", The Times of India, (New Delhi), 14 January 1981.

*Madhu, Limaye*, "India's China Policy", The Illustrated Weekly of India, Vol. XIIX (The Times of India Press, Bombay, November 12- 18, 1978), p. 6.

*Manchanda, Rita.*, "The Ugly Indian Image Remains", The Hindustan Times (New Delhi), 28 July 1997.

A. *Menon, N. C.*, "An Unequal Bargain", The Hindustan Times, 3 November 1997.

*Mohanty, Manoranjan.*, "China Commentary-Course of Sino-Indian Normalisation", The Amrit Bazar Patrika (Calcutta), 19 May 1978.

*Muni, S. D.*, "A Common Destiny" The Times of India (Patna), 23 April 1989.

... "Chinese Arms pour into Nepal", The Times of India, 1 September 1988.

*Nayar, Kuldip.,* "Estranged Neighbour : The Arrogant India", The Indian Express, 12 December 1994.

*Noorani, A. G.,* "India-Nepal Relations : The Heart of the Matter", The Indian Express, 11 April 1989.

*Patterson, Gorge N.,* "A Himalayan Confederation", Far Eastern Economic Review, Vol. 47-48, 1968, pp. 275-82.

*Poole, Peter A.,* "Communist China's Aid Diplomacy", Asian Survey, Vol. 7, No.11, November 1966, pp. 622-29.

*Poulose, T. T.,* "The Politics of Nuclear Freezone in South Asia" Pacific Community (Tokyo), Vol. 6, April 1977, pp. 541-60.

*Puri, Rakshat.,* "Delhi's Kowtowing to Beijing", The Hindustan Times, 12 November, 1997.

*Rao, P. V. Narasimha,* "Nepal-India Relations", Nepal Council of World Affairs Journal, Souvenir Issue, December 1981.

*Sahay, S.,* "A Close Look Indo-Nepal Relations", The Statesman 10 December 1981.

*Shaha, Rishikesh.,* "The Nepal-India Imbroglio", The Indian Express, 24 June 1989.

*Sharma, R. S.,* "Process for formulation and execution of National Security and Defence Policies in the 1990s", Kouser J. Azam., ed., India's Defence Policy for the 1990s (New Delhi, 1992) p. 27.

*Singh, S. Nihal,* "India-China : Time of Move Forward", The Statesman, 22 May 1979.

*Swarup, Rama.,* "Red China Builds a Bridge to Nepal, An example of Peking Aided Projects", Issues and Studies, Vol. 4, 1967, pp.15-18.

*Thapa, Bhekh Bahadur,* "Foreign Aid and Economic Development in Nepal", Souvenir Issue, The Nepal Council of World Affairs Journal, Kathmandu, June 1971.

. . . "The Soviet Union and Nepal", Central Asia Review, Vol. 10, 1962, pp. 294-96.

*Thapliyal, Sangeeta,* "Nepal in India's Security Parameters", Strategic Analysis, Vol. XVIII, No. 9, December 1995 (Institute for Defence Studies and Analysis, New Delhi, 1995), p. 1201.

**C. Newspapers**

Amrit Bazar Patrika (Calcutta).

The Ceylon Daily News (Ceylon).

The Commoner (Kathmandu).
The Dawn (Karachi).
Dainik Nepal (Kathmandu).
Everest News (Kathmandu).
The Financial Times (London).
Gorkhapatra (Kathmandu).
Hal Khabar (Kathmandu).
Himali Bela (Kathmandu).
The Hindu (Madras).
The Hindustan Times (New Delhi).
The Indian Express (Delhi).
The Indian Nation (Patna).
The Motherland (Kathmandu).
Nagpur Times (Nagpur).
Naya Samaj (Kathmandu).
The National Herald (New Delhi).
Nepal Samachar (Kathmandu).
Nepal Times (Kathmandu).
The Nepali (Kathmandu).
Newyork Times (Newyork).
The Rising Nepal (Kathmandu).
The Sunday Standard (New Delhi).
The Statesman (Delhi).
Swatantra Samachar (Kathmandu).
The Times of India (New Delhi).
The Times (London).
The Tribune (Chandigarh).
Xinhua (Peking).

**D. Periodicals**

American Political Science Review (Newyork).
Eastern Economists (Bombay).
Economic and Political Weekly (Bombay).
Foreign Affairs (Newyork).
Foreign Policy Report (New Delhi).
Illustrated Weekly of India (Bombay).

India Today (New Delhi).

Indian Journal of Political Science (Hyderabad).

International Affairs (Moscow).

International Studies (New Delhi).

Link (New Delhi).

Modern Review (Calcutta).

Pacific Affairs (Newyork).

Political Science Quarterly (Newyork).

Time (Newyork).

The News Week (Newyork).

SAARC News (Calcutta).

Survey of China Mainland Press (Peking).

World Politics (Prenceton).

World Today (London).

**E. Digests**

Asian Recorder (New Delhi).

Keesings Contemporary Archives (London).

Nepal Trade Directory (Nepal Trading Corporation, New Delhi).

# INDEX